Making World English

Making World English

Literature, Late Empire, and English Language Teaching, 1919–39

Michael G. Malouf

BLOOMSBURY ACADEMIC
LONDON • NEW YORK • OXFORD • NEW DELHI • SYDNEY

BLOOMSBURY ACADEMIC
Bloomsbury Publishing Plc
50 Bedford Square, London, WC1B 3DP, UK
1385 Broadway, New York, NY 10018, USA
29 Earlsfort Terrace, Dublin 2, Ireland

BLOOMSBURY, BLOOMSBURY ACADEMIC and the Diana logo are trademarks of
Bloomsbury Publishing Plc

First published in Great Britain 2022
This paperback edition published 2023

Copyright © Michael G. Malouf, 2022

Michael G. Malouf has asserted his right under the Copyright, Designs and Patents Act, 1988, to be identified as Author of this work.

For legal purposes the Acknowledgments on pp. xxi–xxii constitute an extension of this copyright page.

Cover design: Rebecca Heselton
Cover image: Class with mistress in a mofussil or up-country girls' school, Bombay, c. 1873 © British Library Board. All Rights Reserved / Bridgeman Images

All rights reserved. No part of this publication may be reproduced or transmitted in any form or by any means, electronic or mechanical, including photocopying, recording, or any information storage or retrieval system, without prior permission in writing from the publishers.

Bloomsbury Publishing Plc does not have any control over, or responsibility for, any third-party websites referred to or in this book. All internet addresses given in this book were correct at the time of going to press. The author and publisher regret any inconvenience caused if addresses have changed or sites have ceased to exist, but can accept no responsibility for any such changes.

A catalogue record for this book is available from the British Library.

A catalog record for this book is available from the Library of Congress.

ISBN:	HB:	978-1-3502-4385-9
	PB:	978-1-3502-4389-7
	ePDF:	978-1-3502-4386-6
	eBook:	978-1-3502-4387-3

Typeset by Integra Software Services Pvt. Ltd.

To find out more about our authors and books visit www.bloomsbury.com and sign up for our newsletters.

For Kristina

Contents

List of Illustrations	ix
Preface	x
Acknowledgments	xxi

Part I Managing English

1 Pioneers and Heretics — 3
   Introduction — 3
   An Anglophone Empire? — 6
   Harold Palmer: The Palmer Method and English in Japan — 9
   Michael West: The New Method and English in India — 12
   C. K. Ogden: Basic English and Artificial Languages — 17
   Conclusion — 23
   Notes — 24

2 Word Lists, Vocabulary Control, and Colonialism — 31
   Colonial Linguistics and Vocabulary Control — 31
   Lemaire, Behaviorism, and Palmer's *Principles of Language Study* — 35
   Michael West: *Bilingualism* and Indirect Rule — 45
   Ogden and Richards: *Meaning of Meaning* and Primitivism — 58
   Word Lists: From Theory to Experiment — 65
   Conclusion — 74
   Notes — 75

3 Readers, Literary Simplification, and the Global Subject — 83
   Introduction — 83
   Auxiliary Reading: West's New Method Readers — 88
   Basic Commodities: *Carl and Anna* and the *Basic Way Reading Books* — 106
   Simple Improvements: Palmer's Poe Test — 118
   Notes — 136

Part II Making English

4 Ogden Agonistes: Basic's Critics and the Problem of World English — 145
   Introduction — 145

	Faucett and the International Turn	149
	Aiken's Englishes	150
	"Think Englishly": West's "English as a World Language"	156
	West and Swenson's *Critical Examination*	158
	Ogden's *Counter-Offensive*	166
	Conclusion	170
	Notes	171
5	The Carnegie Conference and Its Discontents	175
	The Title	175
	The Corporation	178
	The Conference	187
	The Record	194
	The Report	208
	Conclusion	221
	Notes	224
6	After Carnegie: Masking English	231
	Ogden's Mask	231
	West's Mask	238
	Notes	242
Bibliography		244
Index		259

Illustrations

1. *David Copperfield*, New Method Supplementary Reader, Cover — 16
2. Charles Lemaire, word list from *Vocabulaire Pratique* — 39
3. Michael West, *Bilingualism*, "Third Test: First Teaching Experiment" — 58
4. Michael West, Bilingualism, "An Individual Reading Profile" — 59
5. C. K. Ogden and I. A. Richards, *The Meaning of Meaning*, "Triangle of Interpretation" — 61
6. Basic English Vocabulary — 68
7. Basic English diagram of "Operation-words" — 70
8. Basic English diagram of "Direction-words" — 71
9. Herman Bongers' literal translation using Basic English from his *History and Principles of Vocabulary Control* [1947] — 107
10. "The Hurricane Conference." Cartoon. Warwick ELT Archive — 220
11. Ogden receiving reporters in his Greek mask, *The Picture Post*, October 23, 1943 — 233

Preface

In a prefatory "notes on terminology" in his definitive *History of English Language Teaching*, A. P. R. Howatt aptly remarks about the origins of the term, "English as a *Second* Language," as a solution proposed by the colonial educator Michael West to "the problem of using the word 'foreign' in an imperial context."[1] This book is an elaboration on this problem and West's solution. In the century since West made his suggestion for the 1919 Imperial Conference on Education, the definition of Global English has undergone vast changes from an instrument of "soft power" during the Cold War to its image as a commodity in the era of neoliberal globalization.[2] Yet in spite of its changes in form and application, and despite what some predict about its future (decline and fragmentation, or increasing power), the ideology of Global English as a neutral, instrumental, auxiliary language that is a required *skill* for modernity persists.[3] *Making World English* explores how this "second" version of English was conceived during the period after the First World War by educators, linguists, anthropologists, foundations, and governments seeking to maintain English hegemony during a period of contestation in Europe and in the colonies. This study examines how literature, late empire, and modern ideas of pedagogy and internationalism contributed toward an ideology of English as this special type of world language.

Critical accounts of English as an international language have often focused on either the nineteenth century and the introduction of English education in India, or on the post-war development of English as a form of cultural imperialism through organizations like the British Council or the Voice of America. The interwar period has been of interest mainly for ELT historians like A. P. R. Howatt and Richard Smith, and in the controversial postcolonial histories by Robert Phillipson and Alastair Pennycook in the late twentieth century. Phillipson and Pennycook lend significance to the rise of applied linguistics and ELT during the interwar period, but their primary interests are with the persistence of colonial practices in post-war language policies in the later twentieth century. Smith's five volumes on the *Pioneers of ELT*, published in the early 2000s, collected the primary works from Harold Palmer, West, and Lawrence Faucett, and along with his contextualizing introductions, supplemented Howatt's account of this period while acknowledging postcolonial criticisms of the field's origins.[4] Smith also lent a new significance to the Carnegie Conference by including its report in the fifth volume, *Towards Carnegie*. As a literary scholar interested in the politics of English as a global language, I have found this archive from ELT and the contrasting perspectives from Pennycook, Phillipson, Howatt, Smith, and the applied linguist Janina Brutt-Griffler whose *World English* also deals with the early twentieth century, to suggest new ways of seeing the linguistic landscape of the interwar period for postcolonial and modernist literary histories.

But while this study uses postcolonial theory and is set in the modernist period, it is not concerned directly with modernist or postcolonial writers. Rather, this study traces a parallel history in which a different set of actors— educators, anthropologists, philosophers, colonial officials, and linguists— are concerned with similar problems about the paradoxes of linguistic simplicity and complexity, monolingualism and multilingualism, standards and vernaculars that literary critics have long explored as key problems in the modernist and postcolonial canon. Research into the history of applied linguistics reveals that there is another story to be told about the diverse ways that forms of colonial knowledge were inscribed into an ideological conception of a language. This microhistory of English seeks to give a material shape and coherence to an aspect of Global English as a continuation of colonial rule developed during a specific time and place. Investigating one area of English language practice, and focusing on a single conference, it is possible to see the "world" and "English" as constructed together.[5] I am not arguing that this event "made" all of what we know of today as Global English; rather, it is one instance in a Western cultural and social logic of controlling language identity and use in the world that offers insight into the structure of our language debates today.

The bookend dates of the title refer to the post-war ascendancy of English after the First World War, when it supplanted French as the diplomatic language at the Paris Peace Conference, and it concludes with the beginning of the Second World War, after the Carnegie Conference in 1934 and the appearance of the Carnegie Report. The book focuses specifically on two language educators, Harold Palmer and Michael West, and the linguist and philosopher, C. K. Ogden. Along with the literary critic I. A. Richards, the language educator Lawrence Faucett, and the influential educational psychologist Edward Thorndike, they have been categorized together as the Vocabulary Control movement because of their interest in teaching language through the use of limited, graded vocabularies. Although their methods and practices were influential on the post-war development of the field, which changed drastically after the Second World War, I find these word lists, Simplified Readers, and language textbooks to be suggestive of more than just how to teach language. As attempts at "applying" language in multilingual, global contexts, their theories and methods represent an important social and political dimension of language that is normally left out of traditional literary historical accounts of interwar linguistics that privilege formal and philosophical contributions by Saussure, Wittgenstein, the Vienna Cirle, and the Modernist avant-garde.[6] In this book, I use the Carnegie Conference, which Robert Phillipson identifies as "the first reference to English as a world language" that was "specifically aimed at establishing close collaboration between the USA and the UK to achieve global impact,"[7] as a locus for examining the shift that occurs between the wars in the conception of English from a national to an international language. The first part of this book attends to the colonial influences on the methods of Palmer, West, and Ogden with special attention to their use of Simplified Readers for working out their theories of auxiliary English. The second part draws on the Carnegie Corporation archives to explore the conference from its initial planning to its meetings and the writing of the Carnegie Report. Admittedly, the two parts are uneven due to the necessary contextualization in the first part, and while the chapters can be read for their individual topics, they are intended to be read as a continuous narrative in which the events of the first part gain in significance when seen through the deliberations at the Carnegie Conference that legitimated the concept of English as a world language. It is my hope that this approach will bring the history of ELT and these provocative concepts from its early practitioners into the purview of literary critics concerned with the role of language in the world. On the other hand, this outsider perspective on the history of ELT might suggest an awareness of the role that literature has played in its development as well as a sense of how its own institutional and theoretical history fits into other disciplinary contexts.[8]

The exact role played by empire in fostering English as a global language has been debated since Gauri Viswanathan's *Masks of Conquest* first drew attention to the colonial basis for English studies.[9] The emergence over the past decade of the field of World Literature in English (WLE) out of postcolonial studies and comparative literature has led to criticism of both the "world" part of the designation and, increasingly, to the meaning and status of "English."[10] As the postcolonial literary scholar Aamir Mufti remarks about the role of English in comparative literary studies, too often "English" has been assumed as the "ether that permeates the space of world literature."[11] A lot of the scholarship on the latter has been divided, like much of applied linguistics, around questions of agency and structure: the users of the language or the social role of the language. The former have been influenced by a World Englishes approach associated with the work of the sociolinguist Braj Kachru on the plurality of Englishes in the world. Because this method privileges the role of agency in language appropriation, it makes sense to be used to discuss forms of literary invention by authors writing out of multilingual contexts. This has also been used to counter a deterministic view of language that the postcolonial scholar Bill Ashcroft summarizes as the belief that "[c]olonialism imposed a way of talking about the world that privileged certain kinds of distinctions and representations and debased others." Rather than seeing English as a prison, Ashcroft argues that language should be seen as "a tool, and often a weapon."[12] Recent scholarship has turned toward theories of the anglophone that seek to, as Simon Gikandi puts it, "deprive the language of the ecumenical status of the global and to represent [English] as one language among many."[13] However, writing about English as a Lingua Franca (ELF) methods, the applied sociolinguist Ruanni Tupas expresses concern that this agent-centered approach risks obfuscating the role of empire and its persistence in Global English.[14] Considering this same dilemma, the literary critic Rebecca Walkowitz argues for a historical and theoretical understanding of the Anglophone, suggesting that "[i]nstead of promoting two or three or ten Anglophones ....we would do better to make the Anglophone less than one."[15] In order to "reduce" the anglophone, it is necessary to understand how it receives its shape and authority. As the applied linguist Marnie Holborow argues, "English's historicity counters claims of its 'neutrality,'"[16] and, in this spirit, this book's account of one particular moment in the making of this "entrenched ideological view of English" reveals how these ideologies came to adhere to English in the world. In the process, I have had to remember that this was not a project about "English" as a cultural system of grammar, syntax, and phonetics, but rather about the uses of English. As the applied linguist François Grin puts it, the problem "is not with English, *per se*, but linguistic hegemony." In this sense, Walkowitz argues that we need to understand English as "neither denotative nor fixed" but as a heterogeneous "target language" with a hegemonic role in shaping the world that writers and texts inhabit.[17] It is through these interwar debates about the role of English in the world that we can see this linguistic hegemony being imagined, developed, and implemented.

Preview

This book follows the trajectory established in Smith's volumes by making the movement "Toward Carnegie" its central organizing principle. The first part of this book attends to the colonial contexts in which Palmer, West, and Ogden developed their methods, with special attention to their use of limited word lists and Simplified Readers for working out their theories of auxiliary English. The second part examines the debates over Basic English and draws on the Carnegie Corporation archives to explore the 1934 conference from its initial planning to its meetings and the writing of the Carnegie Report. It is in this archival narrative that it is possible to see the deliberations that legitimated the concept of English as a world language that became utilized after the war. As this description suggests, the methodology for this book involves a hybrid critical approach that utilizes geopolitics, economics, biographical analysis, postcolonial critique, rhetorical analysis, archival research and is also a history of ideas, disciplines, and institutions. My interpretations, especially in Part II, are particularly sensitive to the ways that private and public debates function as forms of legitimation. It is in this sense that I use the letters and memos in the Carnegie archives along with the published writings by West, Ogden, and Palmer to understand how the public performance often plays out private desires, resentments, and anxieties. The archival analysis that provides background to the Basic English debates in 1933 and 1934 allows for an interpretation of gender and linguistics during the interwar period that has been otherwise neglected. In a related sense, the close readings of the word lists and Simplified Readers reveal the ways that colonial and domestic racial hierarchies were transferred into the construction of linguistic hierarchies that are not as visible as the usual debates over standardization. Admittedly, I drew on a similar mixture of formal, historical, archival, and biographical methods in my first book, on Irish nationalism and Caribbean modernism. While I hesitate to make meta-critical statements, it does appear that, for my part at least, such a mixture of critical and theoretical methods offers a flexible and generative means for making sense of the postcolonial modernist archive from the first part of the twentieth century.

The first example of this method can be found in the first chapter, "Pioneers and Heretics," which provides a biographical and intellectual background to Palmer, West, and Ogden with a particular attention to their formative experiences with International Auxiliary Languages (IALs), colonialism, and psychology. Chapter 2, "Word Lists, Vocabulary Control, and Colonialism," connects the intellectual context provided in Chapter 1 to the colonial legacy of linguistics that influences the rise of Vocabulary Control in the 1920s. After an overview of the history of colonial linguistics, I provide a contrapuntal analysis that situates their primary works (Palmer's *Principles of Language Study*, West's *Bilingualism*, and Ogden and Richards' *Meaning of Meaning*) in relation to this colonial history and to diverse colonial contexts such as the Belgian Congo, British India, and the Dutch Indies. For all of their respective differences in philosophy and purpose, all three works create a divide between auxiliary and native or mother tongue languages that follow from the developmentalist history of language by the Danish linguist Otto Jespersen. The final section examines how they come together around the methodological turn toward a limited word list or controlled vocabulary for teaching. I argue that the significance of the word list far exceeds its role as a banal list of primary words and phrases; rather, it is a proxy for arguments about the place of English in the world and the type of English-speaking subject it seeks to create. This argument about their methods and word lists is continued in Chapter 3, "Readers, Literary Simplification, and the Global Subject," in terms of their other contribution to language teaching, the development and use of Simplified Readers. The chapter is framed by Palmer's plan in 1931 for the three competing ELT methods to all adapt the same literary work, Poe's "The Gold Bug," and includes a brief introduction on the colonial history of abridged Readers and textbooks; sections on West's New Method Readers, Ogden's Basic English literary "translations" and *Basic Way Readers*, Palmer's *The Grading and Simplifying of Literary Material: A Memorandum*; and a comparative analysis of all three versions of Poe's story.

The second part of the book marks a change of tone and direction as it begins to focus on the controversies produced by Basic English and the debates over the status of English as a World Language that took place in New York and London in the 1930s. I argue that the controversy over Basic English legitimated the idea of a standardized international English. Chapter 4, "Ogden Agonistes: Basic's Critics and the Problem of World English," introduces three new figures: the linguists and educators Lawrence Faucett, Elaine Swenson, and Janet Rankin Aiken. The first section details the shift in the late 1920s toward the idea of an "international" English rather than the area-based concept of a English as a foreign language (i.e., English for India, English for Japan) through the syncretic work of Faucett. It then turns to a less well-known figure, the Columbia University linguist Janet Rankin Aiken whose critical essays on Basic English in 1933 and 1934 were the first rejoinder from professional linguists to publically contest its applicability. The following two sections document the ensuing controversy over Basic English from the *Critical Examination of Basic English* published by the New York University linguist Elaine Swenson and West that was followed by Ogden's vituperative response, *Counter-Offensive: An Exposure of Certain Misrepresentations of Basic English*. My close reading of Aiken's essays, West and Swenson's *Bulletin* articles, and Ogden's responses, seeks to raise these debates out of their trivialities and to show how they provide the rhetorical structure for an anglophone ideology. It is through the banal terms of the debate—word counts and word definition, grammatical English, commercialism, and market value—that they rhetorically construct the anglophone as coherent and stable. In this sense, the Basic English controversy cannot be separated from the Carnegie Conference that was being organized at the same time and was caught up in similar debates and concerns.

Drawing extensively on the Carnegie Archives, Chapter 5, "The Carnegie Conference and Its Discontents," examines the 1934 Conference in all of its aspects from the history of the Carnegie Corporation, its organization (including its participants and the debates over its title), the proceedings of the conference, and the final report that consolidated all of this background into a document to be used for teaching English around the world. I focus primarily on two elements: the transatlantic power struggle over the conference's terms and Ogden's influence on the events despite his absence from the proceedings. In response to these conditions, there emerges a corporate, neutral model of English that is de-territorialized and at the same time refashioned as the "anglophone." I trace this ideology from this interwar period to the present in a brief concluding chapter that argues for recognizing how contemporary debates over English hegemony are shaped by the arguments and positions that were taken in the Carnegie battles.

A Brief Note on Terminology

The terms around World English in this study should be understood as a species of what Michel Rolph Trouillot described as "North Atlantic Universals": "words that project the North Atlantic experience on a universal scale that they themselves have helped to create."[18] Howatt observes that the terms used for ELT differ in the United States and the UK and that in the latter, those choices have been influenced by colonialism. But because this study moves between past and present, there is potentially some confusion over terminology due to changes in meaning over the course of the century. The most obvious is the description of the phenomenon it purports to study. My title uses the phrase "World English" in reference to the sense used at the time, as seen in West's 1934 essay, "English as a World Language," and in correspondence around the Carnegie Conference. As such, it should not be confused with the contemporary use of World English connected to the journal of that name established in the 1980s. There are other terms from this interwar period that are deployed today with a different set of meanings, such as Auxiliary English, Simple English, Plain English, English as a Lingua Franca, English as an International Language, and International English. Other terminological problems arise with descriptions of Palmer and West as either educators or applied linguists; they saw themselves as language educators, yet their work extended into fields that would be developed after the Second World War. For instance, they are seen today as part of the practitioners of English Language Teaching, though that term was not widely used until 1946 when it was adopted as the title for the journal of that name by the British Council; their methods are also similar to those of Applied Linguistics, a term often used to describe the Vocabulary Control group, although its origins as a discipline date from the 1940s with the engagement in language teaching by the linguists Laurence Bloomfield and Charles Fries.[19] I refer to them as English language teachers, educators, and applied linguists depending on the aspect of their work under consideration. As this brief note on terms demonstrates, this was a period of interregnum between conceptions of language study and teaching, not to mention conceptions of English, that provides the foundation for and resonates with the ways that we engage with language today.

Notes

1 A. P. R. Howatt, *A History of English Language Teaching*, second edition with H. G. Widdowson (Oxford: Oxford University Press, 2004), xvi.

2 For theories of Global English that chart its origins and post-war development, see Robert Phillipson, *Linguistic Imperialism* (New York: Oxford University Press, 1992) and *Linguistic Imperialism Continued* (New York: Routledge, 2009); Alastair Pennycook, *The Cultural Politics of English as an International Language* (London: Longman, 1994) and *English and the Discourses of Colonialism* (London: Routledge, 1998); Vaughan Rapatahana, et al. *English Language as Hydra: Its Impacts on Non-English Language Cultures* (Bristol: Multilingual Matters, 2012); Marnie Holborow, *The Politics of English* (London: Sage, 1999); Janina Brutt-Griffler, *World English: A Study of Its Development* (Clevedon, UK: Multilingual Matters, 2002); David Crystal, *English as a Global Language*, 2nd edition (Cambridge: Cambridge University Press, 2002).

3   There are many examples of this ideological view of English associated with British Council publications; this one came from David Graddol, *English Next* (British Council, 2006).

4   See Richard C. Smith, *Teaching English as a Foreign Language, 1912–1936: Pioneers of ELT*, 5 volumes (London: Routledge, 2003). This project is indebted to Smith's editions as well as his introductions to each volume that altogether constitute an important supplement to Howatt's history. Because I am using primary works from Palmer and West as they are reprinted in Smith's volumes, I will cite them hereafter by author and title and then as included in "Smith, *Pioneers of ELT*, volume number, page number" using the numbers in Smith's editions, not in the primary texts.

5   On microhistory, I am using the sense of the term as defined by Karl Appuhn, as "a historical method that takes as its object of study the interactions of individuals and small groups with the goal of isolating ideas, beliefs, practices, and actions that would otherwise remain unknown by means of more conventional historical strategies." See Appuhn, "Microhistory," in Methods & Theory/Periods/Regions, Nations, Peoples/Europe & the World, edited by Peter N. Stearns, 105–12, in Vol. 1 of *Encyclopedia of European Social History* (Detroit, MI: Charles Scribner's Sons, 2001), *Gale eBooks* (accessed February 12, 2021).

6   Formalist accounts of modernism and language include R. M. Berry, "Language," in Bradshaw and Dettmar, *A Companion to Modernist Literature and Culture* (Malden, MA: Blackwell Publishing, 2006), 113–22; April McMahon, "Language: 'History Is a Nightmare from Which I Am Trying to Awake,'" in David Bradshaw, *A Concise Companion to Modernism* (Malden, MA: Blackwell Publishing, 2003), 138–57.

7   Robert Phillipson, "English, the *Lingua Nullius* of Global Hegemony," in *The Politics of Multilingualism: Europeanisation, Globalisation, and Linguistic Governance*, edited by Peter A. Kraus and François Grin (Amsterdam/Philadelphia: John Benjamins Publishing, 2018), 282.

8   This project is indebted to a diverse range of scholars in sociolinguistics and applied linguistics that follows in the wake of Phillipson and Pennycook, though often at a critical angle: Mario Saraceni, *World Englishes: A Critical Analysis* (Bloomsbury, 2015); the essays in Braj Kachru et al., *Handbook of World Englishes* (London: Blackwell, 2006); Janina Brutt-Griffler, *World English*; Suresh Canagarajah, *Translingual Practice: Global Englishes and Cosmopolitan Relations* (London: Routledge, 2013); Holborow, *The Politics of English*; Peter Ives, *Gramsci's Politics of Language* (Toronto: University of Toronto Press, 2004); on the interconnection of economic and sociolinguistic inequalities with language policy, Allan James, "Theorising English and Globalisation: Semiodiversity and Linguistic Structure in Global English, World Englishes and Lingua Franca English," *Apples: Journal of Applied Linguistics* 3, no. 1 (2009): 79–92; Jan Blommaert, *The Sociolinguistics of*

Globalization (Cambridge: Cambridge University Press, 2010); the essays collected in Ruanni Tupas's *Unequal Englishes: The Politics of Englishes Today* (London: Palgrave Macmillan, 2015) and in Peter Kraus and François Grin's *The Politics of Multilingualism*. On ideologies of the Mother Tongue and myths of the "native speaker," Thomas Paul Bonfiglio, *Mother Tongues and Nations: The Invention of the Native Speaker* (Boston: De Gruyter, 2010) and Alan Davies, *The Native Speaker: Myth and Reality* (Clevedon, UK: Multilingual Matters, Ltd., 2003). On language rights, Stephen May, ed., *Language Rights* (New York: Routledge, 2017); Lionel Wee, *Language without Rights* (New York: Oxford University Press, 2011).

9 Recent works on global English and world literature that are particularly relevant for this project include David Damrosch, *What Is World Literature?* (Princeton: Princeton University Press, 2004); Pascale Casanova, *The World Republic of Letters* (Cambridge: Harvard University Press, 2004); Franco Moretti, *Distant Reading* (London: Verso, 2013); Rebecca Walkowitz, *Born Translated* (New York: Columbia University Press, 2015); *The Routledge Companion to World Literature*, edited by Theo D'Haen et al. (New York: Routledge, 2012); Aamir Mufti, *Forget English!*; Simon Gikandi, "Provincializing English," *PMLA* 129, 1 (2014); David Huddart's *Involuntary Associations* (Liverpool: University of Liverpool Press, 2014); Fiona Doloughan's *English as a Literature in Translation* (London: Bloomsbury, 2016); Bill Ashcroft, *Caliban's Voice: The Transformation of English in Post-Colonial Literatures* (New York: Routledge, 2009); and Brian Lennon's *In Babel's Shadow* (Minneapolis: University of Minnesota Press, 2010). On language standardization, vernaculars, and modernism, see Michael North, *The Dialect of Modernism: Race, Language and Twentieth Century Literature* (New York: Oxford University Press, 1994); Joshua Miller's *Accented America* (Oxford: Oxford University Press, 2011); Barry McCrea's *Languages of the Night* (New Haven, CT: Yale University Press, 2015). On postcolonial studies of language education, see Ben Baer's *Indigenous Vanguards* (New York: Columbia University Press, 2019); Shondel J. Nero and Dohra Ahmad, *Vernaculars in the Classroom: Paradoxes, Pedagogy, Possibilities* (New York: Routledge, 2014).

10 Aamir Mufi does both in Chapters 1 and 3 in *Forget English!*; also, see Pheng Cheah, *What Is a World?: On Postcolonial Literature as World Literature* (Durham: Duke University Press, 2016).

11 Aamir Mufti, *Forget English!* (Cambridge: Harvard University Press, 2016), 19.

12 Ashcroft, *Caliban's Voice*, 4.

13 Gikandi, "Provincializing English," 13.

14 For this and other critical approaches to pluralist approaches to WE, see Ruanni Tupas and Rani Rubdy, "Introduction," in *Unequal Englishes*, 2–6; Ryuko Kubota, "Inequalities of English, English Speakers, and Languages: A Critical Perspective on Pluralist Approaches to English," in *Unequal Englishes*, 21–41; François Grin,

"On Some Fashionable Terms in Multilingualism Research: Critical Assessment and Implications for Language Policy," in *Politics of Multilingualism*, 247–74. For a neutral description of WE, see Saraceni, *World Englishes*, 71–134.

15 Walkowitz, "Response," *Interventions* 20, no. 3 (2018): 364.
16 Holborow, *Politics of English*, 191.
17 Walkowitz, "Response," 362.
18 Michel-Rolph Trouillot, *Global Transformations: Anthropology and the Modern World* (New York: Palgrave Macmillan, 2003), 35.
19 Howatt, *History of English Language Teaching*, 302–3. Note that I will be using both editions (1984 and 2004) of Howatt's history.

Acknowledgments

This book could be described as a long answer to a short question put to me by my former advisor, Gauri Viswanathan, after I had presented my initial research on the Carnegie Conference and global English. Her query sent me, as always, back to the archives, and what had started as a curiosity became a book. As many of her students can attest, this is typical of the many ways that her example as a scholar are inspirational. My debt extends to the friends and colleagues who helped along this project in so many ways, Dohra Ahmad, Eric Bulson, Joshua Miller, and Cóilin Parsons. I am grateful to Jahan Ramazani, for his consistent support and interest in the project. My thanks to Maria Frawley and the Migrations Seminar at George Washington University for inviting me to present my work in progress. I also appreciate the patience of Gerry Kennedy and the other members of the Poe seminar at the ACLA; this work was improved by your comments. Parts of Chapter 3 draw upon material from my article, [Malouf, M. (2020). "The Poe Test: Global English and The Gold Bug." *The Cambridge Journal of Postcolonial Literary Inquiry*, 7(1), 35–49 © Cambridge University Press, 2019], reproduced here with permission.

This book was first developed and later completed during leaves of absence supported by the Provost's Office at George Mason University for which I am grateful. I also could not have written this without the support of conference and research travel funds from the George Mason University English Department. In many ways, this is a work that could only have come about at GMU due to its diverse students and faculty. I want to thank the students from my Global English courses over the years who provided unique and valuable perspectives that shaped my approach to the problems of language. I am grateful for all the helpful conversations with my colleagues in the GMU Linguistics program, particularly Steven Weinberger, for his patience with my questions. Of course, any errors and mistakes remain mine. I also want to extend thanks to all of my colleagues at Mason, whose inquiring scholarship and attention to multilingualism in all of its forms provided a rich background for my thinking. I want to especially thank Eric Eisner for his friendship and hospitality when I was doing research in New York.

I could not have completed this project without the generous support of the ELT historian Richard C. Smith who made his Warwick ELT Archive available to an interloping American and for his support for this project. Similarly, I could not have uncovered the mysteries of the Carnegie Conference without the assistance of Jennifer S. Comins, the Archivist for the Carnegie Collections at the Columbia University Rare Book and Manuscript Library. My thanks to Ben Doyle and all of the editorial staff at Bloomsbury Publishing for believing in this work and making it possible. I appreciate the advice of the external readers of the initial chapter and proposal and of the final MS that helped me to see this project into its final form.

The final year of this project was spent working under the pandemic conditions of 2020–1. I want to acknowledge the library staff and research librarians at GMU's Fenwick Library for working under these conditions and always tracking down books and resources at a time when I did not have access to the library.

For my family, I appreciate their patience for my writing while we were all home together during this strange year. To my sons, Liam and Alex, my gratitude for keeping me sane and happy throughout the many years that this book grew alongside you both. To Isabelle, for her inspiration. Finally, my thanks and love to Kristina, my first and best reader, for her endless supply of faith, humor, support, and belief.

Part I

Managing English

1

Pioneers and Heretics

Introduction

In October 1934, the Carnegie Corporation convened a conference on the teaching of English as a world language at their offices in New York City. It was organized by Michael Philip West, the developer of the popular New Method English textbooks, who had recently been appointed as Professor of Languages at the University of Toronto after twenty years as an English-language instructor, school inspector, and teacher trainer in Bengal. The conference met for a week in New York City and then a subcommittee traveled to the University of Chicago and the University of Ohio to consult with statisticians and linguists. A follow-up conference was held in June 1935, at the Colonial Offices in London, this time hosted by Sir Percy Nunn and the Advisory Committee on Education in the Colonies. As this itinerary suggests, this was a transatlantic endeavor that sought to combine progressive American methods of education with traditional British expertise and institutional structures in order to create a consensus around what form of English should be taught to the world. Despite insisting that their goal was "the simplification of teaching, not language,"[1] they were also aware that, as the educator Edward Thorndike remarked, "some universal form of English might ultimately result from [our]work, but that would be an accident."[2]

The Carnegie Conference was the culmination of over fifteen years of innovation and development in the field of English Language Teaching (ELT) that had taken place in dispersed locations all over the world. Its attendees included many figures who were active in the rapid development of linguistics, language teaching and policy during the interwar period. Its chair was R. H. Fife, Professor of German at Columbia University, who had led the effort to secure modern language teaching in the United States after the isolationist attacks against it in the First World War.[3] Among its participants were Thorndike, "the Father of curriculum," who created the influential *Teacher's Word Book*, and the anthropological linguist Edward Sapir, who created the first dictionaries of American Indian languages. The British contingent was represented by Arthur Mayhew, a member of the Colonial Office advisory committee on education in the colonies and the author of *The Education of India* (1926) and *Education in the Colonial Empire* (1938). As illustrious as Sapir, Thorndike, and Mayhew were at the time, the principal figures were West and his rivals in the nascent field of ELT: Harold Palmer, founder of the Institute of Research in English Teaching (IRET) in Tokyo, and Lawrence Faucett, the creator of the *Oxford English Course*. Most notably, however, were two absences: C. K. Ogden and I. A. Richards, the inventors of Basic English, who were invited yet declined to attend. The reasons behind their refusal and the significance of Basic for the conference play an important role, I argue, in defining the conference's purpose and its conclusions.

Using the Carnegie Conference as its focus, *Making World English* examines the process that brought all of these figures together (or not) around this shared purpose and what it tells us about the ideological structure and definition of Global English today. Mainly of interest for histories of ELT, the Carnegie Conference also has relevance for understanding Thorndike's reference to a "universal form of English." In the decade before Carnegie there was a range of experimentation in modern language teaching that prepared the foundations for the post-war teaching of English as an auxiliary language.[4] Most of the models developed in the 1910s and 1920s were designed with a regional focus: English for France, or India, etc. The "world" version of English imagined at Carnegie was a reduced vocabulary that could be used by educators to create primers and tests in any part of the world. One of the difficulties posed by such a universal mandate is the problem of selecting words that are relevant, relatable, and, most importantly, non-offensive. It also involves developing a consensus on how to teach, particularly in classrooms that are large and have non-native speaking instructors. Finally, there is the question of the existing languages in the nations where this English will be taught: what does this World English mean for their status as languages of instruction or their applicability to science, business, and politics? In this way, it is possible to understand how in the process of answering such questions one might "accidentally" create a universal form of English. Even as an expression of disavowal, Thorndike's statement could only be made because the ideological conditions of the time had already granted permission.

Understanding how these ideological conditions were created is the purpose of the three chapters that make up Part I. This first chapter provides an initial introduction to the status of British English after the First World War, and to the careers and contributions of the members of the Vocabulary Control movement: Palmer, West, and Ogden. The first part, "An Anglophone Empire?," situates the conference politically in terms of transatlantic relations, late empire, and governmental and private support for language teaching. The rest of the chapter discusses the Palmer Method, West's New Method, and Ogden's Basic English in terms of their respective intellectual backgrounds with particular interest in the role of their locations in their thought: pre-War Belgium and Imperial Japan for Palmer, colonial Bengal, before and after the war, for West, and early twentieth-century Cambridge for Ogden. Because they were developing their theories independently, without any disciplinary consensus, these diverse locations played a role in their theories of language and their conception of English's role in the world. This chapter introduces their main concepts and situates them in their personal, political, and social contexts.

Chapters 2 and 3 explore the politics of Vocabulary Control through an exploration of their main products: word lists (Chapter 2) and Simplified Readers (Chapter 3). Part II of this book focuses more directly on the controversies over Basic English and the proceedings and aftermath of the Carnegie Conference. These parts are linked by the imperialist ideologies that inform the methodological debates and shape the choices made about a world English. This study views the Carnegie Conference as the culmination of the experiments in language education from the 1920s and as an ideological limitation on the kind of universal English promised by the disruptive influence of Basic English. My study follows Janina Brutt-Griffler's insight that English language spread in the colonies was *managed* through a process of withholding it from the general population, and controlling the type of English that was taught to the elites.[5] In this sense, the Carnegie Conference was as much about halting a form of International English as it was about creating one, even accidentally.

At the time that this study begins, in 1919, the Carnegie Corporation is still finding its place in a post-war world after the death of its founder, Arthur Carnegie. It would find this new purpose in the figure of Frederick P. Keppel, a former Provost at Columbia University and Foreign Secretary during the First World War. As President of the Corporation from 1923 to 1941, Keppel expanded its scope from its initial purpose, the creation of public libraries, to supporting library infrastructure, adult education, and to fund scholarly studies of educational methods that might be implemented all over the world. Most importantly, Keppel consolidated Carnegie as a grant-making institution with a specific interest in international education including funding education grants in sub-Saharan Africa and South Africa as well as the Swedish social economist Gunnar Myrdal's influential study of segregated education in America.[6] As I discuss more fully in Chapter 5, this 1934 conference on English language teaching fit Keppel's vision of the Corporation as an innovator in global education alongside and outside traditional colonial lines. In this sense, it exemplifies the late imperialism of the 1920s and 1930s when the metropole renegotiated some control over education to the peripheries as part of the policy of the Dual Mandate. Carnegie's internationalism is suggestive of a larger tension that arises during the interwar period between the two transatlantic powers. While the English language in 1919 is enjoying a moment of international prestige as it supplants French from its place as a diplomatic language during the Peace Conference, it is not immune from this world of transatlantic politics, as I discuss in the next part of this chapter.

An Anglophone Empire?

The linguist David Crystal, who has written many popular books on the evolution of the English language, describes Global English as "primarily the result of two factors: the expansion of British colonial power, which peaked towards the end of the nineteenth century, and the emergence of the United States as the leading economic power of the twentieth century."[7] From the perspective of the twenty-first century, it is easy to grasp this general narrative of Global English as a sequence of anglophone empires, yet from the perspective of the interwar period, the status of their relations was not as clearly defined, nor was the use of the English language as a mode of cultural imperialism so obvious. During the interwar period, this succession of empires was still in a state of negotiation and ambivalence and transatlantic relations were strained due to contestations over trade markets, naval dominance, and currency valuation that extended to their so-called shared language.[8] For example, in 1923 a US congressman proposed officially renaming the language of the United States as "American" as part of the country's "mental emancipation" from the UK.[9]

The historian Anne Orde argues that while the United States emerged from the end of the First World War as a world power, "the course of world affairs in the 1920s left room for doubt" over the balance of power between the two countries.[10] Their tensions over trade and naval supremacy in particular nearly led to open conflicts as did the United States' apparent financial and commercial dominance by the end of the decade.[11] Despite their increasing international power, the United States during the interwar period was intensely isolationist passing a range of exclusionary policies on immigration, race, and language that Joshua Miller describes as "an interwar ideological constellation that set new limits on US citizenship and civic participation according to language."[12] This English-only ideology extended to US colonies such as the Philippines. English-language education was implemented, it was claimed, to provide a common lingua franca, though Vincente Raphael also noted that it was a means of countering Filipino insurgencies and associating the Philippines with "anglo-saxon values."[13] According to a 1925 *Survey of Education in the Philippines* by Columbia University, the project was largely a failure and it resulted, by the 1930s, in a stratified society with an English-speaking elite and a majority population limited by what the *Survey* reported as a "foreign language handicap."[14] According to Brutt-Griffler, American language policy in the Philippines was motivated by ideology while the British imperative was largely economic. As Timothy Parsons observes about British calls for colonial education in Africa in the 1920s, the goal was to "create a new generation of westernized Africans ... to assist in economic development."[15]

After the Great War, Britain possessed an expanding empire and over-extended resources. Because of their repressive colonial policies adopted in reaction to anti-colonial nationalist movements, including activities such as the Anglo-Irish War and the Rowlatt Acts in India, their military was dispersed thinly around the world.[16] It was further diminished by disarmament in the 1920s and the depression in the 1930s. Britain's interwar empire was defined by the contradiction of this repressive anti-colonial legislation, on the one hand, and Liberal conceptions of a civilizing empire that was leading its subjects toward self-rule, as described in the 1919 Chelmsford-Montagu Reforms and Lord Lugard's *Dual Mandate* from 1922.[17] Responding to anti-colonial criticism from within the colonies and from the United States and Soviet Union, Lugard argued that their purpose was to "develop African resources for the greater good of Britain and the global economy while simultaneously acting as the 'trustee for the welfare of the [native] masses.'" His argument updated late nineteenth-century New Imperialism that was based on the civilizing mission of empire and the policy of Indirect Rule, in which it was the responsibility of empire to protect traditional native ways of life from modernity. In terms of education policy, the Dual Mandate sought to counter nineteenth-century efforts to educate native elites: "Prosperity, combined with the wrong system of education and widespread illiteracy, has indeed like in Ireland, in Egypt, and in India, invariably given rise to unrest and sedition."[18]

As a result, there was an awareness that Britain needed a cost-effective means of expanding influence in order "to win hearts and minds" that was different from the colonial education policies of the past. The "blue-print for the British Council" was developed in the immediate aftermath of the war in the form of the Tilley Report in 1920, which articulated a need for cultural outreach through support for foreign students in England. It was not until the 1930s, when political concerns about competition with the French over cultural influence in Egypt that there was support for an "institution to undertake cultural relations."[19] In 1934, the same year as the Carnegie Conference, the *British Committee for Relations with Other Countries* was formed. At its inauguration, the Prince of Wales declared that the "basis of our work must be the English language."[20] It received permanent status in 1941 as the British Council. This history illustrates the degree to which English language promotion as a form of foreign policy was not a simple continuation of the British empire but was in fact a departure from the past and developed in response to the political conditions of the interwar period.

One of the first Chairs of the British Council was Frederick Clarke, a British educator who wrote the introduction to the Carnegie Report. This is just one of the ways that the Carnegie Conference played a significant role in consolidating transatlantic purpose in English language teaching. Robert Phillipson identifies the Carnegie Conference as "specifically aimed at establishing close collaboration between the USA and the UK."[21] Phillipson was correct in his description about the transatlantic collaboration; it is just that it was not without tension and suspicion, as I document in Chapter 5 in the discussions over the scope of the conference, its participants, and manner of distribution. The differences between the two powers were economic as well as political. The economist Giovanni Arrighi describes the British empire during the interwar period as an "extroverted economy" that was built upon strong links with foreign and colonial economies. In contrast, the United States was "autocentric" with economic activities organically integrated from center to periphery.[22] This difference can be seen in the contrast between the regional practices of ELT by Palmer and West, and the centripetal integration of practices that comes from the intrusion of the Carnegie Corporation into language teaching. The Carnegie Corporation and the Rockefeller Foundation were active in the promotion of education during the 1920s and 1930s, especially in Africa and Asia.[23] In this sense, the Carnegie Conference was not so much a confirmation of transatlantic unity as much as it was a consolidating and legitimating event that made the idea of a continuous anglophone power possible.

Harold Palmer: The Palmer Method and English in Japan

As with so many influential British artists and intellectuals of the modernist period, Palmer, West, and Ogden are products of late Victorian England, shaped intellectually by Edwardian reactions to nineteenth-century orthodoxies, the New Imperialism and the Boer Wars, and the destruction of the First World War.

Palmer was the elder statesman, born in 1877 in London and raised in the southern coastal town of Hythe where his father, a French scholar who had received the *Palmes Académiques* from the French Academy, started up a school and served as its Head Master before founding a newspaper, *The Hythe Reporter*.[24] It would appear that Palmer inherited his father's linguistic and entrepreneurial talents. In keeping with this unconventional middle-class upbringing, Palmer was educated outside of the Oxbridge system. He attended private schools until his teens, when he was sent to France to perfect his French. He excelled in all of his subjects but was particularly interested in art (his mother was a painter), drama, and languages. After school, he worked for his father's newspaper until his mid-twenties when he decided to enter language teaching.

In 1902, he began teaching at the *École Internationale des Langues Vivantes* in the town of Verviers in southeast Belgium. Like his father, he established his own school in 1903 where he taught French, English, and Esperanto. He became engaged with the latter through the *Societe Polyglotte de Verviers*, "an association dedicated to internationalism and encouragement of internationalist attitudes through language learning."[25] It was during this formative period in Belgium that he developed an individual style of teaching and made contacts with leading linguists in the field such as the phoneticist Daniel Jones at the University of London, who invited him to give lectures on language teaching during the war. These lectures were published as *The Scientific Study and Teaching of Languages* in 1917. He published *The Principles of Language Study* after the war as a synthetic and philosophical statement of what would become known as the Palmer Method (though he never used the term himself). Pennycook summarizes Palmer's achievement as "the attempt to develop forms of simplified English as a particular type of standardization, the emphasis on oral language as primary, and the call to make the study of language teaching scientific."[26]

When Palmer began language teaching at the *fin de siècle*, there were two dominant methods of language teaching: the Classical Method (also known as the Grammar-Translation method) and the Direct Method. The first was modeled on the way that classical languages like Latin or Greek were taught through the translation of model sentences, rote memorization, and the recitation of grammatical forms. As the linguistic historian Norbert Schmitt explains, "This method focused on the ability to *analyze* language, not to *use* it."[27] In the 1880s, the turn toward phonetics leads to the Reform Movement formed by Henry Sweet and Daniel Jones in London, Otto Jespersen in Denmark, Paul Passy in France, and Wilhelm Viëtor in Germany. There were three main principles to the Reform movement: the primacy of speech; the use of the "connected text," rather than isolated sentences; and primary use of the target language for instruction. The fundamental problem with the Reform Method was how to apply it to the classroom. It was difficult, for instance, to teach a connected text without breaking it up into smaller parts, or teach without translating at all, as many Reform advocates insisted. In rejecting the Classical Method, Reform also rejected any curriculum or textbooks. Instead, it depended on native-speaking instructors who could invent a productive class experience through the force of their own personality.

In the 1890s, two British Civil Servants in India, Percival Christopher Wren and Horace Wyatt, developed a curriculum to bring Reform principles into the classroom. Wren and Wyatt's system became known as the Direct Method, an inductive, oral-based curriculum based in contemporary research in phonetics that emphasized the monolingual classroom and reduced the role of literature. Wyatt's advice to teachers characterizes the utilitarian principles of efficiency associated with early twentieth-century language teaching methods: "The only true economy is to teach one language thoroughly, and that must be the language needed in practical life."[28] Consigning the vernacular to the middle stages of the English course and Literature to its highest, in the University, Wyatt's system updated the socially stratified model of education that had long been a part of the colonial curriculum.

Palmer was introduced to the Direct Method for the first time when he began teaching in Belgium. He had started by teaching in the Berlitz method, which preceded Reform but shared its emphasis on the monolingual, oral classroom. Although Palmer successfully taught English, French, and Esperanto for twelve years in Verviers mostly through the Direct Method, he soon realized the degree to which it depended upon a subjective and unique classroom experience rather than an objective, scientific pedagogy. Palmer's *Scientific Study* criticized and adapted the Direct Method in several ways. Most importantly, he broke with its emphasis on the connected text using instead sentence patterns based on his "ergonic method." But the influence of the Direct Method is evident in Palmer's course design with its oral emphasis, beginning with speech and the repetition of sentences before introducing any grammatical rules.

English in Japan

It was because of his popular adaptation of the Direct Method that Palmer was recruited in 1921 by a wealthy Japanese businessman, Matsukata Kojiro, the head of the Kawasaki Shipbuilding Company, to advise the Japanese Government Ministry of Education.[29] The businessman was concerned with the "commercial implications of spoken English."[30] This sentiment linking language and business runs deeply in Japan. The first schools to teach economics were originally language schools: Keio Gijuku, founded by Fukuzawa Yukichi in 1858, and Tokyo Imperial University, which developed out of Bansho Shirabesho, the Institute for the Study of Barbarian Writing.[31] The first business school was founded by the first Minister of Education, Mori Arinori, in 1875. Like Matsukata, he was a progressive Liberal who sought to Westernize Japan. As the economic historian Liah Greenfeld notes, this desire was so strong that "he was willing to consider replacing Japanese with 'a rationalized version of English' as the national language (on the grounds that Japanese could not support the modern economic and political discourse)."[32] This interest in a limited model of English for purposes of trade would influence the role of English in Asia in the 1920s and would reappear in the initial interest in Basic English in China.

As part of the prominence of both English and economics in the new Japanese universities in the nineteenth century, American and British professors were recruited to teach economics. Matsukata Kojirohe was the son of Matsukata Masayoshi, the finance minister responsible for the privatization of Japan's industries in the 1880s. Like many children of the elite at that time, Matsukata studied in the United States and France between 1884 and 1890 where he became a famous collector of Western art; it is his collection that provides the basis for the Museum of Western Art in Tokyo, designed by Le Corbusier and built in the 1950s after his death. Despite this Westernization, he was known for embodying a modernized samurai ethic of *bushido*, as Greenfeld describes it, the ethic's traditional devotion to duty "was now interpreted as service to the nation."[33] Recruiting and financing Palmer indicates the persistence of this *bushido* ethic that combines Japanese nationalism and an openness to Western liberalism.

However, just as Matsukata's pre-war Liberal internationalism was contested in the 1920s by Japanese nationalism, Palmer's status as linguistic advisor to the Ministry was never fully accepted. Soon after Palmer arrived, Howatt reports, he suggested using "a controlled vocabulary of 3,000 words" to improve English teaching in Japan. Not only would this mean revising all of the existing schoolbooks it also met resistance from officials who saw him as intentionally limiting Japanese students from acquiring "full English."[34]

An unintended consequence of his ambivalent status as a consultant but not a full minister in Japan was that Palmer had financial support to experiment with language teaching methods, which allowed him to use this second phase of his career to establish language teaching as a profession through the Institute for Research in English Teaching (IRET) that he founded in Tokyo. Palmer's Institute created language materials for Japanese schools while remaining autonomous from the Ministry, but it was mainly a site for experimentation. Most importantly, the IRET published the first international journal on research in language teaching, the IRET *Bulletin,* that provided the model for the British Council's journal *ELT* founded by Palmer's former assistant at IRET, A. S. Hornby.[35]

Palmer stayed in Japan for fourteen years before leaving with the rise of Japanese nationalism in the 1930s. According to Smith, his record in Japan is mixed: there was no large-scale reform of Japanese English language education to a Direct Method curriculum, yet the research and experimentation into language teaching methods influenced later developments in Japanese teaching.[36] Palmer's career marks the changes in the field from the amateur linguists of the nineteenth century who began as language teachers like himself, to the professional field of applied linguistics.

Michael West: The New Method and English in India

At the same time that Palmer was in Japan developing his oral methods for teaching English, West was in Bengal developing his own program for teaching English with an emphasis on "reading first." Despite these divergent approaches, they shared a desire to develop the field of applied linguistics around scientific means of word definition, language acquisition, and pedagogy.

Like Palmer, West was the son of an educator. His father, a Church of England minister, was the headmaster at Ascham School in Bournemouth. Unlike Palmer, West was educated through the Oxbridge system: he attended Marlborough College and then studied English at Christ Church College in Oxford. He joined the Indian Education Service (IES) in 1912 with an assignment at David Hare Teachers' Training College in Calcutta. After a year, he was transferred to a Teachers Training College in Dacca. The IES had a mixed reputation when it came to its officers. As Clive Whitehead documents, there were many brilliant talents that burned out after only a few months in the service and some less bright talents that lingered on.[37] I raise this point not to disparage the IES (whose history I discuss more fully in Chapter 2) but to reinforce Richard Smith's observation that West took "his duties as a colonial educator very seriously," as evident by the fact that he learned Bengali before his appointment to India.[38] Smith sees West in the tradition of Wren and Wyatt, as IES officers who grappled with the problems of language education as part of the larger system of education rather than just a linguistic challenge. In 1914, he had already written his first book, *Educational Psychology*, a subject which he taught himself, that reflects the progressive theories of education that were coming out of American institutions like Columbia's Teacher's College and would not enter the British education system for another generation.[39] His service was interrupted by the war and in 1919 he took part in a survey of primary education in Bengal, inspecting schools in Calcutta and Chittagong. Along with his interest in psychology, his observations during this period shaped the educational program that he developed in the 1920s in his position as a Principal of the Teachers' Training College in Dacca.

English in India

West was a late arrival in the history of English language teaching in India. The rise of English as an integral part of rule in India was a feature of the late eighteenth and early nineteenth centuries, primarily through the influence of Charles Grant, a member of the Clapham sect in England, who sought to reform Indian morality through instruction of an elite class in English. This became known as the Anglicist argument for reforming Indian education that was later adopted famously by Thomas Macaulay (son of Zachary Macaulay, a member of the Clapham sect), during his time serving on the Supreme Council of India. Opposed to the Anglicists were the "Orientalists," whose views had a longer history in the East India Company going back to Warren Hastings and William Jones in the eighteenth century who sought "native" languages that could be used for the purposes of treaties over property, taxation, and trade.[40]

Macaulay's arguments on the superiority of English for the Anglicists are often cited in histories of English as a world language because of his explicit claims for the superiority of English over vernacular languages.[41] Despite his arguments for English education, Macaulay admits that the funds allowed for education were insufficient to teach the entire population. Therefore, he suggests limiting education to "a class of interpreters" who would be "a class of persons Indian in blood and colour, but English in tastes, in opinions, in morals and in intellect."[42] This became the basis of what became known as the Filtration Method adopted by William Bentinck when he implemented English-language education in 1839.[43] It became even more necessary in 1844 when English was made a requirement to work in the Indian Civil Service which created an increased native demand that could not be met by existing institutions. Sir Charles Wood's Education Despatch of 1854 sought to reverse the Filtration Method by expanding vernacular primary education through new economic incentives for building private schools. Numerous reforms followed, and are discussed more fully in Chapter 2 in relation to West's *Bilingualism*, but they did not reverse the trend wherein secondary education exceeded primary education, creating what the economic historian Latika Chaudhary calls "a mixed picture of lopsided progress."[44]

West developed his New Method in response to this "lopsided" nature of English education in India, and as an alternative to the Filtration Method and the Direct Method. During his work as an inspector of schools, he saw these two theories as leading to wasteful education in both English and the vernaculars. Students in the native schools who do not learn English are kept within menial positions while students who get into the English schools only learn enough English to pass exams for civil service positions. As West described the failure of the Filtration Theory: "Education does not filter downwards; it produces crowding upwards."[45] In terms of the Direct Method, he criticized its oral methods as ill-suited for the crowded classrooms led by non-native speakers. Because the Direct Method rejected the use of connected texts, students mainly learned how to speak short phrases while slowly building their vocabulary. However, in a school system where students only have English for a year or so before leaving for work, it is inefficient. Instead, he introduced the concept of "reading-first" as a means of exposing students to a wide vocabulary in a short period of time. By de-emphasizing pronunciation and practicing speech, the New Method also de-emphasizes the teacher and promotes the status of the textbook, the "surrogate Englishman" in the classroom.[46]

West based his New Method on observations and quantified data collected in Bengali classrooms, which he published in 1926 as a Government of India Occasional Report titled *Bilingualism (with special reference to Bengal)*. He wrote this extensive report with graphs and charts demonstrating his data as an Oxford dissertation. However, as Smith notes, it was turned down by examiners who were wary of his use of statistics and quantitative methods for analyzing education. He was able to get it accepted in 1927 after it was reviewed by different examiners, and soon after he published *Bilingualism* and an abridged version,

Learning to Read a Foreign Language. As an example of the divergent trends in transatlantic philosophies of education, *Bilingualism* was widely accepted in the United States where "a trend toward focusing on reading at the expense of other skills was gaining ground within modern language teaching."[47] West tested his thesis through the production of a series of textbooks, *New Method Readers*, published in India in 1926-7, that were piloted with Bengali students. West's Readers were the first significant development in ELT Readers since Wren had remarked around twenty years earlier that "the days were over when works like Lamb's *Essays* or Burke's *Reflections on the French Revolution* could be regarded as suitable introductions to modern English for Matriculation students."[48] The Readers begin with fables and fairy tales before adding longer works usually with an adventurous theme like *Robinson Crusoe* and *The Deerslayer* and then canonical British novels such as *David Copperfield* and *Silas Marner* (see Figure 1). West's contribution was to grade his Simplified Readers by a "plateau" or graded system of vocabulary. Thus, a student would learn 1,000 words and then use the reader to reinforce those before moving on to the next "radii" of vocabulary. As a result, West popularized the two main features of vocabulary control, the word list and the simplified reader.

The Readers became successful in their own right and had their own success outside of the classroom. After the course that they were to supplement had been discontinued in the 1930s, West remarked that "the potted books go on and on."[50] Reportedly, the New Method Readers saved its publisher, Longmans, from financial ruin and got it a foothold in an emerging English as a foreign language market.[51] Their success gained many imitators, including an attempt to be bought out by Oxford University Press, which was just starting its own efforts in English language teaching in Africa. The American linguist Lawrence Faucett, who would become known as the third "pioneer of ELT" after West and Palmer, approached West with a proposal for an "all-in joint account" between the New Method Readers and the Oxford English Course that he was developing.[52] Longmans' rejection of Faucett's proposal is significant for understanding how the education textbook market drove the competition among teaching methods. Longmans, known colloquially as the "ship" because of their logo, responded that "the world be divided in Ship and Press areas";[53] that is, the colonial markets were to be divided by geography: Longmans in India, Oxford in Africa, Royal Readers in the West Indies and the Dominions. This accounts for the way that different language teaching methods were associated with specific publishers and locations. It also reflected the dominant belief among language teachers that language should be taught for the specific region. That is why West tested

Figure 1 *David Copperfield*, New Method Supplementary Reader, Cover. During the interwar years, these were in use in India, Ceylon, Palestine, Persia, Nigeria, Kenya, and Uganda.[49]

his Readers with Bengali students; the system was based on his research on classrooms in Calcutta, therefore the content selected in the stories and the range of words employed would reflect the culture and needs of Bengalis, including, as I discuss in Chapter 3, their resistance to British colonialism.

Ironically, the success of the New Method Readers led to the end of West's career in India as he was forced to resign his position at the Dacca Teachers' Training College in 1932. Colonial education authorities saw a conflict of interest in the fact that he was making money from textbooks that he was also training teachers to use in the classroom.[54] Aside from its immediate context, West's resignation might also be seen as anticipating a shift taking place at the time from a bureaucratic, regionalist, colonial model of education in which local authorities decide on modes of teaching within a particular sphere to a centralized, market-based system driven by metropolitan publishers such as Oxford and Longmans. What West had started as part of a local economy—publishing and using his Readers in India—had expanded beyond its peripheral status. It is fitting that after leaving India, West takes a position at the University of Toronto that was funded by the New York-based Carnegie Corporation. He has moved from a British model of colonial imperialism to the "soft" imperialism of the United States. In 1934, when he convenes the Carnegie Conference, it is ostensibly an attempt to synthesize the transatlantic methods of teaching that were divided regionally around the world. It can also be seen as anticipating a shift in relations between the center and periphery that would become apparent with the new economic order after the war.

C. K. Ogden: Basic English and Artificial Languages

In the late 1920s, the nascent ELT profession was defined by a dichotomy between the Palmer Method and the New Method: what was to be emphasized: speech or reading? Was the teacher an active presence as in the Direct Method, or should the classroom be "learner-centered," as it was conceived by West? This methodological dichotomy was not to last long, however, as a new way of thinking about English in the world was to emerge in 1930 with the publication of C. K. Ogden's *Basic English*. Basic originated as an intervention into Artificial Languages like Esperanto and Volapük, not as a form of ELT. However, its fame had the effect of disrupting the field even in its serial publication in the *Cambridge Magazine*, and it was not long before Ogden began adapting Basic to ELT purposes.

According to I. A. Richards, the idea of a minimal language came to them while writing the chapter "On Definition" for their 1921 book on semiotics, *Meaning of Meaning*, and finding "a limited set of words reappearing"[55] with each definition suggesting the possibility of an essential vocabulary. Ogden began the project in earnest in 1925 working on the formula until early 1928 when, Ogden writes, "it became clear that 850 English words, put into operation by the Basic system, would give us something which was supported by science while offering to teachers and businessmen what they had been looking for."[56] Although it was a language system, not a means of teaching language, Ogden's reference to "teachers" in this quote suggests that it would be used in classrooms for teaching English.

Artificial Languages

Although the search for an ideal international language has its roots in the biblical story of Babel, there was a particular flourish of interest in constructed languages in the late nineteenth and early twentieth centuries. The first universal language to gain widespread popularity in Europe was Volapük, or "worldspeak." Developed by a German priest, Johan Martin Schleyer, in 1879, Volapük was not intended to act as an auxiliary but was an attempt to restore the single language that was destroyed by the curse of Babel. Its principal method was to employ common English and Germanic roots and to add prefixes and suffixes in order to change their purpose or meaning. This root system was used by many of the later constructed languages, including Basic. According to Michael Gordin, within its first ten years, Volapük had over two hundred thousand students and published newspapers in disparate locations from North America to China. However, it was not destined to last as Schleyer feuded with his followers and, as one observer recalled, "in 1888–89, it seemed as though it would conquer the world: in 1890 it was dying."[57] As we will see, the reason for its failure was a common one for constructed languages—a resistance to reform by the original creator.

The most well-known constructed language, Esperanto, followed soon after Volapük's demise, appearing in the famous pamphlet by "Doktoro Esperanto," a.k.a. Ludwik Lejzer Zamenhof in May 1887. Unlike Volapük, Esperanto was intended as a universal auxiliary, not a universal language. It uses a root system drawn from all the European languages with suffixes in form of letters—"o" for noun, "a" for adjective, "e" for adverbs—as well as circumflexes to signify pronunciation. Its value, as Gordin notes, is that it is easy to learn because of the number of words that can be devised from a small number of roots that are themselves easy to learn with a dictionary. The widespread popularity of Esperanto has been well-documented by Gordin and others. For our purposes, it is notable that Palmer taught Esperanto and, as is discussed in Chapter 2, was friends with Charles Lemaire, a Belgian linguist who advocated for what was known as "French Esperanto." Esperanto was also undone by internal divisions over reform that were suggested anonymously by the Nobel Prize-winning chemist Wilhelm Ostwald, at a general meeting in 1907. The changes were intended to "purify Esperanto," yet, when Zamenhof refused to make any reforms, it led to an irrevocable divide in the language movement and the creation of Ido as a rival language.

The split between the Idists and Esperantists weakened the movement but its internationalist idealism effectively ended with the First World War. Even Ostwald, the German creator of Ido, chose nationalism over internationalism. Abandoning Ido, he argued for an international scientific language, *Weltdeutsch*, a simplified German. According to Gordin, he based the language on the pidgin English used by the British as a mode of communication in Africa, a common source for simplified languages as discussed in Chapter 2. One of Otswald's sources for justifying his simplified German was one of Ido's most important followers, the Danish linguist Otto Jespersen, whose work, influenced by Darwin, argued that languages simplify as they evolve. Taking this as a "natural law of development" Ostwald suggested taking out "all the avoidable diversity, all that 'richness' of the language so charming for aesthetics."[58] Despite his disappointment with Ostwald's break, Jespersen would still support Ido up until 1929 when, at the same time as Ogden publishes Basic English, he created his own artificial auxiliary language, Novial. Jespersen's artificial language came out of a different spirit of internationalism than its predecessors. Where Volapük, Esperanto, and Ido were imagined as the languages of a positive, internationalist future based in science and technology, the artificial languages in the 1920s came out of a more desperate post-war internationalism whose political counterpart was the movement for the League of Nations and whose purpose was to prevent another war.

The experiences of these artificial language movements are instructive for understanding Basic English and the development of English as a world language. As with the early languages, Volapük and Esperanto, Basic was conceived as a language for specialized use (hence the acronym: Business, Applied, Scientific, International, Commercial) and like Novial, it views the lack of a common language "the chief underlying cause of War," as Ogden puts it.[59] In one of the most thorough studies of Basic English, James McElvenny concludes that Basic "occupied a curious place in relation to ... the international language problem":

> While in his preference for "analytic" structure with minimal morphology Ogden conformed to the established design aesthetics of the mainstream international language movements, in his abandonment of the ideal "international" compromise in discovering *ap posteriori* forms he abnegated one of their dearest principles.[60]

One reason McElvenny suggests is that "his attitude was typically British," the arrogance of an imperial power that believed in its deserved place in the world.

But it also shared with those earlier languages the fault of a creator, Ogden, who was resistant to any reforms. Ogden put a copyright on Basic so that he could bring legal action against any imitations. For instance, when Palmer offered to experiment with Basic in Tokyo, Ogden refused, threatening, "Take care, or our lawyers will be prosecuting you for infringement of copyright."[61]

Unlike Ogden, Richards was less interested in Basic English as a business or a form of ELT and more idealistic about its purpose as a transformative language system.[62] It was Richards who probably did the most to spread Basic English through his work in China and his numerous publications on Basic in the 1930s as well as the textbooks that he made with Christine Gibson at Harvard in the 1940s.[63] But he consistently distinguished his purpose in promoting Basic from that of the ELT profession. In a foreword he wrote for Palmer's IRET vocabulary, he argued that "the two aims are in no way in opposition" distinguishing between word lists of languages in their "normal form" designed for learning full English and lists such as Basic English's which he describes as "a minimum mnemonic apparatus" for a "world auxiliary language."[64] Yet opposition was how Ogden saw it.

The Heretic

With a few exceptions, C. K. Ogden has been largely neglected in accounts of the modernist period, or at least rendered secondary status behind the more well-known Cambridge intellectuals of his time such as Richards but also Bertrand Russell, Ludwig Wittgenstein, Bronislaw Malinowski, F. R. Leavis, and J. M. Keynes. Even his acolyte, the mathematician Frank Ramsey has recently been the subject of a major reassessment. When he appears in recent scholarship, it is usually as an interlocutor (e.g., Russell), a collaborator (Richards or Joyce), or a translator (Wittgenstein).[65] In histories of British linguistics, he is mentioned as part of the London school and as a precursor to J. R. Firth. Possibly, his main impact comes from publishing Malinowski's influential essay on primitive languages as an appendix to *Meaning of Meaning*, which is discussed in the following chapter. In philosophy, he appears to be more well-known as an editor than as an original thinker. His main contribution was in reviving utilitarianism by editing and reissuing several key volumes by Jeremy Bentham. The complexity of Ogden's mediating role is nicely captured by the philosopher Nomi Stolzenberg who remarks that "it could justly be said that it was Ogden who wrote *Bentham's Theory of Fictions*."[66] Similar questions about where the original leaves off and Ogden emerges also arise regarding his controversial translation of Wittgenstein's *Tractactus*.[67] Maybe Ogden's most important roles have been as an editor, first, of *Cambridge Magazine* and of the *Psyche* series on psychology and science for Routledge. It is only when Ogden's career is viewed through the lens of ELT history rather than modernism or philosophy that he has specific agency, though even in this area he is often neglected in favor of Richards. In this study, I take Ogden seriously as an important syncretic philosopher of language and semiotics who was also a complicated personality. Normally, this latter point would be irrelevant; however, when it comes to the institutional processes behind the making of English as a world language, his personality has as much significance as his ideas.

Ogden's background as a Cambridge "heretic" and as a pacifist during the First World War helps to explain this personality, particularly his rejection of academic norms and use of polemical rhetoric in support of Basic. Just like Palmer and West, Ogden was the son of a headmaster. Tragically, when he was a teenager, he suffered from rheumatic fever and was forced to live "confined to a darkened room"[68] for two years (Richards, too, was homebound with tuberculosis as a teenager). Ogden's biographer, and the editor of his works in linguistics, Terrence Gordon, sees these years of solitude as important on his intellectual precocity, though it is also possible that spending these formative years in seclusion also explains his independent streak and his social eccentricities. The latter were evident soon after he enrolled at Cambridge in 1908 to study "the influence of the Greek language on Greek thought."[69] The answer, he found, was not much; yet Basic English was predicated on a relationship between thought and language, as Richards would claim, "Basic was a tool to think with."

It was at Magdalene College that he founded the Cambridge Heretic Society, a group whose "purpose was to challenge authority in all forms."[70] He extended this reactionary attitude to the *Cambridge Magazine* when he became editor in 1912. The magazine ran articles on athletics and academics but it also conveyed

Ogden's interests in philosophy, psychology, aesthetics, religion, educational reform, and foreign policy. In a precursor to Basic English, Ogden ran a mock advertisement in the *Magazine* for the "Cambridge Oratorical Bureau" that would "arrange other peoples' words."[71] Despite its humorous tone, the concern was one that Ogden took seriously as can be seen in the fact he often used meetings of the Heretics to espouse the theories of language and mind by Lady Welby known as "signifies."

Born into the aristocracy (she was a former maid of honor to her godmother, Queen Victoria), Lady Welby began her studies late in life and is now mostly remembered due to her correspondence with the American philosopher, Charles Sanders Peirce. Lady Welby and Peirce independently developed similar theories of meaning based on a triadic sign. In addition to the synchronicity of their ideas on meaning, Peirce and Welby also had in common their status as outsiders to the academy. Their concern with the relation between language and thought and their belief in reforming philosophy from metaphysics to pragmatism naturally makes Peirce and Welby the philosophical parents to Ogden. Gordon observes that even though she is hardly mentioned, Welby's ideas are integral to *Meaning of Meaning*. This is evident in her critique of language. Unlike semantics, which linked the problem of meaning to grammar and vocabulary, she argued that words alone were not sufficient to account for misunderstanding. In her 1903 entry in the *Encyclopedia Britannica* on "Signifies," she characterizes the "Significian" as more than a detached philosopher but as a radical social reformer with a noble purpose.

> The first duty of the Significian is, therefore, to deprecate the demand for mere linguistic reform, which is indispensable on its own proper ground, but cannot be considered as the satisfaction of a radical need such as that now suggested. To be content with mere reform of articulate expression would be fatal to the prospect of a significantly adequate language; one characterized by a development only to be compared to that of the life and mind of which it is or should be naturally the delicate, flexible, fitting, creative, as also controlling and ordering, Expression.[72]

One can see the influence this type of philosophical engagement might have on Ogden who combines an interest in mind and language with a streak of anti-authoritarianism. Her dismissal of "mere linguistic reform" suggests a key distinction between Ogden's Basic English and other efforts at reforming English such as George Bernard Shaw's efforts at simplifying spelling or other nationalist attempts at simplifying English.[73] Her phrase, "a significantly adequate language," encapsulates Basic English's purpose to create a language that "signifies" in itself, and is "adequate" to its purpose of "controlling and ordering expression." By teaching language as it relates to thought rather than to formal principles of grammar, then education can train students in how to think by teaching them how to use words rather than separating these as distinct activities. Lady Welby viewed semiotics as more than an academic concern; rather, the misuse of language was the cause for "the wide-spread and all-pervading havoc in modern civilization." Both Ogden and Richards similarly describe their purpose as trying to save Western culture in the face of modernity. In this way, Basic English is similar to two other modernist works, Pound's *Cantos* and Joyce's *Finnegans Wake*, that attempted to prevent another world war by inventing syncretic international languages. Yet where they adopted obscure, multilingual, private languages, Ogden emphasized a simple, public, monolingual, auxiliary language.

As this background illustrates, although Ogden was an outsider to the language teaching profession in other ways, he was an "insider" in other ways. While Palmer and West were in the peripheries of Tokyo and Dacca, he was ensconced in the imperial center with offices in London and the cultural and linguistic authority of Cambridge behind him as well as his connections with publishers like Routledge, Kegan, Paul where he was editor for their highly profitable *Psyche* series of books on philosophy, science, and psychology. He also had Richards, the most famous literary critic at the time, as a collaborator and advocate. In very little time, Ogden had established "Orthological Institutes" all over the world, secured publishing contracts, and received funding from the Rockefeller Foundation. Most importantly, Basic English was reviewed and discussed in newspapers and on the radio on both sides of the Atlantic, which helped to spread its fame as "a world tongue" based on "850 English Words."[74]

Conclusion

Basic English's relative popularity disrupted the field of ELT, even as much as it declared that it had different intentions. This disruption made vocabulary matter for more than just its practical effects on a curriculum. Now it had a commercial relevance in terms of access and publicity. Palmer and West had already been interested in lexical simplification: Palmer said as much when he arrived in Japan in 1923, and for West it was necessary for his reading method. Both had arrived at their methods and the value of word lists through their experiences in these locales—either responding to the limitations of Bengali classrooms in the case of West or meeting the expectations of the Japanese

Ministry, in the case of Palmer. And despite their experience, Howatt observes, neither Palmer nor West was "in the position to exploit their research work in the production of language teaching materials on a wide scale"[75] as the challenge from Basic demanded.

This intersection of interests cannot be separated from the interwar social, political, and colonial contexts in which these figures are producing their theories and methods. Each of them inhabits a distinct sphere within interwar modernity: Palmer as the scientist using the latest concepts from phonetics, Saussurean linguistics, and behaviorism; West is the "new" imperialist, updating Liberal models of education with insights from educational psychology and economics; and Ogden is the modernist, challenging traditions of language and identity and creating a brave new world with his invented language. The fact that their work intersects is more a product of markets and the dispersed, undefined field of language teaching at the time. The following two chapters examine the materials that they produced in the 1920s and early 1930s—their word lists and simplified readers—as expressions of these diverse modernities within the frame of late empire.

Notes

1. Lawrence Faucett, Harold Palmer, Edward Thorndike, and Michael West, *Interim Report on Vocabulary Selection for the Teaching of English as a Foreign Language*, in Smith, *Pioneers of ELT*, vol. v, 389. The phrase is from Dr. Ballard quoted in the Introductory Statement.
2. "Record of an Informal Conference on the Teaching of English to Non-English-Knowing Pupils," Box 140, Folder 6, Carnegie Collection, Columbia University Rare Books and Manuscripts Collection. Hereafter "CCNY."
3. Fife was the chair of the committee whose extensive survey resulted in the foundational *Summary of Reports on the Modern Foreign Languages* (New York: Macmillan, 1931).
4. Howatt notes that the first works in ELT in the 1950s were "based on the spadework done in the 1930s." See *History of ELT* (2004), 296–7.
5. Brutt-Griffler, *World English*, 78. I am following Richard Smith's application of her concepts to the response to Basic English by West, Palmer, and Faucett. See Smith, Introduction, *Pioneers of ELT*, vol. v, xxv.
6. The quote on Keppel is from "Our Past Presidents," the Carnegie Corporation of New York, at https://www.carnegie.org/about/our-history/past-presidents/. On the African and American education projects, see Richard Glotzer, "A Long Shadow: Frederick

P. Keppel, the Carnegie Corporation and the Dominions and Colonies Fund Area Experts 1923–1943," *History of Education* 38, no. 5 (2009): 621–48.

7   Crystal, *English as a Global Language*, 59.
8   On transatlantic relations between the wars, see Anne Orde, *The Eclipse of Great Britain: The United States and British Imperial Decline, 1895-1956* (New York: St. Martin's Press, 1996), chapters 3 and 4.
9   Joshua Miller, *Accented America: The Cultural Politics of Multilingual Modernism* (New York: Oxford University Press, 2011), 10.
10 Orde, *The Eclipse of Great Britain*, 70–1.
11 Ibid., 91.
12 Miller, *Accented America*, 37.
13 Vincente L. Raphael, *Motherless Tongues: The Insurgency of Language amid Wars of Translation* (Durham, NC: Duke University Press, 2014), 43–6.
14 Ibid., 45, 51.
15 Parsons, *The Second British Empire : In the Crucible of the Twentieth Century* (Lanham, Maryland: Rowman & Littlefield, 2014), 96. Brutt-Griffler, *World English*, chapter 3.
16 Parsons, *Second British Empire*, 64. Parsons notes that "the regular British army shrank from a wartime high of 3.5 million to 370,000 men by 1921."
17 Ibid., 64.
18 Quoted in Parsons, *Second British Empire*, 57.
19 See Cyril J. Weir and Barry O'Sullivan, *Assessing English on the Global Stage: The British Council and the English Language Testing, 1941–2016* (Sheffield, UK: Equinox Publishing, 2017), 6.
20 Ibid., 7.
21 Phillipson, "English, the *Lingua Nullus*," 282.
22 Giovanni Arrighi, *The Long Twentieth Century: Money, Power, and the Origins of Our Times* (New York: Verso, 2010), 290–2. On how this British economic model worked under Lugard's Dual Mandate, see Parsons, *Second British Empire*, chapter 3.
23 On the Rockefeller foundation's interests in China, see Koeneke, *Empires of the Mind*, 94–9; on the Carnegie Corporation, see Glotzer, "A Long Shadow," 621–48. For foundations and colonial education, see Edward H. Berman, "Educational Colonialism in Africa: The Role of American Foundations," in *Philanthropy and Cultural Imperialism: The Foundations at Home and Abroad*, edited by Robert F. Arnove (Bloomington, IN: Indiana University Press, 1992), 179–232.
24 Dorothée Anderson, "Harold E. Palmer: A Biographical Essay," in Harold E. Palmer and H. Vere Redman, *This Language-Learning Business* (George Harrap and Co., 1932), edited by Roland Mackin (London: Oxford University Press, 1969), 133–60.
25 Smith, Preface, *Pioneers of ELT*, II: xi.

26 Pennycook, *The Cultural Politics of English*, 129.
27 Schmitt, *Vocabulary in Language Teaching*, 12.
28 Horace Wyatt, *The Teaching of English in India*, in Smith, *Pioneers of ELT*, vol. I, 266.
29 While there is some debate among Western and Japanese historians over whether bringing Palmer was Matsukata's idea or the Ministry's, Howatt notes that "either way, Matsukata paid the bills." Howatt, *History of ELT* (1984), 232.
30 Ibid.
31 Liah Greenfeld, *The Spirit of Capitalism: Nationalism and Economic Growth* (Cambridge: Harvard University Press, 2001), 353–4.
32 Greenfeld, *Spirit of Capitalism*, 354.
33 Ibid., 341.
34 See Howatt, *History of ELT* (1984), 233. Harold Palmer, "The History and Present State of the Movement towards Vocabulary Control," in Smith, *Pioneers of ELT*, vol. 5, 373.
35 Howatt, *History of ELT* (2004), 294.
36 Smith, "Introduction," *Pioneers of ELT*, II, xvi–xvii.
37 Clive Whitehead, *Colonial Educators: The British Indian and Colonial Education Service, 1858–1983* (London: I.B. Tauris, 2003), 11–4.
38 Smith, "Introduction," *Pioneers of ELT*, vol. III, ix.
39 See Richard Glotzer, "The Influence of Carnegie Corporation and Teachers College, Columbia, in the Interwar Dominions: The Case for Decentralized Education," *Historical Studies in Education/Revue d'histoire de l'education* 1, nos. 1/2 (2000): 93–111.
40 On William Jones, see Joseph Errington, *Linguistics in a Colonial Context: A Story of Language, Meaning, and Power* (London: Blackwell, 2008), 103–4.
41 See Stephen Evans, "Macaulay's Minute Revisited: Colonial Language Policy in Nineteenth-century India," *Journal of Multilingual and Multicultural Development* 23, no. 4 (2002): 260–81.
42 Ibid., 171.
43 The Filtration Method was derived from the Bell-Lancaster system—another educational system that was developed in India and then returned to England. It was developed by Andrew Bell, a superintendent of the Madras Male Orphan Asylum during the late eighteenth century as a means of dealing with the disparity in teacher-student ratio. "Bell, Andrew (1753–1832)." *The Hutchinson Unabridged Encyclopedia with Atlas and Weather Guide*. Abington: Helicon, 2014. *Credo Reference*. Web (accessed Feb 23, 2015).
44 Latika Chaudhary, "Caste, Colonialism, and Schooling," in *A New Economic History of Colonial India*, edited by Latika Chaudhary, Bishnupriya Gupta, Tirthankar Roy, Anand Swamy (London: Routledge, 2016), 162–3.

45 West, *Bilingualism*, in Smith, *Pioneers of ELT*, vol. III, 42.
46 I borrow this phrase from Antoinette Burton and Isabel Hofmyer who use it to describe the book in the British empire. See Burton and Hofmyer, eds., *Ten Books That Shaped the British Empire: Creating an Imperial Commons* (Durham, NC: Duke University Press, 2014), 1.
47 Smith, "Introduction," *Pioneers of ELT*, vol. III, xiv.
48 Quoted in Rimi Chatterjee, *Empires of the Mind: A History of Oxford University Press in India under the Raj* (New Delhi: Oxford, 2006), 329.
49 Smith, "Introduction," *Pioneers of ELT*, vol. III, xvi. Cover from Michael West, *New Method Readers. Supplementary Reader. David Copperfield. Grade 5.* (London: Longmans, Green and Co., 1940).
50 See Smith, "Introduction," *Pioneers of ELT*, vol. III, xvii.
51 See Smith, "Introduction," *Pioneers of ELT*, vol. III, xvi. This is also suggested by Chatterjee, *Empires of the Mind*, 345. We cannot know for sure since Longmans' records were destroyed in December 1940 after a bombing during the London Blitz.
52 See Chatterjee, *Empires of the Mind*, 346. Faucett's OEC would have a longer lasting effect than West's NMRs as it was adopted by many postcolonial African countries.
53 Quoted in Chatterjee, *Empires of the Mind*, 348.
54 See Smith on West's complaints about being "up on the mat" for his work as well as his own regrets about how his service concluded. Smith, *Pioneers of ELT*, III: xviii.
55 John Paul Russo, *I. A. Richards: His Life and Work* (New York: Routledge, 1989), 398.
56 C. K. Ogden, *Basic English: An International Second Language*, edited by E. C. Graham (New York: Harcourt, Brace and World, 1968), 88. This edition is a revised and expanded version of *The System of Basic English*, last published in 1944, and contains *Basic English, A Short Guide to Basic English, The ABC of Basic English, The Basic Words*, sample adaptations.
57 Quoted in Michael D. Gordin, *Scientific Babel: How Science Was Done before and after Global English* (Chicago: University of Chicago Press, 2015), 117.
58 Quoted Gordin, *Scientific Babel*, 161.
59 C. K. Ogden, *Debabelization* (London: Kegan Paul, Trench, Trubner & Co., 1931), 13.
60 James McElvenny, *Language and Meaning in the Age of Modernism: C. K. Ogden and His Contemporaries* (Edinburgh: Edinburgh University Press, 2018), 81–2.
61 Quoted in Howatt, *History of ELT* (1984), 233.
62 For example, his one work that is supposedly about teaching, *Basic in Teaching: East and West* (London: Kegan, Paul, 1935) has more to do with semiotic questions about logic and psychology than with teaching.

63 This study does not examine Richards' contribution to Basic English because he remained outside of the English language teaching debates that influenced the Carnegie Conference. Also, his work on Basic has already received excellent attention in biographical works by John Paul Russo and Rodney Koeneke. He has also been criticized from the Chinese perspective for cultural imperialism, see Shu-mei Shih, *The Lure of the Modern: Writing Modernism in Semicolonial China, 1917–1937* (Berkeley: University of California Press, 2001); Q. S. Tong, "The Bathos of a Universalism: I. A. Richards and His Basic English," in *Tokens of Exchange: The Problem of Translation in Global Circulations*, edited by Lydia H. Liu (Durham, NC: Duke University Press, 1999), 331–54; Yunte Huang, "Basic English, Chinglish, and Translocal Dialect," in *English and Ethnicity: Signs of Race*, edited by Janina Brutt Griffler and Catherine Evans Davies (New York: Palgrave Macmillan, 2006), 75–103; for a recuperative account of Richards' engagement with China, see Ming Xie, *Conditions of Comparison: Reflections on Comparative Intercultural Inquiry* (New York: Continuum, 2011), chapter 1. Also, see the essays collected for the special journal issue, "Cambridge and China: A Conversation," *The Cambridge Quarterly* 41, no. 1 (March 2012).

64 I. A. Richards, "Foreword," in *Interim Report on Vocabulary Selection submitted to the Seventh Annual Conference of English Teachers* (Tokyo: Institute for Research in English Teaching, 1930), 2.

65 See Megan Quigley, *Modernist Fiction*, esp., "James Joyce, Ludwig Wittgenstein, and C. K. Ogden." Peter McDonald, *Artefacts of Writing : Ideas of the State and Communities of Letters from Matthew Arnold to Xu Bing* (Oxford: Oxford University Press, 2017). On Ramsey, see Cheryl Misak, *Frank Ramsey: A Sheer Excess of Powers* (Oxford: Oxford University Press, 2020). A relevant source that appeared too late for me to incorporate is Aarthi Vadde, "Language's Hopes: Global Modernism and the Science of Debabelization," in *The New Modernist Studies*, edited by Douglas Mao (Cambridge: Cambridge University Press, 2021), pp. 200–24.

66 Nomi M. Stolzenberg, "Bentham's Theory of Fictions: A 'Curious Double Language,'" *Cardozo Studies in Law and Literature* 11, no. 2 (1999): 223–61. McElvenny, *Language and Meaning*, 94.

67 See Gordon, "Introduction," *C. K. Ogden and Linguistics*, 5 vols., edited by W. Terrence Gordon (London: Routledge/Thoemmes Press, 1994), vol. 1, xiii.

68 Ibid., vii.

69 Ibid.

70 Ibid., ix.

71 Ibid., x.

72 On Lady Welby and Ogden, see McElvenny, *Language and Meaning*, 28–34. On Lady Welby, see "1911_Encyclopedia Britannica_Significs," WikiSource, last edited 24 Oct. 2012, accessed Nov. 26, 2018. https://en.wikisource.org/wiki/1911_Encyclop%C3%A6dia_Britannica/Significs.

73 On modernist writers and language purification, see Morag Shiach, "'To Purify the Dialect of the Tribe': Modernism and Language Reform," *Modernism/Modernity* 14, no. 1 (2007): 21–34.
74 See L. H. Robbins, "850 English Words: A World Tongue," *The New York Times*, Nov. 20, 1932, 149. https://nyti.ms/34OrpeY.
75 Howatt, *History of ELT* (2004), 286.

2

Word Lists, Vocabulary Control, and Colonialism

Language was always the companion of empire ... language and empire began, increased, and flourished together.
— Anton de Nebrija to Queen Isabella (1492)[1]

Colonial Linguistics and Vocabulary Control

In the battle for English's primacy as an international auxiliary language, the weapon of choice was the most banal instrument one can imagine, the limited vocabulary word list. While word lists had existed as long as there have been organized language systems, there was an increase in the value of English-language word lists among ELT and IAL practitioners during the interwar period. This reflected the fact that the post-war consensus around English as an international language coincided with a quantitative turn in the social sciences. In this chapter, I situate their methods in relation to their basis in behaviorist psychology, economics, anthropology, and philosophy, as well as colonial practices and theories of language and identity. Through individual studies of their major theoretical works, Palmer's *Principles of Language Study*, West's *Bilingualism*, and Ogden and Richards' *Meaning of Meaning*, this chapter traces a persistent dichotomy in all of their works between a nativist model of a premodern, static "mother tongue" language and a modernist, flexible, deterritorialized, "auxiliary" language. Drawing on Joseph Errington's *Linguistics in a Colonial World*, this chapter argues that this dichotomy should be seen as a legacy of colonial linguistics that informs their methods and word lists. Despite the internal conflicts among Palmer, West, and Ogden that are described in the later chapters, they are viewed in this chapter as sharing a positivist view of language and learning efficiency that they inherit from the history of colonial linguistics and that they each adapt in their own way for the twentieth century. Overall, this chapter demonstrates how their theories of language and education draw on behaviorism, primitivism, and colonial linguistics to create an evolutionary conception of the "mother tongue" to describe all non-auxiliary languages.

Word collections, dictionaries, spelling lists, or specialized vocabularies have existed at least since Roman times.[2] In contrast to modern word lists, these collections subordinated vocabulary to syntax due to the influence of the medieval teaching of Latin that emphasized syntax and grammar through rote memorization.[3] The classical grammar-translation method was transferred to other languages like English with "the intent of purifying English based on Latin models."[4] Because of this emphasis on grammar, vocabulary lists were relegated to the purpose of standardizing national languages as in eighteenth-century prescriptivist works such as Johnson's *Dictionary* (1755) and Lowth's *Introduction to English Grammar* (1762). In this way, the history of language learning in English primarily focused on cultural nationalism through purification and standardization.[5]

One of the original uses for the printed Latin grammars was their application in the linguistic contact zones of the first European colonies. In his valuable history of the intersection between linguistics and colonialism, Joseph Errington describes how the Spanish Conquistadores and missionaries used Latin and the early Castilian grammar by Anton de Nebrija to structure and describe the indigenous languages that they encountered. It was unusual at the time to have a grammar for a vernacular language. Nebrija sought to use his Castilian grammar to educate the sons of Aztec chiefs. In this way, the creation of the grammar and its deployment in the colonies were united. As Walter Mignolo writes about Nebrija: "He knew that the power of a unified language, via its grammar, lay in teaching it to barbarians, as well as controlling barbarian languages by writing their grammars."[6] It also established the colonial practice of educating native elites in the imperial language that was to persist into the methods of ESL in the twentieth century.[7] Ultimately, a hybrid of Nuahatl based on Castilian grammar was adopted because it already functioned as a link language among elites connected to the court and was associated with authority by the people. Errington writes that it "was recognized by the Spaniards as what they called the *lengua general* of Mexico: 'a principal intermediary language' or, to use a more recent phrase ... a 'language of wider communication.'"[8] Language of Wider Communication (LWC) is a contemporary term used to describe non-native languages later endorsed by colonial governments in the twentieth-century such as Malay, Swahili, and English. It applies here because the Nahuatl example resonates with later colonial vocabularies due to the imposed limits and selections made by the Spanish friars who wrote the native grammars. In the process, they elevate a specific dialect of a native language to a position of authority, a recurring feature in any process of language standardization. At the same time, by transcribing the indigenous language into a Latin-based grammar, they incorporate it into a system of European literacy. Errington describes this as the act of "reducing speech to writing" which stands at the heart of colonial linguistics, especially when it is seen in the context of developing a standardized language as a means of controlling a native population.

The structure of the Spanish-Mexican experience of language politics has been identified by Errington and other linguistic historians in a wide range of colonial contexts, from British India and Ireland in the nineteenth century to the Dutch East Indies, French Algeria, and US Philippines in the twentieth.[9] While each colonial power had its own distinctive language policy, they each had a need for a language of wider communication to command and control their population. Where the English and French tended toward using their own languages—in different degrees at different times in their respective Empires—the Germans and Dutch preferred to withhold their languages and create intermediary languages. In any case, whether the colonizer uses their own language or invents one out of a single or combination of indigenous languages, they have the effect of formalizing a language within the standards of European literacy (i.e., a grammar or vocabulary on the Latin model) that develops prestige and dominance over time. The other, nondominant languages, of all different forms—including nonstandard versions of the dominant language—are relegated to the status of "other." This might be done with explicit racist purposes, such as the German belief that their language would be ruined if spoken by an African, or with a Christian sense of civilizing purpose as in William Jones' invention of Hindustani.[10] These linguistic hierarchies contribute to making the colonized into objects of knowledge for the colonizer. As Errington puts it, philology was an aid for Europeans to make language difference go hand in hand "with the creation and reification of social groups."[11]

This colonial process of codifying native languages was also integral to the creation of European nationalisms in the nineteenth century. Benedict Anderson's well-known theory of imagined communities argues that the combination of vernacular languages and print capitalism led to a sense of shared identity among people across territorial boundaries.[12] In addition to the newspapers, novels, and journals that Anderson describes there were also more official modes of standardization like dictionaries and grammars. Behind all of this was a romantic conception of language as organically connected to territorial identity and race. German philologists (or proto-philologists) such as Herder, von Humboldt, Schleicher, and the Grimms and Shlegels built upon the comparative philology begun by William Jones in India by emphasizing language origins and their organic development. Even before Darwin's *Origins of the Species* appeared, they had developed an aryan theory of the Indo-European tree in which languages were subject to the laws of evolution where, as Schleicher wrote after reading Darwin, some "genera of speech disappear, and ... others extend themselves at the expense of the dead."[13] The "transformational" view of evolution that Schleicher and others adopted was quite distinct from that of Darwin's own variational account; however, it was influential as an argument that could justify nationalist identities.[14] This combination of organic metaphors of language and evolutionary theories of selection that was applied to European nationalism was also integral to the civilizing mission of late nineteenth-century imperialism. Language provided evidence that their cultures had developed from primitive to civilized. In the colonial sphere, philology legitimized imperial missions as "uplifting" rather than exploitative. As Errington argues, philological theories raised the status of national vernaculars, while also keeping native languages from achieving equality with European languages.[15]

The bridge from Jones and Herder to language teaching in the 1920s is in the work of the Danish linguist, Otto Jespersen. One of the most influential linguists in the late nineteenth and early twentieth centuries, Jespersen modernized language study by adapting the evolutionary theory of language change from organic metaphors of racial difference to positivist, scientific theories of selection based on efficiency. The evolution of languages, he argues, comes through a process of reduction and refinement. Instead of baroque phrases or multiple words for single items, progress in languages was marked by survival of the fittest in terms of the most economical principle such as the often-cited example of the historical change from the Gothic *habaidedeima* to the modern English *had*.[16] Jespersen's developmentalist perspective on language fit with other modern tendencies toward efficiency and rationality. This was the same logic used by the Artificial Language movements to justify their languages as modern and scientific.

Jespersen was personally involved in arguments for Esperanto including the decisive split that led to the creation of Ido in 1907. In 1928, he proposed his own language, Novial (*nov*=new, *ial*=International Auxiliary Language), that was designed to correct the flaws from previous attempts. Auxiliary languages emphasized morphology rather than grammar or syntax.[17] The linguist Edward Sapir, who would participate in the Carnegie Conference in 1934, wrote a memorandum about auxiliary languages in which he held up Chinese and Chinook as ideals because he viewed them as "highly analytical languages" that valued simplicity.[18] Jespersen also argued for simplicity of words as the basis for an auxiliary language: "we must make the interlanguage of the future more perfect, i.e. simpler [...] The simpler the morphological structure is, the less inducement will there be to make grammatical mistakes."[19] These evolutionary arguments that value "simplicity" and the "word" or vocabulary as marks of linguistic progress influence the movement for language simplification in the interwar period.

This brief history of early colonial linguistics, nineteenth-century philology, and early twentieth-century artificial languages demonstrates a consistent interest with "reducing speech to writing" as a means of legitimating and conveying power within the context of linguistic diversity. Much like other modernist aesthetic arguments for a return to classical simplicity and order, Jespersen argued that linguistic progress was marked by a tendency toward clearer and fewer words.[20] Palmer, West, and Ogden share this positivist, utilitarian view of language as part of their desire to align language teaching with scientific methods. While nineteenth-century philologists were inspired by nationalism, these linguists followed Jespersen in adapting this evolutionary logic to internationalism. Just as Jespersen argued that language progresses from "primitive musical utterances" to words, so do the word lists and pedagogical methods of the vocabulary control movement depend upon a concept of "natural" speech that participates in the same developmentalist model. This chapter explores the place of the "mother tongue" within their respective theories and how the technology of the word list reinforces its place within a linguistic hierarchy that privileges an auxiliary version of English.

Lemaire, Behaviorism, and Palmer's *Principles of Language Study*

Palmer provides an interesting case to consider the issue of colonial linguistics and ELT since, unlike West, he did not serve in the colonies as an educator, and unlike Richards in China, whom many Chinese perceived as a cultural imperialist, his time in Japan, while controversial in some quarters, did not rise up to any such recriminations.[21] I want to suggest that if Palmer was not actively complicit in empire, he presents a case study in the significance of proximity to empire. In this section, I read his foundational work for ELT, *Principles of Language Study*, as exhibiting certain colonial forms of knowledge. This can be seen in its rhetoric and argument which it inherited from the tradition of colonial linguistics just covered, but also in its paratextual features, namely, its *Préface Dédicatoire*, written to a friend, the Belgian Charles Lemaire, who was complicit in some of the worst aspects of empire.

According to the linguist and editor of Palmer's works, Ronald Makin, Palmer began writing *Principles of Language Study* after the war during a visit with Lemaire, an old friend from his days as a language teacher at Vervier. Makin writes that Palmer was so "impressed by Lemaire's fervour and by the similarity of their views" that "he began to write [*Principles*] the same day."[22] Palmer's daughter recalls Lemaire as "a specialist in the teaching of French as a foreign language,"[23] who was one of her father's closest friends in Belgium with whom he shared similar views on language and classical music. Missing from this estimation is the fact that Lemaire had been a Lieutenant in the Belgian Army during one of its most violent periods of rule in the Congo. It is not my interest to impute his crimes onto Palmer but rather to trace the influence of the ideas about language that he developed in the Congo into Palmer's rhetorical imagery. Palmer writes in his preface to Lemaire that in this work "[y]ou will find your own words and the echo they have awakened in me."[24] The forms of colonial knowledge that inform *Principles* are indeed the "echoes" of colonialism, not their fact or policy—as it is with West, or with Lemaire. The coincidence of Palmer's meeting with Lemaire provides another coincidence that is relevant to the topic of this chapter: word lists. Lemaire's interest in language learning and acquisition came from his time in the Congo where he had devised one of the first and most popular language guides for use by colonial officials. Lemaire's *Vocabulaire Pratique* is a word list using simplified French and English to translate African tribal languages. While the vocabulary control word lists that I examine in this chapter are properly situated in the interregnum between late empire and a nascent globalization, their roots are in the colonial setting, like Lemaire's, in the Congo. For this reason, I want to explore Lemaire, not only because of his influence on Palmer, but as a significant figure linking the old colonial linguistics to the new internationalist model represented by Palmer.

Lemaire's *Vocabulaire Pratique*

Before he became the retired elder statesman discussing language teaching with Palmer, "the multi-talented Charles Lemaire" was a "prolific colonial propagandist" as well as a "soldier, explorer, cartographer, and amateur ethnographer."[25] As a young man, Lemaire took part in the first exploration of the Congo's interior by Henry Morton Stanley and became responsible for drawing up colonial boundaries in the southern Congo until rising to become a highly respected Lieutenant in the Belgian Army. After his return to Belgium in the early twentieth-century, he became one of the "key figures of an imperial *tiers-parti*—colonialist but anti-Free State—championing an undiluted Belgian annexation of the Congo against anticolonial critics and the hard core of the king's admirers," according to the Belgian historian Vincent Viaene.[26]

While serving in the Congo Free State during the 1890s, Lemaire compiled one of the first language guides for sub-Saharan Africa. Published in 1894, and again in 1897, Lemaire's *Vocabulaire Pratique* was among the earliest and most popular guides adopted in the region and, according to the anthropologist Johannes Fabian, became the standard for all incoming colonial servants.[27] Fabian observes that the "compiling of word lists had become a common practice in this expansive phase of colonization."[28] The shift from geographer to linguist is not all that unusual since Lemaire would have encountered a wide diversity of languages and needed to develop practical modes of communication while exploring the interior. At the time, Belgian policy discouraged the use of French or Flemish and sought to create native languages, such as Lingala, as the colonial lingua franca. As the historian William Samarin notes, the concept of an intercultural lingua franca would have been new to the Africans living and working in the Congo as they traditionally used translators, gestures, or other means of communicating.[29]

Samarin argues that while the language guides arose out of necessity—colonial officials could not expect to be fluent in all of the languages in which they came into contact—they were also based on language policies informed by colonial racist assumptions on the part of the Europeans that distinguished, as Samarin puts it, "between speaking to and understanding blacks."[30] The Belgians distrusted African translators since it was believed that they "deliberately altered their speech out of mistrust for whites."[31] The approach used in the early days of Belgian colonization was to limit the words used in their exchange with the Africans as a way of controlling the range of reference. Samarin argues that Europeans believed that 500 words or less was all that was necessary because of the "Africans' limited needs and rudimentary sentiments." They claimed that "with three little vocabularies in the languages of the Upper Congo ... a voyager had all the indispensable elements for making himself understood by natives."[32] It is this role that was fulfilled by Lemaire's *Vocabulaire Pratique*.

Lemaire's guides and word lists were intended for new soldiers arriving in the Congo. As he writes in the Preface to the 1897 edition:

> Knowledge of native languages (*idiomes*) is without any question of utmost importance to those who go to Africa. Every candidate for service in the Congo must study them as early as possible. The more the Independent State develops the less time it can give its agents to acquire the experience everyone needs before he becomes useful.[33]

The rationale here is practical and administrative since there is little training and high turnover and a need to gather a workforce from multiple language communities. Fabian summarizes Lemaire's advice:

> As soon as he has been accepted for service in Africa, the future agent should learn English so that he can communicate with anglophone Protestant missionaries, Scandinavian sailors and West Africans. He should also take up Fiote, "the language of the region of caravans." After arriving at Boma—then the administrative base of the Free State—he may continue with other languages according to his assignment, for instance, those who go on to the region taken back from the Arabs "will study Swahili (*le zanzibarite*)."[34]

Lemaire's advice on learning English suggests its early role as a European *lingua franca* and also implies the fear of English's encroaching dominance—an anxiety that would inform Belgian language policy from its earliest founding into its later colonial education policies. Fabian argues that the Belgian promotion of Swahili as an LWC was an attempt to counter the encroaching prominence of either English or French in the colonies.[35] In view of this type of pressure, the perceived multilingualism of Lemaire's guide served another purpose in so far as it diluted the languages and limited the influence of any single European language.

This purpose can be seen in the design of Lemaire's *Vocabulaire Pratique*. It consisted of 500 words listed in columns of French, English, Swahili, Fiote, Kibanga, Mongo, Bangala with two blank columns on the page so that soldiers could add newly acquired words as they encountered them. Over thirty pages, it is alphabetically ordered according to the French words with the other languages listed in rows for easy translation (see Figure 2). In comparison to previous guides such as Dutrieux's *Vocabulaire francais-kisouahili*, published in 1880, which Fabian defines as an "open" vocabulary of the "military-expedition type," Lemaire's guide included less blank space for the addition of new words and phrases.[36] Fabian characterizes the reduction of words and limited space for addition as "indicative of a transition" in the purpose of these vocabularies

— 6 —

ıÇAIS	ANGLAIS	ZANZIBARITE	FIOTE	KIBANGI IRÉBOU
	one	môdjia	môci	môko
	two	bili	zôlé	mibari
	three	tatou	tatou	misatou
	four	nné	ïa	miné
	five	tano	tano	mitano
	six	sitta	sambano	môtôba
	seven	sâbba	sâm'bwadia	n'sambou
	eight	nané	nana	mo'âmbi
	nine	tissa	voi	iboua
	ten	koumi	koumi	djoumi
	eleven	koumi na môdjia	koumi na môci	djoumi na môkc
	twelve	koumi na mbili	koumi na zôlé	djoumi na miba
	thirteen	koumi na tatou	koumi na tatou	djoumi na misa
	fourteen	koumi na nné	koumi na ïa	djoumi na miné
. . .	. . .	. . .	. . .	. . .
	twenty	ichrini	makou môlé	makwa bâri
t	twenty one	ichrini na môdjia	makou môlé na môci	makwa bâri na
	twenty two	ichrini na mbili	makou môlé na zôlé	makwa bâri na n
. . .	. . .	. . .	. . .	. . .
	thirty	selasini	makou ma tatou	boëli
	forty	aroubaïni	makou ma ïa	niou miné
	fifty	h'âm'sini	makou ma tano	niou mitano
	sixty	sittini	makou ma sambano	niou môtôba
	seventy	sabaini	lousâm'bwadia	niou n'sambou
gts	eighty	samanini	lou'nana	niou louasi
	ninety	tissini	lou'voi	môbôa
	hundred	mïa	n'kâma	mo'n'kama
	hundred one	mïa môdjia na môdjia	n'kâma na môci	mo'n'kama na n
. . .	. . .	. . .	. . .	. . .
et un	hundred twenty one	mïa môdjia na ichrini na môdjia	n'kâma na makou môlé na môci	mo'n'kama makwa bari ı
. . .	. . .	. . .	. . .	. . .
s	two hundred	mïa mbili	n'kâma zôlé	n'kama mibari
. . .	. . .	. . .	. . .	. . .
	thousand	elf	founda	n'kôto
. . .	. . .	. . .	. . .	. . .

Figure 2 Part of the comparative vocabulary from Charles Lemaire's *Vocabulaire Pratique* (1897). The first column, cut off here, has the French word.[37]

"from 'communication to command.'"[38] Lemaire's guide casts language as an "instrument for colonial agents who have begun to cover the immense area of the Congo" and who need to "dicate their terms to the natives."[39]

The purpose of this "closed" guide is reinforced by the ten pages of phrases that follow the vocabulary. For example, here are the phrases as they appear in English:

What is that?—What is his name? What is the name of this thing?
That is to me.—The palm-wine is good.—Who did so?

The pieces are in the box.—The palm-wine is no good.
He has two knieves.—I am the chief.—The soap is on the table.
The work is finished.—He is coming.—Call Tonio.
The fowl gave one egg.—The goat brought forth young one.[40]

The short phrases with their active verbs and direct objects convey the "practical" purpose of the vocabulary to give directions to a multilingual workforce. This emphasis on control and command is evident in other phrases such as

"Stretch out your arms"
"Do not laugh.—Rise up.—Sit down"
"Follow me.—Go at the head.—Stay behind"
"I am tired; prepare my bed"
"Stand out of my way"[41]

Fabian notes that Lemaire's *Vocabulaire pratique* was the first within a "military-expeditionary genre" with an aim toward "command" that reflected the changing economic role of King Leopold's Free State. Published after the expeditionary phase of the 1870s and before the consolidated role of the Belgian colony in the 1900s, Lemaire's language guide was popular during the most rapacious period in Belgian rule. Politically, the goal was to establish Belgian dominance over the region against other European powers, and economically, its purpose was to collect raw materials, mainly red rubber and palm oil. Collecting rubber meant utilizing multilingual workforces that needed to be mobile as they collected rubber far inland and moved across the Congo as they depleted resources in each area. A polyglot language guide of commands and directives served this economic and administrative mission. However, Lemaire's diary demonstrates the limits to a language guide in the face of indigenous resistance to labor conscription. In his memoir, he reflected on the brutality of his service: "As soon as it was a question of rubber, I wrote to the government, 'To gather rubber in the district … one must cut off hands, noses, and ears.'"[42] Lemaire's colonial career as a linguist and colonial officer serves as a reminder of the continuity between colonial linguistics and colonial brutality.

The association of Lemaire's language guide with this brutal period of rule comes about because language guides change with colonial policies. After the transfer of power over the Congo from King Leopold to the Belgian Parliament in 1908, there was a shift from rubber to mining natural minerals which required a more fixed labor population. In turn, colonial policies turned toward the creation of monogamous, stable families by way of cultural forces such as religion and language. It is during this time, Fabian points out, that the existing language divisions in the region were consolidated and the state deployed Swahili and Langala as "languages of wide communication," to be used by labor, military, and administration. He argues that these local lingua francas circumvented the rise of English and kept the region isolated from other African populations as a means of consolidating colonial power.[43] In this way, these LWC made the old colonial language guide unnecessary though still fulfilling the same task of isolating and managing a local labor force.

Lemaire's interest in language and the Congo did not end upon his return to Belgium. As the historian Vincent Viane notes, he was part of a family and social context imbued with Liberal internationalist politics and debates over the status of the Congo Free State. Along with his step-brother, "Félicien Cattier, a lawyer for the (liberal) Free University of Brussels, who helped to provide the legal underpinnings for the *système domanial* before turning into a renowned critic of the abuses it engendered," Lemaire was one of the "key figures of an imperial *tiers-parti*—colonialist but anti-Free State—championing an undiluted Belgian annexation of the Congo against anticolonial critics and the hard core of the king's admirers."[44] Indeed, after his retirement from the army in 1907, he wrote and lectured considerably about the Congo for Belgian audiences. Yet his interest in language continued even into this sphere as he composed his memoirs about the Congo in Esperanto. Lemaire was among the first to introduce Esperanto into Belgium through newspaper articles (collected as a pamphlet, *L'Esperanto, solution triomphante du problème de la Langue Universelle [ne acêtebla]e*) and a magazine he founded, *Belga Sonorilo*.[45]

What are we to make of the incongruity between Lemaire's linguistic endeavors? The colonial purpose of the *Vocabulaire* appears a world away from the goal of universal peace associated with Esperanto. They do not seem so incongruous once one considers the different versions of Esperanto that were circulating in the *fin de siècle*. Lemaire was follower of the French Esperantist Louis de Beaufront whose interpretation of the International Language's purpose differed from the religious sense cultivated by its founder, Zamenhof. For French Esperantists, the language was seen "as a practical form like a telegraph."[46] In this sense, the *Vocabulaire Pratique* and Lemaire's vision of Esperanto share an instrumental vision of language as utilitarian, pragmatic, and quantifiable. Also, as noted about the language guide, which had the ulterior purpose of limiting the spread of French, Esperanto was also a means of establishing Belgian independence from French. This is Fabian's point about how the invention of

Swahili as an LWC came about because the problems of national language identity in Belgium extended to their language policy in the Congo. In Lemaire's case, Esperanto is another LWC to be used in the center and the peripheries. The example of Lemaire in his different guises as the "colonial linguist-esperantist-language teacher" suggests some ways that we can see colonial linguistics and artificial languages as similar attempts to modernize language for use in multilingual contexts.

Lemaire and the Palmer Method

Palmer dedicates *The Principles of Language Study* to "Commandant Lemaire" because, he writes, he was so inspired by their conversation in 1919 in the Fange forest in southern Belgium. Writing in French, Palmer opens the preface by recalling that meeting:

> Do you remember my last visit to you at *Sources Fraîches*, after the five tragic years we had experienced? I remember it like it was yesterday. You had suffered; I found you weakened, and I feel even now the profound pain in which I found you at that time, which I contrast with the spirit in which I left you in 1914.[47]

Palmer and his family had narrowly escaped Belgium in 1914. It is not lost on Palmer that the main events of the war, such as the horrific Battle of the Bulge, had taken place close to where they were meeting. Palmer expresses the elegiac mood common after the war and identifies the older Lemaire with the pre-war European "spirit" that has been lost. Palmer reports that they discussed the ideal conditions of language learning to which Lemaire developed a "thesis, supporting it with facts collected during [his] long years of observation in the heart of Africa" that "Nature must … be our inspiration." Palmer quotes Lemaire as saying that "Nature … is a fertile source of teaching and method—she is the only teacher for blacks" and that the example of "primitive life" offers "superior" examples of education.[48]

The comments about natural learning conditions are not unusual for Palmer since he had already emphasized those qualities of "natural" learning through phonetics and orality in his first book, *The Scientific Study and Teaching of Languages* in 1917. Where one might detect Lemaire's influence could be in the rhetorical form that Palmer gives his argument in *Principles*. Some of the chapter titles—"Our Spontaneous Capacities for Acquiring Speech," and "The Supreme Importance of the Elementary Stage"—reflect Lemaire's discourse on "Nature as our best teacher" even though they also resemble typical statements for Palmer who often refers to "spontaneous capacity" as the ability to absorb a second language in the mimetic, unconscious method by which an infant acquires language. The goal of the Palmer Method is to create the conditions through which the adolescent or adult learner can tap into this "spontaneous capacity."

Where *Principles* differs from Palmer's traditional arguments and evokes Lemaire's "own words" are in the additional references to the "barbarian," "savage," and "primitive" alongside the figure of the infant as spontaneous masters of the "art" of language acquisition.

> This art, we are told, requires no intelligence on the part of the one who is learning it; on the contrary, the least intelligent often prove to be among the most successful adepts, notably very young children, idiots, or barbarians of the lowest scale.[49]

Although Palmer's intention here is to congratulate the "least intelligent" as "the most successful adepts," it is framed by an evolutionary paradigm inflected by colonial discourse. He emphasizes this category again when he asks, referring to the "art of using the spoken and everyday form of any given language," he writes, "show me the child of three years of age, the madman, or the savage, who is not an expert at it!"[50] He develops this analogy by arguing that children are able to acquire speech while lacking powers of reason, he similarly writes about the "savage":

> By definition he is unintelligent, he has never learnt to think logically, he has no power of abstraction, he is probably unaware that such a thing as language exists; but he will faithfully observe to the finest details the complexities (phonetic, grammatical, and semantic) of his "savage" language. He will use the right vowel or tone in the right place; he will not confuse any of the dozen or so genders with which his language is endowed; a "savage" language (with an accidence so rich that Latin is by comparison a language of simple structure) will to him be an instrument on which he plays in the manner of an artist, a master: and we are speaking of a savage, mark you, whose intelligence is of so low an order that for him that which is not concrete has no existence![51]

There are quotation marks around "savage" before its modification of language yet none around the use of the savage himself. Palmer's qualification suggests Jespersen's cultural relativist perspective on the complexity of the savage's language as part of what marks its inferiority. In examples possibly gleaned from Lemaire, Palmer refers to the "grammatical system of the Bantu languages" and how "no Bechuana or Matabele native, illiterate as he may be, will ever commit the slightest error in the use of his tones."[52] Palmer draws on this ethnographic perspective in order to make his argument for non-intellectual, sensual processes of language learning. In this latter sense, all of Palmer's *Principles* derive in some way from this initial comparison to the "savage."

From the emphasis on orality, elementary stages of learning, and spontaneity there is a clear correlation between this evolutionary paradigm and his pedagogical emphasis on habit. Howatt surmises that Palmer's use of "habit" derived from several sources including the theory of associationism that first appears in William James's *Principles of Psychology*, and is applied to language by Lawrence Bloomfield in his influential 1914 book, *An Introduction to the Study of Language*. Notably, Howatt connects Palmer's behaviorism with the work from that period, not the psychological behaviorism of the 1920s. These foundational works in behaviorism were both published in 1913: J. B. Watson's article, "Psychology as the Behaviorist Views It," and Edward Thorndike's *Psychology of Learning*.[53] In these theories, the concept of "habit" came from studies of animal intelligence. Watson's thesis was that psychologists needed to "apply the rigorous methods of experimental animal psychology to their work."[54] Thorndike revolutionized the field of animal studies and educational psychology through his "puzzle-box" experiments with cats, dogs, and monkeys where he tested their ability to learn how to escape confinement to reach food. His original insights into animal intelligence radically challenged Victorian approaches to animal intelligence, which mainly consisted of anecdotal description that explained animal behavior by endowing the animals with human motivations. In order to test whether the animals could understand the consequences of escaping the box, which they were to do by lifting up a latch, Thorndike experimented with animals in different states of starvation or panic. The fact that these conditions did not affect their ability to escape (but did increase their probability), he countered Victorian accounts of extreme forms of animal intelligence and demonstrated that animal behavior was random with repetition of the response coming through experience of satisfaction.

According to the historian of science Bennet Galef, Thorndike's main contribution to comparative psychology was the invention of quantitative measures of performance.[55] This will have implications later, as we will see at the end of this chapter, for understanding Thorndike's contribution to quantitative methods of measuring language. Thorndike's work helps to locate Palmer's concept of habit-formation in the early behaviorist movement because of his methods that bring together educational psychology, associationism, and animal studies. It is important to consider also, the role of evolution in shaping Thorndike's associationist and behaviorist views. Galef argues that Thorndike adopted Spencerian, not Darwinian, understanding of phylogeny at the same time that he shifted his interests from animal studies to educational psychology, viewing evolution as a form of linear progress from simple organisms to complex humans.[56]

We can see this positivist view of language development reproduced in Palmer's method of language teaching. As Jespersen put it: "that language ranks highest which goes farthest in the art of accomplishing much with little means."[57] According to this logic, it is possible to understand Palmer's evocation of the innate complexity of primitive languages in *Principles* as also a means of measuring social and developmental inferiority. A key part of the ideology of English as an auxiliary language is the reification of the *first* language as a "mother tongue" that is complex, baroque, premodern, and incapable of development. In contrast, the universal *lingua franca*—English, for Palmer, or Esperanto for Lemaire—becomes the language that is capable of achieving a linguistic ideal of concision and simplicity. The ideology requires this version of the mother tongue language in order to distinguish its own auxiliary form of language. The more that a behavioral account of instinctual, spontaneous language learning can be made, then the auxiliary language can assume its role as a transactional language. In this way, the Palmer Method inherited this tradition of early twentieth-century thinking about evolution, science, and progress.

At the time of this inspirational meeting in Verviers, Lemaire was about to begin his position as the first director of the newly established Colonial University in Antwerp.[58] Coincidentally, Palmer was also about to take up a new position, as an advisor to the Ministry of Education in Japan. This post-war meeting between Palmer and Lemaire might be seen as capturing a transitional moment in language teaching from its colonial past to its internationalist future and how two concepts from the former—word lists and primitivism—make their way into the latter.

Michael West: *Bilingualism* and Indirect Rule

At the same time that Palmer was in Japan developing his methods for teaching English through "speech first," West was in Bengal developing his own program for teaching English with an emphasis on "reading first." West founded his theory of language teaching on first-hand experience from over twenty years working as a teacher, inspector, and instructor in Bengal. As a colonial educator in India, West was participating in a drastically different intellectual and social context than Lemaire, a colonial officer in the Congo, and Palmer, a teacher and researcher in London and Tokyo. In this section, I examine West's neglected major work, *Bilingualism, with Special Reference to Bengal*, from 1926, as a key text for understanding the change in colonial attitudes toward language and education during late empire that prepared for the ideology of international English developed in the 1930s. Based on research he conducted in Bengali schools between in the early 1920s as part of his Oxford dissertation, *Bilingualism* provided the rationale for his New Method Readers. Drawing on similar arguments about the mother tongue as Palmer, and using Ogden and Richards' own arguments for instrumentalized language, West provides a model of language teaching that will be readily adapted to the arguments for World English in the 1930s. Yet it is significant that he does not arrive at his method while at the University of London or Cambridge. Rather, West developed his New Method while training teachers in Dacca within the context of anti-colonial nationalist movements and declining British influence. As a result, his method, which was adapted (by him and by others) for use in Africa and the Middle East, provided a blueprint for managing British cultural imperialism after the empire. In this way, West's study is not only about language teaching, it also projects a strategy for adapting British influence during a tumultuous period of Bengali anti-colonial nationalism following the 1919 Montague Reforms.[59]

Of course, West was not the first to reform English in India, nor was his method all that new. As Alok Mukherjee has demonstrated, English language textbooks and readers were circulating in India even before Lord Auckland passed the policy of English language instruction in 1839.[60] Indeed, as covered in Chapter 1, West comes late in the long history of English language education in India that has been well-documented by historians and scholars of the British Empire, English language teaching, and contemporary Indian education.[61] In this chapter, my interest is with those elements of the history that West considered relevant to his arguments such as policies on teacher training and the role of the vernacular in the classroom.

At the level of colonial policy, British education in India was always defined by questions over whom to teach, in what language, and how to pay for it. All of these contradictions were present from the first policy of English language instruction in the 1835 English Education Act that was implemented in 1839, to the 1854 Despatch and the subsequent reforms in the 1882 Hunter Commission Report, the 1904 Raleigh Commission and the 1919 Calcutta University Report. All of these sought to affect change by revising funding for primary education and by expanding universities and the curriculum.

To understand this change, it is useful to compare it to pre-Empire Indian education, which had been localized and diverse. The subjects and the languages taught varied depending on the caste, area of training, and region. As the South Asian linguist E. Annamalai explains, "The language taught was also the medium for teaching. It was Sanskrit for the priestly Brahmins, Pali for Buddhist monks, and the local language for others engaged in farming, trade and artisan work. Education served the purpose of preparing the different groups of people to perform their socially ascribed roles, and the choice of language to be taught was the one needed for those roles."[62] I cite this description of a local, linguistically specific and socially stratified educational tradition to illustrate the significance of British policies introduced in the nineteenth century that centralized education to states, standardized modes and languages of instruction, and directed its purpose to serve the colonial state. Despite debates over the actual effectiveness of British colonial education (e.g., when compared to the influence of private, missionary schools, or in its purpose of assimilating Indians into colonial subjects[63]), the overall disruption of traditional systems of education cannot be disputed nor can the fact that the introduction of a centralized, technocratic, exam-based, English-focused educational system has remained an integral part of the postcolonial state into the twenty-first century.[64]

As Gauri Viswanathan demonstrated in *Masks of Conquest*, when English education was first offered, English literature, not language instruction, was the priority. The English language teaching at the time was based on the Classical Method using textbooks like Lindsley Murray's *English Grammar* and George Campbell's *Philosophy of Rhetoric*.[65] As Viswanathan notes, this priority was to change with Wood's 1854 Despatch. She describes the reforms as a turn toward a system that is utilitarian and "functionalist in character":

> The rhetoric of morality gave way to the demands of political economy, from which evolved a scheme of education set out to create a middle class serving as an agency of imperialist economy and administration and, through it, to initiate social change through a process of differentiation.[66]

In addition from changing the content—from literature to language—it also changed the subjects of the education: Chaudhary notes that these reforms marked a shift from a policy of "a very high degree of education for a small number of natives in the English medium" to "expanding vernacular primary education to the rural population."[67] The subsequent reforms in 1882 and 1904 continued to expand access to centralized primary education using local vernaculars as the medium of instruction. However, due to the increasing demand for English schools because of the promise of government jobs more secondary schools were being built than primary schools, which undercut the expansion of vernacular schooling. As Annamalai argues, this created a persistent "conflict between the goal of mass education through native languages and elitist education through English."[68]

To rectify this divide reforms were made in the late nineteenth and early twentieth centuries to increase participation of Indians in education civil service. This led to the creation of two administrative branches of education, originally called the "Superior" and "Inferior" services, which were soon renamed as the Indian Education Service (IES) and the Provincial Education Service (PES), though the new names did not change the inherent bias. The act of naming the IES also captured the contradictions of British education in India. The IES consisted of an Imperialist education determined from London and Cambridge teaching European content in the English language. The only "Indian" education was being performed by the service not named "Indian," the PES.[69] This suggests how, on the one hand, British colonial authorities sought to manage Indian participation in education through distribution of aid, resources, and social difference while, on the other hand, they were cautious about creating an education that might meet disapproval. For its brief history, the IES remained understaffed and underfunded with problems relating to recruitment and promotion as well as a contentious relationship with the PES which took on more of the administrative burden. Finally, the combined effects of Indian calls for nationalizing education and the First World War, which cost a generation of recruits, brought an end to the IES.

West first came to India in 1912 in the midst of these reforms, as a member of the IES with assignments at the Teachers' Training College first in Calcutta and then Dacca. His service was interrupted by the war and afterwards he participated in a wide-ranging survey of primary education in Bengal. It was through this survey that he observed the problems that provided the basis for the criticisms of the Filtration Method and of existing language teaching models that he raises in *Bilingualism*. As Smith notes, West saw the problems of language teaching as connected to larger educational issues from school maintenance, curriculum and classroom management.[70]

West's response to the survey for the Calcutta University Commission in 1919 captures his arguments about language education at the time. According to Smith, a common lament in the 1919 survey was the fact that English was the medium of instruction at the university and college levels even though the students' English was "insufficient for academic purposes." The solutions were divided between expanding vernacular instruction and improving English teaching. In contrast to his peers, Smith notes, West

> argued against the idea of concentrating on English to the detriment of mother tongue instruction. Instead, he stated that he was in favour of making English "the mere second language, in this case not so much a colloquial language as one for reading," thus dooming it, he admitted to its disappearance as a colloquial language. The reasons he gave included the future needs of the country, the present poor state of English teaching, and the fact that increasingly the staff of universities as well as schools were likely to be Indian.[71]

Adopting arguments that would have been familiar to the Orientalists of the 1830s, West criticized the "English-only" bias of his IES colleagues. West even argued that it would be less expensive to train British instructors in local Indian languages than to "pay for a whole educational system" to teach students to speak English.[72] Implicit in this criticism with English-only policies was a criticism of how English was taught through the Direct Method which he argued was not adequate for teaching students in "extreme conditions"—where the teacher was a non-native speaker and the classrooms were too large for systematic oral practice.

In *Bilingualism*, West revisits this history of English education in India emphasizing the failure of Macaulay's Filtration theory. Anticipating contemporary criticism of Macaulay's Minute, West argues that it has received undo attention and should only be seen as one moment in the controversy between the Orientalists and Anglicists. West sees the *dichotomy* between English and vernaculars—not the preference for English—as the central problem for English education in India. He argues that it was institutionalized in the failed compromise of the 1854 Dispatch that created a two-tier education system with English education for the elite and vernaculars for the rest. West suggests that the policy misunderstands the class system in India, neglecting a large middle class of professionals who desire English. In this regard, West expands the 1830s educational debates to include arguments from many interested parties other than Macaulay's—such as Anglicists like Benthune, Orientalists like Princeps, and Indian Anglicists like Rammohan Roy.[73] By describing these early debates as a series of reactions and counter-reactions, West is able to characterize his own concept of bilingualism as a reasonable middle ground.

Like Palmer, West was influenced by early twentieth-century progress in educational psychology. His first book, *Educational Psychology*, published in 1914, was a primer on the new methods of learning that emphasized the student's role in the classroom. Smith summarizes West's philosophy as a "learner-centred view of education" with a "sceptical attitude about the abilities of teachers."[74] This was not only true for native teachers in India, but all teachers who were prone to "talking too much." In contrast, West supplemented his use of psychology with quantitative methods from economics. This innovation created some problems with his Oxford dissertation readers who rejected *Bilingualism* when it was first submitted in 1925 because they objected to his use of statistics and tables as too "American." The resistance to West's methods demonstrates the difference at the time between British and American theories of education. The rise of Columbia's Teacher's College, discussed more fully in the fifth chapter, based in the work of Edward Thorndike, influenced West's practice. Smith notes that West's *Bilingualism* and a nontechnical version, *Learning to Read a Foreign Language*, were well-received in the United States.[75] This disparity remains apparent ten years later in the transatlantic organization of the Carnegie conference around US statistical methods and the traditional expertise of the British colonial educators.

West's study took two years and "involved the use of thirteen different tests of reading applied to various groups of children from a few hundreds in number up to 4,000."[76] The study led him to conclude that the Filtration Theory was a "failure" in theory and practice. He argued that in the dichotomous colonial education system, "Education does not filter downwards; it produces a crowding upwards."[77] The structural incentives for learning English were too great due to the increase in government services, industrialization, and the increasing number of European businesses in Calcutta (who were also offering scholarships for learning English) had made English education nearly compulsory for Indians. All of this made the vernacular-English, popular-elite dichotomies illusory; instead "[t]here was only one popular form of education—namely English education; it grew and became the only form of education."[78]

As the Calcutta survey demonstrated, the Filtration Theory had few defenders by the 1920s, but the solutions remained focused on elite education. In contrast, West wanted to create a method of teaching English for younger students who only attend school for a few years before working or going to the English high schools. In the current educational context, students going to the high schools had insufficient English and those who left school lacked serviceable English for working in a modernizing Calcutta. The solution, for West, was to make English language education efficient so that it would yield a high "surrender value." Borrowing this term from economics, West defines it as: "the proportionate amount of benefit which will be derived by any pupil from an incomplete course of instruction in that subject." In Bengal, West writes, English instruction needs to be designed "in such a way that the surrender value shall at every point be as high as possible" so that whenever "a boy may abandon school, he must carry away something of permanent value and utility from his study of English."[79] The concept of surrender value means that the type of English taught for a student who takes it for "five years" and becomes a "skilled labourer" would be different than that for a student who completes his education and becomes a professional or joins the civil service. His criticism of the Filtration Theory upended a tradition of colonial education policy based on withholding English from the masses and derived from a revisionist perspective on the colonial modes of knowledge that assumed the need for an elite class of Indians to act as translators.

West's argument against the Filtration Method extends to its role in turning Indians against English and Western education altogether. By failing to create adequate institutions for vernacular learning and limiting English education to "a useless literary training," West argues, the Filtration Theory sacrificed the goodwill that nineteenth-century Liberal Bengalis had toward Europeans.[80] According to West, Bengalis in the 1860s–80s were "enamored with Europe and English" and turned toward anti-colonial nationalism out of frustration and disappointment.[81] West cites the influential figure of Rammohan Roy, considered the father of Indian nationalism, who supported English language education in the Liberal, enlightenment belief that it would help to modernize India. However, in the late nineteenth century, Bengali intellectuals turned away from Roy's universalism and toward a "new cultural nationalism." Partha Chatterjee describes this as "the story of nationalist modernity in Bengal":

> [That] began in the 1870s as a self-conscious and idealist critique of the universal abstract subject of Western modernity and became a project for constructing a modern subject that was specifically Indian in its cultural practices and moral values. Nationalist modernity, in other words, was premised on a necessary rejection of the early liberalism of men like Rammohan.[82]

This cultural nationalist movement peaked with the Swadeshi movement in the early 1900s, an "ethical political economy"[83] that cast British imperialism as the purveyors of industrial capitalism and a dehumanizing commercialism. While the boycotts ended several years before West arrived, the impact of Swadeshi's demand to develop indigenous manufacturing was still felt intellectually and culturally. These nationalist economic concepts took refuge in cultural debates over Bengali regional, class, religious, and linguistic identities.

The Bengali historian Sabyasachi Bhattacharya locates this shift with the 1919 Government of India Act that extended the franchise to a population of non-English speaking Bengalis.[84] This Act increased the number of Bengali language newspapers and the expectation that public discourse would be in Bengali, not English. As Bhattacharya puts it: "The ideal of oratory, an art much overrated in Bengal, was no longer the Gladstonian language of Sir Surendra Nath Banerjea, but the chaste Sanskritic Bengali of C. R. Das, or the Bengali closer to the people's language used by A. K. Fazlul Huq."[85] The 1919 reforms were intended to provide a pathway to independence for India by further devolving responsibilities such as education from British control to local governments. Criticized by the Indian National Congress as far short of actual independence, the reforms offered a form of dyarchy in which power was shared between provincial governments, which were reshaped by expanded franchise and took over responsibility for public works, and the GOI which was responsible for military and foreign affairs. Despite its claims of self-governance, the British maintained systematic administrative control and its reforms were matched by repressive legislation that severely limited civil rights such as the Rowlatt Acts.[86]

It is in this late imperial context that we have to consider West's New Method. As a colonial educator during the period of Indirect Rule, West seeks to bring English to the masses of Bengalis without threatening, nor encouraging, national identities. As Indirect Rule maintains rule by decentralizing power, his New Method seeks to promote English by destandardizing it. His criticism of Macaulay's Filtration Theory as inefficient suggests a break with Liberal universalism of the first empire that persisted among colonial educators despite the efforts of numerous utilitarian reforms. The title of his work, *Bilingualism*, conveys this revisionist sentiment (even though West mostly treats Bilingualism and Multilingualism as synonymous) that an educational system predicated on multilingualism rather than a monolingually defined dichotomy will have greater success during a time when English is both desirable professionally and repellant politically. The basis for his argument for bilingualism is that Indian national feeling can coexist with the English language and that learning English will not "de-nationalize" Bengalis.

For West, the impetus toward multilingualism is not based on ethics nor assimilation to British culture, but access to a specialized language. Just as one learns Latin or Sanskrit or Arabic as a religious language, one learns English as the specialized language for modernity. This is the rhetoric of English as a "skill" that is still used today in neoliberal discourses of Global English. West even articulates this view through a vision of English as the language of modernity and internationalism, writing that English is a specialized language and that "under the conditions of modern life everyone is a specialist."[87] Unlike Macaulay's explicit association of Europe with Modernity, West's modernity is global: "Modern Industrial organisation demands the elimination of provincial and national boundaries: the whole world has become one vast interdependent commercial organisation, a 'Great Society.'"[88]

West's reference here is to the 1914 book of that title by the Fabian socialist Graham Wallas. Combining psychology and economics, *The Great Society* represents a pre-war analysis of the effects of modernity and industrialization on "the individual psyche." Wallas argues that as aspects of everyday life such as producing food or finding labor have become internationalized and commodified, people are sensing a loss of agency and are "affected by this ever-extending and ever-tightening nexus."[89] While the promise of the Great Society in nineteenth-century progressivism was supposed to exchange the "romance and intimacy of life" for greater material security, Wallas argues that it has come at a psychic cost, "a deeper anxiety," that the world is no longer in one's control. Wallas draws on social psychology to suggest ways that humans can adapt our "dispositions" such as habit and fear to the new social conditions.

Like Wallas, West sees modernity as a force that destroys local affiliations and produces existential feelings of despair. He writes that "Man's individual soul is a naked, sensitive thing, intensely conscious of itself" and that "a man hates to be herded, indexed, treated as an interchangeable unit" as occurs under modernity. It is in reaction to this depersonalizing modernity that individuals turn toward a romantic past associated with a national or cultural language. West casts this as a desire for "differentiation." In a section of *Bilingualism* on the "Need for a Sense of Individuality," West characterizes the recovery of a national language or culture as that of a "clique" asserting "their difference from the common herd."[90] Drawing on Freud's account of the Ego and Group Psychology, West portrays the small group as a way of expressing individuality. In the spirit of Wallas's modernist analysis, West's purpose is to re-direct this romantic desire for individual expression toward adaptation to this alienating modernity. In this way, he trivializes the "revival of obsolete nationalist and tribal languages" as egoistical acts of "self-expression." Rather than seeing language revival as a form of "de-Anglicization," as the Irish nationalist Douglas Hyde describes the revival of the Irish language, West views the sentiments "I am a Welshman," "I am a Cornishman" as simply "expressions of a desire to be different."[91]

West does not refer to the needs of empire, or English or Western values but instead he refers to "Modernity" and "Internationalism." An international lingua franca is a necessity for maintaining, not creating, globalization: "As regards its material interests and the means of supplying the whole world is one: it is only linguistic barriers and the artificial boundaries of tribal feeling that separate."[92] In his chapter on "Bilingualism and National Culture," he sympathizes with nationalism and recognizes that national languages are important in so far as they reflect "the nature of people's thought."[93] In the European tradition, this argument was used to raise minor languages to up the status of major languages so that the Latin vernaculars were equal to Latin or that the Germanic languages might justify a unified national identity. Instead, West uses this logic to argue for the intrinsic strength of national languages. The difference lays in how language is used to legitimate evolutionary theories. In Europe, linguistic diversity indicates the paths that individual nations have taken to reach modernity. Abroad, in the colonies, linguistic diversity indicates arrested development, a stubborn inability to evolve. West sympathizes with nationalism as long as it remains within its local frame of reference and acknowledges that its limits require the use of an auxiliary supplement. In this way, West's "new" method reflects the late imperialist policy of Indirect Rule.

What is referred to as Indirect Rule was part of what Timothy Parsons calls the "second British Empire," that revises the Liberal policies of the early nineteenth century. As Partha Chatterjee describes it, there was a "hardening of imperial attitudes" after the mid-century rebellions in India and Jamaica that criticized "the alleged sentimentality of the liberal pedagogical project of culture." In its place, "the new alibi of empire was the protection of people living in traditional society from the destructive consequences of modern commercial and property regimes."[94] As a consequence, British imperialism sought to mitigate the impact of modernity on traditional societies and, in those areas not saturated by imperial rule already, the "British colonial power came to see itself in the special role of protector of the local tribal communities against planters and traders."[95]

The division of responsibilities for governance instituted in the 1919 Act resembles West's vision of Bilingualism. Using the pragmatic and culturalist rhetoric of late imperialism, West describes multilingualism as reflecting different functions:

> The first language is the vehicle of thoughts about the home life, and perhaps of a literature expressive of emotions and ideas connected with the home; while the second language is a vehicle of communication for matters of government,

commerce, industry, scientific thought and higher culture generally. There may be a third language which is a medium of communication for international relations and higher education, and a fourth necessary for the religion and ancient culture of the people.[96]

This neat categorization of languages as based on need allows West to imagine that each sphere remains independent of any other. Similarly, the 1919 Act tries to avoid any inherent contradiction between the local and international spheres of power.

This comes through in his argument about the divide between national and international spheres of culture and identity. Rather than arguing for the superiority of English culture over other national cultures, as Macaulay does, West acknowledges cultural nationalist claims for national languages as "an expression of the colour of national thought." It is due to this connection between language and feeling that nationalists, he argues, express a "fear of Renationalization" by acquiring English.[97] West argues against the "fallacy of renationalization" by appealing to psychology. Nineteenth-century Liberal colonialism, he argues, used an educational psychology based in Locke's theory of the mind as a *tabular rasa*. This is the psychology epitomized in Macaulay's infamous statement about an English education that can create "a class of persons Indian in blood and colour, but English in tastes, in opinions, in morals and in intellect."[98] This is the assumption that "the same education everywhere would produce the same type of educated person."[99] West cites modern educational psychologists, including Edward Thorndike, to argue instead for the selection of a certain type of learning for certain type of learners. Fears of renationalization are prompted, correctly, West says, from an assimilationist model of English language education: "a standard course in English, starting with the Direct Method and ending in an M. A. syllabus which includes Old English and Philology."[100] Because the Direct Method depended upon Standard Pronunciation and limited the amount of translation in native languages, it created classroom conditions that promoted assimilation: compelling students to sound and think British.

In its place, his New Method with its differentiated lessons developed for a range of learners and purposes would "select" the education to fit the learner rather than trying to shape the student by the curriculum. The New Method allowed for teachers to use their native languages to explain and translate the material. Because it does not use class time practicing oral competencies, the reading method was more efficient allowing students at different stages to acquire a grade-level competency in reading English. West estimated that by using his reading method that students could learn with more efficient use of class time and acquire a greater "surrender value." West anticipated the criticism that the New Method's "simplified" English would receive from contemporary critics of ELT such as Pennycook and Phillipson.

> There is a danger that the present book may create a false impression in the minds of some, especially in Bengal. The author may be accused of advocating a "dumb" knowledge of English, so that "Bengalis will not learn to speak English and their command over English as a means of expression become even less than it is at present," etc.[101]

His response is that the New Method should not be viewed as acting with the same intentions of the old Liberal models of assimilationist education. It is not a universalist approach wherein all Bengalis only have limited reading ability in English. It is a selective approach so that all Bengalis, not just an elite class, receive a useful, functional amount of English approximate to their age and need. The goal is that over time Bengali boys will read English at the same grade level as their English counterparts. Rather than the universal plan of the old colonial English education, the New Method is a strategic plan to meet current "extreme conditions" of poverty, classroom conditions (with non-native speakers), and the particular needs for English in a colonial society. In this sense of educational psychology, West appears to respect anti-colonialist criticism of English education as a logical response to an outdated curriculum based on a discredited educational psychology of learning. It follows from this that the "fear of renationalization through language" can be assuaged with the proper educational curriculum.

However, this rationalization might not be so compelling when considered within the accepted ideas of educational psychology such as Thorndike's. A leading member of the New York chapter of the eugenics movement known as the "Montrose Colony" in the Hudson Valley, Thorndike's theories of education were rooted in the belief that teaching needs to be adapted to the student's level, but cannot expect that it will improve them.[102] As he wrote in a 1927 article,

> Men are born unequal in intellect, character, and skill. It is impossible and undesirable to make them equal by education. The proper work of education is to improve all men according to their several possibilities, in ways consistent with the welfare of all.[103]

As an expression of the "new education psychology" that West espouses in *Bilingualism*, Thorndike's argument that education needs to be selective, not universal, assumes that the learners remain in their particular place within the hierarchy. West was certainly not a eugenicist like Thorndike, just as Palmer cannot be held accountable for Lemaire's actions. But in this way, West's New Method expresses the late nineteenth-century criticism of Liberal colonialism that was represented in the theories of Indirect Rule. His educational model argues against assimilating natives to English modernity and alienating them from their national and cultural languages. His argument for a second language depends upon an argument for a first, mother tongue, language similar to the way that Indirect Rule justified its power through the rhetoric of protecting natives from modernity. His notion of an auxiliary language depends upon an ethnographic and depoliticized view of a national language as a mother tongue language. It is because the mother tongue has such an intrinsic connection to the individual's identity and thought that it resists any potential threat from a second language. But his multilingualism is predicated on a hierarchy in which these languages remain in their place and acknowledge that their limits require the use of a supplement. The mother tongue, like the imagined native cultures under Indirect Rule, can be protected from modernity; they just cannot be imagined as adapting to it, or existing without it.

The "second language" approach reflects the "dyarchy" of responsibilities instituted in the 1919 Act between the local, provincial, and international British spheres of power. However, this second, auxiliary language that is differentiated by learning level and intentions needs its own set of vocabularies. If the old assimilationist model depended upon a "standard" English, then it is necessary to create new vocabularies that do not seek to change the student (from inside out), but rather that can be used by the learner. West used reading and testing experiments with Bengali students to measure reading speed and comprehension that he made up in a series of tables and graphs (see Figures 3 and 4).

These are only two examples of the many tables and graphs used by West to display the results of his tests. The appearance of the boys' names in the columns, and the detail given to each child, as can be seen in Figure 3, suggests an attention to detail and a recognition of individual difference that was surely lacking in the racial profiling of entire groups by Macaulay. Nonetheless, it creates a new means of sorting. If not by race and religion, then it is by grade, gender, region all subject to objective measurement and quantification. Because American researchers were the leaders in reading assessment, the tests that West used were the Kansas test, developed by F. J. Kelly in 1916, and the methods of analysis from Thorndike's research on measurement scales of assessment for American

Name of pupil.	THIRD TEST (OCTOBER 5TH AND 6TH 1923).								Name of pupil.
	Burt's Directions.		Burt's Vocabulary.		Prince and Crow.		Prince and Tiger.		
	Expt.	Cont.	Expt	Cont.	Expt.	Cont.	Expt.	Cont.	
1. Manik	...	...	...	...	...	...	...	...	Jitendra.
2. Susil	4	3·5	30	20	4·5	5	17	14	Jyotirmay.
3. Samarendra	3·5	—	26·5		5	...	16·5	...	Gandreram.
4. Prodyot	3	1·5	21	22	1·5	1	8	4·5	Ashutosh.
5. Oahidur	3	2·75	16·5	19	5	1 5	15·5	9	Parimal.
6. Karim	4	3	28	20·5	5·5	4	17	15	Amulya.
7. Amjad	2·5	1	16	19·5	2	1	13	10	Rohini.
8. Haripada	3·5	3·75	28	25	6·5	5	16	13·5	Sukhada.
9. Barendra	3·5	2·5	25	22·5	4	0	15	7·5	Animesh.
10. Mahiuddin	...	...	...	...	...	2	...	9	
Mean	3·4	2·6	23·5	21·2	4·1	2·5	14·5	10 5	
Superiority of Experimentals to Controls.	30·7 per cent.		10·8 per cent		65·7 per cent.		38·1 per cent.		

TABLE 78.—First Teaching Experiment. Result of the Third Test.

Figure 3 An example of the type of quantitative methods used by West that were considered controversial to some of his dissertation readers at Oxford. "Table 78: First Teaching Experiment. Result of the Third Test" from West, *Bilingualism* (1926).

schoolchildren.[104] In this sense, despite his desire to differentiate his work from that of his predecessors, West's *Bilingualism* follows in the colonial tradition of viewing India as an "epistemological space," as Bernard Cohn describes the act of using the colonies as a site to develop new forms of colonial knowledge. The right to do the measuring and assessing for this particular purpose, of learning an imperial language, remains unquestioned.

Ogden and Richards: *Meaning of Meaning* and Primitivism

The second part of West's argument against the "fallacy of renationalization" is the "fallacy of Word Magic" which he defines as "the tendency to assume that a word has a fixed connexion with its referent and that by acquiring the word one acquires the referent."[105] A key term in their influential work on language and thought, *The Meaning of Meaning*, Ogden and Richards define Word Magic as the belief in words as spiritual: "The whole human race has been so impressed by the properties of words as instruments for the control of objects, that in every age it has attributed to them occult powers."[106] West argues that it is Word Magic that leads Bengalis to confuse the symbolic and the evocative

Vocabulary Control and Colonialism

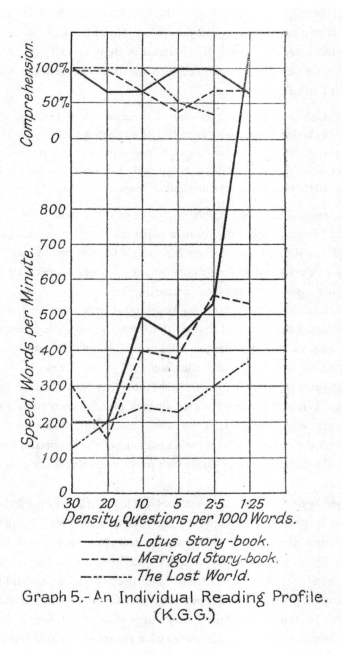

Figure 4 "Graph 5: An Individual Reading Profile," from West, *Bilingualism* (1926).

elements of language. Following Ogden and Richards's contextual definition of language, when a language is decontextualized, it loses its power to determine thought. Therefore, when English is learned in Bengal, "away from English scenery, English life, English people" then the language becomes refracted through the Bengali mind so that

> ... the English language becomes adapted to express Bengali thought. The English may be indistinguishable from that of an Englishman; if however the accompanying imagery and ideas could be thrown upon a lantern screen, the difference would immediately become apparent. The words are the words of England, but the thoughts are the thoughts of Bengal.[107]

As a result, anyone learning English "out of context" in India cannot be "de-nationalized." English words do not necessarily lead to English "thoughts." In this line of reasoning, West reverses Macaulay's famous formulation: rather than a native exterior and an English interior, he proposes a superficial English exterior—language—and a "spiritual" native interior.

A "nice half-brick"[108] of a book, *Meaning of Meaning* consists of ten chapters deriving from articles first written for *Cambridge Magazine* as well as five appendices and two supplemental essays. Since this is a key text for West's argument and, later, for Basic English, I want to examine how the mother tongue—auxiliary language dichotomy fits into their philosophy of language. Where Palmer draws on images of African primitivism and West engages with Bengali nationalism, Ogden and Richards find an anthropological parallel in Malinowski's account of the Trobriand Islanders that is one of the supplemental essays, as a proof for their theory of language and meaning.

Described by one reviewer as a "handbook of logic," *Meaning* might be most well-known for its introduction of C. S. Peirce's tripartite theory of the sign to a wide audience. Gordon argues that similar to Peirce, Ogden and Richards approached sign theory as an extension of Logic.[109] Peirce's triangle of meaning had three parts—a sign, an object, and an interpretant—with the definition of a sign as anything that depends upon an object for its existence and has an effect upon a person. For example, smoke depends upon an object, fire, and an interpretant, a person who determines what the relationship is between the two things; for example, is the fire dangerous or not? Their theory is similar to Peirce's in that they include a mediating interpreter as part of the construction of meaning. Where they differ is in how the three parts connect. As can be seen in Figure 5, their triangle has direct lines from Symbol to Thought and from Thought to Referent; however, these causal relations contrast with the "imputed" relation between Symbol-Referent, which is represented by a broken line. This indicates an indirect relation between Symbol-Referent; that is, the symbol does not have a *determining* relation to the Referent. This is an important distinction for their theory since the ordinary use of "meaning" in the dictionary sense assumes a direct line between word-symbol and referent. This ordinary conception of meaning, which they elsewhere refer to as the "fixed meaning fallacy," ignores the fact that all meaning is indirect and contextual. Word Magic occurs when the interpreter assumes there is a direct line between symbol and referent either in a dualistic or monist interpretation the sign. The broken line between symbol and referent demystifies the magical properties of the word by showing the indirect, contextual basis for the word's "power." The word as found in the dictionary, or in a word list, as we will see, consists of a reification of the word as a thing. Attention to the context of interpretation prevents this mistaken assumption and allows us to see words as only having meaning depending on their use.

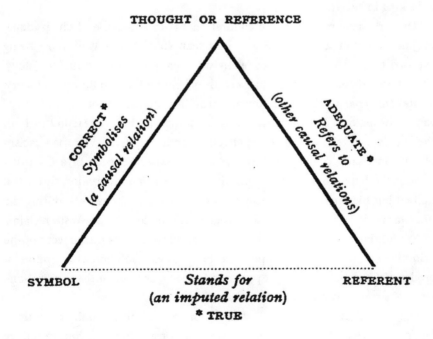

Figure 5 C. K. Ogden and I. A. Richards, *The Meaning of Meaning*, "Triangle of Interpretation." Ogden and Richards' semiotic triangle follows Peirce's triadic interpretation of the Sign.

All of *Meaning of Meaning* could be summed up as a description of the phenomenon of Word Magic and prescriptions for its prevention. The term appears most prominently in an encyclopedic chapter, "The Power of Words," where Ogden and Richards draw on examples of illogical language use from antiquity, medieval religious texts, and cultural anthropology. Word Magic and primitivism come together in their criticism of Saussure and his dualist theory of signs. They view Saussure as a victim of "the tyranny of language" because of his treatment of abstract terms such as *la langue* as an object in queries such as, "What is the object at once integral and concrete of linguistic?" Ogden and Richards respond, "[h]e does not ask whether it has one, he obeys blindly the primitive impulse to infer from a word some object for which it stands, and sets out determined to find it."[110] This description of Saussure's thought as "primitive" is one of several uses of the word in the opening pages of the book along with related evolutionary terms like "civilized man" or reference to American Indian languages. For example, they cite Herbert Spencer's distinction between Primitive and Greek thought as the capacity in the latter to separate the name from the object. All of these citations take the primitive view of language as lacking in "ideas."[111]

Their rhetoric resembles the cultural relativism and sense of civilizational decline common among interwar European intellectuals who were being exposed to the ideas of cultural relativism from anthropology and sociology. The cultural theorist Victor Li, in his study of primitivism and European theory, locates this change of attitude toward primitive models of society with postwar anthropology. Li summarizes this modernist period as reacting to both the "noble savage" ideal of the eighteenth century and the Victorian racism of the nineteenth century. Where the former existed outside of a Christian society, the latter connected the primitive to Christian civilization through a unified but hierarchical view of mankind. In contrast, Li observes, during the interwar period, the concept of the savage was used to critique Western claims to "civilization": "To the intelligentsia of the interwar years the concept of the primitive could no longer support the progressive, evolutionary narrative of modern Western civilization; it provided instead a critique of that civilization's sense of superiority and faith in progress."[112]

Ogden and Richards suggest the importance of this imminent critique for their project when they chose, in revising for a second edition, to reduce drastically the examples from antiquity, religion, and ethnography in Chapter two on Word Magic. Where the extensive list of examples in the first edition suggests a universal human error across time and cultures, the revision, with only a few paragraphs with examples from Ancient Egypt and the Old Testament, allows them to shift the focus of their analysis to the "persistence of the primitive outlook"[113] in the twentieth century. Like the use of Fetishism by Marx and Freud to describe atavistic habits within Western civilization, Ogden and Richards' "Word Magic" similarly uses the stigma of premodern irrationality to demonstrate the need for an antidote of rationality.

Malinowski and Basic English

The two supplemental essays included as appendices to *Meaning of Meaning*—Bronislaw Malinowski's "The Problem of Meaning in Primitive Languages" and F. G. Crookshank's "The Importance of a Theory of Signs and a Critique of Language in the Study of Medicine"—were considered by Ogden and Richards to be so integral to the whole that when they were asked to reduce the original for the second edition, they chose to cut their own work and retain these essays in full. Although the essays were solicited after most of *Meaning* had been written, they were seen by Ogden and Richards as valuable reinforcements, a "sort of footnote,"[114] to their arguments about the role of context in creating meaning. Malinowski offers evidence in the form of language use in the Papua tribes he studied in New Guinea while Crookshank criticizes medical language for its inaccuracies and dependence on Word Magic. It is notable that their subjects—the primitive and the scientific—replicate the dichotomy between ideological conceptions of "native-primitive-national languages" and the "modern, scientific, instrumental, auxiliary languages" implicit in the vocabulary control movement.

Born in Krakow, Bronislaw Malinowski helped to found British social anthropology and methods of fieldwork in the early twentieth century. He developed a theory of structural functionalism which held that social practices persist because they serve a useful function. As we will see, Ogden adapts this functionalist theory to language in Basic English, as, for example, when he remarks that "the word has no value when not in use."[115] According to Richards, Malinowski had just returned from the Trobriand Islands when they were writing *Meaning* and was staying in Ogden's Cambridge apartment.[116] He read the essays that were published in *The Cambridge Magazine* and noted similarities between his own ethnographic work and their theory of language. Malinowski's essay seeks to demonstrate the parallels between his work as an "ethnographer studying primitive mentality, culture, and language" and their theory of signs.[117] Malinowski's interest in primitive languages came out of his experience translating fieldwork. Finding so much of the primitive expressions untranslatable led him to be skeptical of linguistic theories based on the study of words and grammar alone. Instead, he focuses on language as speech—or, as it would later be adopted within British linguistics—as speech *acts*. In contrast to Saussure's *langue*, for Malinowski, there was only *parole*.[118] Meaning, in this analysis, connects speech to a host of non-linguistic contexts such as gesture, facial expression, environment, and audience that defy word-to-word translation.

In "Primitive Languages," Malinowski uses the example of a fishing expedition by the natives of the Trobriander islands to illustrate this problem with translation. The approximate English word-for-word translation of this expedition only amounts to "a meaningless jumble of words," as he puts it: "We run front-wood ourselves; we paddle in place; we turn we see companion ours; he runs rear-wood behind their sea-arm Pilolu."[119] Malinowski notes that it becomes more comprehensible when presented as an ethnographic description of ceremonial bartering and overseas trade. In addition to grammatical relations, it is necessary to describe the "wide fields of custom, of social psychology, and of tribal organization,"[120] or as he puts it elsewhere, "the general conditions under which a language is spoken."[121] As a result, "linguistic analysis inevitably leads us into the study of all the subjects covered by Ethnographic field-work."[122] If Ogden and Richards' theory has its psychological (word magic) and behaviorist elements, Malinowski's essay illustrates the latter. Where Ogden and Richards posit thought as the crucial intermediary between word-stimuli and the referent (the role of interpretation), Malinowski does not see words as related to thought at all. Instead, he argues that language in primitive societies can *only* function in relation to action. Therefore, linguistic meaning depends on the context of situation that relates to the act being performed, in this case, the trading expedition. As he writes in "Primitive Languages," "the utterance has no meaning except in the *context of situation*."[123]

In his later theories, developed in *Coral Gardens* from 1933, Malinowski goes further in denying any symbolic use of language, reducing it to "an ordinary tool."[124] For Malinowski, "Word Magic" derives from a deep association of the words with the "context of situation" so that one comes to mistakenly believe that the word creates the situation, rather than the other way around. He uses the example of the child who learns that speaking the word "Mama" makes the mother appear. Malinowski argues that "the first contexts of situation that the child experiences are magical ones" where experience teaches the child that "a name has the power over the person or thing which it signifies."[125]

There is a circular logic to Malinowski's context theory of language that relates to the paradoxes of Basic English. In his example of the Trobriand fishing expedition Malinowski notes that the "technical language ... acquires meaning only through personal participation in this type of pursuit. It has to be learned, not through reflection but through action."[126] For Malinowski, language and culture are intimately linked to such an extent as to make translation impossible. As linguistic historian Terence Langendoen summarizes: "in order to understand Trobriand fishermen while they fish, one must oneself be a Trobriand fisherman."[127] This culturally determinist view of language resembles West's characterization of national languages in *Bilingualism* as so irreducible to their local contexts that they cannot be translated outside of the small community of users. If language is so limited that "one learns through action not reflection," then one cannot use a language for actions not already part of its culture. As we have seen with Palmer's theory of language acquisition and West's conception of national languages, Malinowski theory depends upon a primitivist category in which certain languages are not capable of adapting to modernity.

Word Lists: From Theory to Experiment

Around the same time as West's *Bilingualism*, Palmer was in Japan developing curriculum for teaching English in Japanese middle-schools and building the discipline of English language teaching through the Institute for Research in English Teaching (IRET) and its journal, the IRET *Bulletin*. In Cambridge, Ogden was beginning to publish his earliest articles on Basic English in *Cambridge Magazine* and *Psyche* while I. A. Richards was taking his first, formative trips to China. This chapter has sought to describe the origins of their theories through the lineage of colonial linguistics, psychology, anthropology, and philosophy that they inherited as early innovators in a field that was still being defined as a discipline with its own methods and practices. Although they are all developing unique language models in different parts of the world, this shared inheritance entails an ideological conception of an evolutionary fixed mother tongue language.

After this theoretical phase, comes the experimental phase, defined by word lists, textbooks, and simplified readers. If the purpose of colonial linguists was to "reduce speech to writing" in order to create languages of "wider communication," as Errington puts it, then that same process applies to the making of world English out of "full English": the vocabulary control movement "reduces" English through the making of word lists. The Vocabulary Control word list was more utilitarian, technological, and positivist than its romantic, nineteenth-century predecessors. My interest here is with Palmer's criticisms of these methodologies and how he resolved these issues while developing the IRET list that appeared in 1934. In his critique, Palmer exposes significant methodological problems with the "objective" methods of counting words by Thorndike and Horn as well as the limitations of the subjective lists created by Ogden and West. For the purposes of understanding how these word lists relate to the formation of anglophone ideology, Palmer's criticism reveals the structural dependency of these auxiliary languages on the mother tongue they supplement. Palmer himself would decide that the only way to judge among these word lists would be to test them through a process of adapting them to literary texts. The result of this test is the subject of the following chapter. For now, I want to conclude this chapter on mother tongues by considering how they are reinvented into auxiliary languages through the logic of word counts.

Counting Words Objectively: Thorndike

There were four major word lists developed in the 1920s: Edward Thorndike's Teacher's Word List from 1921, Michael West's New Method reading vocabulary from 1925, Horn's Basic Writing word list from 1926, and Ogden's Basic English word list from 1929.[128] Palmer began experimenting with word lists after arriving in Japan but did not produce a definitive list until the 1932 IRET list. Word list methodologies were divided at the time among a series of approaches and systems that strove to answer two questions: Why these words? Why this number? Two schools of thought, objective or subjective methods of word selection, sought to answer the first question. The limits to the list were based in principles of frequency, range, and coverage.

The most famous modern word list was created by Edward Thorndike in his *Teacher's Word Book* from 1921. This is the same Edward Thorndike who was discussed earlier in this chapter as a founder of the behaviorist psychology that influenced Palmer and whose quantitative methods influenced West. One of his initial projects took the form of a word list designed for teaching reading and spelling through a statistical measurement of word frequency. He did this by creating an algorithm for measuring a "value" for a word by designating it with a "merit number." The calculation ran as $MN = f/10 + r$ (f = frequency; r = number of sources in which the word appeared). This seminal list first introduced an astonishing 10,000 words (revised 1931 to 20,000 and in 1944 to 30,000 words) compiled from forty-four sources out of 4 million words. Thorndike defined a word as all units that appear in a text regardless of size, derivation, or syntactical purpose, and as the formula reveals, his emphasis was on *frequency*.

Thorndike's textbooks influenced the teaching of spelling in the United States, where elementary school textbooks used his list into the 1970s, but, through his participation in the 1934 Carnegie Conference, also the teaching of English around the world. Thorndike's word list was part of a quantitative turn in Education studies connected to the rise of Teacher's College at Columbia in the 1910s. The significance of Teacher's College is discussed more fully in Chapter 5 because of its connection to the Carnegie Corporation. In terms of word lists, this might be reflected in the texts that he uses and his emphasis on frequency rather than other values such as coverage or range. For instance, Thorndike's 1921 edition drew 3 million of its 4 million words from the Bible.[129] Since his goal is to teach spelling for purposes of a general education then Thorndike relies on the Bible as a common cultural indicator of norms. Thorndike's lists reflect Gramsci's definition of language as "a multiplicity of facts more or less coherent and co-ordinated" which is organized to reflect a "single cultural climate."[130] Word lists based on frequency reflect the value of consensus and hegemony with the aim of social reproduction. Hence one of the foremost criticisms of objective lists is that, according to one comprehensive study of word lists, they "tend to reflect the subjectively chosen sources and categories."[131]

All of these questions of word value change in their significance when the interest is with teaching language, particularly in non-native English contexts. For instance, as discussed in the Palmer section of this chapter, the words selected by Lemaire for his *Vocabulaire Pratique* were determined by frequency in so far as they were tied to the specific, repeated tasks that were demanded of the natives. As indicated by the multiple languages used in the cross-reference tab, the word list also needed to account for coverage (i.e., different tribal territories and European languages). In order for the word list to truly be *pratique*, it needed to be applicable to the language variety throughout the Congo. West, Ogden, and Palmer all have their own solutions to the frequency/coverage problem that are suggestive of the changing purpose of word lists.

Counting Words Subjectively: Ogden

According to Richards, the idea of a minimal language came while they were writing the chapter "On Definition" for *Meaning of Meaning* and finding "a limited set of words reappearing"[132] with each definition suggesting the possibility of an essential vocabulary. Unlike frequency-based word lists like Thorndike's, they used a definition test: "if a word could be defined in a descriptive phrase of ten words or less, the phrase words were kept and the word thrown out."[133] While Ogden believed the word list could have been reduced even further, to 200 words, the value of 850 as a marketing tool cannot be underestimated. Ogden repeatedly mentions the 850 words that fit on the "single sheet of notepaper" in the promotional materials and the graphic image of the list (as seen in Figure 6) captures its modernist efficiency.

BASIC ENGLISH

OPERATIONS etc.	THINGS						QUALITIES	
100	400 General				200 Pictured		100 General	50 Opposite
COME	ACCOUNT	EDUCATION	METAL	SENSE	ANGLE		ABLE	AWAKE
GET	ACT	EFFECT	MIDDLE	SERVANT	ANT	KNEE	ACID	BAD
GIVE	ADDITION	END	MILK	SEX	APPLE	KNIFE	ANGRY	BENT
GO	ADJUSTMENT	ERROR	MIND	SHADE	ARCH	KNOT	AUTOMATIC	BITTER
KEEP	ADVERTISEMENT	EVENT	MINE	SHAKE	ARM	LEAF	BEAUTIFUL	BLUE
LET	AGREEMENT	EXAMPLE	MINUTE	SHAME	ARMY	LEG	BLACK	CERTAIN
MAKE	AIR	EXCHANGE	MIST	SHOCK	BABY	LIBRARY	BOILING	COLD
PUT	AMOUNT	EXISTENCE	MONEY	SIDE	BAG	LINE	BRIGHT	COMPLETE
SEEM	AMUSEMENT	EXPANSION	MONTH	SIGN	BALL	LIP	BROKEN	CRUEL
TAKE	ANIMAL	EXPERIENCE	MORNING	SILK	BAND	LOCK	BROWN	DARK
BE	ANSWER	EXPERT	MOTHER	SILVER	BASIN	MAP	CHEAP	DEAD
DO	APPARATUS	FACT	MOTION	SISTER	BASKET	MATCH	CHEMICAL	DEAR
HAVE	APPROVAL	FALL	MOUNTAIN	SIZE	BATH	MONKEY	CHIEF	DELICATE
SAY	ARGUMENT	FAMILY	MOVE	SKY	BED	MOON	CLEAN	DIFFERENT
SEE	ART	FATHER	MUSIC	SLEEP	BEE	MOUTH	CLEAR	DIRTY
SEND	ATTACK	FEAR	NAME	SLIP	BELL	MUSCLE	COMMON	DRY
MAY	ATTEMPT	FEELING	NATION	SLOPE	BERRY	NAIL	COMPLEX	FALSE
WILL	ATTENTION	FICTION	NEED	SMASH	BIRD	NECK	CONSCIOUS	FEEBLE
ABOUT	ATTRACTION	FIELD	NEWS	SMELL	BLADE	NEEDLE	CUT	FEMALE
ACROSS	AUTHORITY	FIGHT	NIGHT	SMILE	BOARD	NERVE	DEEP	FOOLISH
AFTER	BACK	FIRE	NOISE	SMOKE	BOAT	NET	DEPENDENT	FUTURE
AGAINST	BALANCE	FLAME	NOTE	SNEEZE	BONE	NOSE	EARLY	GREEN
AMONG	BASE	FLIGHT	NUMBER	SNOW	BOOK	NUT	ELASTIC	ILL
AT	BEHAVIOUR	FLOWER	OBSERVATION	SOAP	BOOT	OFFICE	ELECTRIC	LAST
BEFORE	BELIEF	FOLD	OFFER	SOCIETY	BOTTLE	ORANGE	EQUAL	LATE
BETWEEN	BIRTH	FOOD	OIL	SON	BOX	OVEN	FAT	LEFT
BY	BIT	FORCE	OPERATION	SONG	BOY	PARCEL	FERTILE	LOOSE
DOWN	BITE	FORM	OPINION	SORT	BRAIN	PEN	FIRST	LOUD
FROM	BLOOD	FRIEND	ORDER	SOUND	BRAKE	PENCIL	FIXED	LOW
IN	BLOW	FRONT	ORGANIZATION	SOUP	BRANCH	PICTURE	FLAT	MIXED
OFF	BODY	FRUIT	ORNAMENT	SPACE	BRICK	PIG	FREE	NARROW
ON	BRASS	GLASS	OWNER	STAGE	BRIDGE	PIN	FREQUENT	OLD
OVER	BREAD	GOLD	PAGE	START	BRUSH	PIPE	FULL	OPPOSITE
THROUGH	BREATH	GOVERNMENT	PAIN	STATEMENT	BUCKET	PLANE	GENERAL	PUBLIC
TO	BROTHER	GRAIN	PAINT	STEAM	BULB	PLATE	GOOD	ROUGH
UNDER	BUILDING	GRASS	PAPER	STEEL	BUTTON	PLOUGH	GREAT	SAD
UP	BURN	GRIP	PART	STEP	CAKE	POCKET	GREY	SAFE
WITH	BURST	GROUP	PASTE	STITCH	CAMERA	POT	HANGING	SECRET
AS	BUSINESS	GROWTH	PAYMENT	STONE	CARD	POTATO	HAPPY	SHORT
FOR	BUTTER	GUIDE	PEACE	STOP	CART	PRISON	HARD	SHUT
OF	CANVAS	HARBOUR	PERSON	STORY	CARRIAGE	PUMP	HEALTHY	SIMPLE
TILL	CARE	HARMONY	PLACE	STRETCH	CAT	RAIL	HIGH	SLOW
THAN	CAUSE	HATE	PLANT	STRUCTURE	CHAIN	RAT	HOLLOW	SMALL
A	CHALK	HEARING	PLAY	SUBSTANCE	CHEESE	RECEIPT	IMPORTANT	SOFT
THE	CHANCE	HEAT	PLEASURE	SUGAR	CHEST	RING	KIND	SOLID
ALL	CHANGE	HELP	POINT	SUGGESTION	CHIN	ROD	LIKE	SPECIAL
ANY	CLOTH	HISTORY	POISON	SUMMER	CHURCH	ROOF	LIVING	STRANGE
EVERY	COAL	HOLE	POLISH	SUPPORT	CIRCLE	ROOT	LONG	THIN
LITTLE	COLOUR	HOPE	PORTER	SURPRISE	CLOCK	SAIL	MALE	WHITE
MUCH	COMFORT	HOUR	POSITION	SWIM	CLOUD	SCHOOL	MARRIED	WRONG
NO	COMMITTEE	HUMOUR	POWDER	SYSTEM	COAT	SCISSORS	MATERIAL	
OTHER	COMPANY	ICE	POWER	TALK	COLLAR	SCREW	MEDICAL	
SOME	COMPARISON	IDEA	PRICE	TASTE	COMB	SEED	MILITARY	
SUCH	COMPETITION	IMPULSE	PRINT	TAX	CORD	SHEEP	NATURAL	
THAT	CONDITION	INCREASE	PROCESS	TEACHING	COW	SHELF	NECESSARY	
THIS	CONNECTION	INDUSTRY	PRODUCE	TENDENCY	CUP	SHIP	NEW	
I	CONTROL	INK	PROFIT	TEST	CURTAIN	SHIRT	NORMAL	
HE	COOK	INSECT	PROPERTY	THEORY	CUSHION	SHOE	OPEN	
YOU	COPPER	INSTRUMENT	PROSE	THING	DOG	SKIN	PARALLEL	
WHO	COPY	INSURANCE	PROTEST	THOUGHT	DOOR	SKIRT	PAST	
AND	CORK	INTEREST	PULL	THUNDER	DRAIN	SNAKE	PHYSICAL	
BECAUSE	COTTON	INVENTION	PUNISHMENT	TIME	DRAWER	SOCK	POLITICAL	
BUT	COUGH	IRON	PURPOSE	TIN	DRESS	SPADE	POOR	
OR	COUNTRY	JELLY	PUSH	TOP	DROP	SPONGE	POSSIBLE	
IF	COVER	JOIN	QUALITY	TOUCH	EAR	SPOON	PRESENT	
THOUGH	CRACK	JOURNEY	QUESTION	TRADE	EGG	SPRING	PRIVATE	
WHILE	CREDIT	JUDGE	RAIN	TRANSPORT	ENGINE	SQUARE	PROBABLE	
HOW	CRIME	JUMP	RANGE	TRICK	EYE	STAMP	QUICK	
WHEN	CRUSH	KICK	RATE	TROUBLE	FACE	STAR	QUIET	
WHERE	CRY	KISS	RAY	TURN	FARM	STATION	READY	

Figure 6 The famous 850-word Basic English vocabulary was promised to fit on a "single sheet of notepaper."

Basic English is organized around three parts: 600 "Things," 150 "Qualities," and 100 "Operations." Ogden uses "Things" to refer to noun-forms divided into 400 "General" words and 200 "Pictured" words. The latter refer to concrete items that can be touched and seen; the "General" words refer to a range of word forms that mainly have in common the fact that they are "less suitable for pictorial representation."[134] Some of the words are tangible (mine, road) but are not picturable, but most of them are nouns that Ogden calls "fictions." These are nouns like harmony, quality, nation, hope that "do not stand for anything concrete, though all languages by a convenient make-believe have treated them as though they did."[135] The "Qualities" or adjectives are divided into 100 "General" and 50 "opposites" to facilitate learning. Operations refer to what Ogden calls "operation-words": verbs, prepositions, and directions. Basic's main innovation was the reduction of verbs to only eighteen (though the notesheet boasts that "there are no 'verbs' in Basic English").

Richards viewed the reduction of verbs as the "key to the discovery of Basic."[136] They were able to eliminate 4,000 common verbs by a process of substituting them with a combination of 20 prepositions and 16 verbs. For instance, verbs that involve direction were substituted with the direction: hence "jump" can be "go up/down." Ogden's antipathy toward verbs comes from his interest in the utilitarian philosopher Jeremy Bentham whose "theory of fictions" influenced his view of language. Ogden liked to quote Bentham's comment that "A verb slips through your fingers like an eel"[137] suggesting a skepticism about verbs as a reliable aspect of language. Ogden implies this distrust of verbs while also justifying the reduction of verb forms as part of making the language more efficient for new learners. In *Basic English* he explains that "the verb-form has hitherto been one of the great barriers to all attempts at simplification"; "that verbs involve a wasteful vocabulary"; and he echoes Bentham in arguing that verbs "may lead to confusion of thought at any stage of symbolization."[138] Just as some General words become naturalized as "fictions," so it is partly through verbs that the obfuscation of Word Magic occurs.

Instead, Ogden used a system of "Operations" to reduce verbs to the "fundamental operations of physics": "moving, pushing, and pulling." The Operations diagram (in Figure 7) demonstrates how this works through a series of oppositions.[139]

The figure of the body here is interesting for what it says about the conception of Basic as an instrumental language. The kaleidoscope of hands in the diagram suggest the primacy of tangibility and intentionality. The point here is to illustrate verbs but it also assumes a singular, coherent, intentional

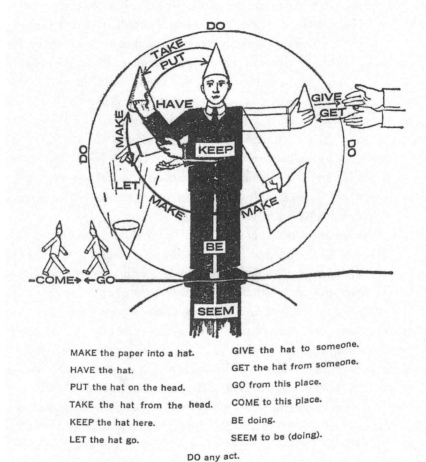

Figure 7 Diagram of Operation-Words from *Basic English* (1930).

subject whose significant actions are all contained within the sphere of "being" as conveyed by the "Be" verb at his feet. The word "seeming" in the opposite, mirrored reflection that only shows his feet, suggests the world of fictions, magic, illusions as a kind of underworld (the reflection of "seem" could have been a vertical mirror) in which the self is fragmented and lacking signification. This utilitarian, instrumentalized world is also conveyed in the image for "Directions" (see Figure 8).[140] The operation words for "directives" are used in

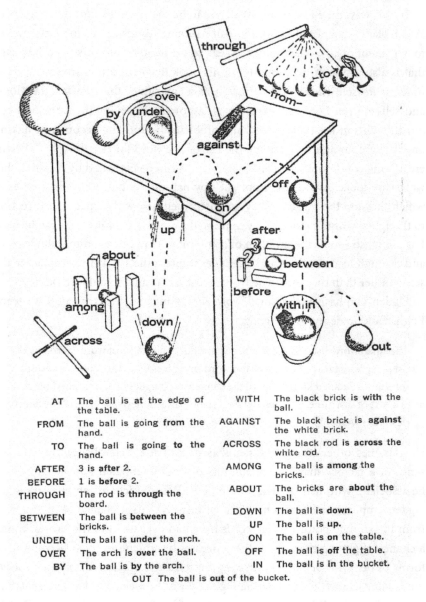

Figure 8 Diagram of Direction-words from *Basic English* (1930).

place of prepositions and similarly emphasize physical movement and impacts. The danger of these directives, Ogden writes, comes from their "expansion and metaphor" which "frequently take the form of fictional analogies" such as "*Thoughts come into the mind, Get at the details.*"[141]

In this way, the Basic word list strives to be the corrective for the dangers of Word Magic diagnosed in *Meaning of Meaning*. By trying to force the writer to act intentionally, Basic English seeks to create a system of shared language that is also a system for thinking. In his book devoted to this argument, *Basic Rules of Reason*, Richards describes it as a "machine" that can facilitate logic and self-control. Logic, he explains, is "a power of keeping divisions between our thoughts in the right places" and problems in thinking occur from "taking one thought for another through the use of one word for two thoughts."[142] This creates the conditions for Word Magic which can be corrected by recalling that words are tools: "Words have not got—by natural design as it were—senses of which they are the owners. They are instruments by which men give direction to thoughts, nothing more."[143] By limiting the amount of words that can be used Basic English avoids the problem of combining two concepts into a single word and through its operations and directives it forces the speaker to emphasize the sense rather than the word. The word is just an ornament to the sense.

Ogden emphasizes the small word list as integral to its purpose to teach English and to demystify language:

> The small word-list of Basic has a special value at all stages of word-learning. The list is representative of every sort of word, and gives us all the material necessary for a more detailed knowledge of the behavior of languages of unlimited range. It is a sort of instrument for testing the use of words in newspapers and the effects desired in verse.[144]

He classifies other learning systems as part of the "school-machines" in the sense of a factory mass-producing bits of undifferentiated knowledge, which he associates with lists such as Thorndike's. Where Richards emphasizes logic, Ogden emphasizes liberation: "Basic at last gives us a chance of getting free from the strange power which words have had over us from the earliest times; a chance of getting clear about the processes by which our ideas become fixed forms of behavior *before we ourselves are conscious of what history and society are making us say.*"[145] The relation Ogden posits between speaker and structure situates Basic English as part of a critique of language as ideology. For Ogden, Basic English represents a competing system to put up against the cultural system that codifies language and action. His analysis of "*the process* by which our ideas become fixed forms of behavior" suggests Gramsci's argument about the distinction between language and ideology. As Marnie Holborow puts it, for Gramsci, "language sedimentizes ideology" but it should not be mistaken as ideological.[146] What Ogden describes in this sentence is the mode by which, in Gramscian terms, the hegemonic class seeks to garner consent from the governed by assuming control over language and meaning. The Basic English word list is the antidote to this type of ideological word magic.

Palmer's Critique

Although Palmer was the last of the Vocabulary Control movement to publish a vocabulary, he had experimented with word lists as early as 1906 with a "learner's vocabulary in Esperanto" and then created a French list for English-speaking students of French "inspired by the Berlitz selection," which used a "rational" list of 100 words. This was followed by an expanded list of a 500-word English vocabulary.[147] These word lists were developed with frequency as the primary measurement but were designed, as the Berlitz method, as a list of "words we speak with."[148] As a result, he was in a good position to criticize word list constructions when they emerged in the 1920s as the principal method for ELT textbooks. Palmer was critical of both Thorndike's and Ogden's methods of creating word lists not to mention West's use of Thorndike's list as the basis for his 3,000-word reading vocabulary. Subjective lists like Basic's, he argues, are too artificial and objective lists cannot escape being *subjective* in so far as the selection of source material is based on individual judgments. As an example of the latter, he criticizes a word list by R. C. Eldridge based on statistical analysis of American newspapers because the word "*police*" appeared among the 100 most frequently occurring words.[149]

However, his primary concern with all methods of word list construction is that they were focused on word value rather than word definition. Palmer considered the concept of the word as "vague and impossible of definition,"[150] arguing that a word is only an accident of "graphic continuity." Thus, the real problem for word list construction was the paradox over word identity and form: what is the relation between root words and their plurals, preterites and antecedent forms? Are all of them one identity or are they all separate words? "What is to be reckoned as *one word, something less than one word* and *something more than one word?*"[151] To a non-native speaker, words like "go, goes, went" all appear as distinct words. Palmer preferred to use lexicological units he defined as "monologs, polylogs, and miologs": *Monologs* refer to simple units that do not have any break or space such as "dog, good, up"; *Polylogs* are phrases or word groups that function like a monolog such as "in case, of course, every year"; *Miologs* are affixes like "-ly" endings, which Palmer categorizes as units in themselves, not as parts of words. Ogden would later mock Palmer's theory of word definition as indicative of academic pedantry, though his own theory that "the word has no value when not in use"[152] is not that different from Palmer's own skepticism of the reified dictionary concept of the word.

Because of the skepticism toward limited vocabularies that Palmer encountered from the Japanese ministry, and his own concerns with word list methods, Palmer took four years to prepare the *Interim Report on Vocabulary Selection* of 3,000 words in 1931. The list combined objective measures of word frequency with subjective judgments about the place of the word in the list.[153] Around the same time, Lawrence Faucett and Itsu Maki developed their own word list by combining the Thorndike and Horn lists, using "range of usefulness" as a guide for the subjective placement of the word list. Faucett would use this list in his *Oxford English Course*. These two lists, IRET and the Faucett-Maki, would be the basis for the Carnegie word list.

As a sign of the predominance of Basic English, Palmer prefaced the IRET *Interim Report on Vocabulary Selection* of 3,000 words with a foreword by I. A. Richards clarifying that the IRET list and Basic English were "independent of each other and designed for different purposes."[154] I noted this in Chapter 1 as an example of Richards' desire to remain aloof from ELT. For Palmer, Richards's foreword also helps to distinguish his own claims for language teaching and limit Basic to its original purpose as an international auxiliary language. It also played a legal role since, as I already noted, Ogden had already threatened to sue Palmer if he adapted Basic English for use in Japan.[155] As Smith notes, although West and Palmer developed word lists independently and prior to Basic, the decision to develop an authoritative word list at Carnegie was motivated largely by "the rapid rise of Basic English."[156]

Conclusion

The task of colonial linguistics was to "reduce speech to writing" through the creation of word lists, vocabularies, and grammars. As the role of empire changes in the early twentieth century, the role of these collections also changes. Where it had sought to use a linguistic national identity (i.e., Hindi, Swahili, Malay) to manage and control native cultures during the first phases of imperialism, its purpose in late empire was to create an auxiliary form of language as a means of curbing anti-colonial aspirations.

Word lists are an example of how the global spread of English was managed. It is through word lists that debates over the role of English in the world took place. As the place of English as an auxiliary "world" language, rather than just a "foreign" language, becomes more widely accepted, its justification rested upon the capacity of a pedagogical word list suited to this particular purpose. The word list was important for establishing language teaching as a science by drawing on the turn toward quantitative methods of statistics and measurement that signified scientific work at the time. In this way, the early twentieth-century word list was not only a model of the modern obsession with efficiency but also uniquely suited to the devolved interwar empire, as scientific, modular units that can travel easily and align English with North Atlantic modernity rather than traditional conceptions of the British empire.

Notes

1. Quoted in Errington, *Linguistics in a Colonial Context*, 18.
2. James DeRocher, Murray S. Miron, Sam M. Patton, Charles C. Pratt, *The Counting of Words: A Review of the Techniques and Theory of Word Counts*. Prepared for the Defense Language Institute (Syracuse, NY: Syracuse University Research Corporation, 1973), 1–4.
3. Schmitt notes that here are two notable exceptions from the Renaissance including William of Bath's book on vocabulary acquisition and Comenius's Latin textbook that used a limited vocabulary as part of an inductive approach to language learning. See Norbert Schmitt, *Vocabulary in Language Teaching* (New York: Cambridge University Press, 2000), 11.
4. Ibid.
5. See Linda C. Mitchell, "Grammar Wars: Seventeenth- and Eighteenth-Century England," in *The Handbook of World Englishes*, edited by Braj Kachru et al. (London: Routledge, 2006), 475–95. For an alternative account of the 18th century "progress of English", see Alok Yadav, *Before the Empire of English: Literature, Provinciality, and Nationalism in Eighteenth-Century Britain* (New York: Palgrave, 2004), chapter 1.
6. Walter Mignolo, "Nebrija in the New World. The Question of the Letter, the Colonization of American Languages, and the Discontinuity of the Classical Tradition," *L'Homme* 32, no. 122 (1992): 195.
7. See Weir and O'Sullivan, *Assessing English*, 31–2.

8 Errington, *Colonial Linguistics*, 39.
9 See Errington, *Colonial Linguistics*, 68–9; on French Algeria, see Mohamed Benrabah, *Language Conflict in Algeria: From Colonialism to Post-Independence* (Bristol: Multilingual Matters, 2013), specifically chapter 2, "Frenchification: Annihilating Indigenous Languages," 21–50. English is currently becoming one of the languages competing for status as LWC in Algeria, see Benrabah, chap. 4, 87–125; and Kamal Belmihoub, "English in a Multilingual Algeria," *World Englishes* 37, no. 2 (2018): 207–27. On how French language teaching informed anti-colonial concepts, see Baer, *Indigenous Vanguards*.
10 On German linguistic colonialism, see Sara Pugach, *Africa in Translation: A History of Colonial Linguistics in Germany and Beyond, 1814–1945* (Ann Arbor: University of Michigan Press, 2012). As she writes about the practice of Afrikanistik, "it was not the language of the colonizer but of the colonized that was being put to use in the service of the imperialism. Missionaries, lay scholars, and colonial officials all wanted to use African languages to extend European power" (5).
11 Errington, *Linguistics*, 69. Pugach notes that "German images of Africans and their languages shifted over time, as biological race grew increasingly important to linguistic description" (5).
12 Benedict Anderson, *Imagined Communities: Reflections on the Origin and Spread of Nationalism* (London: Verso, 1983).
13 Quoted in Errington, *Colonial Linguistics*, 82.
14 Ibid., 82–3.
15 Ibid., 68.
16 Quoted in Errington, *Colonial Linguistics*, 131. On Jespersen, Ogden, and modernism, see McDonald, "Independence, Dependence, and Interdependence Day," in *Artefacts of Writing*.
17 See Otto Jespersen, *An International Language* (New York: Norton, 1929).
18 Julia S. Falk, "Words without Grammar: Linguists and the International Auxiliary Language Movement in the United States," *Language and Communication* 15, no. 3 (1995): 245–6.
19 Quoted in Falk, "Words without Grammar," 246. From Jespersen, *An International Language* (London: George Allen & Unwin, 1928), 25.
20 Errington, *Colonial Linguistics*, 131.
21 On responses to Richards, see Tong, "The Bathos of Universalism," 331–54.
22 Roland Mackin, ed., Editor's Introduction, in Harold Palmer, *Principles of Language Study* (Oxford: Oxford University Press, 1921:1964), v.
23 Dorothée Anderson, "A Biographical Essay," in Harold Palmer and H. Vere Redman, *This Language-Learning Business*, edited by Roland Mackin and Peter Strevens (London: Oxford University Press, 1932:1969), 137.
24 Harold Palmer, *Principles of Language Study* (London: George Harrap & Co., 1921), reprinted in Smith, *Pioneers of ELT*, vol. II, 5. Hereafter cited as *Principles*.

25 Vincent Viaene, "King Leopold's Imperialism and the Origins of the Belgian Colonial Party, 1860–1905," *The Journal of Modern History* 80, no. 4 (December 2008): 767.
26 Viaene, "King Leopold's Imperialism," 767.
27 Johannes Fabian, *Language and Colonial Power* (Cambridge: Cambridge University Press, 1986), 20.
28 Ibid., 21.
29 William Samarin, "Language in the Colonization of Central Africa, 1880–1900," *Canadian Journal of African Studies/Revue Canadienne des Études Africaines* 23, no. 2 (1989): 235.
30 Samarin, "Language," 234.
31 Ibid. Cohn has also pointed to this colonial mistrust of native translators as the impetus for Jones to learn Sanskrit; see Cohn, *Colonialism and Its Forms of Knowledge: The British in India* (Princeton: Princeton University Press, 1996), 29.
32 Samarin, "Language," 235.
33 Quoted and translated by Fabian, *Language and Colonial Power*, 20.
34 Fabian, *Language and Colonial Power*, 21.
35 Ibid., 11. And also to prevent the spread of English from the British or United States, see Fabian, *Language and Colonial Power*, 65, n.15.
36 Ibid., 17, 18, 21.
37 Ibid., 21.
38 Ibid., 22.
39 Charles Lemaire, *Vocabulaire Pratique: Francais, Anglais, Zanzibarite (Swahili), Fiote, Kibangi-Irébou, Mongo, Bangala*. Second Edition (Brussels: CH. Bulens, 1897), 6.
40 Lemaire, *Vocabulaire Pratique*, 38.
41 Ibid., 42, 44, 46.
42 Quoted in Adam Hochschild, *King Leopold's Ghost: A Story of Greed, Terror, and Heroism in Colonial Africa* (New York: Mariner Books, 1998), 227–8. Elsewhere, Viaene refers to Lemaire's sexualized, "tasteless prose" such as: "the belly of Africa, which barbarism sterilized, has become fecund and will soon bring forth incalculable riches." Quoted in Viaene, "King Leopold's Imperialism," 783. Colonial historians consider Lemaire's diary to be one of the most brutal and thorough accounts of this destructive period in the Free State. Also, see Hochschild, *King Leopold's Ghost*, 227–8.
43 Fabian, *Language and Colonial Power*, 41.
44 Viaene, "King Leopold's Imperialism," 767.
45 *The Geographic Journal* vol 29 (1907) *Tra Mez-Afriko. (A travers l'Afrique centrale) Par le Commdt. Ch. Lemaire* [In French and Esperanto] size 11x 8 1/2, pp. 86. Map and Illustrations. Presented by the Author. "An account of Major Lemaire's journey given before the Geneva Esperanto Congress in September, 1906."

46 Christer Kiselman, "Esperanto: Its Origins and Early History," in Andrzej Pelczar, ed., *Prace Komisji Spraw Europejskich PAU* (Krakow: Polska Akademia Umiejeno, 2008), 17. For more on French Esperanto and the influence of de Beaufront, see Gordin, *Scientific Babel*, 122.
47 Harold Palmer, *Principles*, 5.
48 Palmer, *Principles*, 5–6. My translation.
49 Ibid., 34.
50 Ibid., 34–5.
51 Ibid., 37.
52 Ibid., 38.
53 Ibid. Howatt notes that behaviorist is "a label that [Palmer] would have accepted."
54 John A. Mills, *Control: A History of Behavioral Psychology* (New York: New York University Press, 1998), 65.
55 Bennet G. Galef, "Edward Thorndike: Revolutionary Psychologist, Ambiguous Biologist," *American Psychologist* 53, no. 10 (1998): 1130.
56 Ibid., 1132. On Thorndike and eugenics, see Geraldine Jonçich Clifford, *The Sane Positivist: A Biography of Edward L. Thorndike* (Middletown, Conn: Wesleyan University Press, 1968), 544.
57 Quoted Errington, *Linguistics in a Colonial World*, 130.
58 The *École Coloniale Supérieure* was established in 1920 for the training of senior officials in the colonial administration and was restructured as the *Université Coloniale de Beglique* in 1923. Lemaire served as director until his death in 1926. See Marc Poncelet, "Colonial Ideology, Colonial Sciences, and Colonial Sociology in Belgium," *The American Sociologist* 51, no. 148 (2020): 162; "A Brief History of 50 Years of Development Studies," Institute of Development Policy, University of Antwerp, Website, https://www.uantwerpen.be/en/about-uantwerp/faculties/institute-of-development-policy/about-iob/history-development-studies/ (accessed October 18, 2019).
59 Michael West, *Bilingualism (with Special Reference to Bengal)*, Bureau of Education, India, Occasional Reports, no. 13, Calcutta: Government of India Central Publication Branch. Reprinted in Smith, ed., *Pioneers of ELT, Vol. III*, 1-392. Hereafter cited as *Bilingualism;* page references are to the Smith edition.
60 Alok Mukherjee, "Early English Textbooks and Language Policies in India," in *Language Policy and Education in India: Documents, Contexts and Debates*, edited by M. Sridhar and Sunita Mishra (London: Routledge, 2017), 9–25.
61 On English language education and empire, see Gauri Viswanathan, *Masks of Conquest: Literary Study and British Rule in India* (New York: Columbia University Press, 1989); Sanjay Seth, *Subject Lessons: The Western Education of Colonial India* (Durham: Duke University Press, 2007); Mukherjee, "Early English Textbooks," Chaudhary, "Caste, Colonialism, and Schooling"; Indra Sengupta and Daud

Ali, editors, *Knowledge Production, Pedagogy, and Institutions in Colonial India* (London: Palgrave Macmillan, 2011); Zastoupil and Moir, *The Great Indian Education Debate*; on gender politics of English language in India, see Shefali Chandra, *The Sexual Life of English: Languages of Caste and Desire in Colonial India* (Durham: Duke University Press, 2012); on English language policies under colonialism and their effects on contemporary Indian education and the sociology of English in India, see Krishna Kumar, *The Political Agenda of Education: A Study of Colonialist and Nationalist Ideas* (New Delhi: Sage Publications, 2005); Chaise LaDousa, *Hindi Is Our Ground, English Is Our Sky: Education, Language, and Social Class in Contemporary India* (New York: Berghahn Books, 2014); Sridhar and Mishra, *Language Policy and Education in India: Documents, Contexts and Debates* (London: Routledge, 2017); Svati Joshi, *Rethinking English: Essays in Literature, Language, History* (Delhi: Oxford University Press, 1995); Krishnaswamy and Archana, eds., *The Politics of Indians' English* (Delhi: Oxford University Press, 1998).

62 E. Annamalai, "Nation-building in a Globalised World: Language Choice and Education in India," in *Decolonisation, Globalistion: Language-in-Education Policy and Practice* (Bristol, UK: Channel View Publications, 2005), 20.

63 J. A. Hayden Bellenoit argues that colonial education was limited due to its lack of knowledge about Indian society, see *Missionary Education in Late Colonial India, 1860-1920* (London: Pickering and Chatto, 2007), chapters 5 and 6. Sanjay Seth has noted the repeated claims of failure by British educators and colonialists, see *Subject Lessons*, 22–6. Latika Chaudhary argues that the economic impact of education was minimal when compared to legal and land reforms, see "Caste, Colonialism, and Schooling," 175.

64 On the role of English in the persistence of a divide between elite and mass education in India, see LaDousa, *Hindi Is Our Ground, English Is Our Sky*; Kumar, *The Political Agenda of Education*; Sengupta, *Endangered Languages*; Annamalai, "Nation-building."

65 See Mukherjee, "Early English Textbooks and Language Policies in India," 21.

66 Viswanathan, *Masks of Conquest*, 146.

67 Chaudhary, "Caste, Colonialism, and Schooling," 162.

68 Annamalai, "Nation-Building," 22.

69 Whitehead, *Colonial Educators*, 11.

70 Smith, *Pioneers of ELT*, Vol. III, ix.

71 Smith, *Pioneers of ELT*, III: x.

72 Ibid., x–xi.

73 West, *Bilingualism*, 35–40.

74 Smith, "Introduction," *Pioneers of ELT*, Vol. III, xiii.

75 Ibid., xiv.

76 Ibid., xiv.
77 West, *Bilingualism*, in Smith, *Pioneers of ELT*, Vol. III, 42.
78 Ibid., 44.
79 Ibid., 132.
80 Ibid., 46.
81 Ibid., 48.
82 Partha Chatterjee, "The Curious Career of Liberalism in India," *Modern Intellectual History* 8, no.3 (2011): 695.
83 See Andrew Sartori, *Bengal in Concept History* (Chicago: University of Chicago, 2008), 23, 168.
84 Sabyasachi Bhattacharya, *The Defining Moments in Bengal, 1920–1947* (New Delhi: Oxford University Press, 2014), 26. According to Durba Ghosh, "Bengal's Legislative Council was enlarged to 139 members, as many more property holders, businessmen, lawyers, and professionals were rendered eligible to vote." See Ghosh, *Gentlemanly Terrorists: Political Violence and the Colonial State in India, 1919–1947* (Cambridge: Cambridge University Press, 2017), 28. On Indian reaction to the reforms, see Parsons, *Second British Empire*, 57.
85 Bhattacharya, *Defining Moments*, 26.
86 See Ghosh, *Gentlemanly Terrorists*, 27–59.
87 Bhattacharya, *Defining Moments*, 29.
88 Ibid., 32.
89 Graham Wallas, *The Great Society: A Psychological Analysis* (London: MacMillan, 1914), 4.
90 Ibid., 31.
91 Ibid., 32.
92 Ibid., 32–3.
93 Ibid., 38.
94 Partha Chatterjee, "The Curious Career of Liberalism in India," 689.
95 Ibid., 691.
96 West, *Bilingualism*, in Smith, *Pioneers of ELT*, Vol. III, 13.
97 Ibid., 60–1.
98 Macaulay's Minute, 171.
99 West, *Bilingualism*, in Smith, *Pioneers of ELT*, Vol. III, 63.
100 Ibid., 66.
101 Ibid., 342.
102 See Richard Glotzer, "A Long Shadow," 624–6.
103 Quoted in Ann G. Winfield, "Resuscitating Bad Science: Eugenics Past and Present," in *The Assault on Public Education*, edited by W. H. Watkins (New York: Teachers College Press, 2012), 147.
104 See West, *Bilingualism*, in Smith, *Pioneers of ELT*, vol. III, 141. E. L. Thorndike, "The Measurement of Ability in Reading," *Teachers College Record* 15 (1914): 1–70;

F. J. Kelly, "The Kansas Silent Reading Tests," *Journal of Educational Psychology* 7 (1916): 63–80 https://doi.org/10.1037/h0073542. See Nancy Scammacca et al., "A Century of Progress: Reading Interventions for Students in Grades 4–12, 1914–2014," *Review of Educational Research* 86, no. 3 (2016): 756–800, doi: 10.3102/0034654316652942.

105 West, *Bilingualism*, in Smith, *Pioneers of ELT*, vol. III, 63.
106 C. K. Ogden and I. A. Richards, *The Meaning of Meaning: A Study of the Influence of Language upon Thought and of the Science of Symbolism* (New York: Harvest, 1989), 4.
107 West, *Bilingualism*, in Smith, *Pioneers of ELT*, vol. III, 64.
108 Richards quoted in Gordon, Introduction, *Meaning of Meaning, C. K. Ogden and Linguistics*, vol. III, xx.
109 W. Terrence Gordon, "Linguistics and Semiotics I: The Impact of Ogden and Richards' *The Meaning of Meaning*," in *History of the Language Sciences* (New York and Berlin: De Gruyter Mouton, 2006), 2586.
110 Ogden and Richards, *Meaning of Meaning*, 24.
111 Ibid., 7.
112 Victor Li, *The Neo-Primitivist Turn: Critical Reflections on Alterity, Culture, and Modernity* (Toronto: University of Toronto Press, 2006), 9.
113 Ogden and Richards, *Meaning of Meaning*, 29.
114 Quoted in John Paul Russo, *I. A. Richards: His Life and Work* (New York: Routledge, 1989), 119.
115 C. K. Ogden, "To the Reader," in *The Gold Insect* (London: Kegan Paul, 1932), 7.
116 I. A. Richards, "Co-Author of the 'Meaning of Meaning,'" in *C. K. Ogden: A Collective Memoir*, edited by P. Sargant, Florence, P. Sargant, and J. R. L. Anderson (London: Pemberton Publishing Co. Ltd., 1977), 103–4.
117 Malinowski, "The Problem of Meaning in Primitive Languages," in C. K. Ogden and I. A. Richards, *Meaning of Meaning*, 299.
118 Jerzy Szymura, "Bronislaw Malinowski's 'Ethnographic Theory of Language,'" in *Linguistic Thought in England, 1914–1945*, edited by Roy Harris (London: Duckworth, 1988), 108.
119 Malinowski, "Primitive Languages," 300–1.
120 Ibid., 302.
121 Ibid., 306.
122 Ibid., 302.
123 Ibid., 307.
124 Quoted in Szymura, "Malinowski's 'Ethnographic Theory of Language,'" 130.
125 Malinowski, "Primitive Languages," 320.
126 Quoted in Terence D. Langendoen, *The London School of Linguistics: A Study of the Linguistic Theories of B. Malinowski and J. R. Firth* (Cambridge: M. I. T Press, 1968), 21.

127 Langendoen, *The London School of Linguistics*, 22.
128 For a complete discussion of word lists, see DeRocher et al., *The Counting of Words*, and Herman Bonger, *The History and Principles of Vocabulary Control: As It Affects the Teaching of Foreign Languages in General and of English in Particular* (Woerden, HL: Wocopi, 1947).
129 Ibid., 10.
130 Antonio Gramsci, *Selections from the Prison Notebooks of Antonio Gramsci*. Translated by Quintin Hoare and Geoffrey Nowell-Smith (New York: International Publishers, 1971). 349.
131 DeRocher, *Counting of Words*, 91.
132 John Paul Russo, *I. A. Richards: His Life and Work* (New York: Routledge, 1989), 398.
133 Ibid.
134 Ogden, *Basic English*, 20.
135 Ibid.
136 Quoted in Russo, *I. A. Richards*, 400.
137 Ogden, *Bentham's Theory of Fictions* (London: Kegan Paul, Trench, Trubner, 1932), cvii.
138 Ogden, *Basic English*, 25.
139 See illustration from Ogden, *Basic English*, 27.
140 Ibid., 30.
141 Ibid., 31.
142 I. A. Richards, *Basic Rules of Reason* (London: Kegan Paul, 1933), 9–11.
143 Ibid., 14.
144 Ogden, *Basic English*, 60.
145 Ibid., emphasis added.
146 Holborow, "Language and Neoliberalism," 53.
147 Palmer, "History," 372.
148 Ibid., 371.
149 Palmer, "History," 372; DeRocher, *Counting of Words*, 88.
150 Palmer, *Scientific*, 11.
151 Palmer, "History," 373.
152 Ogden, "Preface," Gold Beetle, 7.
153 "The Institute for Research in English Teaching, Its History and Work" (Tokyo: IRET, Department of Education), 1934. In Smith, vol. 5, 245.
154 Ibid., 375–6.
155 See Howatt, *History of ELT* (1984), 233.
156 Smith, Introduction, vol. V, xx.

3

Readers, Literary Simplification, and the Global Subject

Introduction

In a 1935 essay reflecting on the history of the Vocabulary Control movement, Harold Palmer recalls the significant moment in 1931 when he recognized that the problem of word lists was "intimately" associated with the development of Simplified Readers:

> I remember well the place and time I did this. It was during the course of a voyage from San Francisco to Yokohama on the *Chichibu Maru*, and one of my fellow passengers was Dr. Sanki Ichikawa. I showed him the manuscript and method of working, and he warmly approved of it–and indeed the following year expressed his approval in the course of a lecture at the Ninth Annual Convention of the I.R.E.T.[1]

Known as the "grandfather of English studies in Japan," Dr. Ichikawa was a leading Japanese linguist who had studied English with Dr. John Lawrence at Tokyo Imperial University in the 1910s. Succeeding Lawrence as the Chair of English Language and Literature in 1916, Ichikawa sought to modernize the study of English in Japan through philological and grammatical studies of English. It was Ichikawa who first met Palmer at the pier in Kobe when the British linguist arrived in Japan in 1922 to assume his position as advisor to the Ministry of Education. In addition to publishing English grammars and dictionaries (including the first phonetic dictionary of English pronunciation), Ichikawa wrote annotations for the sixty-volume series *Kenkuysha's English Classics* as well as a series of Shakespeare plays beginning in 1921.[2] What Palmer was proposing, however, was neither a philological project, nor an abridged version of English classics. For this reason, Ichikawa's approval was important because of the resistance to the Palmer Method by some Japanese education ministers.

Palmer's recollection illustrates the many contradictory factors at play in the making of Simplified Readers as part of the system of Vocabulary Control: they use canonical Western works yet do not reproduce them in full; they are not "abridged" versions but revised according to scientific methods; they need to appeal to a native audience who resent "dumbed-down" versions. Finally, the Readers are not determined by their story as much as they are determined by the pedagogical word list. As Palmer wrote in his essay, "This was indeed the germ of the idea that I had been developing over twenty years earlier, and that the compilers of the scheme called *Basic English* had also developed later on similar lines but in a special way."[3]

What Palmer had in mind was the publication of Basic English "translations" through Ogden's Psyche series with the publisher Kegan Paul that began in 1930 with a translation of the popular German romance, *Karl und Anna*, by Leonhard Frank. The significance of this literary project for Ogden is evident in the fact that it appeared in the same year he introduced the famous 850-word list and the first Basic English textbooks.[4] Ogden himself was inspired by Michael West's New Method Readers, which were first published in 1927 by Longmans in India. West's New Method Readers adapted British novels and world literature to his 3,000-word New Method vocabulary. Because his system was based on "Reading First," West's New Method Readers played a more significant role in his language system than previous colonial textbooks and abridged readers had for the practitioners of the Grammatical Method, or certainly for the speaking-first Direct Method. As we will see, West's New Method Readers were enormously successful for Longman, and led to even more famous imitators such as the Oxford English Course, which the linguist Laurence Fawcett created for the British colonies in Africa. Ogden recognized West's success and very quickly adopted literary Readers to accompany his Basic English textbooks leading to a large catalog of Basic English versions of Western classics from Homer to Shakespeare and the Bible.

The place of literary texts within colonial English education has been controversial ever since the first use of literature as the basis for English education in India. For critics of ELT, the use of Simplified Readers as supplements to language learning textbooks performs the structural inequality of the colonial relationship. In their work on Global English, both Phillipson and Pennycook cited West's New Method Readers as examples of the colonial relationship implied by ELT methods. Examining West's adaptation of *Robinson Crusoe*, Phillipson views Crusoe's teaching Friday as an allegory for the "assumption of mastery" that pervades the ideology of global English.[5] Pennycook expands this interpretation of *Crusoe* to consider postcolonial readings of Defoe's novel that problematize the relationship between Friday and Crusoe recognizing the degree to which the control over language marks the limits to Crusoe's mastery. Although I generally agree with these interpretations, the fact that they are based on readings of Defoe's novel, not West's adaptations, makes them more valuable as allegories of Global English ideology than as arguments about West's New Method Readers. It is difficult to make an interpretation based on just one text out of the entire corpus, even if it was the "first" New Method Reader,[6] and it also should be considered that *Robinson Crusoe* had been circulating in the colonies for decades already in an abridged form. This latter point raises the question that underlies my argument in this chapter: what makes West's New Method Reader *Crusoe* distinct from the abridged version?

This question suggests my interest in this chapter with the Simplified Readers produced by West, Palmer, and Ogden as more than just allegories for the colonial experience but as sites of experimentation for their word lists and theories of language. Building on this traditional criticism of Simplified Readers as colonial discourse, I view the vocabulary control Readers and textbooks within the context of late imperialism and the second language ideology of the auxiliary. The purpose of these Readers is not as much with the relation of the colonizer and colonized, as allegorized by Crusoe and Friday, as it is with the colonized and modernity depicted through pedagogical scenes of language use and concepts of tradition or nativism. Also, unlike Phillipson and Pennycook's readings of *Robinson Crusoe*, I am interested in the Readers themselves, not the "original" books that they have adapted. In this sense, I treat them as translations with an interest in their decisions for what to include or exclude, or choices for rendering into their vocabularies. As experimental texts, the purpose of these Simplified Readers and textbooks is to test their respective vocabularies, as conditions for verifying the applicability and range of the word lists.

In a literal sense, Palmer viewed the Simplified Readers as experiments. As he documents in his essay reflecting on the history of vocabulary control, he approached literary readers with the same methodological scrutiny that he took to the word lists. Indeed, he saw the two methodological problems as linked: the problem of assessing value to a word list complemented the problem of assessing the effectiveness of a supplementary reader. Palmer saw this as an opportunity for a kind of methodological experiment. The Readers, he argued, should be composed rigorously—according to rules governing plot, subject matter, types of English used—and should also have an experimental purpose—that is, as a means of testing specific vocabularies.

In 1932, IRET published its first simplified Reader under this plan, a version of Edgar Allan Poe's 1843 short story, "The Gold Bug," re-titled as "The Gold Beetle." Palmer also published a companion volume, *The Grading and Simplifying of Literary Material: A Memorandum*, which first appeared in two issues of the IRET journal, *Bulletin*, in 1932, and published by IRET as a single volume in 1934. Despite its title, the IRET *Memorandum* is not just a review of best practices for the making of supplementary Readers. Palmer uses it to repeat his critique of word list methods, to reprise his theories of the "word" as a linguistic symbol, and to define a new pedagogical purpose for literary material in the language learning classroom. Palmer draws many of these arguments from his previous work in *Scientific Study and Teaching of Languages* and *Principles of Language Study*, and from the methodological debates over word lists in the 1920s. He acknowledges "the co-incidence of several more or less independent factors" from the objective word lists by Thorndike, Dewey, and Horn and the "series of reading-texts with vocabulary limitations composed by Dr. Michael West in India" and "the project called 'Basic English.'"[7] As a result, he approached A. P. Rossiter, a Cambridge scholar of Shakespeare and friend of Ogden's who happened to be in Japan for the year, with the idea that each method within the Vocabulary Control movement—IRET, Basic, and the New Method—should test their respective word lists by applying them to an adaptation of "The Gold Bug." Thus, within a couple of years, there appeared Palmer's "The Gold Beetle," Ogden's "The Gold Insect," and West's "The Gold Bug."[8]

However, Palmer's coordinated effort provides insight into more than just bugs, beetles, and insects. This turn to literary source material is revealing in that it is a kind of admission of methodological limits for Vocabulary Control. Where is the "vocabulary" that they can define? In managing language one has to invent it at the same time. Ironically, Palmer reverses the conditions that he criticized in Thorndike's objective method of composing word lists. As discussed in Chapter 2, Palmer argued against its objectivity since the researcher was responsible for selecting the literary material (e.g., the Bible and Shakespeare) that was to be the basis for the statistical collection. But when it comes to using Readers, Palmer now argues that literary material can be used at the other end of the process: as a test of the word list. Rather than a word list drawn from literary material, he offers literary material made from a word list. The "test" of the word list comes from the degree of difficulty for the adapter in re-writing literary material within the given limited vocabulary. A low degree of difficulty in composition and ease of comprehension means that the word list would have a low degree of difficulty in learning and being used in conversation. The fictional world, specifically, realism, acts as a site of experimentation for reality. The capacity of words to create a viable "reality effect" is the means of measuring their effectiveness for reality, that is, to be used in real-world situations. This assumption might be one of the most convincing demonstrations of faith in the tenets of the realist novel.

Palmer's experiment raises the question: what is the relationship between a novel and the words it uses? Normally, we subsume the latter into a more general observation about "language" or "voice." The novel uses a national language, or a particular regional, racial, or vocational vernacular. The "words" are symbols of a language-type. But what about when the words are not the servants but the masters of the text? For example, one of West's New Method readers for children is *Jack and the Bean Plant* mainly because "stalk" is a relatively infrequent word by comparison and thus not included in his word list. Similarly, two of the titles for the Poe story change the Saxon "bug" to the Latinate "Insect" and the more descriptive and specific "Beetle." In these cases, their changes from the canonical title draw attention to the word in a way that lends them status for their selective difference and emphasize the word list that the adapted text is meant to convey. In this sense, for these language methods getting the title "wrong" is a feature, not a bug.

This chapter develops the arguments made about the colonial and racial history of Vocabulary Control word lists from Chapter 2, through close readings of their accompanying literary texts and textbooks. The chapter opens with an analysis of West's New Method Readers, and the Basic English translations and textbooks, before returning to Palmer's *Memorandum* and a comparison of their three versions of Poe's short story. As argued in Chapter 2, Vocabulary Control depends upon a developmentalist perspective of "mother tongue" languages inherited from colonial linguistics. The word lists depend upon "mother tongue English" and "foreign mother tongues" as a means of distinguishing their collection of words as unthreatening *supplements* that have the capacity for adaptation and change. But the Vocabulary Control word list is limited in its ability to argue for how these "supplementary words" or Auxiliary English should be used. It is the purpose of the Simplified Reader to illustrate the value to be found in using an auxiliary language, indeed, in the value of the "auxiliary" toward a modern and internationalist perspective on the world. Therefore, as these comparisons demonstrate, the simplified literary texts are not supplemental but integral to these word lists. They determine the value of the words in the list and mediate and validate a nascent ideology of the anglophone.

Auxiliary Reading: West's New Method Readers

For as much as it emphasizes its "newness," West's New Method Readers were, like the late imperialist context in which they appear, very late arrivals to the history of English novels and language education in India. In fact, the first English work printed in India was Thomas Dyche's *Guide to the English Tongue* in 1716.[9] Language teaching, colonial policy, and English books have been intimately linked at least since the establishment of Government-run Anglophone schools in 1835. As a result of this "educational nexus," as Robert Fraser puts it in his history of the book in India, books in English and imported British books were widely circulated and consumed since the middle of the nineteenth century.[10] They were sold at bazaars, loaned at public and private libraries, and assigned as required texts for the Civil Service exams. During the nineteenth century, fiction had almost no place in university exams in India. According to one record "up to a third of the courses should be devoted to poetry which 'aids in the formation of taste, as well as in the acquirement of words and ideas.'"[11] Curricular debates in British India resembled those in England at the time over the proper method of literary instruction, specifically philology versus criticism or historicism. Genres like fiction were outside their scope altogether as was the question of how to educate below university levels. The fact that West was using fiction and directing his efforts at primary and secondary learners already made his efforts "new."

According to Priya Joshi's authoritative study of Indian reading habits in the nineteenth and twentieth centuries, Indians read British fiction with more regularity than readers in England. Notably, their canon of British writers was distinctly unique from that of the metropole. From her analysis of library requests, publishing records, and reviews by Indian readers, Joshi notices that didactic and melodramatic works were popular genres. The didactic works often in vernacular translation such as *Robinson Crusoe*, *Pilgrim's Progress*, and *Rasselas* originated with colonial sponsorship yet persisted as popular afterwards. In contrast, melodramatic and romantic works by authors like Scott, Dickens, and Fielding, but more significantly, non-canonical, popular writers like G. M. W. Reynold, Marie Corelli, and translations of Dumas, were not officially sponsored readers and yet were even more widely circulated.[12] The popularity of Reynolds and other less well-known Victorian writers represented a divergence from British reading habits. What those readers did with these melodramatic and romantic works was also not in line with the ideological tendencies of the genre which tended toward narratives about social mobility, marriage, and domesticity. For Joshi, Indian readers remade British fiction according to their own, sometimes subversive, imaginations: "Indian readers' manipulation of their reading matter was an inadvertent and unpremeditated act of subversion that successfully sabotaged the dominance of the colonial apparatus."[13]

Joshi and other scholars of the history of the book also acknowledge the role of British publishers in the formation of the English-language literary landscape in India. The three leading publishing firms were Macmillan, whose "Golden Treasury" of English classics was the most widespread publishing series in India beginning in the 1880s; the Oxford University Press, which established its own branch in India in the 1910s; and Longmans, which specialized in language teaching textbooks and published West's New Method Readers.[14] Kegan Paul, which inherited a list of publications going back to the East India Company, forsook the Indian market after being acquired by Routledge.[15] Macmillan's Colonial and Home Library began in the 1870s and, with the exception of competition from Kegan Paul's Indian and Colonial Series in the 1880s, it was largely dominant. As Joshi notes, they were responsive to their Indian readers' preferences for romantic and melodramatic literature.

The Indian market largely determined the shape of Macmillan's list including a reactionary tendency toward "anti-realist" literature that led them to neglect modernist developments in fiction in favor of authors and styles from the late nineteenth century. For example, one of their most popular authors was F. Marion Crawford, whose entertaining and didactic novels were celebrated in the 1880s but were soon forgotten in England and the United States. Nonetheless, his books persisted on the list of Macmillan's Colonial Library, which published forty of his forty-four novels.[16] In contrast, Oxford and Longman mainly focused on education, language teaching, and histories until the 1910s when the colonial language teacher Percival Wren advised Oxford that "the days were over when works like Lamb's *Essays* or Burke's *Reflections on the French Revolution* could be regarded as suitable introduction to modern English for Matriculation students."[17] As a result, Oxford adopted fiction in the form of a series titled *Stories Retold*, which not surprisingly were abridged versions of works like *Ivanhoe*, *The Cloister and the Hearth*, *Gulliver's Travels*, *King Solomon's Mines*, and even an edition of *Indian Heroes*, many of which were adopted as school readers and also adapted by West for his New Method Readers.[18]

In *Bilingualism*, West notes that there already exists "a very large output of English books 'abridged and simplified for Indian students,'"[19] which the

Calcutta University Commission suggested should be subsidized. However, he argues that they are inadequate:

> Such books are already produced in appreciable numbers without subsidy; if they are not produced in larger numbers it is because they do not sell well, — save those few which have the good fortune to be adopted as textbooks for examinations. If they do not sell well, it must be because the Indian student derives no pleasure or profit from them. And if this be the case, we are not surprised.[20]

West examines several books from a variety of publishers, including Oxford's Stories Retold Series, and argues that the simplification is not done with a scientific understanding of vocabulary. Ironically, he notes, the abridged texts are *more difficult* than the original versions. About a simplified version of Cooper's *The Prairie*, he notes that it has a vocabulary "more difficult than an un-'simplified' book of Dickens, Arnold Bennett, or Kipling."[21] Using one of Oxford's first readers, *The Cloister and the Hearth*, West shows the number of words used outside the first 5,000 words of the Thorndike Word Book on just three pages.[22] He revises one paragraph to show how it can be done within the Thorndike list. West claims that "any simple narrative which does not contain too much local colour and has a strong plot can be written within 2,500 or 1,000 [words]."[23]

The emphasis on "strong plot" is important for how West distinguished his Readers from those published by Oxford and others. As the Calcutta Commission recommended, outside reading in English was needed in order to learn. Yet, reading in English in India was largely determined by exams in which case reading itself suffered as students used "cram" study editions sold in the bazaar more frequently.[24] West's emphasis on a "strong plot" reveals a change from the Liberal argument for literature to demonstrate ethics, or the emphasis on grammar and memorization in Wood's Despatch from 1854 that were previously used to justify inclusion of texts on the curriculum. However, any extra curricular reading needs to both be compelling and yet at the correct level for the reader. F. Marion Crawford and other Romance writers were immensely popular among adult Indian readers, but West's focus was on primary school reading, not books for adults or for matriculation.

This question leads to the problem of finding English material with appropriate content and vocabulary. It also points to another factor in using the existing Simplified Readers—and one that was resented by the Indian readers: while they were intended for Indian readers, they were simplified as if for

English children so that surplus texts could be cross-marketed at home. West's New Method Readers would only be intended for use in India and therefore would not have the problem of dueling English audiences. However, this still leaves a discrepancy in the age-reading level and the age of the reader that West refers to as the Age Discrepancy between the level of the vocabulary and the content. If the Readers were to be used by eleven-year-old Bengalis, whose English was at the level of a six-year-old English child, there was the problem of having content in the six-year-old vocabulary that would suitably interest the eleven-year-old. He uses it as a measure for the question of whether the reading material, if translated into Bengali, would be interesting to the age of the student. West resolves this by turning to Thorndike's Word-Frequency List (from *Teachers Word Book*, 1921) and using its Credit-Index as the basis for deciding on the level of the reader.

As discussed in the previous chapter, the turn to word lists was part of Vocabulary Control's scientific method for language teaching. In creating his New Method vocabulary, West recognized the limitations of a system that merely applied an objective word list directly onto a text. He acknowledges that the "commonest words" in Thorndike's list are determined through literary material and that the list is short on technical and scientific material. West cites Thorndike's comment that if it were more representative of useful speech, then "*Angels* would go down and *bricks* would go up."[25] West integrates this problem in Thorndike into his own method by saying that the measure should not be to follow the word list strictly but rather to avoid "all avoidable words."[26] Citing the example of "albatross" in Coleridge's "Ancient Mariner," a word that would not be on a word frequency list but which is obviously necessary to the poem, West argues that the criterion "needs to be just to the authors."[27] West's method then sought to balance this concern with maintaining the uniqueness of the work with a prevailing concern to avoid offending his Bengali audience. As for the latter, he could not publish a series that was seen as "dumbing down" the native education or he might be at risk of inciting further anti-colonial criticism, as was occurring elsewhere in the empire.

In *Masks of Conquest*, Gauri Viswanathan charts the contradictions and controversies in using English literature in colonial education. As her book first demonstrated, English literary studies originated from the turn toward a British literary education as a means of avoiding charges that the anglophone schools would be used to convert students to Christianity. Literature's original purpose was to teach Western, Christian-based ethics without imposing religion. This led to other forms of surveillance of vernacular literature as well, to the point of creating a canon of colonially sanctioned Indian literature.[28] British textbooks constituted a "paper empire," as Antoinette Burton and Isabel Hofmyer have argued, that lent the book "English manly authority" as "it was the very emblem of imperial sovereignty—with the rigorous spine a testimony to its singularity, its probity, its titular power."[29] As we will see, this does not assume that colonial knowledge was unitary or hegemonic. Rather, as Sanjay Seth and others argue, most Indians viewed colonial education mainly as a vehicle to status and a necessary requirement to enter the Civil Service.[30] Nonetheless, controversies over British textbooks were proxy battles for colonial power. At the height of the anti-colonial pressures in the 1920s, in particular, education was a flash point for criticism by the emerging middle-class.

To understand the larger imperial context in which West was operating, it is useful to compare his New Method to a contemporary textbook series, the red-covered editions of *Nelson's West Indian Readers* that first appeared in Trinidad beginning in 1927, at the same time as West's New Method Readers. Thomas Nelson and Sons began their readers in Canada during the 1880s, where they integrated regional literary and geographical sources into the material. In Trinidad, the West Indian Readers were edited and written by Captain James Oliver Cutteridge whose three books—*Nelson's West Indian Readers* 1-6, *Nelson's West Indian Maths*, and *Nelson's Geography of the West Indies and Adjacent Lands*—were used throughout the Anglophone Caribbean for thirty years and became identified with racist colonial education. Criticism of Cutteridge was rampant among the first postcolonial generation from politicians like Eric Williams, and is cited by Kamau Brathwaite and V. S. Naipaul, not to mention, most famously, by the Calypsonian Mighty Sparrow whose 1963 song "Dan Is the Man (in the Van)," calls out Cutteridge directly in its lyrics:

> Captain!
> There's a traitor on board!
> Examine the horn!
> According to the education you get when you small,
> You will grow up with true ambition and respect from one and all.
> But in my days in school, they teach me like a fool,
> The things they teach me ah should be ah block-headed mule ….

The song mocks the use of folk tales and British pronunciation in the elementary school *Readers*. Cutteridge's readers were not trying to teach English, but Sparrow's song title refers to an exercise that sought to create "proper"—British Standard—pronunciation of vowels that was also part of the Direct Method of language teaching. Thanks to Sparrow's calypso, Captain Cutteridge might be one of the most infamous colonial officers from the history of the British Empire and an emblem of racist colonial education that is often equated with the racism in ESL teaching. However, the points of similarity and contrast between Cutteridge's West Indian Readers and West's New Method Readers are instructive for the corrective argument I am making for how we understand the relationship between traditional colonial education focused on British Standard and West's New Method pedagogy focused on auxiliary English.

Captain Cutteridge was a former military officer who arrived in Trinidad in 1921 as the Principal of Tranquility Boys' Model School and rose to become, like West, Chief Inspector of Schools, and later, Assistant Director of Education. Unlike other colonial educational figures, he did not have a university degree, rather, as Robert Fraser puts it "he came equipped ... with a First World War field commission, a fellowship of the Royal Geographical Society, a zeal for educational reform and an eye for a telling picture."[31] This was a particular point of controversy since it appears that the colonial authorities appointed him over a more qualified Trinidadian.[32] However, Cutteridge was not just the no-nothing soldier that was depicted by his enemies. In fact, he was similar to West in that he was inspired by progressive theories of education in England and the United States and sought to implement them in the colonial system. Like West, he sought to reform colonial education by getting rid of rote learning, exams, and the "pay for results" system.[33] The new educational model was based in psychology and was child-centric, seeing them as subjects with their own ideas and beliefs, rather than as a *tabula rasa* to be filled with knowledge. Just as West sought to replace the Grammatical Method of language teaching, Cutteridge modernized the teaching of grammar in elementary schools by emphasizing phonetics. His philosophy of the reforms followed Dewey's belief in the use of handwork as a way of stimulating the brain. Students were constantly drawing, painting, paper cutting, or doing woodwork and gardening. Also, rather than British readings, Cutteridge followed Nelson's policy from their readers in Canada and created localized readers that used Caribbean folklore, history, and geography including Creole folk tales and "Nancy" stories from Africa in the first reader.

Despite his progressive intentions, the reforms were controversially received by the Trinidadians. The 1920s witnessed the rise of both the labor movement and Garveyism among middle-class Blacks in Trinidad. They paid particular attention to issues such as Cutteridge's appointment and lack of traditional credentials as well as teachers' rights and pay. Part of Cutteridge's reforms meant new models of inspection putting the burden on teacher performance, rather than the traditional measure of student performance on exams which, in an era of labor unrest, led to complaints about the curriculum from teachers' unions. All of these administrative conflicts made the controversies over the content of the *Readers* more overt. For middle-class Trinidadians, Cutteridge's curricular emphasis on handwork was interpreted as vocational education, a suspicion that was compounded by the de-emphasis on grammar, all of which implies that students would not be prepared to take exams for Civil Service jobs. And, most controversially, the use of vernacular folk stories in the early readers drew outrage for suggesting that Afro-Caribbeans are backwards and primitive. During a period of Indirect Rule, the curriculum seemed designed to undermine their attempts at self-determination. Cutteridge, who did all the drawings for the readers, made all of this worse when the images of Afro-Trinidadians that appeared in the first reader were seen as racist.[34]

Leaving aside the obvious fact that West's textbooks were primarily for language teaching, there are other differences between Nelson's West Indian Readers and the New Method Readers that help to distinguish West's project from traditional colonial education. In terms of method, for instance, both men sought to implement progressive educational concepts using insights from psychology. But Cutteridge followed in the colonial tradition of imposing the latest metropolitan methods on the locale. In contrast, as *Bilingualism* demonstrates, West used evidence and data to support his claims about teaching language. Cutteridge wrote these textbooks in his own voice, drew the racist pictures, and made the faulty maps and questionable equations all by himself without any prior testing. For instance, even the implementation of phonetics was faulty as is evident in the fact that it is mocked specifically by Might Sparrow's Calypso. For West, the emphasis on pronunciation and its association with a British Standard was one of the faults with the Direct Method that the New Method sought to amend. Another effect of this empirical method is that West's Readers are shaped by his encounter with Bengali nationalism. Where Cutteridge seems to have developed his West Indian Readers in opposition to the Trinidadian middle-class, West's New Method Readers seek to reflect the interests of the Bengali middle-class, as evident in the review of *Bilingualism* by Srinivasachari.[35]

West's New Method Readers differ most significantly in the selection of the reading material. It is not necessarily the case that elementary readers only told stories about England. While this was true for the Victorian-era

Royal Readers, colonial education in the twentieth century, as can be seen in Nelson's *Readers*, sought to make its material regionally specific. This was aligned with the aim expressed in the Dual Mandate to prepare young colonials to run their nations. West's *New Method Readers* differ in that there is little local regionalism in the reading material. The catalog, such as I have been able to acquire, looks like a canonical shelf of British and American classics. There are a few European tales, and *Arabian Nights* is included, but there is not any Indian folk material. Some reasons for this are pragmatic—there is the question of acquiring rights and, as Joshi documents, a history of English fiction as popular among Indian readers—but there are other reasons that have to do with his paradoxical goal of creating English as an auxiliary language. By translating English novels into the limits of his word lists, stripping them of "local colour" he is able to make the language instrumental. The effect is circular: he uses the language to act upon the fiction which he needs in order to trans-value the language.

What was "new" about West's readers had to do with how he exploited the nexus of publishing and education. His Readers offered similar canonical works as Macmillan's *Golden Treasury* yet the simplification was aimed at a younger audience. In terms of education, he deployed contemporary reforms more successfully than Cutteridge did in the West Indies. Like Cutteridge, he reinvented classroom culture, de-emphasizing rote learning and exams. Yet his textbooks did not meet with the same resistance. By 1929, West's New Method Readers were so successful that Longman dismissed attempts by Oxford University Press to co-opt the series. The consequences of its success are notable: it led OUP to abandon India and create its own influential "Oxford Course" of readers for Africa.

One possible reason for its success could be that his emphasis on genres like adventure stories, the Bildungsroman, and exploration was similar to popular forms of Bengali children's literature. In his examination of children's literature in Bengali magazines from the 1910s to 1940, the historian Satadru Sen argues that the editors of the magazines sought to contest British constructions of childhood and to construct "a literary and pedagogical child that is generally Hindu and middle-class." These popular magazines such as *Mouchak, Sandesh,* and *Rangmashal* presented an image of childhood as "plastic" and "mobile" that escaped the limitations of colonialism imposed on adults. Some of the themes deployed in these stories included stories of Indian children abroad, in Oxford or Japan; adventure stories, exploring Africa or the Antarctic; or nostalgic stories set in the Bengali countryside. All of these story forms engage with colonial models in different ways from the anti-colonial stories set in Japan that suggest a model of "Asian modernity" or the colonial mimicry of exploration literature. Sen observes that almost all of the stories feature orphans, which are necessary in order to have malleable, liberated children. As he writes, the possibility of change was a critical feature of the form:

> Children's literature in Bengal between the 1900s and the 1930s was premised on the assumption that children were both reflective and plastic: i.e., although they might inhabit geographies that served as metaphors of the politics of colonized adulthood, they were also capable of growth and transmutation to a degree that was beyond the capacity of adults. Whereas adults could only be (colonized, effeminate, inauthentic, unscientific, urban, earthbound), the child could become (modern, masculine, scientific, authentic, rural, airborne).[36]

The image of childhood created in these Bengali magazines fit well with the implicit assumptions of West's Readers. While his only stipulation for the Readers was that they have "a strong plot" and "not too much local colour," the selection of novels about development like *David Copperfield*, adventure like *Ivanhoe* and *Deerslayer*, and exploration like *King Solomon's Mines* suggests an awareness of these stories as his competition. In all of these stories, the canonical texts in the New Method Readers and in Bengali children's literature, "whiteness, masculinity, and modernity" are "admirable assets," as Sen puts it. The last item listed here, "modernity," is the key feature that links the New Method Readers with Bengali children's fiction. While West includes *Robinson Crusoe* and *King Solomon's Mines*, he does not feature jingoistic stories celebrating England or Empire nor does he refer to it as such in his textbooks. Rather, he emphasizes aspects of modernity such as industrialization and electricity. It is in this vein that he casts language—specifically multilingualism—as a tool of modernity.

The New Method Readers' significance is in how they transition from colonial models of English language teaching to global English by developing the argument made in *Bilingualism* for the distinction between mother tongue and auxiliary languages. As I noted in my analysis of *Bilingualism*, West depends upon literary forms and artifacts to convey this ideological distinction. Unlike the colonial morality commonly found in Cutteridge's textbooks, the ethics of West's readers tend toward models of individual fulfillment. As we will see, character and plot development depend upon narratives of individualism in which change arises through acts of linguistic difference. What we see when we read this catalog through the lens of *Bilingualism* is how he deploys the novel to reinvent English into an international auxiliary language.

Staging English: The New Method Readers

Most of the fiction that West adapts, however, comes from the canon of nineteenth-century British novels. What happens when these novels are simplified? In essence, realistic accounts of setting or forms of characterization through character-speech are de-emphasized and the novels become reduced to their melodramatic plots. For instance, West's adaptation of *David Copperfield*, reducing it to 110 pages and only the words in the New Method stage five vocabulary, downplays the story of David's development in favor of a romantic plot. Similar to the many film adaptations, there is more attention given to his marriages than there is to his education—either at school or in the world. In contrast to what Esty and Slaughter have argued about the uses of Bildungsroman in creating colonial subjects, West's Readers deploy Victorian morality as its model.[37] The Bildungsroman form does not disappear entirely, however, but it is significant that it is subservient to the romantic plot. By doing so, it fits with the conflicted view of individualism conveyed in West's *Bilingualism*. West presents a bifurcated view of individual self-expression—on the one hand, it is part of human nature to desire escape from the crowd—as he cites in his examples from the boarding school and the POW camp. This is seen as one of the reasons he can find for reviving or privileging native languages under the guise of cultural nationalism as a desire to not become subsumed under the communal sign of English.

On the other hand, his argument for English as an auxiliary language depends upon a re-imagining of one's relation to cultural identity as flexible and as permanent: multilingualism does not threaten mother tongues because the latter are permanent, essential parts of our character. Thus, in West's adaptations the *Bildung* is secondary to the marriage plot, or, to put it another way, the maternal language remains primary. The narrative contains the radicalism of affiliation by framing it within a "maternal" romance plot signifying ongoing filiation. In the linguistic allegory, the auxiliary language appears in this narrative as a necessity, while the mother tongue appears as persistent, yet always secondary. This is reinforced by the fact that David Copperfield rises in society by learning a new language, shorthand, which is often cited as an example of an "auxiliary language": the kind of abstract representational expression that allows for communication. In West's version, this aspect of the plot is buried within other, more significant events. In this way, the New Method Reader stages the experience of personal reinvention through the learning of an auxiliary language but in such a way that it does not threaten filial bonds.

In the New Method *David Copperfield*, the development of the individual also takes place within the study questions in the appendix. Here, the questions build on the first-person narrative by moving between first and third person with some questions asking about the character "D. C's" actions (What had D. C been doing?) and asking about the actions by or to an implied "I" (What did P do which hurt me?"). And the third- and first-person voices appear interchangeable, so that a question like "Where will D. C. go?" is followed by "Why were *my* mother's eyes red?" (emphasis added). The persistence of David's voice outside of the text puts the individual reader in the situation of engaging with the fictional character. These direct questions appear intermittently among other basic comprehension questions and in this way, interpellate the reader as a subject akin to David. Rather than a traditional Bildungsroman form in which the reader is educated vicariously, here that Other addresses the reader and implicates him into his subjectivity. In this way, West uses the romance plot to fulfill the principles of his Readers to make a "strong plot without too much local colour" and uses the questions in the appendix to reinforce the underlying message of individualism.

Although learning shorthand is de-emphasized in the New Method edition, in other New Method Readers language—as a form of difference and means of communication—is staged as central to plot and character development. An illustrative case is the New Method version of *Ivanhoe*, a novel in which the original plot centers around language difference. In his "dedicatory epistle" to *Ivanhoe*, Sir Walter Scott famously addresses the problems faced by the novelist writing about historical events that occurred in other languages including earlier versions of a national language, arguing that it is better to sacrifice historical accuracy for the sake of conveying the story in a way that appeals to modern readers. Describing his role as a novelist as akin to that of a translator, Scott extended the necessity of translating to the behavior of his characters as well: "It is necessary, for exciting interest of any kind, that the subject assumed should be, as it were, translated into the manners, as well as the language, of the age we live in."[38] His advice for adapting historical events into modern fiction is similar to West's theories for adapting British fiction into his Simplified Readers. Scott's remarks about the "error of Chatterton" in using ancient dialects in his poetry resemble West's criticism of the abridged Readers that kept the English dialect from the original. Scott's advice to convey ancient plots in a language that is neither obsolete nor distinctly modern suggests West's attempt to steer British plots into a contrived language that is neither Standard English nor an artificial language like Basic English. Scott has been recognized by critics for creating a narrative of modern English as a "master language" in *Ivanhoe* by depicting a historical moment before its individual elements—Saxon, Latin, and Norman-French—were fully integrated. This becomes an essential element to the plot; as Gillen D'Arcy Wood notes, "[i]ts heroes ... are those who intuit and obey the imperative to cross over from their 'home' culture to a new order."[39]

Because of the way that language difference features in its plot, *Ivanhoe* provides an opportunity for a New Method adaptation to represent positive moments of language difference and stage the language conversion implicit in West's *Bilingualism*. For West, adopting English as an auxiliary language is not imperialist. He portrays English in *Bilingualism* as an appropriate "world" language because of its own hybridity, which he implies, means that it cannot displace more pure, native languages. Modernity, then, is associated with a multilingualism that happens to use English rather than English-only monolingualism. West's goal in *Bilingualism* is to focus less on the value of English and more on the necessity for multilingualism. This hybridity is emphasized on the first page of the New Method version which gives a brief account of the context and suggests its concluding moral: "As time went on these two peoples—the Normans and the Saxons—mingled together to make the English nation of to-day; but that mixing had not, at this time, taken place; and there was ill-feeling and hatred between the Norman 'nobles' (or great lords) and the Saxons (the original people of the country)."[40] In addition to the mingling of Saxon and Norman, other languages such as Latin and Arabic are seen as part of the environment. Early on, the plot turns on the Pilgrim warning Isaac about the Templar's plan to kidnap him when he overhears their plans in Arabic.

Yet this act of successful translation is balanced by moments of linguistic confusion and even illiteracy where success depends upon multilingual individuals. The letters exchanged by the outlaws and Front-de-Boeuf reveal the reality of their language difference. The letter from the outlaws has a dichotomy between its formal, legalistic language and the marks and hieroglyphs that stand in for their signatures. It is received with equal confusion by Front-de-Boeuf and De Bracy, who remark, "it may be magic charms for all I know." Scott qualifies this as indicating that De Bracy "possessed his full proportion of the ignorance which characterised the chivalry of the period."[41] In the New Method Reader *Ivanhoe*, De Bracy's comment is not explained, suggesting that he cannot read Saxon rather than being illiterate. The letter that Bois-Guilbert writes back in French is equally confounding since the outlaws are as ignorant as their counterparts in Saxon. The two figures who are able to read across languages—de Bois-Guilbert and the Black Knight—are notably the two most heroic characters. It is more than implied that the age of De Bracy's chivalric ignorance is about to be superseded by a modern, multilingual age.

There is another association between West's conception of a language as an auxiliary and the association made between language and clothing in *Ivanhoe*. For example, when the Hermit protests being sent as a spy into the castle he claims that when he takes off his priestly robes he also loses his ability to speak Latin: "When I put off my hermit's gown, my priesthood, my holiness, even my Latin are put off with it."[42] Scott humorously reinforces this connection when the illiterate Saxon jester Wamba puts on the garments and instantly speaks his pet Latin phrase: "*Pax vobiscum*."[43] Language and clothing relate again in Front-de-Boeuf's threat to Wamba: "Tell me in plain words what numbers there are, or your holy garments will not protect you!"[44] contrasting the ideal of plain speech and priestly robes. When Cedric puts on robes as part of the escape plan, his first thought is how his impersonation will fail because of his illiteracy: "I know no language ... not a word of Latin."[45] Yet he learns "*Pax vobiscum*" from Wamba: "the magic charm lies in two words ... *Pax vobiscum* carries you through all. If you go, or come, or eat, or sleep, *Pax vobiscum* carries you through it all. Speak it thus in a deep grave tone, '*Pax vo-bis-cum*'—it is ir-resist-ible."[46] However, the plan immediately leads to a problem when the multilingual Rebecca responds with the rejoinder from the Catholic Mass and Cedric thinks to himself: "A curse on the Fool and his *Pax vobiscum*. I have lost my spear at the first cast."[47] The last sentence indicates the significance of language in these chapters as taking the place of warfare, as part of the battle, foreshadowing the real battle that follows.

The use of vernaculars, literacy, ritual, voice, and bilingualism in West's *Ivanhoe* signify language as a necessary instrument for negotiating one's way through the world. It is both a cultural native product of identity—as it is for Cedric—yet it is also a weapon that can be deployed strategically, as a tool. This mimics West's claim that auxiliary language can be instrumental and not have any negative effects on identity. Athelstane's speech on the honor of family reinforces this when it does not mention language as a source of pride or distinction—rather it is physical, material ancestry that signifies. The book concludes around another pedagogical scene of language and literacy that has to do with how to read. The letter that the Prior writes to Bois-Guilbert is intercepted by the Grand Master who interprets the phrase about Rebecca, "this witch who has cast a charm on you," literally, that "This Rebecca of York is indeed a witch and practices magic."[48] The Grand Master's religious intolerance extends to his inability to read properly. The association here between literalism and magic suggests Ogden and Richards's theory of Word Magic, quoted by West in *Bilingualism*. That is the belief that words are essentially linked to the objects they identify. It is this belief in "word magic," West argues, that impedes understanding language as an instrument.[49] The adaptation concludes all of these pedagogical scenes with an example of a proper use of language in Rebecca's letter which is direct and simple in its speech.

The ELT historian A. P. R. Howatt considers the New Method Readers an important innovation in language teaching that laid the groundwork for later ESL instruction; however, he notes that they never truly fulfilled West's pragmatic vision: "there were too many Black Beauties and not enough manuals for fixing bicycles."[50] But there is another way of seeing these Readers as developing the ideological, if not pragmatic, purpose from *Bilingualism*. The adaptations of classic British fiction like *David Copperfield* and *Silas Marner* into "strong plot[s]" convey the sense of language as instrumental. West's insight was the same as that recognized by all genre writers which is that by making words serve the plot, they become almost invisible. In conveying these stories with as little "local colour" as possible, West is also able to reach a wider foreign audience by making them less about "England" than about their characters.

It is also significant that many of the novels like *Ivanhoe*, and, as we will see, "The Gold Bug," stage pedagogical scenes of language instruction, literacy, and multilingualism. In this way, the reader takes on the message of multilingualism as part of an allegorical plot about auxiliary language. The capacity for characters like David Copperfield, Rebecca, Wamba, and Legrand to transform their situations through the use of another language suggests that language might be "used" but not come to re-define the essence of a character. This reinforces West's distinction between English as a second, or auxiliary language, versus English as a foreign language. Where the latter is based in Standard English, the former is based on word lists like Palmer's. The reader of West's New Method Readers is congratulated for learning the words, not for learning a language. The confident blurb at the end of each book "You know ALL the words in this book" addresses the reader as a repository for *words* not as a learner of a *language*. The reader can absorb *all the words* without feeling that there was any threat made to one's identity. At the same time, the need to "stand out from the crowd" that might find expression in support of a minor world language (though major locally) finds compensation in the cultural capital of the British canon.

In *Bilingualism*, West imagines the Bengali reader as needing English "for international and interprovincial trade."[51] To understand how this view of modernity is put into practice, it is necessary to look at the New Method textbooks, not just the literary readers. The New Method Readers were designed to inspire reading for pleasure, outside of school. The textbook was an important pedagogical intervention on the part of West that came out of a tradition of teaching in India. For example, let's consider New Method Reader VI, originally published in India in 1937, written for twelve- and thirteen-year-old Bengali boys. The contents include stories from the Bible, from Kalidasa, a story by H.G. Wells, and poems by Milton, Wordsworth, and Tagore alongside articles about "Power" and "Electricity." Overall, it seems to provide a balance of India and England with accounts of industrial modernity. In this way, it is an exemplary form of what Krishna Kumar, a historian of Indian education, calls "textbook culture," developed first in 1845 and reinforced as part of the 1857 educational reforms. Its effect, Kumar argues, was to create a role for the colonial state within the classroom. The textbook was perceived as "a sacred icon of required knowledge,"[52] whose authority took precedence even over the teacher, who "could not be trusted."[53] The textbook was part of a centralized, bureaucratic system of education that served the exams needed for entering into colonial civil service. The standardization was necessary because the exams were taken all over the country. The teacher's role was to prepare the students for the exams by rote memorization of the material in the textbook. There was no reading allowed that was outside the textbook. As a result, "for both teacher and pupil the textbook was the curriculum. ... All other forms of knowledge were thus invalidated by the 'textbook culture.'"[54] West's New Method Reader VI opens with a "Note to the Teacher" that summarizes the goals of the textbook to "build up vocabulary" and to "improve word density" including advice on how often to revise vocabulary and even giving permission to study word lists. This is followed by a Preface on "What this book teaches" that states in its subheading that it should be read by the entire class so that West is able to speak directly to the class in the place of the teacher.

In his Preface, West explains that one goal of the textbook is to teach the reader how to independently find out the meaning of words that are not included on the grade-level word list but which they will encounter when reading non-prepared materials. This involves introducing the idea of a dictionary and how it can be used. The paradox of a dictionary is that it explains English words in English; also, West argues that access to a dictionary cannot be assumed when reading. Therefore, he uses the Preface to explain how to gain understanding of a new word by looking at its context on the page or by "un-fold-ing it."[55] He demonstrates the latter by showing the students that they have learned parts of words that are combined in new ways (e.g., prefix as learned as "pre" and as "fix" in Reader III). The independence preached in the Preface persists in the fiction, poetry, and non-fiction readings. The contents include the Old Testament story of Samson paired with Milton's poem "Samson"; H. G. Wells' short story, "The Country of the Blind"; Wordsworth's poem "Upon Westminster Bridge"; two chapters on "Power," and "Electricity"; a classic Indian play by Kalidasa, *Sakuntala*; and finally, two poems by Tagore.

Despite the relative diversity of the forms and their authors, all of these works narrate stories about the relationship between the individual and the crowd and the transition into modernity. The biblical story of Samson and the Philistines shares many themes of the individual struggle against mass conformity apparent in Wells' story about Nunez' defiance of the morality of the blind village. While *Sakuntala* should be very different from these Western narratives, its adaptation in the textbook focuses on Sakuntala's departure of the hermitage for the "real world." In this way, she leaves a premodern Eden in much the same way as Nunez leaves the blind village. Like the other New Method Readers, all three stories have romantic plots, yet in this case, they do not end with marriage. Samson and Delilah, Nunez and Medina-Sarote, and Sakuntala and King Dushyanta are all stories about doomed romances. Sakuntala, of course, does end with her leaving for marriage but the conclusion emphasizes the pain of departure and does not depict the final romance, which, in the complete version, only arrives after a series of conflicts.

As for the poems, these also share an emphasis on individualism through their use of lyric voice. In the context of the other readings in the textbook, the Wordsworth poem, "Upon a Westminster Bridge," conveys not so much the emphasis on England typically found in colonial Readers as much as it reveals the value placed on the city and urban living. For many of West's readers, who do not live in Calcutta, this poem would be an advertisement for living in the city. This is significant since that is part of West's argument for auxiliary English in *Bilingualism*: the need for a common language among newly urbanized populations in India. As part of this celebration of the modern, urban city, Wordsworth's poem depicts the city as an aesthetic site for personal contemplation.

Milton's poem "Samson" is presented after the story of Samson from the Bible which is only one of the multiple frames used: it is introduced with the setting of the poem, then the first eleven lines are quoted and then followed by a line-by-line paragraphs, which is repeated for the remaining sixteen lines. This is then followed by a transcription of the poem emphasizing pronunciation, with syllables in bold. In this way, it balances the use of a religious text with a secular adaptation that draws attention to the singular individualism of Samson as a heroic individual resisting the crowd. In its use of multiple frames—the Bible story, the paraphrase, and the phonetic transcription—the poem conveys West's message about multilingualism to show how these other versions can be both related to and independent of the main poem. Story is not tied to form, just as languages are also forms that are not tied to content. The story of Samson is translated from the Bible, again by Milton, and then finally into pronunciation and paraphrase—sound and sense—without changing the source.

The final two lyrics from Tagore that conclude the textbook would appear to be on a different order than the Wordsworth and Milton poems. They are not followed by a lesson, nor are they framed by an explanation or instructions for reading aloud. Yet they replicate the same theme of the individual against the crowd as in the first poem, a prayer from Tagore's *Fruit Gathering*, "Let me not look for allies in life's battlefield, but to my own strength"; and in the second selection, from *Gitanjali*, the desire is for the Lord to "Give *me* strength…". These selections are not rewritten in the New Method vocabulary, yet it draws on the prestige of Tagore, whose image graces the selection, as the exemplary New Method poet: he translated his own work into English to international acclaim. Tagore represents West's ideal balance of the mother tongue and the auxiliary language: where the latter provides raw material for translation into a new, modern, secular code. In all three lyrics, its ideological association with Bakhtinian monolingualism, subjective experience and dense "untranslatable" language is activated as a stand-in for a "mother tongue" language that needs to recognize its perennial need for a modern, supplemental prothesis.

The two nonfiction sections on "Power" and "Electricity" are coincidentally placed after related fictional material: "Power" follows the two lessons on Samson and the lesson on "Electricity" follows Wordsworth's poem and its homage to "bright and glittering" London. In this way, they reinforce similar themes of individualism and modernity. The lesson on "Power" emphasizes the transition from the story of Samson by referring to "men in ancient times" first celebrating how they used their bodies to accomplish tasks, then lamenting at length the deprivations of the premodern condition such as being "at the mercy of the weather" and lacking books. This sets up the contrast with "modern man" whose life is described as a futurist utopia where man is not "hunted by wild beasts" but the master of machines: "His clothes and most of the comforts which his home contains are made by machines. Machines bring him food from all parts of the earth, or carry him to all countries of the world. The modern world is a world of machinery, with man the master of machines."[56] The narrative of how this world was created includes references to the water mill in *Robin Hood* in an earlier New Method Reader and mainly features southern England as the unique location for the industrial revolution. The lesson proceeds historically, explaining the evolution from water power and steam engine to coal and the spread of railways from England to Africa and Asia. An entire section is devoted to the disadvantages of coal and the steam-engine including the difficulties of mining conditions for workers—all to demonstrate the efficiency and "modernity" of the oil-engine. The progressive narrative concludes with a section on the motor engine and the innocent image of the "smoke of waste gas coming out in little puffs."[57] Just as in the stories, the lesson demonstrates knowledge as an evolutionary progress from premodern, tribal, communal living to a modern, individualized, international, and rational world. After reading this lesson's account of the premodern past, the reader is prepared to see the blind villagers in "Country of the Blind" not as an Edenic retreat from the world, but as regrettably backwards and premodern.

The lesson on "Electricity" similarly gives an English-based, developmentalist account of the spread of electric power along with explanations of how it works and relates to its sources of power. Most importantly, it concludes with a "moral lesson to be drawn from the two lessons."[58] Turning to the second person point of view, West writes: "You are living in an age of machinery, and by the time you reach manhood the world will be even more mechanical than it is now."[59] He continues by asserting a generational divide:

> There are some men and women who seem quite content to remain hopelessly ignorant of all mechanical matters. They press the button of the electric bell, but they do not know how it works; they turn on the electric light, they do not know how it works; they use a motor-car, they do not know how it works; and if it goes wrong they cannot repair it. These people may know a lot about books, and perhaps a lot about nature—about trees and flowers and insects—but in regard to machinery they are hopelessly ignorant—mere fools. It is just as bad to be a fool in regard to books and school-work—in some ways worse, for when it comes to earning a livelihood, a person who can make and repair machines is paid far better than a clerk who has mere book learning.[60]

This emphasis on useful knowledge goes directly against the Filtration Theory approach to education which focused on classic texts for civil service exams. It also comes into conflict with Indian complaints about colonial education using vocational training as a way of keeping them out of political roles. Here West addresses the student directly, using the textbook's power within the classroom to override the native social and cultural authority of teachers and parents. The fact that he connects these two chapters by literature shows its role in developing this "moral lesson." The "mere fools" in the electricity lesson are the characters from the literary examples: the Philistines, the blind villagers, and the hermit Kanwa. The student is implored to break with this previous generation and to identify with Milton's Samson, Wordsworth's speaker, Wells' Nunez, and Tagore's devotee to individualism. As each lesson concludes with the number of words that the reader "knows," West reinforces the connection between this heroic individualism and the English language. Although the ostensible purpose of the textbook is to provide instruction in English and technical knowledge, it links the two so that the language becomes a kind of *techne* that is associated with a conception of global modernity rather than imperialist morality.

Basic Commodities: *Carl and Anna* and the *Basic Way Reading Books*

While West's New Method Readers were a success within the ELT market, they were largely unknown outside of the field. The same is not true for the Basic English texts which are still studied by scholars in fields ranging from modernism to technology and early twentieth-century language movements.[61] The Basic English bibliography extends to over thousands of titles ranging across genres from literary classics to the sciences and history. Unlike West's New Method Readers, the Basic English readers were not intended for elementary or middle-school audiences. As a result, the purpose of the adaptation differs significantly from the New Method. Where West's readers were designed around a graded development of vocabulary and changing skill level, the Basic English books appeared to be working from the same vocabulary.

It is questionable whether this was ever the case. In what might be seen as a ruse of what one critic calls "the Basic English sales and marketing division," very few of the Basic English books are in fact written in the famous 850 words. Ogden created specific supplemental word lists for the Readers that made the translations into something like normal English possible. This was in response to an underlying concern for Basic which is that as an International Auxiliary Language (IAL) it might be closer to the original IALs, pidgins, than to its purported referent, Standard English. This was an anxiety that is deferred onto the Basic books that comes from the popular parodies of Basic as a pidgin form of English. In his history of the Vocabulary Control movement, Herman Bongers gives an example of a non-expert translation of Standard English using only the *Basic Dictionary* (see Figure 9).[62]

Because Basic excludes common English words such as "eat," "stand," "sit," "husband," and "wife," among many others, it leads to absurd versions of normal expression. The complicated circumlocutions that are necessary to convey information without using these common words or the verbs that make up a third of the language lead to an unnatural form of English. The orthodox Basic response to these parodies is to lament the author's naive understanding of translation. By rendering classic and contemporary works with high cultural capital into Basic, its supporters are able to claim that Basic can work as a form of

1000-word Standard English Text	Basic English as a Non-Expert would write it
She counted the names of the people her husband had asked to dinner that evening. Then she began to get excited and said to him: "What do you mean by asking so many! I can't give them much to eat; they can have a dish of meat and vegetables; that is all." Mr. Jones was standing near the window; he was not listening to his wife and he wanted to go and lie down.	She got the number of the names of the persons of whom her married man had request the company at the important meal of the dat that nightfall. Then she made as start to get worked up and said to him: "What is your purpose in requesting the company of such a number? I am not able to give them much food to take. They will be able to have vessel of meat and garden produce; that is all." Mr. Jones was upright near the window; he was not giving ear to his married woman. He had taken a midday meal of great weight and he needed to go and be stretched on his bed.

Figure 9 Herman Bongers' literal translation using Basic English from his *History and Principles of Vocabulary Control* [1947].

translation, if done properly. Drawing on the prestige of "experts" and of "literary language," Ogden was able to make an impact on a number of important figures within the British elite, if not among linguists.

But the reality was different than Ogden claimed. He was only able to manage his translation through the supplemental lists of idioms and specialized vocabularies. For the science and technology books for adults such as *The Chemical History of a Candle* by Michael Faraday, *Electricity and Magnetism* by H. S. Hatfield, and *Science and Well-Being* by J. B. S. Haldane, the editors included a Basic Science word list. For the Basic version of Edgar Allan Poe's *The Gold Bug*, *The Gold Insect*, which I examine later in this chapter, he included a supplemental list of idioms. Similarly, the Basic English version of the Bible added 100 poetry words and 100 "Bible words" to the standard 850. Most of the books were translated within a word count of over 1,000 words. Despite Ogden's justifications and the rationales he would offer in the introductions to these editions, it is still a tacit admission that the Basic vocabulary was insufficient as a literary or scientific language. Also, non-specialist attempts at translating Standard English into Basic using the 850-word limit often ended in ridiculous parody rather than the more natural sounding translations done by Ogden's network of experts. This raises the question: if the literary translations are not true renderings of Basic English, then what is their purpose?

It is not my interest, of course, to simply examine Basic English's texts for their infelicitous use of English. Instead, I want to examine two texts—one literary adaptation and one set of Basic ELT readers—to consider the ways in which Ogden sought to use fictional and non-fictional texts as a means of legitimizing Basic as part of a late imperialist, global world order. As with the New Method Readers, the Basic English Readers are not only interested in teaching English but with marketing the language system. They are a necessary source of financing and popularizing the specific method. Using the celebrity of authors and famous titles are ways to expand the market for their language systems beyond the bureaucracy of government education ministries. This comes through mainly in the turn to the Bible and classical epic. These canonical translations demonstrate Basic English as an intrinsic part of Western culture, not its dangerous opposite. Where Ogden's polemical tracts about Basic depict it as revolutionary, the literary translations depict Basic as essentially conservative. Ogden suggests this contradiction in his introduction to *Basic English* where, after lamenting the state of language he writes:

> But if we are agreed that they are ruins, the case for a newer edifice is all the stronger. If, however, we can build on the old site, so much the better. We may even be able to preserve the old bricks, so that our children's children may say, "this was known to Johnson, to Webster," or "Here Bentham, here Runyon fought and won." The strength of Basic English lies in its determination to discard nothing that is essential from the standpoint of continuity.[63]

In addition to the cultural capital gained by the literary translations, Ogden depended upon them for financial capital, especially as support from the Rockefeller Foundation ended in the late 1930s and the Orthological Institutes struggled to survive. In this way, the Basic books functioned similarly to the simplified readers for Palmer and West—as a means for gaining cultural and financial capital, and as sites for deferring contradictions within their language systems and working out anxieties over the worlds they are creating.

I want to consider this in terms of Basic by looking closely at their first literary work, an adaptation of Leonhard Frank's novella, *Carl and Anna*, from 1930, and *The Basic Way Reading Books* from 1940, which accompanied *The Basic Way* textbooks. This comparison will illustrate the dual purposes of literary material for Basic English. On the one hand, canonical literature was used to promote Basic English though it could also, as with the New Method Readers, act as didactic texts training its readers to accept an auxiliary language model. On the other hand, the educational textbooks use narrative form to align its international language with an ideological view of the international. Both turn on the mother tongue/auxiliary dichotomy as a means of constructing their ideologies of how language conveys the modern and the global.

Carl and Anna

Ogden's industriousness was legendary among his peers. Between 1929 and 1940 he was a publishing industry all by himself—writing dozens of books, pamphlets, and textbooks. I. A. Richards also published several books directly about Basic such as *Basic Reason* and *Teaching with Basic*, and also indirectly in his book on the Chinese philosopher Mencius. In addition, there were several Cambridge figures like the Shakespeare scholar, A. P. (Arthur Percival) Rossiter and J. A. Lauwerys who contributed to the Basic library in its wide range of subjects from the sciences (the *Basic English Applied: Science*) to economics and literature.

Many of the early Basic English textbooks and literary translations were done by L. W. (Leonora Wilhelmina) Lockhart, who only graduated from Girton, the Cambridge women's college in 1929. Her 1931 book, *Word Economy: A Study in Applied Linguistics*, is credited with being the first use of the term "applied linguistics" (ironically, she named the field that would define itself by rejecting Basic English).[64] The daughter of a decorated British Naval officer, Murray MacGreghor Lockhart, Lockhart was mostly raised in South Africa where her father had retired after the First World War. Her mother, also named Leonora, was a socialite and, after they returned to the UK, was friends with intellectuals like Bertrand Russell, which may explain Lockhart's personal connection to Ogden.[65] Despite the celebrity of her parents, she gained some fame of her own as an undergraduate at Girton when she was part of a select female debate team that toured colleges in the United States debating male clubs.[66] As Carly Woods notes in her history of co-education in the early twentieth-century, their tour, which ranged from the east coast to the south and the Midwest, received press attention. Woods quotes the *New York Times* describing Lockhart as a passionate debater in the Oxford style. The common debate topic was co-education which she argued against, claiming that the presence of men distracted women from learning because of the pressure for dating and marriage. Her favorite line of argument was to quote a coed from a midwestern university who said that she had gone on "72 dates in 60 days" to which Lockhart would wittily respond that one should "never have more dates than there are dates."[67] As the founder of the Heretics club, Ogden was also a skilled debater and must have appreciated the same set of skills in Lockhart. Indeed, the rhetorical style of Basic English could be described as that of a British debating club. As we will see more fully in the next chapter, the polemical tracts by Ogden, Richards, and Lockhart in the 1930s feel like an ongoing series of debating points against its opponents whether it is other International Languages, the Vocabulary Control movement, or other philosophers and linguists.

One of Lockhart's first projects for Basic was to translate the German novella *Karl und Anna* by Leonhard Frank. First published in Germany in 1926, Frank's melodramatic novella was one of the first works in Germany to deal with the effects of the First World War on the homefront. Despite its localized subject matter, *Karl und Anna* was an international success. Within just a few years, it was adapted into a play, a major film by UFA (*Heimkehr* [Homecoming], directed by Joe May), and was widely translated, appearing in an English translation by Cyrus Brooks in 1929.[68] In the tradition of *Le Retour de Martin Guerre* and *Enoch Aden*, *Karl und Anna* is a love story about a soldier, Karl, who returns from the war disguised as another man and successfully persuades the man's wife, Anna, into accepting him. Anna's husband, Richard, had told Karl so much about Anna during their time together in a POW camp that Karl fell in love before ever meeting her. Once he escapes from the camp, Karl uses all that he learned from Richard about Anna to convince her that he is in fact her husband. Unlike the duplicitous Martin Guerre, Frank's "returning soldier" is depicted as a truly honest man who is forced into this imposture by his love for Anna. Frank is, as the critic Brian Murdoch puts it, the "husband who both is and is not the right husband."[69] In the end, when Anna's real husband returns, she chooses to run away with Frank.

In his introduction, Ogden remarks on the importance of this translation for Basic English. Claiming that "this volume was undertaken as a literary experiment, the first of its kind," he uses the introduction to explain the system of Basic English.[70] It is clear that for Ogden, the function of the literary translations is mainly to promote Basic, as he states rather directly: "Though Basic English was not, and is not, designed to deal with 'literature,' it was decided early in 1930 to make an appeal to the public with a literary model."[71] For Ogden "the success of *Carl and Anna* with the general reader recommended it for this first attempt."[72] It is interesting that in comparison to West's New Method Readers that used the traditional British canon as its subject material, Ogden drew on a text that was European and popular and that could be considered a work of world literature because of how quickly it was translated and adapted. In this case, it makes sense that Ogden would want to introduce an international language through a work that already had an "international public"[73]—a concept that was something new at the time. Ogden uses this introduction to repeat many of his standard arguments for Basic; however, because of the brevity of the space, he is more direct here than elsewhere, notably about the necessity of a universal language for "world peace" and the efficiency of using English since "it starts with over half the civilized world 'converted,' as it were, by the unconscious labour of five centuries" and because "no other European language can dispense with 'verbs'; no Eastern language can cope with science."[74] In only a few sentences, Ogden repeats many classic tropes of Global English from the "accidental" nature of its spread to the racist judgments about premodern Eastern languages that he appears careful to avoid stating so directly in the Basic English textbooks.

Other than its popular appeal, *Carl and Anna* also works for Ogden because its plot makes these same arguments. For instance, Ogden's reference to Basic English and world peace is a reminder of its origins in Ogden's pacifist criticism of the war (and accusations that he was pro-German) comes through in the novella's criticism of the war as harmful for both the soldiers who undergo radical changes in personality and on the home front as well.[75] The novella also makes available an allegorical reading about substitution that resonates with Ogden's remarks about the relation of Basic English to Standard English. Notably, Frank's revision of the returning soldier theme tells a story about a deception that does not end with a tragedy. Unlike Martin Guerre, there are no beheadings. Instead, there is an ambiguity over the status of truth and knowledge in the fact that Anna is always aware that the man she accepts as her husband is not actually him. For the novella, Anna's choice to flee with Karl at the end suggests the power of love over truth, yet for Basic English, it is also a deliberate choice of the "replacement" over the original, or as it might be called, the "standard." There are a few ways that Richard as Standard English and Karl as Basic English resonate. One has to do with communication: Richard "over-communicates" in telling Karl all about his wife, while Karl, who speaks briefly and concisely, uses direct speech and confession to seduce Anna into loving him. Accepting Basic English as an auxiliary language requires a similar leap of faith that the doppelganger will improve that which it resembles. The allegory of family, nation, and language also comes through in the truth of Richard as a husband is the truth of language as a form of national identity. The novella suggests that the post-war world requires re-imagining familial and nationalist bonds. Similarly, Ogden argues that the post-war world requires a language that is not based on filial connections; rather, it needs an affiliative language based on logic, reason, and science.

This condition of the uncanny might also be applied to all Basic English translations. Because they are produced as part of the general literary marketplace and are not solely limited to education, like the New Method Readers, they appear to be passing as normal translations. But when the reader comes across a footnote for a word like "frogs," or reads that Carl had washed and "taken the hair off his face," it appears as an uncanny version of Standard English. Unlike a translation of a foreign language where the target seeks to appear as normative as possible, to erase any sense that it is a translation at all, Basic draws attention to its status as a translation, as if Standard English itself was a foreign, mother tongue language. To adapt Murdoch's description of Carl, as a substitute for a kinship language, Basic is both not a language, yet wants to be the right language.

The Basic Way Reading Books

Lockhart produced *The Basic Way Reading Books* for the educational publisher Evans Brothers textbooks in the late 1930s and early 1940s. Evans Brothers began educational publishing in the 1930s before entering into the field of African publishing after the war. In this sense, Basic English fits their profile perfectly as an educational textbook directed toward foreign students. This is the latest material covered in this chapter which mainly focuses on the period leading up to the Carnegie Conference in 1934. Since Basic English was the latest to arrive as part of the Vocabulary Control movement, and was initially intended as an international auxiliary language, not a system for teaching English, it took longer to produce coherent teaching materials and the type of Reader that I am examining with West and Palmer. Despite its late date, the idea of a series of essays in Basic about everyday life was talked about as early as *The System of Basic English*. So even though it came about after Carnegie, the series is consistent with the original rationale that Ogden used to justify Basic English as a form of ELT.

Ogden controlled every aspect of Basic English. In fact, his disputes with Richards were often over disagreements about the materials that Richards made for China. However, the *Basic Way Books* are works clearly written in Lockhart's voice and reflect her economists' view of the world. There are two books divided into four parts each (there is an additional fifth part in book two). The student was to read the book after completing the corresponding set of lessons in the *Basic Way to English* textbook; for instance, after completing the "five steps," for each lesson stage, the "sixth step" is a "reading stage" using all the previous words—about 400 English words per stage. While this roughly follows the stages learning model set up by West and used generally for language teaching, it is not as strict in its limitations. For instance, since the student would be reading the book while learning new vocabulary in the next stage, the book also includes "surprises" with words from the new lessons they are learning. Also, traces of Basic English as an IAL are apparent in its desire that the essays appear "smooth and natural" despite its teaching purpose. Most importantly, they differ in their subject matter. Unlike the fictional content in West's New Method Readers, the *Basic Way Books* consist of short, nonfiction essays. As Lockhart describes it in the introduction, the point is to give students "facts" and a global view of the world:

> It is hoped that the material of *The Basic Way Reading Books* will be interesting to boys and girls everywhere. These books give facts—facts about events which have taken place in history and about things which go on in different parts of the Earth. In them everyone will probably come across some things which are part of his everyday experience and others which are strange to him. And so, through his reading, he will get a wider knowledge not only of the English language, but of the doings of other men, learning in turn of the orange farms of Spain, of the oilfields of America, of the silk industry of Japan. In this way, at a very simple level, he will be using Basic as an instrument for the questioning mind.[76]

The subject matter reflects Basic English's original purpose to act as a language for science and business. It makes sense therefore that the learning material engage with that purpose; however, the emphasis on "facts," "events," and "history" suggests more than exposure to the world but also a way of viewing it. Even though the books are not as revolutionary as Ogden's early polemical writings on Basic English, Lockhart's use of "surprise" words in the essays and content that is "strange" to the student certainly expresses similar modernist values of defamiliarization and internationalism.

The books have three types of essays that might be classified as commodity narratives, on topics like rice, oranges, wool, cotton, silk, oil, fish, and tin; nature essays on weather, astronomy, insects, trees, waterways, and "earthshocks"; and civilization essays on money, writing, newspapers, play, and hospitals. The latter essays appear in the second book mimicking a developmentalist parallel between progress in vocabulary and progress in subject. This evolution similarly matches the cultures investigated in the essays that begin in book one with accounts from India, China, Nigeria, the West Indies, and northwest Canada and Australia while the second book mainly refers to Europe. The essays are accompanied by photographs that were selected with "special care." Lockhart writes that "They are a camera record for those who are unable to make journeys to far places, of some of the interesting things which may be seen there. In addition to increasing the attraction of the pages, they give details of dress, of men's faces, of the country-side, which are not readily put into words."[77] Typically, the black-and-white photographs depict the natural resource such as the cotton plant, or fish, and show either the artisans making the product such as a pot-maker or brick-maker, or they show the laborers collecting the product from rice or cotton fields. Almost all of the topics are depicted in economic or ethnographic terms. Even in the more scientific essays "A Look at the Sky" and "The Journey of Birds," the natural phenomenon is described in terms of human observation or utility.

The commodity narrative essays describe with some detail the way that commodities come from sites of labor and nature such as "tin mines," "rice fields," and "wool from sheep." The tone strives for empirical distance and an ethnographic sympathy with the producers and their difficult conditions of labor. Yet the repeated narrative connection made between the native or local cultures that have the task of collecting and refining natural resources for sale in the metropole creates an indelible association between the people and the resource. For instance, the essay "Thread Which We Get from a Plant" contains eight paragraphs with six about the natural process such as the conditions in which the cotton plant grows, the color of its flowers and the opening of the seed-vessels, and two paragraphs on the laborers who harvest the cotton. While the essay mentions that cotton production is based in Egypt and the American South, it only addresses the latter and does so in frankly racist terms describing how the "black families do their work very happily" and despite the hard labor, "they go back to their houses with smiles on their faces."[78] It should be noted that this is an unusually extensive account of the laborers and their attitude toward their conditions. In the other commodity narratives, the description of the laborers is limited to their functions and actions. They are described by their gender roles—the women, girls, and boys who collect oranges or palm oil and the men who pick up the natural resource from the farm or the men who fish in the north sea or collect lumber in Canada. The laborers are described as naturally suited to the tasks. Black women in the South are described as valuable for their "small fingers" to pick cotton, or "all the men" in Newfoundland are fishermen. Not only are they reduced to existing in a state of nature, their value as people is tied to the commodity's value in Europe.

The photographs reinforce these racialized accounts of the global commodities. The images tend to depict the artisan working at a loom, or making a pot at a wheel, showing pre-industrial labor conditions that belie the technology and trade described in the essays. In a couple of the essays the image contrasts the narrative in ways that illuminate conclusions that are otherwise unstated. For instance, the essay on brick-making has a photograph of an Indian brick-field opposite a paragraph stating that "In Africa and India one sees only a small number of brick houses, but in a great number of towns in Europe all the buildings are of brick."[79] Most of the commodity essays conclude with someone bringing the rice, wool, lumber, or fish away from the place where it is produced either to market or to a refinery. This contrast between the prose and image states most directly the ideological condition that sites of production cannot also be sites of consumption. Similarly, the essay on cotton provides an example of how the photograph allows the text to depict race and class relations in a way that the prose cannot. For instance, Lockhart writes that the Black laborers put the cotton into "great baskets" and "when the baskets are full they take them to the cotton house where someone sees how much cotton is in every basket."[80] On the opposite page, there is a photograph showing a white man in a hat and tie weighing a bag of cotton while surrounded by Black field workers. Under the image is a caption that reads "someone sees how much cotton is in every basket."[81] The value of Basic English's word economy comes through in this case where the euphemism for "white man" can simply be "someone." The relation here between the image, caption, and text is a stark example of Lockhart's statement that the photographs "give details ... which are not readily put into words."[82]

The essays on civilization in book two are similarly organized around economic themes, particularly the creation of value through trade and international circulation. The latter as a condition of the commodity is the basis for many of the essays, especially, of course, the one on Trade and Transport and Money. But also the essay on Stamps emphasizes the value in collecting and trading them, and the essay on Money notes that the value can change depending on circulation. The essays on Newspapers and Writing also draw attention to their economic aspects such as the role of advertising in newspapers and the way that writing becomes a valuable commodity. While focused on consumption and the commodity itself, these essays do not lose sight of the source narratives from book one. The essays do this in a number of ways such as contrasting places where the commodity does not exist, drawing attention to laborers using the instrument, or emphasizing the subject's modernity in contrast to a prior period or place rendered unmodern. The essay on Fire, for example, has two images side by side—one of Australian aboriginals making fire with a stick and the other of a bourgeois Western family sitting in front of a fireplace. Modernity and its lack come through in the essay on Electricity that notes that not all places have electricity, or the essay on Hospitals that emphasizes the horrific state of hospitals before modern conditions of sterilization were instituted. The Electricity essay also has an image of servants using electrical devices as if to suggest that they have not been replaced by machines.

The second book includes a fifth essay, "Twenty-four Hours in Newtown" that is longer and more extended than the others. Written in the first person plural, "we," the essay describes a tourist's trip to a major city. The purpose of the essay is to demonstrate the fifty "international words" that are not on the Basic English word list because they are already internationally known. Similarly, the fictional city of Newtown is described as an amalgamation of common features found in all of "the great towns" in the world from London to Buenos Aires. In keeping with the Readers' economic perspective and her overall celebration of commodity capitalism, Lockhart describes these international towns as "the towns of the money-makers" and, lest we forget, "money-making is an international business."[83]

This is a fitting description because the entire trip is viewed through the lens of class, wealth, and privilege. When the tourists first arrive, they find that "the part of the town near the station is dirty and not very interesting," worse the "boys and girls playing in the roadway have no shoes or stockings, most of the houses are in need of a coat of paint, the stores are small and have cheap goods in the windows."[84] The poverty of the children evokes the children described in the other essays who work in the fields using their small hands to pick cotton or oranges. For elementary students in non-Western countries learning Basic English, childhood has few charms.[85] Where the other essays lump together women and children as performing similar modes of labor, here they are separated to represent class differences. After leaving the impoverished children near the station, they come to an upscale shopping district where "on the sidewalks well-dressed women were looking at the beautiful clothing, leather-work, jewels, and other things on view in the windows." In contrast to the women as laborers, here she represents the idle consumer. This contrast between poverty and wealth helps situate the narrator as firmly middle-class: a person who finds the poverty "unpleasing" and the wealth obscene—"we were pleased that our taxi went past them [the expensive stores] without stopping."[86] The presence of class attitudes pervades the rest of their trip from their hotel to the restaurant and then when they attend a play and visit a nightclub. The next morning, they stroll through a park and see the university and government buildings before leaving.

In addition to the emphasis on class, the essay conveys a strong presence of time. Their day is regimented by the sound of "the Great Clock" and at the end of their trip they derive their greatest satisfaction from the fact that "not one minute had been wasted."[87] That efficiency is valued so much should not be surprising for an auxiliary language system based on eliminating wasteful words. Throughout the essay the international words that are being taught appear in boldface. As with the use of time in the essay, these international words are aligned with modernity. They appear as consumable commodities produced from colonialism (coffee, chocolate, tobacco), technology (automobiles, zinc, aluminum, radio), or elements of the European nation-state system (passport, police, war, colonialism). By situating these elements within a narrative form, Lockhart associates modernity with these forms of gender and class division. Implicit in these representations is the language that the student is learning: it is not merely describing modernity but conveying it as well. The association here between the narrator's perspective and the language system being used implies that Basic English can describe modernity objectively and bring the student to Newtown where he can experience it himself. In the Carnegie Report discussed in Chapter 5, one of the justifications for a world English is the need for an auxiliary language to be used in urban cities where people come from rural spaces with their own languages and vernaculars. The essay on Newtown presents this most explicitly, conveying the sense that only Basic English can both negotiate modernity and correct it.

Maybe the most important part of the perspective in "Twenty-four Hours in Newtown" is that it is a view from somewhere else. Where the commodities in book one never make it past the farm or local market, in this essay we see them arrive in shop windows and in restaurants ready for consumption. This "somewhere else" that marks the narrative "we" in the essay defamiliarizes received reality just as we have seen Basic English make Standard English strange and uncanny. The tourist can be aligned with a series of "others" that appear in Basic English texts from Richard, the legal husband, to the African American cotton pickers and other laborers who exist in a natural connection to the land and resource. Opposite them are their "translations": their same forms but in an auxiliary, modern conception: as Carl, the replacement husband, or the commodity that "replaces" the labor and resource. Both Carl and the Commodity in these essays are marked by leaving, though in the Newtown essay it is the narrator who leaves the city. But in that case it is the city that appears to be in flux, not the narrative voice. As auxiliary forms of the husband or the resource, the commodity narratives described in both the literary and the language lesson gain value by mobility and circulation. In this way, the unstated lesson of the *Basic Way Reading Books* appears to be that language itself should be seen as another raw material that can be remade into a commodity which gains value by mobility. The dichotomy between mother tongue and auxiliary is symbolically reinforced by these commodity narratives that are based on similar parallels between primitive and modern cultures, sites of production and consumption, and natural resource and commodity.

Simple Improvements: Palmer's Poe Test

Palmer's Poe Test, mentioned at the top of this chapter, brought all three language teaching methods to bear upon a single story, Poe's "The Gold Bug." While I examine the Basic and New Method versions of "The Gold Bug," I am primarily interested in Palmer's rationale and explanation in his *Memorandum* on how to simplify literary material for the purpose of evaluating word lists. Because of its own complex language politics, Poe's story presents a provocative case study for the relationship between auxiliary and native languages. I demonstrate through the adaptations and Palmer's commentary the ways in which the story symbolically stages the argument over auxiliary languages made by Vocabulary Control.

"The Gold Bug" was a popular story from its first serialization in two editions of Philadelphia's *Dollar Newspaper* and later the *Saturday Courier* in June and July 1843, to the publication of Poe's *Tales* in 1845, where it is the first story in the collection. It is a story of a treasure discovered through the clever decoding of a cryptograph left behind by the pirate Captain Kidd. The story is narrated in the first person by an unnamed character who lives in Charleston and has become acquainted with an eccentric named Legrand, an impoverished former plantation owner from Louisiana with Huguenot ancestry. Legrand lives on Sullivan's Island, just a few miles off of Charleston's coast, with his Black servant, Jupiter. As a sign of his former wealth, Jupiter was a slave on the family's estate in Louisiana and, despite being freed, continues to serve Legrand. The mystery begins when they find a gold-colored bug on the beach. The paper that they use to catch it reveals the cryptograph that Legrand deciphers to find the treasure. However, while figuring out the code, Legrand pretends to be mad so that nobody suspects what he is up to, including Jupiter, who at one point threatens to beat him back to his senses. After he figures it out, Legrand still keeps his purpose a secret as he enlists the narrator, who also begins to suspect Legrand's sanity, to help him dig out the pirate treasure. After they discover the treasure, Legrand appears to return to his senses and, in an extended denouement, he explains the cipher and his method of decoding it.

While we cannot know the intentions Palmer had in selecting this story, it just so happens that he chose one that exhibits all the concerns with vernacular, race, translation, and codes that are apparent in the history, theories, and methods of Vocabulary Control. It is through these versions of this story—and Ogden and Palmer's accounts of their purpose and process—that we can see the role of literary form as mediating the contradictions of Vocabulary Control most fully enacted.

Palmer's *Memorandum*

Palmer situates his Simplified Readers in the nineteenth-century tradition of abridged elementary readers adapted from Dickens and Lamb. Since classical times, pedagogy has been based on the idea of graded reading from the simple to the complex. He distinguishes the IRET simplified readers from this tradition due to the modern, twentieth-century interest in word lists and in the pedagogical reading texts made by West's New Method series and Ogden's Basic English. This creates two expectations about the production of such texts: first, that the vocabulary would be controlled by the logic of statistical frequency counts, and second, that the text would be pedagogically efficient. Palmer wants to use these Readers and his *Memorandum* to critique both methods. The Readers, along with the *Memorandum* and the 3,000-word IRET list that accompanied it, were his salvo in the word list debates. His purpose is to justify the use of literary Readers as a means of resolving the dispute between objective and subjective methods of creating word lists while at the same time promoting his own Palmer Method and vocabulary.

The first part of the *Memorandum* addresses the Vocabulary Control debates that I discussed in Chapter 1. He criticizes both objective and subjective methods for the fact that neither one has a theory of what it is measuring; that is, they lack a definition of the "word." As a result, almost half of Palmer's memorandum is devoted to a "brief lexicological survey" that reviews the analytical terms of "alogs," "monologs," "pliologs," and "miologs" that he introduced in his *Scientific Study of Teaching of Languages* in place of the grammatical terms for "words" and "sentences." Rather than conceiving of the Readers as based on a limited word list, he argues that they should be based on these linguistic symbols so that what may be "expressed in one language by a specific word may be expressed in others by a *miolog*, an *alog*, a *collocation*, or a *construction-pattern*." Instead of using a word list to create a Simplified Reader, the educator would use the appropriate linguistic symbols available to the learner at their given stage.[88] Palmer is trying to create an abstract model for words that is similar to what the International Phonetic Alphabet does for sound. If both the source and target languages can be broken down into their *miologs* and *alogs*, then they can be matched up in a way that is not limited by available vocabulary. This interest in first principles of word definition distinguishes Palmer from West and Ogden who are more pragmatic and utilitarian, if not mercenary, in their approach to word lists.

Palmer criticizes objective methods of creating word lists, such as Thorndike's, by pointing out the degree to which they are subjectively determined insofar as they select the source material from which to draw their measurements. Palmer argues that subjective measures need to rely on statistical measures as a means of grounding this judgment. He summarizes these two sides as such:

> The "objectivists" claim that subjective lists have little or no validity because they must, from their very nature, be haphazard and random lists. The "subjectivists", on the other hand, claim that objective lists have little or no validity because they must, from their very nature, be based on insufficient material and inadequate principles.[89]

Palmer's insight is that the key to resolving this methodological divide is in finding a means of testing the respective lists. The "main issue," he argues, is "whether a given list has been tested in practice or not so tested."[90] One should be able to take a word list, whether subjective or objective, apply it to "a quantity of literary material" and if it "proceed[s] rapidly and naturally" then it can be considered successful, "it *worked*."[91] Success is measured by the efficiency of the "linguistic symbols" in the list. The list should not be lacking in needed symbols nor should there be "superfluous" symbols. As Palmer blithely concludes, "Just as the proof of the pudding is in its eating, the proof of the vocabulary is in the degree of its smooth and natural functioning when put to the test."[92] In this way, the debates over word list methods are resolved through literary material and the act of translation. By acting as a site of abstraction, the literary text functions in a way that could be seen as similar to the grammatical structure of the *miologs*. Palmer seeks a machine-like instrument for evaluating vocabulary. Where the *miolog* structure offers a machine for breaking words down, literary texts are machines for combining them. Either way, words are entered into these machines as data and the word list is measured by its capacity for translation.

This leads to the premise for selecting an appropriate text. Palmer writes that the material must be

> interesting for the sort of reader whom we have in mind, either because it tells him things that he wants to know, describes things that he wishes to have described

to him, relates a story that keeps him in a state of pleasurable anticipation, or in other ways makes enjoyable reading."[93]

Fiction fulfills all of these categories as Palmer asserts, "Narrative material is more suitable than descriptive." He favors "[a] well-told story" rather than "the depicting of scenery … the analysis of character … [or] [t]exts the chief charm of which lies in their stylistic value, such as poetry."[94] While all of this makes plausible sense in terms of engaging the reader, it also appears here as a distinct issue from the previous concern with subjective and objective methods. It is also possible to consider that fiction has other formal characteristics that suit Palmer's purpose. The use of narrative, for instance, that uses different registers of third-person perspective, from the more objective mode of omniscient narration to the mixture of first and third person in focalization, replicates formally the quandary of objective and subjective methods. The "omniscient" statistical measurement of word frequency is synthesized here with a "focalized" subjective perspective. In this way, narrative formal divisions are analogous to the methodological divisions that Palmer identifies in Vocabulary Control debates. These methodological differences in word counting are not resolved as much as they are deferred into narrative.

Palmer describes the process of this deferral as consisting of "two procedures: *deletion* and *replacement*." The purpose of the rewriting is to create "facility in reading" and any word or phrase that inhibits this aim should be either removed where it is possible or replaced by a "linguistic symbol" from "within the predetermined radius."[95] Deletion comes from deciding whether or not the "text will not materially suffer by its absence" and by assuming the position of the author: "We feel that the author of the original text might have done as we are doing, that he might just as well have omitted it."[96] For Palmer, simplification is not only about creating a readable text but, more importantly, about improving on the literary text, almost as an editor might, by striving for "clarification" as much as simplification, a word that he uses synonymously. Palmer sees it as more than just a supplement to the simplified text but as competition. In a Derridean formulation, Palmer boasts in the foreword to the Simplified English series that "One not having before him the original version might even suppose that the simplified text was the original."[97] The goal is to produce a version of the literary material which, while ostensibly in the same language, has the status of a translation. It seems that the distinction between a simplification and a translation lies in the status of the target language. A translation has a robust and complex language with a variety and mixture of diction and levels from which to adapt another text. A simplification by definition does not have this level of variety or complexity. Yet, for Palmer, the "simplification-clarification-translation" is not only a revision of an original text into a version drawn from a radius of linguistic symbols, it is also made into its own form of language, what Palmer calls "Plain English."

While Palmer suggests that the simplified text may supersede the original, he does not do this by erasing the original. In fact, in the IRET Simplified Series, the original text appears on the opposite page from the simplification. According to Palmer, this allows the student to learn not only the material in the simplified form but also have a discussion on the impetus behind the revision. As Palmer writes:

> The original version ran thus; the simplified version runs thus: there is a difference between the two; what is the nature of this difference? What is it that is lost on the one hand, and gained on the other?[98]

Palmer refers to this process as "an important form of literary criticism." He does not mean this in the sense of developing insights into the text's meaning, but in managing the student's English. The "original" text functions as a cautionary tale on how *not* to speak and write. It is designed as "a corrective to abuses of stylistics, or, in other terms … to cure lapses into 'foreigners' English."[99] He argues that foreign learners of English speak and write in "Babu English, or Pidgin English, or Japanese English, or French English, or Slavonic English,"[100] dialects that mix high and low forms of diction because stylistic differences "are a mystery." Palmer turns the confusion of styles that the student encounters in reading literature toward a pedagogical purpose by opposing it to the simplified form of Plain English. Palmer takes pains to distinguish Plain English from Standard English, native English, and Basic English. It is a style designed for pedagogical purposes; it is less complex than Standard and is not a vernacular used by native speakers, nor is it a stand-alone vocabulary like Basic. Rather, it is a style that is only used in the foreign-language learning context and only manifests within the narrative form of these simplified readers. Its only purpose is as a protection against the "mystery" of "Babu-English." As a preventative device, Plain English is an example of the way that Palmer's *Memorandum* is yet another example of how Vocabulary Control seeks to manage English.

Palmer's Readers, like West's New Method and the Basic Way Books, use the textbook as a way of substituting for the non-native speaking teacher in the classroom. The use of opposing texts is meant to instruct the teacher as much as the student. By directing the lesson toward the Plain English version on the opposite page, Palmer's method allows for criticism but not for interpretation. The original literary prose does not exist to expand the student's sense of English style but to limit it. In this way, Palmer's simplified texts enact on the page the ideological tension in auxiliary English between its limited instrumental role and the vernaculars, dialects, and national languages that it seeks to supplement and make more efficient.

Improving Poe

Poe's short story is a curious choice for a Simplified Reader, especially one based on these principles of clarity since the story's own language mixes diverse modes of speech including that of the unnamed narrator. In the section of the *Memorandum* on "Choice of Original Material," he rejects texts that rely on "stylistic value" or have "too large a proportion of words, which although comparatively rare, cannot be replaced by commoner synonyms."[101] Most of Palmer's simplification consists in replacing Poe's baroque prose with more commonly known words and direct sentences. Palmer substitutes "cried" for "vociferated"; "instant" for "prevarication"; and replaces phrases with lots of subordination like "I shall be under the necessity of breaking your head with this shovel" with a more direct version: "I shall be obliged to break your head with this spade."[102] This substitution of "shovel" with "spade" is an example of using words that have single references rather than nouns that can also act as verbs.

It is this logic of specification that informs the title change from "Bug" to "Beetle." Of course, the word "bug" derives from old English and exists only as a vernacularized synonym for insect while "beetle" shares the old English heritage yet describes a class of insect. Just as "shovel" has multiple uses and meanings beyond its function as a noun, bug also has multiple uses, and, according to the OED, even precedes its association with insects. Poe's story uses "bug" often and never uses the word "beetle"; the closest usage is when the narrator refers to it as a "scarabeus," which is a genus of beetle. In keeping with the narrator's pretentious speech, the word also evokes orientalist associations lending a strangeness to the scene that anticipates the "death's-head" image about to be discovered on the paper. Beetle exists at the midpoint between the vernacular bug and the genus-specific scarabeus. If simplification is supposed to be accomplished through specificity, then how does beetle improve upon scarabeus? Or, if the other measure is word-frequency, then it would be hard to justify not using "bug." Such are the improvements upon Poe's prose that are made in the name of Vocabulary Control.

The Basic English version by A. P. Rossiter is titled the "Gold Insect." As M. A. K. Halliday notes in a separate discussion, bug and insect are not synonymous, rather "an insect is a more abstract bug. It names a class: a class which can be defined, such that the question 'is this (thing, or kind of thing) an insect?' can be definitively answered—whereas you can't really ask about something 'is that, or it not, a bug?'"[103] Halliday's point is that English has the capacity to create new words, and new semantic meanings, through its use of Saxon, Norman, Latin, and Greek resources to expand its register of discourses. The purpose of Vocabulary Control is to do the opposite, to limit its register and range of reference.

The choice of the Latinate "insect" makes sense for Basic English in so far as it creates an association between a classical international language and its own modernist international language. With its limited vocabulary, Basic avoids specific words like "beetle" and like Palmer, it avoids using words with multiple meanings. Also, the Latinate "Insect" aligns with Basic's self-image as an international scientific language. Similarly, the Basic translator, A. P. Rossiter, uses periodic table notations for the chemicals cited in Legrand's explanation of the changes in the paper and even includes footnotes correcting Poe's science.[104] Rossiter's translation resonates with the impetus behind Basic English—to eliminate ambiguity in language and to make it a scientific instrument for communication.

An example of this correction appears when Legrand explains how he discovered the skull's image on the parchment:

> Zaire, digested in aqua regia, and diluted with four times its weight of water, is sometimes employed; a green tint results. The regulus of cobalt, dissolved in spirit of nitre, gives a red. These colors disappear at longer or shorter intervals after the material written on cools, but again become apparent upon the re-application of heat.[105]

The Basic English translation by A. P. Rossiter uses periodic table notations for the chemicals: "CoO put into mixed HCl and HNO_3 and then taken with four times its weight in water is sometimes used: that gives a blue colour when heated. In the same way $Co(NO_3)_2$ in alcohol gives a blue color."[106] It even goes so far as to include a footnote correcting Poe's science: "Poe says that $Co\ Cl_2$ gives a 'green' colour and that $Co(NO_3)_2$ 'gives a red.' This is wrong. Co salts are light red, but become blue when heated. On colored paper the red may be so thin that it is not to be seen: the blue becomes clear when warm."[107] The Basic translation also corrects Poe's reference to the "Spanish Main" noting that "the use of *main* for 'sea' is a common error: the true sense is the *main-land*—not the islands."[108]

All of this is in keeping with Ogden's belief that Poe is a writer in need of improvement. In his introduction to Rossiter's translation, Ogden demonstrates some areas of agreement with Palmer while also using the occasion to flaunt his cantankerous differences with the linguistics establishment. Ogden considers his adaptation an "improvement" on Poe's style which he describes as "complex, stiff, and frequently not of our time," and relies on Baudelaire's translation as a model for dealing with "Poe's thick masses of words" concluding that "[w]hen such things are cut out, the story is as good as ever."[109] Unlike Palmer's scientific approach to Poe, Ogden approaches him as a literary critic, comparing Poe's style to that of Shakespeare, Sir Thomas Brown, and Conan Doyle, while also situating "Gold Bug" within his overall *oeuvre* of mysteries, and as part of an American literary tradition from "the early days of American writing." In the same vein, he finds the "Gold Bug's" formal value in its "changes in rhythm" and offers measured praise, saying that it is an "important landmark" in the development of crime fiction and "still a good story." However, this is balanced by the fact of Basic's improvement: for instance, the story's "rhythm" comes through more effectively in the Basic translation, which he claims "gives all that is of value in Poe's somewhat unequal work."[110]

Ogden's ambivalence suggests that the translation of Poe was only made because of Palmer's personal request to Rossiter. This may explain why Ogden seems to use the Preface to indirectly criticize Palmer and the professional linguists. He takes a shot at the rival objective, statistical word list in an aside to his discussion of Poe's mistakes with science: "We are so used to our Thorndike and other experts that 'today' even Holmes seems to us improbable, and Poe's errors in chemistry and mathematics may be a cause of amusement."[111] He also alludes to Palmer's theory of word definition as part of an argument for the place of idioms: "this important fact has been very frequently overlooked by those who take the 'word' as the only teaching unit, and whose pages are full of theories about its 'varieties of meaning', 'semantic multiplicity', and so on." In contrast, the utilitarian Ogden repeats the contextual definition from *Meaning of Meaning* in arguing that "the word has no value when not in use."[112] The Basic translation keeps the entire plot of Poe's story, like Palmer does, which reproduces the same language dynamics discussed below. One reason for keeping much of the story is that Ogden sees this translation as useful for "the international reader, no less than for English boys and girls."[113]

By approaching the translation as a means of correcting Poe's errors, Ogden uses facts to compensate for the insignificant effect of the Basic translation. The addition of symbols in scientific notation is more than just a means of dealing with a limited vocabulary; it appeals to another symbolic universal language in order to make a fictional work more accurate. This conception of an "accurate fiction" resembles the anomaly of creating an "unmagical" language: to make language purely instrumental is to neglect its inherently rhetorical character just as introducing scientific accuracy to Poe's story neglects its own fictionality. Ogden operates on the premise that language functions like the cryptographic method used in the story: translating a code into a "real thing" is like transforming form into substance, or in the case of Basic English demystifying "magical" words into an instrumental language brings us closer to seeing words as things.

In his effort at "correcting" Poe, Ogden shares with Palmer the belief that the American writer's value is in the deficiency of his language and arguments that allows for their editing to be seen as improving his text by modernizing it. Because they wanted to foreground the vocabulary, their adaptations focused on the words while keeping the different narrative voices and plot mostly intact. In contrast, West's New Method version levels the narrative voices into a singular, neutral voice and drastically reworks the plot. The different point of emphasis can be seen in his retention of the original title, "The Gold Bug." Most likely he kept "bug" because it appears among the first 5,000 words in the Thorndike word list. He also rarely changed titles to fit his word list, usually adding the title-word as a "new word." Suiting its colonial context, West's version aligns more with the traditional abridged colonial readers with the partial re-telling of the story in only nine pages of text (one page is dedicated to an illustration). The New Method version follows through on West's advice in *Bilingualism* for creating readers by reducing "local colour" and conveying a "strong plot." As a result, the plot focuses on the main events—finding the bug, drawing the picture, digging for the treasure, and recounting the process of discovery. The last part is narrated by Legrand in an active voice without the self-conscious digressions that make Poe's version a long-winded conclusion. This fits with both of West's principles in that it helps maintain a "strong plot" and, more importantly, reduces "local colour" for a foreign readership.

In all three cases, it is more than just the vocabulary that is revised but also the figure of Poe, the status of the work, and its purpose as a work of fiction. Poe's popular status as an American writer of genre fiction makes him amenable to such "improvements" that would not necessarily be stated for revisions of more canonical writers. The story itself changes in each version. In Palmer's case it presents a pedagogical example of bad style; for Ogden, it is a rational text that is improved by correcting the scientific references; for West, it is an adventure story in the colonial tradition of Rider Haggard. All of these adaptations of Poe seek to impose their own auxiliary language as dominant over the original author and his story. Although Palmer's version is the only one that presents both texts on opposing pages, all of them signal that the auxiliary is imposed over a non-auxiliary "other." Like the mother tongue or minor nationalist language that the word lists cannibalize and are defined against, the original story provides the basis for the simplification and is excluded from it at the same time. This supplemental relationship is a contradiction at the center of any simplified text that seeks to impose an auxiliary language over original prose. The site where this contradiction is most apparent in "The Gold Bug" is in the treatment of Jupiter, Legrand's servant, and the rendering of his vernacular.

Translating Jupiter

In addition to the title, the other area in which the three adaptations differ the most strongly is in their depiction of Jupiter, Legrand's servant. As Poe critics have observed, the three characters are marked by distinctive speech habits and vocabulary: for instance, the language of the unnamed narrator, who lives in Charleston, reflects his social position as an urban elite, much as the refined French-English speech of the main character, Legrand, reflects his upbringing as a member of a plantation family in Louisiana with Huguenot ancestry.[114] Yet he is now an impoverished eccentric living on Sullivan's Island, just a few miles off of Charleston's coast, with his Black servant, Jupiter. A former slave who has remained with Legrand out of loyalty, Jupiter speaks a controversial form of African-American vernacular that critics have identified as anything from a minstrelsy stereotype to "a believable Gullah speaker," a creole spoken by Blacks on the coastal islands of South Carolina and Georgia.[115]

Poe helped to promote the latter interpretation by drawing attention to the authenticity of Jupiter's characterization in his anonymous reviews of the story, where he wrote: "The negro is a perfect picture. He is drawn accurately—no feature overshaded, or distorted. Most of such delineations are caricatures."[116] Yet Toni Morrison criticizes Poe's depiction for its use of "eye dialect" (e.g., "nose" for "knows") and for Jupiter's ignorance, which associates him with minstrelsy.[117] Her claim is supported by one linguist, quoted by the Poe critic Liliane Weissberg, who argues that Jupiter uses "such vocables as might have been used by a black sailor on an English ship a hundred years ago, or on the minstrel stage, but were never current on the South Carolina coast." Weissberg concludes that "Jupiter's dialect designates him as different, but it does not ground its speaker in a specific geographic and cultural setting."[118] Thus, it might be most helpful not to think of his speech as representing either a race or a place but cultural expectations about those two things. Weissberg distinguishes between the racism in Jupiter's speech and the fact that Poe creates an African-American character with more freedom of speech than was found in conventional representations. It is here that an auxiliary English interpretation differs from the standard interpretation followed by Morrison and Weissberg. For instance, what happens to the language dynamics once Jupiter's speech is rendered without its dialect markers in simplified English?

This is not to deny the significance of those markers. In fact, one point that becomes clear in the simplified versions is how important Jupiter's dialect is for the story. Jupiter commits malapropisms such as "tin" for "antennae" and "syphon" for "cipher," and, perhaps most significantly, has colorful figurative language such as referring to the bug as "gold." Poe critic Michael Williams observes that Jupiter's speech is limited by admitting only a single reference for a word or sound. For instance, the "tin/antennae" error suggests that he "believes the middle syllable has only one referent." Similarly, Williams argues that Jupiter's misunderstanding of "cause" as "claws" or translating "message" into the dialect "pissel" (for epistle) indicates that he is limited to a naive conception of names, sounds, and their single referents. This also accounts for his mistake with his left and right hands, which occurs when he is dropping the bug through the eye of the skull because, for Williams, "such a linguistic practice also inhibits abstraction."[119] Williams's description of Jupiter's language as naive suits the perspective that Palmer, Ogden, and West had toward all vernacular "mother tongues" that are opposed to global auxiliary forms, which suggests the problems that it poses for their adaptations, particularly Palmer's.

My analysis will focus mainly on Palmer because he discusses it specifically in his *Memorandum on Grading and Simplifying Literary Material* where he advises that any story that has a "considerable quantity of dialect" that is also "essential to the enjoyment of the text" is not suitable for simplification.[120] Because Jupiter provides a quantity of dialect and is essential to the overall story, it is worth wondering why Palmer selected this particular Poe story. He claims it was because of Poe's worldwide celebrity and the value of using a suspenseful story that keeps the reader involved until the end. "A Tell-Tale Heart" or many other Poe stories, however, would have suited these requirements as well, if not better, and did not have any of the drawbacks associated with correcting the story's extensive vernacular. That is, unless one considers performing the rectification of vernacular as integral to the Reader's overall purpose. For these reasons, I believe that Jupiter presented an opportunity for Palmer to more fully demonstrate the strength of his method for simplification. Because the vernacular appears on the opposite side of the page in the IRET version and because the speech is rendered phonetically as eye-dialect, its deviation from Standard English is clearly evident even for a foreign reader, and, as a result, its rectification can be more apparent and particularly suited to his suggested model of "literary criticism."

Palmer addresses Jupiter's speech in a brief section in the *Memorandum* titled "The Rectification of Dialect": "In the simplifying of *The Gold Bug* the negro talk of Jupiter was recast in intelligible English. We may note here that all this negro dialect *necessarily disappears* in the French translation."[121] Nowhere else does Palmer refer to the practice of using a translation as a basis for the simplification (though the French translation is implied in the choice of "beetle," which resembles the French use of "*Scarabée*"). Palmer does not claim that the simplification followed the French translation, but rather cites it to justify his "rectification." As Ineke Wallaert argues, translators reveal an "ideological stance" in the way that they choose to translate or not translate literary sociolects.[122] By referring positively to the way that Jupiter's dialect disappears, Palmer could be arguing for the "necessary disappearance" of all non-auxiliary language forms.

It is no surprise that Palmer would refer to the French translation. Palmer came from a family of Francophiles; his father received a doctorate in French and sent Palmer to live in France after secondary school. Because of his fluency, Palmer would have been familiar with French translations of Poe who was an important author for nineteenth-century French writers. Clayton McKee has noted the nineteenth-century French translations of Poe's story differed in how they treated Jupiter's speech depending on their audiences.[123] The anonymous translation for *Le Magasin de demoiselles* was "intended to educate young, bourgeoisie French women," and therefore it standardizes Jupiter's speech and condenses the dialogue into narrative that minimizes not only his speech difference but his impact as a character.[124] In a way similar to what West does in his New Method adaptation.[125] Palmer was, however, most likely referring to Baudelaire's 1856 translation of Poe's story in *Histoire Extraordinaires*. Baudelaire sought a "*traduction positive*"—a faithful translation—in contrast to the "free" translations of other Poe stories by his contemporaries.[126] According to Léger, Baudelaire was using "positive" to refer to "interested" or "utility,"[127] a sensibility that is shared by these simplified versions. As part of this, Baudelaire avoided using archaisms or slang in order to create a clean, readable version, and like West, he sought to downplay its American context.[128] And, like Ogden and Palmer's boasts about their editorial decisions with Poe's style, Baudelaire saw his translation as improving upon the English original. Yet despite these convergences between the French translation and the English simplifications, it is not exactly the case that the negro dialect "necessarily disappears," as Palmer puts it, in Baudelaire's translation.

Palmer's phrase suggests that Baudelaire removed Jupiter's speech without much thought, yet in fact Baudelaire devotes two footnotes to the problem of rendering Jupiter's speech. The longest is the footnote that appears following Jupiter's "antennae/tin" error where Baudelaire explains that Jupiter's comment is an untranslatable pun (*"Calembour intraduisible"*) and that there is no adequate French equivalent for Jupiter's *"patois anglais."* He explains that it could not be rendered in *"le patois nègre français"* any more than Breton can be used as an equivalent for Irish Gaelic. It is not clear what he is referring to as *"le patois nègre français"* given there was no literary equivalent at the time, according to Waellert and McKee. Although this is in keeping with the belief in the impossibility of translation, Baudelaire does raise another option of reconfiguring the spelling of the words as Balzac has done in his *"orthographes figuratives,"* or creative spellings. He decides against it, however, because it would make the story comical. For our purposes here, it is important to note that Baudelaire's final rendering of Jupiter in normative French speech comes about by default, due to a perceived lack of choice, and that Jupiter's vernacular proved a more complicated question of culture and translation for Baudelaire than Palmer suggests.

Aside from the vernacular, Palmer's simplified version alludes to Jupiter's different status as reinforced by his speech. When he is first introduced in the story, Palmer retains the original sentence except for changing "Massa" to "Master" yet including the former in a parenthetical explanation: "He always refused to abandon what he considered his right to attend his 'Master Will' (whom in his negro speech he called 'Massa Will')." Following this explication, Palmer chooses to keep having Jupiter refer to "Massa Will."[129]

In contrast, A. P. Rossiter, in the Basic English version, changes "Massa" to "Master" throughout. Notably, both replace Jupiter's reference to himself as a "nigger," with "negro." Rossiter also removes the pun on "tin" and "antennae," neither of which fits in the Basic vocabulary. But like Palmer, Rossiter retains almost the entire plot including the interactions between Legrand and Jupiter. As a result, the politics of these adaptations change from questions of linguistic standardization to those of linguistic distribution. It is no longer the *use* of Standard English that distinguishes the characters but rather their ability to manage and control their speech. When seen in terms of the distribution of speech acts, Jupiter's character does not change by being rendered into Plain or Basic English.

In his post-structuralist reading, Williams argues that the three characters are distinguished by their relationship to language. Where Jupiter is limited, as noted previously, and the narrator mired in received language (and opinions), it is Legrand's skepticism about language that distinguishes him as the hero of the tale. In this way, Jupiter plays an important role in the first half of "The Gold Bug" as a motivator to the plot and as an intermediary between the narrator and Legrand. Beyond this role in the plot, however, in a story with three characters whose characterization depends largely upon their relation to language, Jupiter also acts as a supplement to the other characters' modes of expression. In Poe's story, this comes through in his vernacular, which has to be interpreted by the two other White characters. Their ability to decipher Jupiter's speech foreshadows Legrand's interpretation of Kidd's code later in the story.

When the vernacular is removed, however, the difference among the characters in terms of their use of language remains. The narrator possesses and controls language for most of the story until Legrand takes over with the concluding monologue. The narrator's speech mimics an observer's distance from the eccentric Legrand that, as critics have noted, betrays a difference in class. He controls speech yet uses cliché and often appears incapable of interpreting either Jupiter's speech or Legrand's behavior. In contrast, Legrand speaks either in excited bursts or, more often, broods silently in a manner that suggests the withholding of speech rather than its lack. Between these two extremes is the verbose figure of Jupiter, who possesses but does not control language. He has neither the luxury of cliché nor the self-control to remain silent. But it is precisely this negative role that is needed for the plot to take place. It requires his "silly words" about the bug being "gold," his puns on "tin/antennae," and misunderstanding of abstractions such as left and right to create the suspenseful plot. What is created, therefore, is not a relationship of standard to vernacular Englishes but a hierarchy of speech positions within the story that mimics the relation between Poe's variety of Englishes and their adaptation into these auxiliary forms.

In this way, Jupiter is distinguished as much by his role in the story's linguistic hierarchy than by the nonstandard orthography of his speech. This can be seen in the confusing dialogue he has with the narrator when he comes to deliver Legrand's letter. Although already noted for its comical malapropisms and misunderstandings, as well as Jupiter's threat to beat his master, this scene illustrates the story's initial language politics insofar as Jupiter acts as an intermediary between the narrator's conventional urban perspective and Legrand's feigned madness. Yet more than just Jupiter's vernacular leads to the miscommunication between the narrator and Jupiter in this scene; rather, it is Legrand's silence, his refusal to speak, at least to Jupiter, that causes the confusion. The fact that this is not a sign of madness and more about asserting Legrand's control over speech comes through in the fact that Legrand's letter demonstrates his controlled and measured use of language against Jupiter's excitable nature (i.e., "old Jup annoys me").[130] This hierarchy of speech positions might be seen to take an absurd turn if one were to also include the dog, "the large Newfoundland"[131] who accompanies them on their treasure hunting expedition and appears to understand only Jupiter's speech and even to have its own "speech" controlled by Jupiter.

Although Palmer and Rossiter retain the latent master-slave relations from the original, West omits Legrand's plantation background, deracinates the former slave woman who helps Legrand, and removes many of the scenes that humiliate Jupiter either directly or indirectly. For example, Jupiter's "silly words" in Poe stay "silly" in Palmer and are made "foolish" in Basic, but are left out entirely in the New Method version. He is introduced as an "old African man" and, though the narrator refers to Legrand as Jupiter's master, it omits any dialogue where Jupiter himself refers to Legrand as "Master Will." In addition, the references to his violent nature—threatening to whip Legrand and silencing the dog—are removed. West does retain the mistake that is crucial to the plot, where Jupiter confuses his right and left, yet this is simply stated, without the consequence of Legrand's insults; rather, he appears supportive: "Look man—this is your left eye. We must try again!"[132] The treatment of Jupiter changes how we see Legrand's character as well; instead of Poe's unstable character, we encounter a rational leader of men, an ideal image of the colonizer as an intelligent and benevolent master. This reflects the ways in which West's experiences in Bengal made him sensitive to scrutiny for imperialist bias. West anticipates this criticism in the disclaimer on the copyright page of all the New Method Readers, including this one: "Nothing is included in this book which is unintelligible or offensive to any foreign child." Although the pedagogical word lists account for its intelligibility, it is the latter part of the statement that refers to a Global English ideology that distinguishes between English as a language and as a national, cultural identity. Legrand's status within a sociolinguistic hierarchy, then, does not simply reflect colonial status; rather, Legrand's skepticism about language suggests a model attitude toward language as an auxiliary form within a multilingual context. Unlike Jupiter and the narrator, who remain fixed in race and class-determined "mother tongues," Legrand sees language as an instrument and a commodity. For Palmer, Ogden, and West, he represents an ideal global reader within a multilingual society who manipulates language in such a way that will substantially change (or reinstitute) his social position. Yet skillful decoding requires a code. Having established Legrand as the story's model for a reader, now I want to consider the text that he reads and the significant role of cryptography in the story's allegory of English as an auxiliary language.

Secret Writing: Cryptography and English as Code

In the denouement, Legrand explains how he found the treasure by solving the code left by the pirate Captain Kidd. At this point, his tone becomes more balanced and authoritative than its erratic bursts in the first part of the story. He even takes control of the narration, reducing the narrator to merely asking prompting and unctuous questions. Jupiter falls silent, too, essentially disappearing from the story. However, his place in the story's triangulated language dynamics is replaced by the absent figure of Captain Kidd. Where earlier in the story the two white men derived their status by their differentiation from Jupiter's speech, now Legrand acquires it from his ability to decipher and "master" the clues created by the illiterate Kidd. The foremost reason that Legrand gives for attempting to solve the mystery is that he believed Kidd was a mostly illiterate pirate, a "crude intellect."[133] Legrand's success depends upon Jupiter as well because it was "Jupiter's *silly words*, about the bug being of solid gold"[134] that inspired his search. Although Jupiter's figurative use of language is depicted as a form of uncontrolled speech, it is Legrand's ability to decipher such speech that becomes valuable for deciphering Kidd's code. Legrand states that the "first question" of all "secret writing" is the "*language* of the cipher."[135] Although Spanish and French are primarily associated with their geographical locations, he determines that it is English because of the visual-linguistic pun in the goat's head as a crude signature for "Captain Kidd" that leads him to recognize that it *has* to be English, which is the only language in which the pun would make sense. It seems that Legrand's skill in deciphering code derives in part from a lifetime of listening to—even taking inspiration from—Jupiter's speech. The mastery involved in recognizing the serious meaning in Jupiter's "silly words" and in deciphering Kidd's code constitute status, whereas the production of those codes does not. Both of these relationships—to Kidd and to Jupiter—suggest how these three global auxiliary forms depend upon the local vernaculars that they seek to supplement. Not unlike the word list under Vocabulary Control, English is established as the natural target for all of these illiterate codes, and LeGrand stands in for the professional linguist, philosopher, or statistician with the expertise essential for their comprehension.

A hundred years after Poe helped to make cryptograms a national fad, cryptography took on another significance as a source for machine translation. As Rita Raley and others have documented, the "cryptographic-translation idea," as she calls it, was articulated by Warren Weaver in his writings about machine translation in the 1940s where one could input "a text from a source language and [output] the same text in a target language with the basic meaning preserved."[136] Weaver imagined machine translation as producing a mediating, auxiliary language that was neither an invented language, like Esperanto, nor British Standard English. According to Weaver, the machine translation conception of English was not just as a target language but also as a hidden source for all languages: "When I look at an article in Russian, I say: 'This is really written in English, but it has been coded in some strange symbols. I will now proceed to decode.'"[137] By conceiving of translation as a mode of cryptography, Weaver assumes English as both source and target, much as Kidd's English is the source and target for Legrand to decipher. I discuss Weaver's theories more in the final chapter, but at this point, it is worth noting how the story illustrates the ways in which his conception of language as code was always already integral to Vocabulary Control ideology.

Similarly, this assumption that English might function as an auxiliary language because of its infinite adaptability can be seen in Legrand's assumption that the "secret writing" is *really* English. This rhetoric of decoding and cryptography has an allegory in the fact that the treasure has to be converted from foreign currencies into American money just as linguistic value depends on conversion into English. This is particularly important for auxiliary languages; unlike standard languages whose logic is tied to nationalism, an auxiliary language justifies itself through its efficiency in converting expert knowledge.[138] Legrand's expertise comes from his ability to convert Jupiter's speech and Kidd's code into material, practical form. That is the difference between Jupiter's use of "gold" to describe the bug and Legrand's interpretation of it to refer to real gold. Legrand's skill comes in translating Jupiter and Kidd's metaphors into the language of information.

In addition to its allegorical significance, cryptography also offered Palmer a means to resolve the methodological dispute over word lists that divided the Vocabulary Control movement. In a way that suited Palmer, "The Gold Bug" can be seen as performing the dispute between objective and subjective methods of counting words (notably, deciding in Palmer's favor).[139] This can be seen in the way that Legrand uses a mixture of objective statistics and subjective judgment to decode the cryptograph, just as Palmer recommends. In fact, Legrand's mind resembles a word list in that he intuitively understands language in terms of use frequency both at the level of the letter—identifying "E" as the first part of the code—and at the level of the word—arriving at "the" as the second part of the code. He then relies on his own subjective judgment (in Palmer's sense, not Ogden's) to identify the rest of the words. His method corroborates Palmer's solution to the methodological dilemma facing Vocabulary Control: use objective measures to identify the most instrumental features of the language, and then use subjective judgment to create the final list. Legrand resembles the linguists in that he provides a method to decipher a code, yet, like the Vocabulary Control movement, there are limits insofar as that instrumental language depends upon non-instrumental words and phrases to create meaning.

Legrand encounters these limits when he arrives at the part of the code he has translated as "Bishop's Hostel." By inference, he is able to link it to the name of an old family, "Bessop," yet they owned a plantation, not a hotel. In visiting the site of the old plantation he encounters one of its former slaves, an old Black woman, who helps Legrand identify the spot: "At length one of the most aged of the women said that she had heard of such a place as *Bessop's Castle*, and thought that she could guide me to it, but that it was not a castle, nor a tavern, but a high rock."[140] Just as with Jupiter, an illiterate Black figure lends Legrand assistance in explicating a code that they can decipher but not master. As Weissberg acutely observes, this woman preserves the memory of the landscape that is lost to the white characters.[141] I would add that this memory is preserved through an act of translation, from "Bishop" to "Bessop," from "Hostel" to "Castle," and from "hotel" to "a high rock." The phrase "Bessup's Castle" does not refer to a seat of property or power, which might be associated with the language of Legrand and the narrator, but simply a rock. Legrand needed her to decode the doubled meaning of the rock-as-castle, or, rather, a rock in the shape of a chair, the "devil's seat" mentioned in the cipher. Like Jupiter and Kidd, the old woman contributed to Legrand's success because of her historical memory, which provides a similar function as the vernaculars of Jupiter and Kidd. But in the end, she is forgotten by Legrand, who only requires these illiterate figures to provide him with material: coded words for him to decipher. Like Palmer, Ogden, and West, Legrand's skill is in the art of simplification. He does not produce meaning; he reduces it.

In itself, this "castle" has only an indexical value. It matters because of what can be seen from its peak: the spot in the distance where the treasure is buried. Similarly, the vernaculars of Jupiter, Kidd, and the old woman are, by the terms of the story, worthless as rocks, acting only as supplemental labor for Legrand's "expert knowledge," which consolidates it, literally, into a commodity form. Poe's story replicates this conversion in the way that it mixes linguistic and material dominance by having the recovery of Legrand's lost family fortune, which included owning slaves in Louisiana, depend upon using African American vernaculars: a linguistic dominance over Black tongues used to recover material dominance over Black bodies.

If Legrand figures in this allegory as both the ideal colonial figure and the skillful linguist, what is Jupiter and the old woman but the natives about whom Palmer wrote in his dedication to Lémaire, "nature is a schoolmistress"? "The Gold Beetle" adapts Poe's story into an extended metaphor for the ideology and practices of the Vocabulary Control movement. In the process, it evokes unlikely comparisons between antebellum South Carolina to the Belgian Congo in the 1880s and Tokyo, China, and Bengal in the 1920s and 1930s. Through the figure of Harold Palmer, who created the conditions in which Poe's story became a measure for judging English pedagogical word lists, the fraught racial background of Poe's American story evokes the symmetry of codes and Black labor in the early word lists created by Charles Lemaire in the Congo. However unusual it may seem, such a reading comes from the transnational circulation of "The Gold Bug" within a late imperial system that was in the process of transforming into a new global order and inventing new global codes.

Notes

1 Palmer, "The History and Present State of the Movement towards Vocabulary Control," in Smith, *Pioneers of ELT*, vol. 5, 377.
2 See *Collected Writings of Sanki Ichikawa*. The Institute for Research in Language Teaching (Tokyo: Kaitakusha, 1966).
3 Ibid.
4 Leonhard Frank, *Carl and Anna*, translated by L. W. Lockhart (London: Kegan Paul & Company, 1930).
5 Robert Phillipson, *Linguistic Imperialism*, 109.
6 Smith questions whether it was indeed the first Reader published in the series; see Smith, "Introduction," *Pioneers of ELT*, vol. III: xvi.

7   Harold Palmer, *The Grading and Simplifying of Literary Material: A Memorandum*, in Smith, *Pioneers of ELT*, vol. 5 (London: Routledge, 2003), 262. Hereafter Palmer, *Memorandum*.
8   Harold Palmer, *The Gold Beetle, This being the simplified version by Harold E. Palmer of The Gold Bug by Edgar Allan Poe*, vol. 1 (Tokyo: Institute for Research in English Teaching, 1932); A. P. Rossiter, *The Gold Insect. Being the "Gold Bug" Put into Basic English. By A. P. Rossiter*. Preface by C. K. Ogden (London: Kegan Paul, 1932); Michael West, "The Gold Bug," in *Tales of Mystery and Imagination: Edgar Allan Poe*, simplified by Roland John and Michael West, Longman Classics Stage 4 (London: Longman, 1988), 15–27.
9   Priya Joshi, *In Another Country: Colonialism, Culture, and the English Novel in India* (New York: Columbia University Press, 2002), 38.
10 Robert Fraser, 143. Also, see table in Joshi, *In Another Country*, 40.
11 Quoted in J. B. Harrison, "English as a University Subject in India and England: Calcutta, Allahabad, Benaras, London, Cambridge and Oxford," in *The Transmission of Knowledge in South Asia: Essays on Education, Religion, History and Politics*, edited by Nigel Crook (Delhi: Oxford University Press, 1996), 166.
12 Joshi, *In Another Country*, 73.
13 Ibid., 91.
14 On Oxford University Press, see Chatterjee, *Empires of the Mind*; unfortunately our understanding of this history is limited due to the fact that Longman's Indian archives were lost in 1941 during the bombing of London.
15 Joshi, *In Another Country*, 108.
16 Ibid., 123.
17 Quoted in Chatterjee, 329.
18 Ibid., 330.
19 West, *Bilingualism*, 242. I introduce and discuss West's *Bilingualism* thoroughly in chapter 2.
20 Ibid., 243.
21 Ibid.
22 See table on p. 244.
23 Ibid., 245.
24 On British anxiety over the practice of cramming for Civil Service Exams, see Sanjay Seth, *Subject Lessons: The Western Education of Colonial India* (Durham, NC: Duke University Press, 2007).
25 Quoted in *Bilingualism*, 268, n. 1.
26 Ibid., 268.
27 Ibid.
28 See Tapti Roy, "Disciplining the Printed Text: Colonial and Nationalist Surveillance of Bengali Literature," in *Texts of Power: Emerging Disciplines in Colonial Bengal*, edited by Partha Chatterjee (Minneapolis: University of Minnesota Press, 1995), 30–62.

29 Antoinette Burton and Isabel Hofmyer, eds., *Ten Books That Shaped the British Empire: Creating an Imperial Commons* (Durham, NC: Duke University Press, 2014), 1. Introduction, 1.

30 In addition to Seth, *Subject Lessons*, see the essays in Ali and Sengupta, *Knowledge Production*.

31 Robert Fraser, "School Readers in the Empire and the Creation of Postcolonial Taste," in *Books with Borders The Cross-National Dimension in Print Culture*, vol. 1, edited by Robert Fraser and Mary Hammond (London: Palgrave, 2008), 92.

32 Carl Campbell, "Education and Black Consciousness: The Amazing Captain J. O. Cutteridge in Trinidad and Tabago, 1921–42," *The Journal of Caribbean History* 18, no.1 (May 1983): 40.

33 Ibid., 42.

34 Ibid., 45. Campbell and Fraser both offer revisionist accounts of Cutteridge that seek to redeem his Readers and textbooks from this criticism arguing that the fault mainly lays with those middle-class Trinidadians who had "internalized a great deal of the values of colonial English" (Campbell, 60).

35 See C. S. Srinivasachari, "Bilingualism as the Basis of Education" in *The Educational Review* (Madras: S. V. & Co., 1928), 1–6.

36 Satadru Sen, "A Juvenile Periphery: The Geographies of Literary Childhood in Colonial Bengal," *Journal of Colonialism and Colonial History* 5, no. 1 (2004). Project MUSE, n.p. doi:10.1353/cch.2004.0039.

37 See Jed Esty, *Unseasonable Youth: Modernism, Colonialism, and the Fiction of Development* (Oxford: Oxford University Press, 2012) and Joseph Slaughter, *Human Rights, Incorporated: The World Novel, Narrative Form, and International Law* (New York: Fordham, 2007).

38 Sir Walter Scott, *Ivanhoe* (New York: Barnes and Noble, 2005), 18.

39 Ibid., xix.

40 Ibid., 7.

41 Ibid., 240.

42 Walter Scott and Michael West, *New Method Readers Ivanhoe* (London: Longman and Greens), 91.

43 Ibid., 92.

44 Ibid., 93.

45 Ibid., 95.

46 Ibid., 96.

47 Ibid., 97.

48 Ibid., 138.

49 This is discussed at length in chapter 2 in relation to the use of the term in Ogden and Richards's *Meaning of Meaning*.

50 Howatt, *History of ELT* (2004), 283.

51 West, *Bilingualism*, 91.

52 Kumar, *The Political Agenda of Education*, 64.
53 Ibid., 65.
54 Ibid., 67.
55 *New Method Reader VI* reprint (Bombay: Orient Longmans, 1950), 2.
56 Ibid., 21.
57 Ibid., 36.
58 Ibid., 88.
59 Ibid., 89.
60 Ibid.
61 See Gordin, *Scientific Babel*; Liu, *The Freudian Robot*; Quigley, *Modernist Fiction and Vagueness*.
62 For this and other examples of non-expert translations, see Bongers, *History and Principles*, 124; for Chinese parodies of Basic by Lin Yutang, see Huang, "Chinglish," 93.
63 Ogden, *Basic English*, 17.
64 Margie Berns, editor. *Concise Encyclopedia of Applied Linguistic*s (Amsterdam: Elsevier, 2010), 7.
65 According to Dora Russell and others, Ogden's relations with other people appear to be complicated; see Dora Russell, "My Friend Ogden," in *C. K. Ogden: A Collective Memoir*, 86. For one thing, he liked to keep his friends separate and would be angered if he heard that they knew one another. A bachelor, Ogden was known to cut female friends from his life once they were married. For an arresting account of the bewildering experience of being a female friend of Ogden's see Marjorie Todd, "An Improbable Friendship," in *C. K. Ogden: A Collective Memoir*, 110–21.
66 Carly S. Woods, *Debating Women: Gender, Education, and Spaces for Argument, 1835-1945*. Lockhart also wrote several articles for the *New York Times* both making her case about co-education and about her experiences in the United States. Woods lists articles by Lockhart including "American Ideas that Assail the Briton" NYT, May 11, 1930; "Women's Colleges: A Striking Contrast," NYT, May 5, 1929; "An English College Girl Studies Ours," NYT, May 19, 1929. "The Professional Woman: A Contrast," NYT, June 2, 1929.
67 Ibid.
68 Leonhard Frank, *Carl and Anna*, translated by Cyrus Brooks (New York, London: G. P. Putnam's and Sons, 1930).
69 Brian Murdoch, "War, Identity, Truth and Love: Leonhard Frank's *Karl Und Anna*," *Forum for Modern Language Studies* 37, no. 1 (2002): 49.
70 C. K. Ogden, Introduction to Leonhard Frank, *Carl and Anna*, translated into Basic English by L. W. Lockhart, second edition (London: Kegan Paul, Trench, Trubner & Co., Ltd., 1933), 5.
71 Ogden, Introduction, 7.
72 Ibid.

73 Ibid.
74 Ibid.
75 On the interpretation of Frank's novella as a work of war literature, see Murdoch, *Karl und Anna*, 57–60.
76 L. W. Lockhart, *The Basic Way Reading Books*, Book One (London: Evans Bros. Ltd.), 4.
77 Lockhart, "About this Book," *The Basic Way*, Book One, 4.
78 Lockhart, *The Basic Way*, Book One, 45.
79 Ibid., 33.
80 Ibid., 45.
81 Ibid., 44.
82 Ibid., 4.
83 Lockhart, *The Basic Way Reading Books*, Book Two (London: Evan Bros. Ltd.), 89.
84 Ibid., 92.
85 Even the essay on "play" offers an ethnographic account of games that emphasizes their "effect of training the muscles or senses" (Ibid., 78).
86 Ibid., 93.
87 Ibid., 101.
88 Palmer, *Memorandum*, 306.
89 Ibid., 310.
90 Ibid.
91 Ibid.
92 Ibid., 311.
93 Ibid., 312.
94 Ibid.
95 Ibid., 313.
96 Ibid., 313–14.
97 Palmer, *Gold Beetle*, vii.
98 Palmer, *Memorandum*, 272.
99 Ibid.
100 Poe, *Gold Beetle*, viii. Also, see Palmer, *Memorandum*, 333, where he elaborates on this point.
101 Palmer, *Memorandum*, 312.
102 IRET, *The Gold-Beetle*, 21, 30, 33.
103 Ibid., 13.
104 M. A. K. Halliday, "Written Language, Standard Language, Global Language," in *The Handbook of World Englishes*, edited by Braj B. Kachru, Yamuna Kachru, and Cecil L. Nelson (London: Blackwell, 2006), 354.
105 Rossiter, *The Gold Insect*, 62, n. 1.
106 Poe, "Gold Bug," 832.

107 Rossiter, *Gold Insect*, 62.
108 Ibid., 62, n. 1.
109 Ibid., 68, n. 1.
110 Ibid., 11–13.
111 Ibid.
112 Ibid.
113 Ibid., 7.
114 On language politics in "The Gold Bug," see Jennifer Dilalla Toner, "The 'Remarkable Effect' of 'Silly Words': Dialect and Signature in 'The Gold-Bug,'" *Arizona Quarterly* 49, no. 1 (1993): 1–20; Michael Williams, "'The Language of the Cipher': Interpretation in 'The Gold Bug,'" *American Literature* 53, no. 4 (1982): 646–60.
115 Quoted in Liliane Weissberg, "Black, White, Gold," in *Romancing the Shadow: Poe and Race*, edited by J. Gerald Kennedy and Liliane Weissberg (Oxford: Oxford University Press, 2001), 139.
116 Quoted in Terence Whalen, "Average Racism: Poe, Slavery, and the Wages of Literary Nationalism," in *Romancing the Shadow: Poe and Race*, edited by J. Gerald Kennedy and Liliane Weissberg (Oxford: Oxford University Press, 2001), 31.
117 Toni Morrison, *Playing in the Dark: Whiteness and the Literary Imagination* (Cambridge: Harvard University Press, 1992), 13.
118 Weissberg, "Black, White, Gold," 139–40.
119 Williams, "The Language of the Cipher," 650.
120 Palmer, *Memorandum*, 328.
121 Palmer, *Memorandum*. Emphasis mine.
122 Ineke Wallaert, "The Translation of Sociolects: A Paradigm of Ideological Issues in Translation?" in *Language across Boundaries*, edited by Janet Cotterill and Anne Ife (New York: Continuum, 2001), 171. For more on this problem of an "adequate equivalent patois" as well as how nineteenth-century French translations differ in their treatment of Jupiter's dialect, see Clayton Tyler McKee, "Translation and Audience: Edgar Allan Poe's 'The Gold Bug,'" *International Journal of Comparative Literature and Translation Studies* 3, no. 4 (2017): 1–10.
123 McKee, "Translation and Audience," 2.
124 Ibid., 4.
125 Ibid.
126 The phrase "*traduction positive*" is quoted in Benoit Léger, "*Traduction négative et traduction littérale: les traducteurs de Poe en 1857*," *Études françaises* 432 (2007): 97.
127 Léger, "*Traduction négative*," 98.
128 Alistair Rolls and Clara Sitbon, "*Traduit de l'américain*' from Poe to the *Série Noire*: Baudelaire's Greatest Hoax?" *Modern and Contemporary France* 21.1 (2013): 43.
129 Palmer, *Gold Beetle*, 3, 5, 9.

130 Edgar Allan Poe, "The Gold Bug," in *Collected Works of Edgar Allan Poe, Tales and Sketches, 1843–1849*, edited by Thomas Ollive Mabbott, vol. 3 (Cambridge: Harvard University Press, 1978), 813.
131 Poe, "The Gold Bug," 809.
132 West, *The Gold Bug*, 20.
133 Poe, "The Gold Bug," 835.
134 Ibid., Italics added.
135 Ibid., Italics in original.
136 Rita Raley, "Machine Translation and Global English," *The Yale Journal of Criticism* 16, no. 2 (2003): 291. Also, see Liu, *Freudian Robot*, 86–7.
137 Quoted in Raley, "Machine Translation and Global English," 295.
138 This view of English as "a virtual language" for "specialist communication" is one of the definitions of Global English given by James, "Theorising English and Globalisation," 84–5.
139 For other cultural associations with Legrand's methods of deduction, see Shawn Rosenheim, *The Cryptographic Imagination: Secret Writing from Edgar Poe to the Internet* (Baltimore: Johns Hopkins University Press, 1997).
140 Poe, "The Gold Bug," 841.
141 Weissberg, "Black, White, Gold," 140.

Part II

Making English

4

Ogden Agonistes: Basic's Critics and the Problem of World English

Introduction

For most of Part I of this book, "Managing English," I have sought to show the commonalities that Basic English shares with Palmer and West because of their interest in vocabulary control and use of Simplified Readers as methods of instruction. This focus on these shared qualities should not obscure the significant differences in their purposes and intentions. As Ogden and Richards would insist, Basic was developed as an international language system, not a simplified form of English to be used in teaching. The philosophical concerns expressed by Palmer over "the nature of the word" or the pragmatic questions by West on the amount of words that can be learned by a Bengali child are disciplinary concerns for language teachers, not philosophers.[1] However, if theoretically it is a category mistake to compare their language systems, it is not a mistake pragmatically. That is, in order for Basic to succeed as an IAL that uses the English language as its corpus, then it was competing in the same terrain as other methods of teaching English just as it is competing with Esperanto and Novial. It is not that Ogden and Richards were unaware of the ELT profession. Neither Ogden nor Richards masked their contempt of traditional language teaching methods nor of the attempts by their contemporaries to update it on scientific grounds. In other words, that there was a controversy over Basic English should not be a surprise given the instability of the ELT market, the relatively new discipline of applied linguistics, and the status and publicity surrounding Basic.[2]

For most histories of ELT, this controversy is noted for its impact on the Carnegie Conference but is otherwise dismissed as a regrettable distraction because of the way it devolved from intellectual concerns into self-interested, litigious, and *ad hominem* attacks. When I first learned of Basic's role as a disruptor of ELT and the instigator of the Carnegie Conference, I felt similarly, that it was an intriguing side-note of intellectual history, though not substantive. As a non-linguist, I was intrigued by Basic's role as an instance where a modernist experiment, what Howatt aptly calls "a work of intellectual art," had an impact on real-world events in a way that other modernist linguistic experiments like *Finnegans Wake* or the *Cantos* did not. Upon further exploration, I found that this controversy contains within it a neglected history of World English that includes forgotten figures such as key female linguists Elaine Swenson and Janet Rankin Aiken, and overlooked debates about the status of English as an international language that resonate with later criticism of Global English. As histories of ELT have noted, the Carnegie Conference was inspired by the rise of Basic, but that event depended upon the controversy that preceded it in order to legitimate the concept of English as a world language that it would explore.

Basic English came to an official end with Ogden's death in 1959, though its real impact declined after the Second World War when its main supporter, Winston Churchill, lost the 1945 elections. However, it could be argued that Basic English's *annus horribilis* was in 1934 when the Columbia linguist Janet Rankin Aiken published two critical essays (the first was published in December 1933), Michael West and Elaine Swenson published *A Critical Examination of Basic English*, West published his essay on the problems with World English, and he began organizing the Carnegie Conference which first met in October of that year. Ogden spent this year in a defensive position: writing a long, vituperative response to West and Swenson, the 300-page *Counter-Offensive*, in just a few months, and, under his pseudonym of Adelyn Moore, an article criticizing West's *New Method Dictionary* titled "How Not to Write a Dictionary." Ogden believed he was responding to a concerted effort by the ELT profession, supported by the Carnegie Corporation, to destroy him and his language system. He threatened to sue individuals for libel, he wrote pleading and condemnatory letters to the Carnegie Corporation and he tried to influence the British Colonial Office to stop the conference from taking place.

Its legacy has played out differently depending on one's perspective. For ELT historians such as Howatt, it was the definitive blow in the long battle between amateur linguists and language teaching professionals. While he is critical of West for changing his position toward Basic from respectful to critical, he mostly faults Ogden for "losing his temper" and "protesting too much": "His passionate and over-elaborate defence of his system contrasts rather badly with West's heavily studied restraint."[3] For acolytes of Ogden's Basic English, it was a cautionary tale of what happens when a philosopher-king wanders into a cutthroat commercial marketplace. Reflecting back on the controversy from the late twentieth century,

W. Terrence Gordon, Ogden's editor, describes West's criticism as full of errors and misunderstandings and Ogden's friend, J. L. R. Anderson, snobbishly dismisses the criticism as a case of "academic trade unionism."[4] I. A. Richards remained outside the controversy and reflected later that it caused irreparable harm to Ogden because of his obsession with responding personally to all of the criticism. He wondered about this neglect in a short essay written decades later, "Commentary on Ogden's Counter-Offensive": "What surprised me then and has puzzled me through four following decades is that no capable inquirer has yet made a detached, evidenced study of the issues between Ogden and those who then attacked Basic English."[5] While I would not dare claim to be such a "capable inquirer," this is such a study of the issues, even though my interests here are not the defense of Basic that Richards might have desired.

In the context of this study, the controversy over Basic is important for understanding the making of World English. As a disruptive force, Basic pushed the two most influential ELT practitioners, West and Palmer, to work toward the concept of World English, and to do so together instead of as rivals. This leads to other collaborations for West, with Swenson, and with the entire collective gathered at the Carnegie Conferences. For all of their criticisms of Ogden's system, his antagonists acknowledge the power of his arguments on the necessity of a world language and for it being English rather than an invented language. It was through Basic that they focused their own simplified Englishes: West's Definition Dictionary, IRET's 1,000 word "Plain English," Aiken's "Little English," "Swenson's English," the Faucett-Maki and Thorndike lists. All of these versions were in some way addressed and consolidated at the Carnegie Conference. As a key plot point in the historical narrative of ELT and the development of Global English in the latter half of the century, the role of Basic cannot be understated. However, there is another narrative that runs under the surface that consists of misunderstandings, threatening letters, and libelous accusations. If the surface narrative describes the means of making World English as a product that can be taught, this sub-narrative describes the making of World English as a concept. It was through this contentious process that World English was legitimated, validated, and consolidated.

As Howatt and Richards both observe, the controversy was mostly due to Ogden's over-reaction to what might be seen today as a form of peer review. In this sense, the controversy foreshadows the changes occurring in mid-century academia as it transitions from a tradition of *belles lettres* to forms of professionalism based on scientific standards.[6] By contrast, Ogden's behavior coheres with the debate tradition at Cambridge in which he and Lockhart were both trained. It also was a powerful means of control. Fear of his reaction, combined with his influence in the UK among publishers, foundations, educational institutions, journalists, and the colonial office, profoundly shaped the direction of the consensus around a version of deterritorialized English.

It might for this reason that the initial criticism of Basic English came from two female linguists in the United States: Janet Rankin Aiken at Columbia University and Elaine Swenson at New York University. As Americans and especially as female linguists, they were not only well outside Ogden's sphere of influence, their criticism of him as females appears to have been particularly galling, and as we will see, he devotes an appendix to attack each of them personally in his *Counter-Offensive*. This episode is indicative of the role of women in linguistics in the pre-war academy and their influence within Auxiliary language movements due to their exclusion from other spheres. In this chapter, I situate Aiken's influential criticism of Basic English within her own "organicist" language theories influenced by her mother, Jean Sherwood Rankin, and the influential linguist, Louise Pound (the first female PhD in linguistics in America). Like Aiken, Swenson first tried to implement Basic English before turning to criticize it, in her case, along with Michael West. I view their *Critical Examination of Basic English* as a manifesto against Basic but also as a working out of the problems of World English that are raised by Aiken and that West engages in his article, "English as a World Language." The chapter concludes with Ogden's parting salvo, his *Counter-Offensive*, a 300-page line-by-line analysis of West and Swenson's *Critical Examination* which he reportedly wrote in only a month. While it was published in 1936, Ogden was already circulating parts of it privately in the summer of 1934 among his supporters and even sending it to the Carnegie Corporation in the hope of stopping the conference from taking place.

Unlike the pedagogical word lists that Palmer and West developed through years of empirical testing in classrooms in Japan and Bengal, Basic English went straight to publication and advertising without ever being tested. The novelty effect of its 850 words led to headlines about Basic English appearing in UK and US newspapers very soon after its publication. As I discuss in Chapter 1, Ogden was not a traditional language scholar, nor did he conceive of Basic as a conventional language pedagogy. He developed Basic to compete with International Auxiliary Languages like Esperanto, Ido, and Novial. To compete, he secured publishing contracts and quickly opened his "Orthological Institutes" in London, South America, and China. Most importantly, he got copyright on the language and its system which he enforced with utmost scrutiny. To the extent that, in the 1940s, when Richards adapted it slightly to use in his *Language through Pictures* series with Christine Gibson, Ogden broke all relations with him and threatened to sue over the right to use the name Basic in its title.[7]

Responding to Basic as someone involved in language education from both the perspectives of colonial education and commercial textbooks, West saw Ogden's invented English as a threat. From his experience as an educator in Bengal, West was aware of how Basic's limited English would be criticized and resisted by colonial elites for whom access to "full English" was considered a political right. And, as the writer of successful English language textbooks, West knew the value of Ogden's contract with Longmans (his own publisher), not to mention the international value of the Cambridge imprimatur.[8] If Basic were to gain prominence as the face of World English, then it would undermine traditional education efforts like his own.

Faucett and the International Turn

Around the time that Basic English appeared in 1930, the field of English language teaching was already transitioning from regionalist to internationalist language teaching models. This was due to a less disruptive figure, the third "pioneer" in English language teaching, Lawrence Faucett, an expatriate American who studied linguistics at the University of Chicago and the University of London, whose research on word lists and pedagogy began to circulate in the late 1920s. Compared to West and Palmer's regional focus in Bengal and Japan, Faucett traveled widely in the late 1920s, studying and practicing language teaching in China, Japan (with Palmer), and writing materials for use in the Philippines, and later, Africa and Turkey.[9] In contrast to the other members in the Vocabulary Control movement, Faucett did not have an orthodox system such as Basic, the Palmer Method, or the New Method. Instead, he adapted and combined elements of all of them as well as the Thorndike and Horn word counts. After trying to collaborate with West on expanding the New Method, he was hired by Oxford University Press to create readers and textbooks based on West's model for use in Africa. Appearing in 1936, Faucett's Oxford series became the most successful and longest-lasting of these interwar language textbooks.

Following—or in some cases, in response to—Basic's universalism and Faucett's international perspective, Palmer and West began to forsake the regionalism and orthodoxies that had defined their methods. As Richard Smith has observed, both men produced works in the 1930s that crossed their divergent methods: Palmer engaging with reading in *On Learning to Read Foreign Languages* (1932), and West becoming more interested in orality in *On Learning to Speak a Foreign Language* (1933) and *New Method Conversations* (1933). More significantly for our purposes, their interests began to extend to language learning in general, not only to the Bengali or Japanese contexts.[10] This is a crucial shift in the history of ELT as it signals the move from teaching English for a specific region to considerations of a mode of teaching that is universally applicable. The principle behind the change is the recognition that there are common aspects to learning English that precede the content-specific forms needed in particular regions. As teaching models, the Palmer Method and New Method were not regional-specific in their emphasis on orality or reading. Principally, the change was evident in their methodologies, which depended so much upon testing in local classrooms; now, their work becomes more theoretical and collaborative as they move professionally into the center. The problem was that Ogden was already there.

As a result, West took part in an effort to discredit Basic English along with Aiken and Swenson. Although the controversy is always described as between West and Ogden, it was Aiken's articles in Louise Pound's journal, *American Speech*, "Basic English and World English," and "International English" that were the first reproaches to Basic. West's article on "English as a World Language" mostly follows upon and repeats much that is already in Aiken's arguments. Although West is listed as the sole author of the *Critical Examination*, West acknowledges that it was Swenson who instigated the project and did most of the statistical work for their first *Bulletin* report on word values. Despite this fact, it is still West who receives authorship credit for the two *Bulletin* reports. As the linguistic historian Julia Falk has noted, very little is known about female linguists during the first part of the twentieth century.[11] One area of study in which they were able to have an effect was in the field of International Auxiliary Languages that was largely situated outside the academy. Though neither Aiken nor Swenson were interested in IALs such as Esperanto, the structural sexism in the discipline and in the university system (they were both lecturers as women at the time were not eligible for tenure) explains in part their early intervention into the field. In order to understand the trajectory of the discourse on world English, it is necessary to delve into Aiken's work.

Aiken's Englishes

An Instructor in English at Columbia University, Dr. Janet Rankin Aiken was a prolific linguist who wrote several accessible grammar textbooks and histories of English from 1929 until her early death in 1944 at only the age of fifty-two. Her first books, *Why English Sounds Change* (1929), *English Present and Past* (1930), and *A New Plan of English Grammar* (1933) synthesized contemporary research on the history and teaching of English for general audiences. In all of her work, up through her books in the 1940s: *The Psychology of English* (1944; with Margaret Bryant) and *Commonsense English* (1940) Aiken argued against purist criticisms of English. Instead, she advocated for a view of English as organic, illogical, and "messy." As she writes in *English Present and Past*:

> And so at the very outset we must reject the ideal of an inherently pure English. We must view our speech, not as a snow-capped peak of perfection unattainable by common humanity, but as a stumbling, aspiring, living, breathing organism, with which to err is and ever has been not only human but normal.[12]

Notably, the foreword for *English Present and Past* was written by her Columbia advisor and then colleague George Philip Krapp, who had attended, along with George Bernard Shaw and Lord Alfred Balfour, the first conference on International English in 1927. Krapp's earlier books, *Modern English* (1909) and *The English Language in America* (1925), similarly argued for a "modern" attitude toward language by rejecting philology and prescriptivism.

Aiken's social and organic view of language also has other, female, sources, such as her mother, Jean Sherwood Rankin, and the linguist Louise Pound. Aiken published both of her essays in Pound's journal, *American Speech*, and she dedicates *English Present and Past* to her mother, "my earliest teacher of English ... whose work has been a constant inspiration." Both of these influences were midwesterners—Jean Rankin was from Minnesota and Wisconsin and Pound was from Nebraska—and both advocated for an organic view of language. In 1906, Jean Rankin published a series of elementary- and intermediate-level textbooks, *Everyday English*. In the Preface, Jean Rankin describes the need for her "different sort of language training"[13] in terms that would be familiar to her daughter twenty-five years later: educating immigrants through a non-prescriptivist view of language: "we are in the transition period from the time when language was taught as science to that better time when it shall be taught as art."[14] Following the Reform movement, Rankin downplays grammar and emphasizes orality first and writing second. Drawing on copious literary examples as a way to convey idiom, figurative language, and diction, Rankin's textbooks presented a view of English as organic and evolving.

These views were shared by Pound. As the first female linguistic professor in America, Pound had to go to Heidelberg, Germany, to receive her doctorate before returning to the United States where she taught at the University of Nebraska-Lincoln for forty years, specializing in folklore and American dialects. Because of her work on American English, no less an authority than H. L. Mencken asked her to serve as editor for his new journal, *American Speech*.[15] The journal defined itself against both traditional philology and modernist structuralism and sought to further scholarship on dialects while also appealing to a general readership. While Pound stepped down as editor in 1933, the year that Aiken's first essay appeared, the journal continued to reflect her positive attitude toward local languages and dialects. In this sense, it makes sense that *American Speech* would publish these essays by Aiken, West, and Swenson that were critical of an abstract, logically planned version of International English such as Basic. A figure like Ogden—a British philosopher of logic advocating a standardized language system—is the contemporary version of the prescriptivist grammarian or professional formalist that Rankin and Pound actively criticized throughout their careers.

Aiken's essay, "'Basic' and World English" appeared in December 1933, while the second, "English as an International Language" appeared in April 1934. While she opens the essay on Basic English by acknowledging Ogden's "pioneer work" in developing a simplified language with international institutes and financial support, Aiken's goal is to criticize the system thoroughly from its formal construction to its institutional presentation arguing that "the present article is an attempt at setting forth the reasons why the world may still look somewhat askance at this simplified English."[16] Among the reasons that she identifies are Ogden's "idiosyncratic" writing style, confusing definitions, and, false word counts. The latter impacts Basic's image built up in its marketing as the simple system of "850 words." Yet, Aiken argues that this only refers to head words; variations on words such as "he," that is, pronouns like "him, his, she, they" are not included in the count. Criticizing the word count is symptomatic of Aiken's underlying message that Ogden is not operating in good faith. In addition to the misrepresentation of the word count, she criticizes his claim that it can be learned quickly by noting the problems with using the panopticon word wheel (she wonders about sentences like "*May let clean key across horse wisely*"). All of these misrepresentations are significant since, as she concludes in a stinging rebuke, Ogden has a copyright on the system and resists any external modifications (some of which she suggests, such as allowing functional shift):

> Aside from its linguistic and pedagogical shortcomings, an objection to Basic is the fact that through copyright it has been made private property. No textbook

may be written, no use or reproduction of the vocabulary may be made, without the permission of the originator of the plan. If ever the system should become internationally current, it is easy to guess what golden returns it would bring the owners of its copyright. An international language should not be copyrighted. It is too big a thing to be made to pay tribute to any individual.[17]

To understand the significance of Aiken's essay, it is useful to recognize that it was one of the first to criticize Basic from a linguistic and institutional perspective. As Aiken notes in her essay, most of the early reviews of Basic were favorable. The criticism it received mainly came from traditional language purists who were precisely the audience that Ogden sought to shock. Aiken's criticism was unique in that it did not argue from a grammarian, Standard English perspective. Conceding that changes to the language are needed for it to be adopted as a mode of international communication, Aiken argues in "English as an International Language" that Basic's problems are similar to those of other proposals for international modes of English. The essay sets out the claims of the necessity for an international language, reviews past and present attempts, presents both cases for and against English as the international language, then compares the value of invented languages to a simplified English, concluding that "An English modified for world use is unquestionably an answer to the world's need for a common linguistic medium."[18] Recognizing English's "inevitable" role as the future international language, Aiken lists its defects and then turns to three simplified English vocabularies: Basic English, Palmer's IRET list of 600 words, and Elaine Swenson's 900-word "Swenson English." While admitting that Basic was the earliest and "best" of the three, she repeats that it does not stand up to "close analysis" and refers readers to her 1933 article. However harsh her criticism of Basic, she also dismisses Palmer's and Swenson's lists, noting that both are distinct from Ogden's in so far as they were designed for teaching and also they rely on objective word lists. About Swenson's English Aiken notes that it has not been printed separately and can only be judged by its use in her newspaper for immigrants, *The American News*, in which case it "does not indicate by its content and style" to be "an improvement on Basic."[19] As she said about Basic, Aiken criticizes Swenson's lists (she also had a 300-word English) for lacking an appropriate amount of research: "consistent scholarship is lacking, and the organization of the material is seriously defective." Her conclusion points toward the necessity for a conference like the one that West was organizing at that moment. She argues that "the new English cannot be the product of any single individual or group of individuals working without adequate scholarly equipment and background" and, as if calling out to Carnegie directly she concludes: "There is a needed place for a project rightly organized and conducted, having for its objective the creation and establishment of a scientific minimum English."[20] In fact, Aiken sought to do such "research and experimentation" as is evident in research on grammar frequency and, oddly enough, in her own simplified model of English.

Aiken's two articles criticizing Basic English and Swenson's English appear in another light, when it becomes clear that she developed her own simplified English, the 800-word "Little English," not to mention Ogden's critical account of her inquiry about promoting Basic for him in the United States. During the controversy over Basic and organizing of the Carnegie Conference, one of Ogden's salient complaints was the invitation that they made to Aiken to participate. He sent to Keppel, the President of the Carnegie Corporation, an excerpt from the unpublished manuscript of *Counter-Offensive* in which he declared that her criticism of Basic was based in "pride and avarice." Pride because she had only turned against Basic, according to Ogden, after her request to be Basic's US representative had been turned down. In her request, Ogden claims, she wrote that she had studied Basic and "was enthusiastic" about creating course materials and requested £300 for the purpose. Ogden writes that "after careful inquiries as to her capabilities she was informed that the anticipated endowment would not be forthcoming" and it was only then that she wrote her critical essay in *American Speech*.[21] However, even if Ogden is to be believed, Aiken cannot be wholly criticized as inconsistent. According to Ogden, she originally wrote that "what Basic needs is a well-financed organization and lots of usable textbook material," and "I believe Basic is very much in need of a more extensive organization than it now possesses." In her essay on Basic English, she reserves her greatest criticism for its lack of organization and poor teaching materials (like the panopticon). If she originally sought to correct those faults from inside and was turned away, then it is not unfair that she would then criticize those same evident faults from the outside.

What is less consistent with Aiken's criticism and her own linguistic beliefs is that her "Little English" did not appear until January 1935—a year after her criticism of Basic and a few months after the New York Carnegie Conference. In an Associated Press article with the headline, "Reduces English Language to 800 Words, Woman Savant also Is to Produce a Simplified Grammar." The article quotes Aiken remarking that "An 800-word vocabulary is enough for anyone to learn to read the Bible—or Ernest Hemingway":

You might call it Hemingway English or Bible English. The greatest English literature has always been the most simple and direct. The Bible would go into this vocabulary with very little change because it is so simple. Hemingway has gone back to Bible English by using short, simple sentences, very few clauses, and clear, direct language. This is exactly our ideal.[22]

Aiken's comparison follows in the tradition of justifying simplified Englishes through canonical literature. Suggesting that her list comes from Thorndike's word list, Aiken claims that her word list derives from the "greatest English literature." The references to literary tradition reassure anyone who might consider her reduced word list as an artificial language. There is also a presumed morality implied in the reference to the Bible as an example of this ideal of "clear, direct language," which is another way of saying it is not "language" at all but a kind of authentic realism.[23]

According to the AP article, Aiken's "Little English" project was supported by a grant from the Carnegie Corporation. The article drew the ire of Ogden who cited it as a reason to discredit her criticism of Basic and validate his belief in Carnegie's anti-Basic agenda. Other than this article, which appeared in numerous newspapers on the same day, there is no evidence of her "Little English" project. She does not mention it in her essay collection where she reviews other word lists. In correspondence around the Carnegie Conference, the chair, R. H. Fife remarked that he found the news "surprising" and that he wrote to Aiken who was in Paris. The main concern was not so much with the list as it was with the publicity in the article which Fife describes as "very unattractive" and remarks that he doubts she is "altogether responsible" since "she has not been disposed toward this type of advertisement."[24] Implicit in this comment is a jibe toward Ogden who was uniquely disposed in this way, often using journalists, or writing articles under pseudonyms, to publish articles for publicity or controversy. Keppel responded to Fife that Carnegie gave Aiken a subvention for a study of grammar frequency but not for the simplified word list, which, he notes, she had already developed when she applied for her grant.[25]

Absent from this all of this controversy, of course, is Aiken's own voice and account of affairs. Also, we do not have any other evidence of the vocabulary. But, as with Ogden's account of her request to the Orthological Institute, there is a way of understanding her behavior. Unlike those simplified Englishes, Aiken does not claim that her model is ready for implementation; rather, it merely states that she is beginning a process of research with "nine assistants" and plans to experiment with the list in British Universities. Aiken's professional position as a female linguist with a PhD but only Instructor status at Columbia might have made such advertising necessary in order to secure sufficient funding. Aiken's interest in grammar resulted in her *Commonsense Grammar* in 1936. She returned to Basic in her 1940 book, *Psychology of English*, where she explicitly opposes Ogden and Richards as part of the logical tradition of semanticists that focus on vocabulary rather than grammar.[26] Writing with a younger female linguist, Margaret Bryant, an assistant professor at Brooklyn College, Aiken argues that "English language and grammar are the products of the group thinking of billions of people whose minds have worked psychologically rather than logically."[27] This ethical, organic view of English as developed from the bottom up summarizes her anti-thetical position to the hierarchical, singular vision of Basic.

"Think Englishly": West's "English as a World Language"

Like Aiken's two essays, West's essay, "English as a World Language," appeared in *American Speech* in October 1934, the same month as the New York meeting of the Carnegie Conference. The issues it raises are similar to Aiken's and resemble much of the discussion that took place at the Conference. Mainly, his concern is with the problems encountered in preparing teaching materials for a deterritorialized English, namely, pidginization and abstraction. Seeking to avoid any "controversy," he defines World English as "a Minimum Adequate Vocabulary—the smallest set of words adequate for all ordinary purposes."[28] This notion of M. A. V. would inform the Carnegie Conference's conception of its vocabulary as a "General Service List."

To address the problems of creating a word list for international English, he uses as an example the 300, 600, and 900 word lists that Swenson developed for teaching US immigrants. He observes that this vocabulary succeeds because of its specificity, that it was "for a known group of persons in a known environment." The problem with conceiving of a World English comes from its abstraction: "[W]hen we begin to apply such methods to World English, they break down; for we have all mankind and all environments. Miss Swenson has no *donkey* on her list; there are few donkeys in New York; but in Egypt one might as well omit the word *automobile*."[29] This is a odd choice of examples considering that in 1930 there were still carriages in New York City and automobile ownership was increasing in Egypt to the point that traffic in Cairo was already considered "intolerable."[30] While certainly there was a difference in scale between the

23 million cars in the state of New York and the 50,000 cars in Egypt and the building of the Holland Tunnel versus the Cairo-Suez roads, this does not mean that these words are irrelevant. In addition to this misunderstanding of the present, the example also eliminates the possibility of an immigrant referring to his rural past or an Egyptian talking about the country's future.

In order to create a list based on utility it is important, he argues, to know "exactly to whom the words are to be useful."[31] His observation balances two positions in the metropole (Standard English purists or prescriptivists) and the peripheries (the native learner, or user), but contradicts the point made in *Bilingualism* about the second language as an auxiliary form independent from a mother tongue. Here he seems to admit a latency between the native language and its secondary form. Either the World English word is too foreign from Standard English or its contextual obscurity makes it too foreign to its users. What he arrives at is a model of "negative selection" by which words are rejected if they are not useful to "all (or nearly all) the prospective learners."[32] This would also have supplementary vocabularies for different localities. Any omission for an area would have a significant impact on the whole number since there would be many similar or related words left out. The principles behind the limitations that he enumerates are that it would be a form of speech that is always directed *outwards* for international, not internal communication: "The vocabulary is primarily concerned with the European (and American) environment." In explaining this, he notes that "the primary function of World English is to discuss world topics, in particular those which are common between Europe, America, and the rest of the world"; and lastly, "the vocabulary will be primarily urban in its environment" in that "specifically rural affairs seldom enter international debate."[33] He then considers if this simplified World English would be preferable to an artificial language, arguing that artificial languages have more breadth and can delete unnecessary words more efficiently. However, World English has in its favor the fact that it is already so well known. But, he argues, an artificial WE such as Basic is limited by the fact that the learner cannot reasonably progress onto standard English: it is a "language not an education."[34] Anticipating the present, West suggests that over time English will become "so widespread as to render an artificial language unnecessary." It is in this way that Basic English takes West's argument in *Bilingualism* to its logical conclusion: that the role of an auxiliary language is as a supplement, not a substitute. While he proposes arguments for English as a "second" language, he makes clear that this should only be part of a curriculum, not a language system, leading to "full" English.

Finally, West considers a "world English" from the perspective of loss: "universality is a big and dangerous thing ... If universality is to be bought at the price of the essential spirit of the English language, we would rather not have it."[35] Rather, he concludes, "we believe that it is more important that mankind should learn to *think Englishly* than that it should learn merely to speak English."[36] However, this is also the argument used by Ogden and Richards for Basic English. They developed it primarily as a logical language that eliminates cross-cultural misunderstanding. As Richards argued for its implementation in China, Basic offers a way for thinking that follows logic and reason without the ambiguity associated with the vernacular. But Ogden and Richards do not associate Basic English with "thinking Englishly"; rather, they associate it with Reason, which they assume as a universal condition of modernity. In his use of the phrase, West casts Basic English as promoting an alien vocabulary and himself as a defender of the "essential spirit" of the language that he fears might be lost in a World English. This is the paradox in simplification. Like Achilles' ship, how many changes can happen before the language loses its "essence"? In *Bilingualism*, West turned to literary examples as a way of deferring this question. The stories in the New Method Readers staged scenes of language learning and use as a way of dramatizing his message about progress, modernity, and internationalism.

In his postcolonial critique of West, Pennycook would seize on this phrase, "think Englishly" as indicative of West's imperialist attitudes.[37] It certainly reminds one of Macaulay's visions of a native elite that was Indian in "blood and colour, but English in tastes, in opinions, in morals and in intellect." But, as we have seen, this phrase is anomalous for West and his theory of language learning as is evident from *Bilingualism* to his New Method Reader textbooks. The crux of his theory rests on the hold of the national language on processes of thought and as a vernacular expression of emotion. Instead, it might be read as indicating the influence of Basic English on West's thought. Confronted with an image of English as an auxiliary language within an internationalist system, West turns back to an imperialist rationale but one that is caught in the paradox of a late imperialist moment. It is as a result of this exposure by Basic English that West spoke with the director of the Carnegie Corporation in 1935 about plans for a conference that would resolve these problems of English as a world language once and for all.

West and Swenson's *Critical Examination*

While Aiken's essay provided the first disciplinary blowback against Basic, the most detailed criticism came from a special issue of the *Bulletin* of the University of Toronto's Department of Educational Research, *A Critical Examination of Basic English*, that lists as its authors, West, Swenson, K. M. Fawkes, F. L. Russell, and Dr. Jose de Magellanes Wilf. Despite the list of contributors, West was the lead author and the figure Ogden held responsible. Yet on the question of authorship, West himself defers to Swenson. As he notes in the acknowledgments, "This study was outlined and begun by E. Swenson, and later carried on, jointly, by M. P. West, with the help of K. M. Fawkes, F. L. Russell, and Dr. Jose de Magellanes Wilf." The latter specialists helped answer questions about specific sections. The first indication of West's collaboration with Palmer also appears here as it is noted that "he agrees with all said here" except for part of Chapter 4.

West began collaborating with Swenson on the problem of word counting after he had arrived at the Ontario College of Education at the University of Toronto in 1933. As the head of the Language Research Center at New York University, Swenson was actively interested in developing methods for teaching English to US immigrants.[38] This was a highly valued market for all of the ELT professionals and the primary commercial reason behind the entire controversy. Ogden imagined Basic English serving these adult learners who needed a practical, universalist form of English.[39]

Along with Aiken, Swenson was one of Ogden's main targets in his *Counter-Offensive*. According to Ogden, she had, like Aiken, applied to the Orthological Institute for materials in 1933 and then announced her own original system, "Swenson's English," which had graded systems of 300, 600, and 900 words for specific use by US immigrants. He accused her of plagiarizing Basic, and then attacking it as a way to keep Basic out of the potentially lucrative US market. For their part, West and Swenson address this in the first chapter, "The Reason for the Publication of this Study," that the journal issue arose out of Swenson's attempt to apply "the technique of item-counting and word-rating ... to the study of Basic English, with a view to the employment of it, or of a modification of it, in teaching adult immigrants in America." Where Ogden finds Swenson culpable, she finds Ogden incompetent: "The result of this study was to show that the system was unusable for this purpose."[40] They not only find it inadequate as a language system, they also describe it as dangerous in itself—both if it succeeds and if it fails:

> If it succeeds and becomes widely diffused, we believe that its effect upon the correct use of the English language in foreign countries will be disastrous; while, if it fails, it may, by shaking public confidence and frustrating expectations, impede the work of those engaged upon the problem of simplifying language-learning.

As indicated by his own New Method vocabulary, West was never an English language purist, yet he finds that Basic's modifications from "correct use" will impede any development to "full English." Their criticism of Basic's failure stands out in part because most criticism of IALs is formal, looking at the internal logic within the systems and as a result does not consider how it is learned or what happens if it is only learned in part, which is often the case with most second or third languages. The threat of Basic English is that it appears as English yet functions as an artificial language. Its failure as the latter (as is inevitable) resonates against the former.

The risk identified here of "shaking public confidence and frustrating expectations" resonates with West's experience in Bengal. As discussed in Chapter 3, West's theory of Bilingualism and his New Method were developed with the specific conditions of teaching English in Bengal where it competed not only with the local language politics of Hindi and Urdu, but also with a controversial history of teaching English in India. West's perspective had always been about finding ways to make English both desirable—a necessary and attractive language—and unthreatening—its necessity as secondary to issues of religion and politics better suited to one's "mother tongue." Although there was never a demonstrative attempt to introduce Basic English in India, West and Swenson's supposition here is supported by the negative reaction in China as seen in the parodies by Lin Yutang.[41] In terms of imperialist styles, Ogden's Benthamite language system resembles the *one-size-fits-all* land policies that the Raj imposed in the late nineteenth century. Going back to the early nineteenth century, Indian critics of English exams and textbooks had always been suspicious of British withholding of the language from natives. West's own New Method, with its 3,000 words, had been criticized as limited in order to keep Indians at "Babu" status.

Unlike Aiken, whose criticism of Basic was part of an overall criticism of the prospect of an International English, West and Swenson emphasize that they "consider it a matter of urgent, indeed of world-importance" and hope "that it be accomplished as speedily as possible." In their note to this comment, they offer one of the few geo-political rationales for International English:

> The reader may consider for himself the possible consequences of a rapid growth, or decline of successful English learning in the following countries—Germany, Austria, Hungary, Bulgaria, the countries of the Little Entente, Turkey, Tropical Africa, China, Japan, India.[42]

Its elliptical phrasing (the reader may …) and place in a footnote suggest that as academic linguists they do not seek to make public commentary. However, West later mentioned the threat of rising nationalisms and the concomitant decline in English influence as the inspiration for organizing the Carnegie Conference. In a letter where he recalls the origins of the conference he writes:

When I reached Canada, after a long tour through Europe, I saw:—

1. that there was a linguistic war beginning in the Balkans and the Near East. I found French and German being subsidised in Sofia and Istanbul.
2. I noticed the demand for a minimum adequate vocabulary.[43]

Notably, it is only the second concern that appears in the Carnegie Conference Record or the Interim Report discussed in the next chapter. While it could be that West's memory was affected by the context of when it was written, in June 1939, the footnote in the Critical Examination suggests that the impending break-up of Europe and the decline of British influence were on his mind in 1934.

But it can't be forgotten that this sentiment was consigned to a footnote. Their principal concern in the Critical Examination is similar to that found in West's essay "English as a World Language"—the relation of International English to Standard English: "the outcome must not endanger the serviceability and universality of the parent language." The apt metaphor of parent-child conveys the paternalist desire to "manage" the development of English internationally. These two conflicting sentiments—English as a world language and English as a Standard language—define all of these debates over English as an international language during the early 1930s and are captured in their dramatic conclusion to the chapter:

It is very important that mankind should have one language in common—probably English …
It is also important that English should remain one language.[44]

This evokes the reference to the "soul" of English and "thinking Englishly" from West's *American Speech* essay. Here the tension between the "mother tongue" and the auxiliary language previously identified as an aspect of native cultures—that is, West on Bengal, Malinowski on Trobriand Islanders, and Palmer on the vernacular—comes around to the metropole: how far can one go to separate one's language of expression from the purposes of communication? Yet where in the former cases they are describing cultures dealing with a colonizing international language needed for survival in the modern world, in the latter case, it describes the anxiety of the metropole dealing with the risk of an "unmanaged" English in the world. As West notes in his *American Speech* essay, it is understandable that it might be adopted and spoken as a pidgin for internal, domestic communication, but it is unthinkable that such a form of un-English might be actively promoted from the center as a means of international communication.

The provocative title and manifesto-like preface establish a clear sense of opposition ahead of the actual study. However, the examination should be considered not only because of what it reveals about Basic but for its arguments regarding the make-up of World English. West and Swenson have three main criticisms: first, that the word limit of 850 words is misleading; secondly, that Basic is inadequate as either a spoken or a reading vocabulary; third, that Basic is a philosophical language that has not been tested in classrooms. While each of these concerns is distinct, they share a common criticism of the discrepancy between Basic's advertising and its reality which they emphasize by recurring references to its 850 words and the claim that it fits "on the back of sheet of note-paper." As a result, the experience of learning Basic will prove frustrating to students who are promised that all they have to do is memorize the words that fit on one side of note paper. While they are careful not to say so openly, they implicitly accuse him of tricky accounting and of falsely deflating the words as a means of gaining market share.

As discussed in Chapter 3, attempts to define the limits for a word count are often methodologically precarious. It is for this reason that Palmer was skeptical of most assumptions about word definition; West and Faucett pragmatically accepted the Thorndikean objective definition of a word although they were aware of its flaws; Ogden and Richards subjectively judged their words based on their own utilitarian system of word-definition. By relying on a theoretical premise in constituting their word list, Ogden and Richards had to eliminate many words from consideration. Other word lists eliminated specific discourses from consideration in an effort to create lists of generic words (as we will see in the Carnegie list). But because Basic English sought an International list of words, then it assumed entire categories of words as already international and that therefore did not need to be taught. West and Swenson calculate over 1,000 such words from "days, months, numbers," measurements, pronouns, irregular verb tenses, comparatives (better, etc.), "international words," and "onomatopoeic words."

West and Swenson note that what Basic English assumes as "international" should be properly interpreted as "European." For example, loan words such as

"Inferno," "Jazz," and "Chauffeur" are considered "international" because they are used without being translated across Italian, German, French, and English. As a counterpoint, West and Swenson create a table of such words that are not known by non-European children. Such a criticism does more than criticize Ogden's word selection, but portray his entire system as out of touch with what should be its main audience. A similar jibe at its European provinciality comes in the other assumed international words—onomatopoeic words—"not counted by Mr. Ogden because it is assumed that they are so natural as to need no learning." What Ogden considers as "natural" is in fact both deeply cultural and quite arbitrary. In fact, the cultural randomness of "words imitative of sounds" epitomizes the unmanageability of language in general. That Ogden mistakes these as words that can be universal ironically reveals his Anglophilia and his willful blindness to this messy aspect of language. By including their tables on onomatopoeic and non-"international" words, West and Swenson seem to revel in pointing out all the variations on what Ogden considers to be his own definitive, universal list of onomatopoeic words listing European sounds such as crisser, krya-krea, Doong, Pak-pak, Svon, and also pointing out Ogden's Anglophone bias in choosing "Mew" as spelling over the "very international" "Miau." More importantly, they argue, it is not sufficient to "know" a word but to know how to use it. While this is a common issue for all of these simplified English word lists, it is even more of a factor for these sound words that Ogden assumes are "natural."[45]

These two tables contribute to the problem of the overall numbers represented by Basic. When they account for the number of "Items," not just "words," and combine it with grammar items, West and Swenson found 3,925 "Learning Items." In a footnote, West attributes to Swenson the practice of counting "Items" as well as Words. This accounts for the fact that individual English words have multiple uses and references. This is a problem for any simplified English but especially so for Basic which claims that learning the words is sufficient for use. According to West and Swenson, Basic does not follow its own theory. To cite just one example that they raise, *The Basic Dictionary* defines "mine" as "a hole in the ground" and *not* as a personal possessive pronoun, yet in *Brighter Basic* and *The Gold Insect* it is used in the latter sense.[46] Basic also tries to limit its words by allowing prefixes and suffixes to be added on to the 850 words. Yet these do more than just create emphasis, they create new meanings and as a result, a new "learning item" for the student. Also, by allowing these additions to the words, Basic sanctions nonstandard compounds using Un- prefixes ("Unnormal," "Unstraight," "Unelectric," etc.) and "-er" suffixes ("Airer," "Judger," "Rainer") that are both new words and have unclear meanings. Their analysis covers idioms, word developments, duplicate expressions, and shifts of meaning (e.g., "Blow (hit)—Blow (wind)")—all of which are equivalent to "new word meaning" in terms of the learning effort on the part of the student. They conclude that there is no other way to see the system except as a ruse: "Basic English deceives the pupil, and it so happens that its system permits an unusually large measure of deception."[47]

The *Critical Examination* continues this line of criticism with Basic by showing how the word list on the note sheet of paper and Ogden's promises of fluency in one month obscures the actual amount of time needed to learn. West and Swenson counter Ogden's rhetoric about Basic's low word count by referencing instead to "Learning Items." Swenson's method for item counting lends words a monetary value from 1–20 pence with a 20p word as the equivalent of a new word, that is, an item that has its own stand-alone definition and can be built upon to create idioms. For Swenson, a variation on a word may not create a new word of an equivalent value. That is, adding an "Un" prefix to "normal" is not the same as a new word since its meaning depends upon the full value word, "normal." But insofar as it has a unique function in helping a sentence create meaning its word-status is not zero. Using the money metaphor, Swenson argued that there should be a sliding scale for word values so that "Unnormal" may be half the value of "normal"—say 10p. Ogden, they argue, "counts everything under 19s, 11d as nothing." The metaphor of money value for word value gets at the underlying sense of the controversy that all of these word lists are commodified forms of language. Unlike capital value that comes from surplus production, the value that Ogden and the language teaching market have established is one of scarcity—fewer words rather than many—because of its value as perceived by the consumer—the language learner—who wants to maximize efficiency by investing time and money and gaining more communicative range. By reconfiguring Basic's word count 850 as 3,000 Learning Items, West and Swenson devalue Basic's capital by 300 percent.

Their criticism of Basic English also raises a general problem with any international version of English: the impossibility of a universal list of "content" words. In his essay, West erroneously describes this as the problem of "donkey" in New York and "automobile" in Egypt. West and Swenson create two tables in their analysis with "Examples of Content Words in Basic English which are of minor importance to a child living in Turkey, Palestine, Egypt, Sudan, Tropical Africa, India, Burma, Ceylon, Siam, Malaya, China (total population about 900,000,000, or half the population of the world)" and "Items in The Basic Words which might be objected to in the above countries." The examples for the former are the "International" words mostly identified with European culture such as Ballet, Café, Encyclopedia, Jazz, or those associated with modern technology, such as air-cushion, automatic machine, gas cooker, torpedo, radium. The objectionable words that they list assume that they would offend Islamic learners such as references to food (beef, pig), sex (lover, kiss, "make eyes at," "sex-desire," "to have sex relations with"), body parts (backside), and drinking (alcohol, beer, wine). As in their criticism of Basic's word count, the issue is more with Ogden's promises than with the word list itself, as they write: "It is impossible for any vocabulary to be equally suitable for all ages and environments. Mr. Ogden is not to be blamed for having failed in this respect, but it is to be regretted that he has made a claim which is, on the face of it, impossible to fulfil."[48] However, these two lists are possibly their most specious. First, they come from *Basic Words* which is neither the 850-word list nor the text that would be used for a child's lessons. Secondly, they mainly assume—as West does in his essay on World English—that these Oriental locales are outside modernity and they fail to imagine that English language learners in these countries might want to know about European culture and technology. But just because, as they put in a footnote, "Kissing is an indecent act in many parts of Africa," this censure should be replicated throughout the world.

Their one concession to Basic English is that it might function reasonably well as a reading vocabulary. However, this is precisely "the Basic Error of Basic English" that " ... Basic English is primarily intended as a speaking vocabulary. Yet the fundamental principle of its structure ... is *essentially a device proper to a reading vocabulary only.*"[49] In the terms of this study, this unconscious confusion between these two modes of speaking and reading is ironic. As we have seen in Chapters 2 and 3, this is the "Basic Error" of the Vocabulary Control movement as a whole. Now this is not to say that West and Swenson's criticism of Basic English applies equally to all three language systems. Their point here is that Basic English requires its users to perform mental actions of inference and development of words that are more likely (though difficult) to be done as readers but are nearly impossible to do as speakers when we tend to be translating literally from one language to another. Rather, this is to point out that each of their word lists depends upon literary adaptation for legitimacy to such a degree as to create confusion between the two modes. Their capacity to function as speaking vocabularies is measured through fictional dialogue, not actual speakers in real contexts. The inherent confusion comes from the auxiliary reading languages having a parasitical relation to the oral-based "mother tongues" that they seek to replace. The difference with Basic English in this criticism is that unlike the New Method or Palmer's "Plain English," it does not have Bengali or Japanese as its "other"; rather, its "mother tongue" is English itself therefore it has a need of repressing itself.

West and Swenson conclude by returning to the strident tone of the introduction, noting the importance of World English and hoping that the task of teaching will be undertaken "by persons who will not lightly encourage the disintegration of the natural or political language of five hundred million people."[50] It is not hard to fathom how such passages with their unacademic tone of an anti-Basic manifesto would raise the ire of someone like Ogden. While I do not have any manuscript evidence, I attribute these strident passages to Swenson. As with any co-written piece, it is hard to say with any certainty who wrote what sections, these manifesto-like passages may have been written by Swenson as it is not a voice that appears in West's publications. Also, Aiken, in a personal comment to one of her discussions of Swenson's English, describes Swenson's vocabulary as "journalistic, colloquial, vigorous *like herself*—but scarcely suited to Oxford or Cambridge."[51] Indeed, some of the most evocative passages in the *Critical Examination* might also be described as "journalistic, colloquial, vigorous." And Aiken, writing in 1935, must have had Ogden's response in mind when she wrote that it was not a style that could be expected to have a sympathetic reception in Cambridge.

Ogden's *Counter-Offensive*

By the time that Ogden published *Counter-Offensive: An Exposure of Certain Misrepresentations of Basic English* through Kegan Paul in 1935, it had already reached its intended audience, Ogden's friends and supporters, as a manuscript privately circulated in the summer of 1934. Part of the *Counter-Offensive*'s lore among his friends was the fact that it only took him a month to refute a criticism that had taken nearly two years for six authors to complete. Such conceit is typical of Ogden's self-mythology as a Parnassian intellect and marks the supercilious attitude with which he treats his interlocutors in *Counter-Offensive*. We can see in this many of the associated attitudes of the interwar Cambridge intellectual as described by Frances Mulhern—disdain for mass culture, trade, commercialism, unions.[52] From this perspective, West (despite his degree from Cambridge) and his colleagues, especially Swenson, are judged by the fact that they are outsiders and as a result open to having their motives suspected.

The odd title is a good place to begin. The phrase "Counter-Offensive" is a pun directed at West et al., whom he faults for being stuck in the methodology of "word counting." The two sides to "offensive" in the joke—his "counter" to their "offensive," as well as the idea that "word counters" are "offensive"—use battle rhetoric to mockingly suggest the seriousness to which Ogden takes this controversy. Richards considers the title, and other elements of the work, to be an example of Ogden's wit that, he writes, "was a bit beyond most of the readers of *The Interim Report on Vocabulary Selection* to whom it was nominally addressed." But according to Richards, the "real audience was Ogden and his collaborators."[53] The fact is that Richards' explanation offers some insight into Ogden method of argument apparently honed in Heretics Club debates and which is apparent from *Meaning of Meaning* to his Basic English manuals. His writing style is often described as "idiosyncratic" due to his use of puns, long sentences, and shifts in tone. This is due in part to the question of audience that Richards mentions. Ogden occupies an ambiguous place as a Cambridge insider and as a populist outsider as in the promotional work that he did for Basic and for the *Psyche* reading series. This produces a strain in Ogden's writing that is particularly relevant to understanding the eccentricity of *Counter-Offensive*. Since its intended audience was a group of Basic English insiders, and also appears to be written to himself, as a kind of journal, his partisanship appears unusual in an academic publication.

Ogden's critique seeks to cast West and Swenson as representing the worst aspects of modernity: technological, bureaucratic, and commercial. The title alludes to the first element, their orthodox faith in American methods of statistical word counts as Ogden writes that he "rejects *in toto* the spurious method of word-counting current in America."[54] The second aspect appears in his derisive description of them as "this group of teachers" insisting on "correct" English.[55] The third term is the most significant as he dismisses all criticism as a cynical attempt to remove Basic English as competition in the ELT market which he addresses in a preface on "Historical Background" and in an appendix devoted to criticizing "West's collaborators." The recurring theme in these sections is that all of them expressed interest in Basic English and supported it until turning against it.

Ogden finds the criticism of Basic English's misleading word count as false because he does not view Basic English's 850 words as a word list in the sense that West means. He finds fault with the idea that the profession will only allow "one particular sort of word-counting" in its textbooks rather than assessing the vocabulary "by its natural command of common-sense simple English, or the lucidity, conciseness, and appropriateness of its technique."[56] This raises the questions of what a "natural command" would look like and how Basic, with its lack of verbs and abnormal words, qualifies as an example of "common-sense simple English." As to the criticism that Basic uses words and stretches them in such a way as to be impossible for a student to learn, Ogden writes that it "is indeed elastic in the sense that when used by an expert writer it is capable of unexpected achievement" but that it can also be limited "to the absolute minimum."[57] This argument coincides with his complaint that West assumes the 850 words would be used for teaching children when, he claims, a list of 250 words was being developed for that purpose. This is typical of Ogden's mode of argumentation that identifies logical fallacies but fails to address core issues directly. Instead, he offers inflated rhetoric about the "expert writer" and "natural command." For example, he does not address the problem of the time spent by the student learning Basic English. Instead, he repeats the ideal formula of hours and learning times for a self-taught, adult learner that is given in the first *Basic English* textbook. This is followed up by a more extensive criticism of classroom learning and accusations of hypocrisy (that, for instance, West changed the time for his course to compete with Basic). Ogden's system assumes an idealized adult learner whose learning is not corrupted by the "limitations of the routine teacher" or "slower-witted companions."[58] In this way, Basic shares with other artificial languages a skepticism about the classroom and traditional methods of language learning.

To briefly counter Ogden's "counterpoint" here, it is clear from reading West's *Bilingualism* and his essay on World English that he was never an orthodox follower of "American-style word counting." It does seem that he has been converted to Swenson's method of counting "Learning Items," but that is not the same thing as objective word lists such as Thorndike's. West's own New Method word list draws on Thorndike and Horn's lists and supplements them with his own subjective words, a method that admits limitations to the statistical methods that Ogden accuses him of supporting.

If Ogden casts himself as the traditionalist versus the modern Gradgrinds in arguing about word counts, elsewhere Ogden takes on the role of the modernist and his opposition is cast as stodgy traditionalists. This is most apparent in the arguments over "correctness." As discussed, the *Bulletin* pamphlet included several tables of "incorrect" English that was possible with Basic English. Just as he responded to criticism of Basic's misleading word list by discrediting word counting altogether—and denying that the 850 words are a "list"—Ogden responds to criticism of correctness by calling it the "bane of English teaching" and citing linguistic arguments against "doctrines" of usage. Of course, West is not a grammatical purist. The thesis of *Bilingualism* was an argument against the Grammatical Method and in his essay on World English he laments that the greatest impediments to any world English are teachers and their insistence of "full English." Ogden assumes that "correctness" as West and Swenson refer to it is the same as that of nineteenth-century, doctrinaire grammarians and neglects the fact that their criticism comes from the perspective of the student seeking to learn "normal" English and finding it "incorrect." If there is a purist in this debate, it is Ogden and his refusal to compromise on the principles on which he built Basic.

This leads to the third aspect of Ogden's "counter" to the *Critical Examination*—his belief that all of the criticism could only be based on a desire to secure publishing contracts and access to teaching markets. As we have seen, the English language teaching market was regional with single educators often dominating an area with their own textbooks and methods. Basic English was a field disruptor not only in its method but also in the way it changes access and distribution. Ogden founded Orthological Institutes all over the world, not just in single regions, and he designs them to be independent of local educational ministries and bureaucracies. In the Appendix to *Counter-Offensive*, Ogden criticizes West, Palmer, Swenson, and Aiken for having reached out to Basic English and then turning against it. For instance, Aiken wrote to Ogden asking to help with organization and when he refused, she wrote a review criticizing it as disorganized. Similarly, Palmer and West made complimentary remarks about Basic and asked about adapting it only to be threatened with lawsuits by Ogden. Each of these solicitations is perceived by Ogden as threatening. Repeatedly, Ogden refuses collaboration, does not accept criticism, and threatens lawsuits of his copyright. If the ELT practitioners are criticizing Basic for commercial reasons, as he and Richards assume, then he is resisting criticism for the same reason—to keep his monopoly. It is legitimate to question the motives of their criticism since there are obvious market conflicts, but then it is a lack of self-awareness to pretend to be above such interests. An apt example of Ogden's true faith comes in the fact that he sued Richards for misusing Basic. In this act, he treats Richards as another reformist like Aiken or Swenson. He puts the sanctity of the system over its possible effectiveness in the classroom and the privileges of copyright over the value of collaboration.

A recurring point raised by Ogden's supporters is that the *Critical Examination* was pulled from circulation. However, at this point, it had already been widely circulated in North America, the UK, and in Japan and obviously still existed in libraries. Others argue that West later sought to retract his most extreme positions. In his essay from the 1970s, I. A. Richards recalled that in 1935, the "leading traducer sped up to Cambridge to beg me to plead with Ogden to let him off the exposures he deserved."[59] Indeed, West was in London in 1935 for the second meeting of the Carnegie Conference. In a letter from the conference, the Carnegie President Frederick Keppel observed that West's distress was interfering with his ability to participate: "West, who has had a good deal on his mind beside his hat, was in a very jumpy state."[60] West mentions in letters to Keppel and Fife in late 1934 that he is seeking to reconcile with Ogden. Four years later, he was able to say that they were "now on reasonably friendly terms."[61] But it makes sense that West might have feared Ogden's public criticism to which he was much more professionally vulnerable than the Americans, Aiken and Swenson. It is only by virtue of reading his personal correspondence in the Carnegie archives that it is possible to guess at West's ambivalence toward Ogden. As West wrote openly to Keppel, his family was unhappy in Toronto and he was trying to move back to London after more than thirty years away.[62] It is clear that in order to return from the colonial peripheries, he would need academic allies in the metropole like Ogden. West's position in this case makes apparent the center-periphery dynamics that marked the origins of ELT for Palmer and West and suggests why he would turn to an American foundation for support.

Conclusion

In the end, Ogden repeated the mistakes of the founders of other Artificial Languages like Volkapük, Esperanto, and Ido whose refusal to accept any criticism or allow any reforms to their languages led to their fall. If one were to cast Basic in the tradition of other IALs, then Swenson's English and Aiken's "Little English" are to Basic as Ido was to Esperanto—an internal reform that became a separate language due to the resistance of the original creators. As Aiken remarked, controversy is endemic to any language system based on a single individual, particularly someone as abrasive as Ogden.

Despite their criticism, West and Swenson agree with Ogden on the necessity of English as a world language. This reflects a common feature underlying competition within emerging disciplines and fields that has been theorized by Pierre Bourdieu as part of the symbolic violence around the process of legitimation: "It is a very general property of fields that the competition for what is at stake conceals the collusion regarding the very principles of the game. The struggle for the monopoly of legitimacy helps to reinforce the legitimacy in the name of which it is waged."[63] The "game" in this context is the concept of English as an auxiliary language. This chapter has focused on the charismatic figure of Ogden because of the role that his inflammatory reactions have inadvertently played in legitimating the concept of an international form of English. These controversies over word counts, language teaching methods, learning items, and correct English derive their stakes from this fundamental collusion in the making of a symbolic product. By rehearsing the claims for a "World English" as part of their arguments over methods, West and Ogden advance the concept more effectively than their more explicit arguments for auxiliary language. This point can be lost in accounts that focus only on the banality of their subject matter or that reduce the controversy to battles over market share. In this way, the Basic English controversies of 1934 cannot be separated from the Carnegie Conference that was organized that same year. As the by-product of the West-Ogden competition, the conference brings the legitimating authority of the Carnegie Corporation to this symbolic contest. How the Corporation was positioned to grant this legitimation and who was involved in consecrating the concept of World English is the subject of the following chapter.

Notes

1 As Howatt succinctly puts it, "Basic was a separate language into which English had to be translated, whereas the teachers were developing a grading system based on a selection of common words in standard English" (*History of ELT* (2004), 287).
2 Applied Linguistics would gain stature during the Second World War when prominent linguists such as Laurence Bloomfield became interested in language acquisition as part of the war effort. See Howatt, *History of ELT* (2004), 302–3.
3 Howatt, *History of ELT* (2004), 286.
4 J. R. L Anderson, "C. K. Ogden: A Plea for Reassessment," in *A Collective Memoir*, edited by P. Sargant Florence and J. R. L. Anderson (London: Elek Pemberton, 1977), 244.
5 I. A. Richards, "Commentary on Ogden's Counter-Offensive," in *C. K. Ogden: A Collective Memoir*, edited by P. Sargent Florence and J. R. L. Anderson (London: Elek Pemberton, 1977), 227. For the ELT perspective, see Howatt, *History of ELT* (2004), 286–8; Smith, "Introduction," *Pioneers of ELT*, vol. 5, xv–xvii.
6 Peer review as a key feature of this professionalization did not become widespread until later in the twentieth century. See Melinda Baldwin, "Scientific Autonomy,

Public Accountability, and the Rise of 'Peer Review' in the Cold War United States," *Isis* 109, no. 3 (2018): 538–58.
7 Russo, *I. A. Richards*, 439; Howatt, *History of ELT* (2004), 284.
8 The University of Cambridge Local Examinations Syndicate (UNCLES) was founded in 1858 for the purposes of administering proficiency examinations. In 1913 the Certificate of Proficiency in English (CPE) was introduced.
9 Smith, "Introduction," *Pioneers of ELT,* vol v, xii.
10 Ibid., xi.
11 See Falk, *Women, Language and Linguistics*, 5.
12 Aiken, *English Present and Past*, 7.
13 Jean Sherwood Rankin, *Everyday English* (New York: Educational Company, 1906), iv.
14 Ibid., vi.
15 Robert Cochran, *Louise Pound: Scholar, Athlete, Feminist Pioneer* (Lincoln: University of Nebraska Press, 2009), 186–7.
16 Janet Rankin Aiken, "Basic and World English," *American Speech* 8, no. 4 (Dec. 1933): 18.
17 Ibid., 21.
18 Janet Rankin Aiken, "English as the International Language," *American Speech* 9, no. 2 (April 1934): 102.
19 Aiken, "English as the International Language," 109.
20 Ibid., 110.
21 Correspondence from Ogden to Keppel, October 5, 1934, Box 280, CCNY.
22 Typescript of "Reduces English Language to 800 Words, Woman Savant also Is to Produce a Simplified Grammar," Associated Press, *Toronto Mail and Empire*, Jan. 21, 1935, CCNY, Box 140, Folder 6.
23 Aiken develops this linguistic morality fully in a manual of Christian behavior, *Surely Goodness*, published in the 1940s. In extolling her readers to see the world as inherently good, she faults the misuse of language as creating the illusion that the world is predominantly bad: "I would not go quite so far as to maintain the origin of evil is in language. But I do maintain against all opposition that it is language which has given rise to the illusion of evil as prevalent or typical. Subtract language and we are left with living" (5). It is also the purpose of "clear, direct language" to be closer to "living" (certainly a curious argument to make about good and evil in 1942). See Aiken, *Surely Goodness: Sixty-six Little Sketches of Nineteen Ways to Become Good at Living* (Ridgefield, Conn: Quarry Books, 1942).
24 Correspondence from Fifel to Mayhew May 23, 1935, Box 140, folder 7, CCNY.
25 Correspondence from Keppel to Fife, May 1935, Box 140, folder 7, CCNY.
26 Janet Rankin Aiken and Margaret Bryant, *The Psychology of English* (New York: Columbia University Press, 1940), 4.
27 Ibid., 5.

28 Michael West, "English as a World Language," *American Speech* 9, no. 3 (Oct. 1934): 163.
29 Ibid., 169.
30 See Yunan Labib Rizk, "Egypt on Wheels," in *Al-Ahram Weekly*, no. 621, Jan. 16–22, 2003 (Accessed April 18, 2018). http://weekly.ahram.org.eg/Archive/2003/621/chrncls.htm. Egypt was considered an attractive market in the early 1930s by Ford, GM, Chrysler, Fiat, and Mercedes Benz. See Robert L. Tignor, "In the Grip of Politics: The Ford Motor Company of Egypt, 1945–1960," *Middle East Journal* 44, no. 3 (1990): 385–7.
31 West, "English as a World Language," 169.
32 Ibid.
33 Ibid., 170.
34 Ibid., 171.
35 Ibid.
36 Ibid. Emphasis added.
37 Pennycook, *Cultural Politics*, 131.
38 Unfortunately, as with the other female linguists in this study such as Aiken and Lockhart, not much else is known about Swenson other than the article and pamphlet that she wrote with West. Her professional rank is unclear (though she lacks a PhD in 1934 since she is always referred to as "Miss Swenson"). In a letter to Keppel about her status at the Conference, West remarks that "Her ideas as to layers of vocabulary also seem to me sound and I think it is a great pity that she has not got together her work earlier and published it." On the difficulty in writing histories of female linguists in the early twentieth century, the historian Julia Falk has written that a "major obstacle" is "the general absence of accessible records on such women. They did not appear in biographical reference volumes; there were rarely *festschriften* prepared in their honor; the high schools and colleges where they taught kept only the slimmest of personnel files." See Falk, *Women, Language and Linguistics*, 25–6.
39 For more on US language education for immigrants, see Miller, *Accented America*, 57–9.
40 West et al., *Critical Examination*, 5.
41 For more on Yutang's parodies, see Huang, "Chinglish," 93.
42 West et al., *Critical Examination*, 6, n. 3. In an interesting paradox, as Goldin notes, it is due to the rise of nationalism in Germany and Japan that led to the dominance of English in Europe and Asia after the Second World War. See Goldin, *Scientific Babel*, 307–9.
43 West to FPK, June 1939, Box 140, Folder 8, CCNY.
44 West et al., *Critical Examination*, 6.
45 Ibid., 13.

46 Ibid., 15.
47 Ibid., 23.
48 Ibid., 31.
49 Ibid., 44. Emphasis in original.
50 Ibid., 45.
51 Aiken, "International English Grammar," in *Commonsense Grammar*, 259. Emphasis added.
52 See Francis Mulhern, *The Moment of "Scrutiny"* (London: Verso, 1981).
53 I. A. Richards, "Commentary on Ogden's Counter-Offensive," in Florence and Anderson, *C. K. Ogden: A Collective Memoir*, 226.
54 Ogden, *Counter-Offensive*, 6.
55 Ibid., 8.
56 Ibid., 9.
57 Ibid., 6.
58 Ibid., 10.
59 Richards, "Commentary," 227.
60 Correspondence from FPK to John M. Russell, June 20, 1935, Box 140, Folder 6, CCNY.
61 Correspondence from West to FPK, June 1939, Box 140, Folder 8, CCNY.
62 Correspondence from West to FPK, Oct. 3, 1935, Box 140, Folder 7, CCNY.
63 Pierre Bourdieu, *The Rules of Art: Genesis and Structure of the Literary Field*, translated by Susan Emanuel (Stanford: Stanford University Press, 1995), 166–7.

5

The Carnegie Conference and Its Discontents

The Title

Although the Carnegie Conference is generally associated with West, it actually originated from a suggestion by the educational psychologist Peter Sandiford during a visit to the University of Toronto by the President of the Carnegie Corporation, Frederick Paul Keppel.[1] In every other sense, from its purpose to its invitations, the conference became West's creation although, as we will see, his vision was subject to compromise and pressure reflecting the needs of Carnegie and the influence of Ogden. Reflecting upon his original inspiration in a 1938 letter, West writes that he had been provoked by political and disciplinary considerations. Politically, he was troubled by a tour of Europe that he took after leaving India in 1932 where he encountered the rise of nationalism and the decline of English influence citing a "Linguistic war in Balkans and Near East. French and German being subsidised in Sofia and Istanbul." Professionally, within his field of language teaching, he "noticed a need for a minimum vocabulary" and a "simplified literature." Speaking in 1934, at the opening of the conference, West focused more on the disciplinary concerns as its rationale. As recorded in the Minutes:

> for some time past Mr. Palmer, Mr. Faucett and he [West] had felt an increasing need of coordination in the work of English teaching; that this work of English teaching had appeared to them so important that it had got beyond the point at which individuals could make decisions regarding it and its future; that the whole matter should be reviewed by the best qualified persons available. The root of the question, in his opinion, was whether a normal or abnormal form of the language was to be aimed at.[2]

While this does not mention his political concerns, it is implied in the urgency with which they saw the need for coordination. Another unstated factor that made this "so important" was Basic English as is implied by the "root of the question" over "a normal or abnormal form of the language." Not all of these issues that were in the original conception of the conference were there at its conclusion, nor even in its title or agenda.

For instance, there was the question over what the conference should be called. As a litany of memos and letters in the Carnegie Archives reveal, this turned out to be surprisingly difficult to decide. West originally referred to it as a "conference ... to discuss the subject of World English." It evolved over time, in this order, as

> "a Conference on English as World Language,"
> "a conference on the Simplification of English in use in the World"
> "a conference ... for the study of the use of English as a world language."
> "a conference on English as a Means of International Communication"

After opposition from the British Colonial Office, "world" and "international" were dropped from all references and the new titles introduced "teaching" as its purpose, and emphasized the conference as merely provisional:

> "a Conference on the Teaching of English to Non-English Speaking Pupils"
> "an Informal Conference on the Teaching of English to Non-English Speaking Pupils"
> "a Conference on the Teaching of English as a Foreign Language"

The final product was the technical, *Interim Report on Vocabulary Selection for the Teaching of English as a Foreign Language*, colloquially referred to as either the Interim Report or the Carnegie Report. Even the common usage of that latter title was controversial as the Carnegie Corporation explicitly stated that it did not want their name attached to the proceedings. The controversy over the titles suggests the degree to which this was a conference based upon a general disavowal of its purpose and explicit rejection of any association with its final recommendations. In covering the conference from its origins to the final *Interim Report*, this chapter is interested in what these conflicted sentiments and cross-purposes indicate about the nature of how international English was conceived. Why the resistance to these titles? Why this disavowal of agency? What happens to the original purpose to discuss English as a "world language" or as a form of "international communication"? All of these questions bear on how one interprets the two final products—the *Interim Report*, published in 1936, and *The General Service List*, completed in 1953—whose banality as documents is in an inverse relationship to the drama in their creation.

Drawing on the meticulously detailed archive of letters, memos, and records kept by the Carnegie Corporation of New York (CCNY), this chapter argues that the Carnegie Conference's significance in the development of anglophone ideology resides in the *making* of the *Interim Report* more than the report itself. The Conference and the *Interim Report* did not intend to create a standardized Foreign English. Instead, it presented itself as a teaching tool, a beginner's English, and "an experiment" in pedagogy. However, the defensive discourse surrounding and within the conference demonstrate the degree to which this presentation was contrived as protection against any criticism that this is in fact what they were doing.

An important reason for maintaining this division between politics and pedagogy was the participation of the Carnegie Corporation, which funded and hosted the conference. Its charter read that the "corporation is established for the purpose of receiving and maintaining a fund or funds ... to promote the advancement and diffusion of knowledge and understanding" in the United States and the British Dominions and Colonies, "by aiding technical schools, institutions of higher learning, libraries, scientific research, hero funds, useful publications, and by such other agencies and means as shall from time to time be found appropriate therefor."[3] As a non-profit with an interest in education, the Carnegie Corporation was practiced in the art of rhetorically separating politics from pedagogy. The first part of this chapter introduces the context of the conference from the perspective of the Carnegie Corporation including its previous experience with education in South Africa and the internationalist perspective of the President, Frederick Paul Keppel (often referred to as "FPK"). While West was the figure most closely associated with the 1934 Conference, Keppel was its prime mover and benefactor. It was the Corporation that managed the Conference's agenda and public presentation through the participation of a group of scholars personally loyal to the Corporation, and Keppel specifically, Edward Thorndike and R. H. Fife of Columbia, Frederick Clarke of McGill, W. A. Jessup and C. T. Loram at Yale (known as Keppel's "Key Men"). Therefore, Carnegie's combination of a liberal internationalist ideology with a belief in the superiority of Anglo-Saxon culture informed the final shape of the Interim Report.

This influence can be seen in the organizing of the conference, which involved balancing a wide range of interests from outsiders (Aiken and Swenson), experts (West, Palmer, and Faucett), antagonists (Ogden), insiders (the Carnegie Key Men), and the old guard (Arthur Mayhew and the British Colonial Office). There is also an influential voice that is more assumed than heard: the anti-colonial nationalists around the world for whom "World English" appears as a return to the dominant hegemonic mode of the first British Empire.

This chapter has three parts: first, a brief history of the Carnegie Corporation and Keppel. In the 1920s and 1930s, under Keppel's direction, the Corporation was more directly involved in its projects than its postwar iteration, therefore the Carnegie Conference cannot be properly understood without fully understanding the role of internationalism, race, and class as part of the mission of the Corporation during the interwar period. The second part covers two years, from 1934 to 1936, encompassing the planning of the Conference through the meetings in New York and London to the making of the final product, the *Interim Report on Vocabulary Selection*. Drawing largely on correspondence, memos, and the Conference Record, I argue that the debates, threats, and controversies around the conference are more revealing about the shape of anglophone ideology than the final document. The final section looks closely at the *Interim Report* in light of this account of its making to demonstrate the way that consensus over English as an auxiliary language arose out of a complex negotiation between the desire for a world language and the anxiety that it might be English.

The Corporation

For the first ten years after its chartering in 1911, the Corporation focused on local projects such as funding libraries and restoring church organs. Education had always been at the forefront of Carnegie's mission, specifically, adult education. Coming from humble Scottish roots, Andrew Carnegie imagined libraries as a form of "public university" where people of all ages and classes could go for an education and self-improvement. After Carnegie's death in 1919, the Corporation's mission broadened to include funding in the natural and social sciences. Supporting modern, scientific, and secular approaches to social problems, the Corporation was "convinced of the need to increase scientific expertise and 'scientific management'" in the United States.[4] By providing an external source of funding, the Corporation was a leader in the turn toward scientific approaches to race, class, and immigration. The most famous instance was the "Americanization Study" led by Columbia Anthropologist Franz Boas that studied the effects of assimilation on immigrants to the United States. Using scientific measurements of immigrants and their children, the study found that the physical health of immigrants improved after living in the United States, which contradicted contemporary racial theories of degeneration.

In a series of articles in the early 2000s, the educational historian Richard Glotzer documented the active role of the Carnegie Corporation and Keppel in promoting education reform efforts domestically and internationally.[5] He describes a system based in New York City and rooted in a single individual, Keppel, working with an international team of experts, mostly trained at Columbia's Teacher's College, to promote theories of "new education" into rural areas in the United States and the British Dominions. As we have seen in the previous chapters, most innovation in British education was occurring by individuals like West working on their own on the peripheries in response to specific conditions. West's dismissal because of the success of his New Method is symptomatic of the British bureaucratic system's centralized control over all aspects of teaching from training to syllabi and exams. After the First World War, the British could not afford to invest in this bureaucracy much less consider reforming colonial education. As a result, there developed a symbiotic relationship between British colonial education and US philanthropic organizations like the Phelps-Stokes Fund, Rockefeller Foundation, and the Carnegie Corporation.

The latter came with an ideology based in the educational philosophy of Teachers College. As Glotzer writes,

> The "new education" of the 1920s and 30s emphasized child development and closer ties between family, community, and the school. It decoupled subject matter from pedagogical practice, and saw local control of schools as a democratic ideal. The movement produced new educational research, stressed leadership roles, and encouraged professional organization and a professional identity for educators.[6]

As a consequence of early twentieth-century modernization, there was an increased need for mass education with the rise of professional, skilled labor as part of a managerial, Fordist economy. Teachers College also benefited from its meritocratic admissions policy, which allowed it to attract a wide range of students from all over the United States as well as the British Dominions. As a result these graduates brought these progressive concepts of education abroad and extended Teachers College's influence internationally.

As a nongovernmental body, the Corporation was able to spread these progressive tenets by working with individual experts within the countries "behind" the official ministries of education. The organizing mind for this system of worldwide education was Keppel, whose background at Columbia, and experiences in the War Cabinet during the First World War, shaped the

Corporation's involvement in international education and set it up to be the site through which World English might be formed.

Keppel's Education

The son of an ambitious Irish Methodist immigrant who became a successful printer and important social figure in New York City during the 1870s, Frederick Keppel and his brother David were "raised to have a deep affection for their Anglo-Saxon roots," Glotzer writes. A firm believer in the Protestant work ethic, Keppel's father required them to work for two years in his business before beginning college. Keppel and David both attended Columbia University, with FPK, as he was known, graduating in 1898 with a degree in biology. Loyal to Columbia, he joined the administration in 1902 as an assistant secretary to President Seth Low and, later, Nicholas Murray Butler, before becoming the Dean of Columbia's undergraduate college in 1910. An immensely popular Dean, Keppel was, according to some of his friends, in a position to be Butler's successor when the war arose and he enlisted in the Army.[7]

During the war, President Butler, with the support of Trustees, converted the interim Dean of the College to full-time, replacing Keppel who was seen as too liberal for the University. The concern for Trustees like Francis Bang was the increasing number of Jewish students at Columbia. As Dean, Keppel had taken a liberal stance toward the issue even arguing in a 1914 article that the problems were based in class and culture, not inheritance, and that it was "one of the obligations of a public institution ... to provide acculturation."[8] Most damning for the Trustees was Keppel's assertion that "No questions are asked and no records kept of the race or religion of incoming students."[9] As a result, Keppel "was viewed as an impediment to the adoption of exclusionary admissions and residency requirements aimed at increasing numbers of Jewish and other *undesirable* applicants."[10] Glotzer describes this as an intergenerational conflict between old and emerging elites. Keppel's generation recognized the increased need for mass education to help the rise of professional, skilled labor as part of a managerial, Fordist economy. However, despite their differences they shared a belief in the dominance of Protestant, Anglo-Saxon values. Where the former saw these as best protected through segregation, the latter saw the virtue of assimilation and education as vehicles toward a unified culture.

Keppel's wartime duties were also intermingled with US racial politics. He served as the Third Assistant to the Secretary of War, a position created just for him by the Secretary of War, Newton Baker. Keppel's responsibility was "the human relations problems generated by mass mobilization," specifically, racial problems. For part of his time, Keppel served as the assistant to Emmett Scott, a former secretary to Booker T. Washington and appointed as a special assistant to the secretary of war after riots in Houston over the presence of black troops who had been conscripted due to manpower shortages. Keppel's task was to help Scott resolve issues such as discrimination at draft boards, and disputes over scheduled military leave, and the management of segregated blood donations. Glotzer finds that "War time exposure to the depth and seriousness of the country's racial problems left an indelible impression on Keppel."[11]

Carnegie and South Africa

After the war, Keppel worked for the Red Cross and the International Chamber of Commerce in Paris before returning to New York to lead the Russell Sage Foundation. In 1923, he was appointed as the first full-time President of the Carnegie Corporation, replacing the revolving chairmanship that had been in place since Andrew Carnegie's death. In that same year, the Rockefeller Foundation helped to create an International Institute at Teacher's College that created a forum for their international students and promoted work in comparative education.[12] The Institute was an example of the central role that education played in postwar internationalism. Insofar as Western countries sought to maintain the promises of development and self-government made to colonies and dependencies at Versailles, they used the rhetoric of improving education as a gesture (however empty) toward that goal. Within this realm, where governments were reluctant to spend money and individual teachers or schools were isolated, philanthropic organizations like Rockefeller and Carnegie took the lead in connecting individual initiatives to educational systems.

One figure who gave an example of how this might be done was Anselm Phelp-Stokes, a New York philanthropist and personal friend of Keppel's. The Phelps-Stokes Fund had started in 1911 with an interest in the education of blacks in the South. Its members were greatly influenced by Booker T. Washington's philosophies of industrial and agricultural education as well as his belief that there was "no great difference between the native problem there and the Negro problem in America."[13] In the early 1920s, the fund sponsored educational commissions for East and West Africa.[14] Not surprisingly, their recommendations for Native Africans were not that different as those for American blacks: technical and agricultural training for the masses and a full education for an elite group who would become leaders. In terms of language policies, Phelps-Stokes maintained the same Filtration Theory with vernaculars used for the masses and bilingual education in English as already existed in British colonial education.

According to Glotzer, Anselm Phelps-Stokes encouraged Keppel to become involved in African education. Because of his close connections to Teachers College, Keppel learned of the South African situation from a Teachers College professor, Mabel Carbey, who had spent a sabbatical year there and declared it the "second best country in the world."[15] Keppel sent his special assistant, James E. Russell (who had been the first Dean of Teachers College) to make a tour of South Africa and then took a tour himself in 1925 where he met Charles T. Loram, Teachers College 1917 and a State Inspector of Schools, and two professors at the University of Cape Town, Fred Clarke and Ernest Gideon Malherbe (Teachers College 1924). While Loram's interest was in Native education, Malherbe had a proposal for studying the problem of "white poverty" from the perspective of education. At the time, there were 100,000 unemployed Afrikaners and there was a fear of racial unrest.

Carnegie support for Malherbe's "Poor White Project" began in 1927 and culminated in the five-volume *Report of the Carnegie Commission on the Poor White Problem*, published in 1932. Malherbe used the Inquiry and his position at the National Bureau of Educational Research to promote TC concepts of decentralized education and direct Union government projects.[16] Regarding education and race, Malherbe argued against "ethnic division supporting the formation of a single white national identity."[17] Through his efforts and Carnegie support, there was a brief period in the 1930s where South Africa was a significant area for progressive education. Meanwhile, Charles Loram was using his position at the Carnegie supported South African Institute of Race Relations (SAIRR) to improve conditions of "native education." The SAIRR's purpose was not strictly educational but the "outgrowth of action-oriented interracial joint councils seeking to improve race relations."[18] When the SAIRR reports on education began to contradict those sent out by the government's ministers, Prime Minister Hertzog publicly objected to Carnegie's interference in the country. Subsequently, the findings from Malherbe's Poor White Commission Report were used by the South African government as a "rationale for establishing apartheid" against the intentions of its creators.[19] With the Carnegie Corporation as an easy target during this rise of racist, anti-African, ethnic nationalism in South Africa, Clarke left Cape Town for McGill University in 1929, and Loram became the Sterling Professor of Race Relations at Yale in 1931. It is from those new positions, and with these fresh lessons in progressive education and nationalist politics, that they attended the Carnegie Conference on World English in 1934. The Carnegie experiences in South Africa is significant for understanding the 1934 conference insofar as it introduced many of its central figures, such as Clarke and Loram, and for what it taught Keppel about education and international politics.

Keppel's "Key Men"

As the above history demonstrates, the Corporation's strategy during this period was for Keppel to become inspired by a proposal and take direct initiative in appointing talented, ambitious men into position to fulfill its potential. In describing his methods, Keppel referred to the necessity of having around him "key men" whom he can trust to carry out the Corporation's plans.[20] Glotzer defines these experts as "highly qualified individuals able to mobilise their respective educational communities and public and governmental opinion in favour of educational innovation and reform."[21] In addition to carrying out Carnegie projects, they were also "gate keepers" that helped protect the Corporation by defending it publicly and by vetting new proposals and people. By having this network of trusted experts, Keppel could manage the Corporation in an informal and personal manner described by others as "Keppel's Show."[22] While the Trustees had to approve the proposals, the projects were initiated and carried out by Keppel who preferred making quick decisions without too much bureaucracy. Despite this informality, Keppel kept careful records by using the Corporation "Blue Sheets"—blue memo forms on which his secretaries recorded all of his phone and office conversations. Considering how many important decisions were made this way, the fact that these are on file is crucial, particularly for the history of an impromptu event like the 1934 conference.

Keppel's "Key Men" were involved in the conference from the very beginning. It was one, Peter Sandiford, at the University of Toronto, who, West says, first suggested it to Keppel. Sandiford was an example of how Carnegie support helped to spread progressive American ideas about education to the British Dominions. Sandiford's 1928 book *Educational Psychology* is credited with bringing the "science of psychology" to teacher training in Canada.[23] Like other "key men," Sandiford was a Columbia graduate and former student of Edward Thorndike. Thorndike was one of the Keppel's oldest friends and even his neighbor in the community of Montrose, north of the city, where he had bought land and sold parcels to Keppel and other faculty and administrators from Columbia.[24] Glotzer documents the growth of Montrose from its first pioneers, Keppel and Thorndike, to its developing identity in the 1910s and 1920s as the home for professors in the psychology and natural sciences departments at Columbia seeking an escape from the urbanization of Morningside Heights and Harlem in the 1900s.

As discussed in Chapter 2, Thorndike was a proponent of the Eugenics movement, a member of New York's Galton Society, and a leader in behaviorist psychology. His work claimed to use scientific measurements to prove that inherited natures were impermeable to education. As a wide range of educational scholarship of the past thirty years has demonstrated, the ideology of eugenics was integrated into American education during the 1910s and 1920s. Thorndike and others saw it as a form of scientific social engineering that could manage race and class with the appearance of democracy and be safe for capitalism by producing better workers. Angus McClaren aptly summarizes how the Eugenicists rationalized their racial views as progressive:

> Eugenics was, its followers claimed, both an international movement and a science. Most therefore made an effort to distance themselves from simple-minded nationalists. Calls for restriction of immigration based on eugenic arguments, so their proponents suggested, would not be based on prejudice, personal bias, or old-fashioned notions of patriotism but rather on progressive, sophisticated, and scientifically informed analyses of the worth of individual immigrants.[25]

Unlike crude, nationalist forms of racial prejudice, the eugenicists relied on a specific aspect of racial difference—the measurement of intelligence—that could be measured and quantified. Where physical, essentialist racial differences were a risk leading to social degeneracy, mental differences had the advantage that they could be managed through education.

Like Thorndike, Sandiford argued that "Intelligence is a trait that is passed on by heredity."[26] His dissertation for Thorndike had consisted of studies of twins and quintuplets where he argued for the dominance of nature over nature. In a 1927 article on race and immigration in Canada, Sandiford argued that intelligence testing could be used as the basis for establishing reliable immigration quotas by screening out "Russians, Poles, Italians and Greeks" and encouraging "Britishers, Germans, and Danes" so that Canada could avoid becoming "a dumping ground for misfits and defectives."[27] Sandiford conducted a series of intelligence tests on Canadian students in 1924 that he claimed was proof of the greater intelligence of whites from British and Germanic heredity.[28] Sandiford's work was validated by a $31,000 grant from the Carnegie Corporation to the Department of Educational

Research at the Ontario College of Education in 1931 that "put the program on the map." It is through this grant that West arrives at Toronto from India and Sandiford's grant was also used to fund parts of the Carnegie Conference and the writing of the *Interim Report*.[29] When viewed through the lens of this Canadian prehistory, West's comment that the "origins" of the conference was "a suggestion from Sandiford," the conference is dislodged from its specific ELT lineage and seen within the context of early twentieth-century progressive American education with all of its internationalist and racist contradictions.

The two "key men" that Keppel relied upon for the Carnegie Conference were Fred Clarke, Professor of Education at McGill University, whom Keppel knew from South Africa, and Robert Herndon Fife, a Professor of German at Columbia who Keppel suggested as Chair of the Conference. This was an apt choice given Fife's background: while he did not work on teaching English, he had written on modern methods of teaching foreign languages, and he also had administrative experience nationally that demonstrated his agility managing questions of politics, culture, and education. His argument in a 1925 essay "Trends in Modern Language Teaching" follows closely the "new education" emphasis on quantitative measurements, test-taking, and teacher evaluation, and his preference for modern textbooks in German, Spanish, and French that focus on limited words taught in graded methods resembles the pedagogies being used by West and Palmer at the same time.[30] As an administrator, Fife was appointed in 1924 by the American Council on Education to lead a survey on the teaching of foreign language in the United States. A tremendous undertaking, the project was the first attempt at a quantitative analysis of modern foreign language teaching including surveys of current teachers, an overview of the history of language teaching, and a review of teacher training methods. The combination of quantitative and pedagogical methods as well as the emphasis on "experiments" in teaching—rather than prescribing solutions—that Fife developed for the ACE plan resembles the eventual path taken for the Carnegie Conference. Fife's position was also not without controversy.

The *Survey* was an action plan for promoting and defending foreign language study at a time when it was under attack in the United States as a nationalist reaction to the First World War. This took many forms including a 1918 bill that would limit federal education funds to "English-Only" states and bans around the United States on teaching, or even speaking, German. In the most famous instance, Nebraska declared itself an "English-Only" state in 1919, prohibiting teaching in any foreign language and limiting the teaching of languages before the eighth grade. In 1923, a year before the ACE survey began, the Supreme Court ruled in Meyer v Nebraska that the state violated the due process clause of the 14th amendment. This was the first time that the court had "engaged in substantive due process" to protect civil liberties; in this case, foreign languages were protected under the individual's right to "acquire useful knowledge." As a German scholar in an era when the language was under attack, Fife needed to avoid controversy in conducting the ACE survey and his approach, through the quantitative and scientific methods of the day, fits with the Corporation's method in South Africa and elsewhere. After the *Survey* was completed, Fife received funding from Carnegie in 1931 to support "experimental undertakings on a broad scale" following the findings of the report.[31]

As a veteran of Carnegie's experiences in South Africa to which he was connected but not central, Clarke was also an apt figure to bring into the Conference as a someone who could protect and represent the Corporation. After leaving Cape Town, Clarke was an active "key man" for the Corporation. He took part in a year-long tour of the "Southern Dominions" for the Corporation in 1935 and then left McGill to become the head of the University of London's new Institute of Education, which was modeled on Teacher's College and "heavily subsidized by the Carnegie Corporation."[32] Educated at Oxford as a day student, Clarke's working-class origins kept him on the periphery of British academy and like West and Palmer, he had to go out to South Africa and Canada to build his career. After his return to England in 1938, he became an important and influential figure in British education as he brought the social philosophies, comparativist methods, and professional organization that marked the Teachers College tradition to England.[33] Yet for all of his institutional gravitas and the official acceptance signified by his knighthood, his social theories and reformist politics continued to distinguish him as an outsider by the British establishment.[34] The addition of Clarke to the conference adds a class dimension that has not been remarked upon. Insofar as the conference was seen as countering Ogden's Basic English, it pits three British academic outsiders in West, Palmer, and Clarke against the ultimate old-school Cambridge insider. But where West and Palmer tend toward provocation and criticism, Clarke's method—and his value to Keppel—lays in his ability to be conciliatory. This becomes evident in his manner at the Conference but especially in the preface that he writes for the *Interim Report*, which I discuss further below but will note here as considered by Keppel and Fife to be the most important part of the entire document.

The Conference

The Invitations

When Keppel meets with West in 1934 it is fresh after the Corporation's experience with South Africa. In taking up another educational initiative, the Corporation needs to make sure to avoid political conflict with government ministries or any problems with teachers in the Dominions who are likely to object to the imposition of new curricular initiatives from the metropole. There are two other significant risks that are highlighted in the change of titles from "Conference on World English" to "Conference on Teaching English," which I list at the beginning of the chapter, that become apparent in the process of inviting its members. These objections come from England and draw attention to the delicacy of this attempt at Anglo-American cooperation. The first objection is from Ogden who argues that the conference constitutes a partisan attack on Basic English. The second is from the British Colonial Office, represented by Arthur Mayhew, which objects to any appearance that it is promoting a version of World English. As we will see, these two objections are ironic counterparts: Mayhew's fear legitimizes Ogden's claim, just as Ogden's claim undermines Mayhew's participation. If they are *not* creating a World English, as Mayhew's participation predicates, then Ogden has no reason to be concerned that its product, a word list for teachers of English, will threaten Basic English. But as long as Ogden persists in objecting to the conference under the claim that it will replace Basic English as a means of learning English around the world, then that threatens to expose Mayhew's participation as indeed supporting a plan for World English. For the Corporation, these British objections are taken seriously because of the strategic necessity of British cooperation: Mayhew and Ogden's concerns need to be managed in order to get the final product implemented, not because of any deep feelings against World English.

In fact, "World English" appears frequently in the initial discussions of the conference between Keppel and West, including in the first planning meeting in Ontario where they also drew up the original list of invitees. The first item in the memo is that they "Agreed that a conference be called to meet in New York in October 1934, to discuss the subject of World English."

The other question with invitations had to do with the female linguists. One of the first points of discussion between Fife as Chair of the Conference and West as its Covener has to do with inviting women. Of course, their sex is not mentioned as a reason, simply, Fife remarks that there could be one day held as an "open meeting" for nonconference members: "This need not be a free-for-all; but there are undoubtedly some person in or near New York who could make contributions in a critical discussion, e.g. Dr. Aiken, Miss Swenson, Miss Eaton, etc."[35] The "etc." is never embellished upon. West wrote to Keppel directly appealing for the inclusion of Swenson with whom he has been collaborating over the past year.

> [Fife's] paragraph raises the question of Miss Swenson's inclusion either as a member or as an observer. I did not include her name at our first meeting because she was not on par with respect to established reputation with the other members. Dr. Aiken was included later. Miss Swenson has, in my opinion, original and valuable ideas, particularly in regard to word counting. (These have already been set out in our joint bulletin). I think she would be a very useful foil to the tendency to false word counting which has done much harm in this work. Her ideas as to layers of vocabulary also seem to me sound and I think it is a great pity that she has not got together her work earlier and published it.
>
> As regards the present question, shall I ask her merely to make a brief exposition in the open meeting or shall I include her as an observer or as a member?
>
> No question of cost arises since she lives in New York.[36]

Keppel agreed that Swenson "ought to be brought into the picture" but not "*ad eudnum*"—that is, at the same level.[37] Swenson does not appear in any of the records as attending. Eaton does not attend either but supplies a prefatory "Comparative Word Frequency List" that was one of the "papers placed on the table" for the members. Aiken attends for one day of the conference as an "Observer." The rationale appears based on the fact that Swenson and Eaton lack credentials. Even though Aiken has a PhD and had already published several books already, she held the rank of Instructor at a time when there were few female professors at Columbia.[38] Yet despite their relative outsider status in relation to the conference, Swenson and Aiken held an incommensurately high status in the controversy with Ogden.

Other than the female linguists, almost all of the invitees in the original memo attended: Fawcett, Fife, Mayhew, Palmer, Thorndike, and West; all, that is, except Ogden. In response to West's memo, Keppel notes that Thorndike and Stevens are "keen about the idea" and that "Stevens suggested that the list might include the psychologist who has worked with Ogden; if my memory serves me correctly, his name is Richards."[39] Stevens here is David Stevens from the Rockefeller Foundation which was funding Richards's work for Basic English in China. (It is odd that I. A. Richards, probably the most famous literary critic in the world at the time, would be virtually unknown to Keppel and that he would be remembered as a psychologist.)

By the summer of 1934, Ogden, who had been privately circulating his copy of *Counter-Offensive* in response to West and Swenson's *Critical Examination* since May, wrote to Keppel citing his objections to the conference. This was not Ogden's first interaction with Keppel and the Corporation, a history that plays a role in his reaction. In his July letter, Ogden refers meeting with Keppel in 1932 leaving him with some Basic English materials. Two years later, Ogden claims that it was an informal meeting and that he was nonplussed when he received a letter from Keppel stating that the Corporation could not support Basic. He also cites Keppel's positive remarks about Chinese language simplification and about West's favorable opinion of Basic English. Ogden then claims surprise to learn that West's pamphlet claims support from the Carnegie Corporation. Ogden appeals to Keppel to appoint a "neutral representative in London" who might review his lengthy criticism of West's pamphlet (he does not mention Swenson in this letter). He demands that the pamphlet be withdrawn from circulation and that there should not be any mention of Corporation support. The former point appears to be the sole concession that Ogden seems to have received (though, as noted in Chapter 4, it was a pyrrhic victory) and the latter point affects the title of the final product, which is known informally as the "The Carnegie Report" even though, at Keppel's insistence, the Carnegie Corporation was not mentioned in the title. Ogden slanders West, saying that he lacks credentials and—in handwriting explains "as a serious critic in the linguistic field." Overall, Ogden casts the Corporation as being unduly under the influence of West— an illegitimate scholar using the Corporation as a means of eliminating Basic as a competitor for publishers and teaching contracts. The refrain that the Corporation first supported Basic before turning against it, is familiar from Ogden's similar criticism of Aiken, West, and Swenson. In this case, it appears that he is implying that Keppel's mind was turned by West.

However, Corporation correspondence suggests otherwise. After meeting with Ogden, Keppel sent the Basic materials to Fife and the Yale Professor Mark May (a former student of Thorndike's), of the Institute of Human Relations, for their opinions. Both recommended passing on it with Fife's letter coming in November 1932 and May's in January 1933—a year before West and Swenson's pamphlet. Fife's letter offers one of the more astute criticisms of Basic English. Avoiding arcane debates over word counts, he distinguishes Ogden's approach as coming from psychology and metaphysics and not from language teaching identifying many of the same faults in Basic as can be found in Esperanto and other synthetic languages in their neglect of figurative language and idioms. Fife doubts it can succeed in its purpose as a language for scientists except "as a fad." It is his final comment that is most suggestive for the 1934 conference where he remarks: "In case help is given to Mr. Ogden, I hardly need to say that a condition for such support should be that he avoid direct propaganda for English as a world language."[40] As we see, the views in this letter carry over to the planning for the conference as it emphasizes teaching and carefully polices any mention of "World English."

May's opinion, however, fits Ogden's paranoid contention that everyone who is against Basic was once for it. In a letter to Keppel in November 1932, only a few days before Fife's, May wrote about the possibility for funding an educational study using Basic English, which he had just learned about in a *New York Times* article.[41] Fife might have had this full-page article in mind when he remarked in his letter that Ogden is "a man of unusual energy and publicistic ability." Based on this article alone, May wrote that he was "intensely interested" in Ogden's list and would like to "develop a series of language tests based on these words" to help him examine "the correlation between knowledge of English and a list of measurable symptoms of acculturation."[42] May's tests are a proxy for the global English debates that would ensue for the rest of the century: to what degree does learning English make one English? The implied connection between language and thought was an integral concept for Ogden's language system as it was for May's colleague in Yale's Institute for Human Relations, Edward Sapir. Ogden and Richards would probably have argued that Basic was the wrong language system for May to use in his test. According to their rationalist vision, the auxiliary form of Basic English insulates from any nationalist identity formation. Richards argues that this is why Basic is suitable for the Chinese to use: by using Basic they are not using an imperialist English but a language that inherently conveys Western logic and reason. Only a few months later, May changed his mind, writing to Keppel that "on first blush [Basic] sounds good" but that he agreed with Fife and that he had discussed it with colleagues at Yale "most of whom express grave doubts as to the ultimate success of the enterprise."[43] Like other critics of Basic English that Ogden resents, May appears to have been intrigued with the system based on Ogden's publicity and then found it wanting after analyzing it further.

Richards turns down the invitation from West implying that their projects—teaching of English and Basic English—are inherently different from one another. Richards states respectfully that the dates conflict with start of term at Cambridge and that he did not see how "the discussion—as envisaged in the suggested Agenda—would be likely to advance the matter in view of the position which it has already reached and the work that has been done upon it."[44] West responded by noting that the date had been changed by a week to accommodate Faucett's schedule and writes defensively (and not entirely truthfully) that he was not responsible for the list of members. West also wrote a conciliatory letter to Ogden saying that if it would make him feel more favorable about the conference, that he would not attend and would accept whatever it decided.[45] These letters have no effect on Ogden who is busy showing Keppel's friend Burgess Johnson, other letters from West, written before the pamphlet appeared, asking to split royalties with him. Johnson spoke with Keppel explaining that Ogden wants Keppel to ask for these letters.

There is a full effort in August and September of 1934 to assuage Ogden despite the opinion of Columbia English Professor William Greet that "Ogden was a sort of sore head anyway."[46] At this point, after Ogden's July letter attacking West and implicating the Corporation, the issue has less to do with Ogden's attendance than the appearance that he was deliberately uninvited. Thorndike explained to Keppel that "the danger of the whole scheme is that the Corporation will find itself in a row, not with competing scholars, but with competing publishers."[47] On the other hand, the publishers could not afford for there to be a battle in the small ELT field over competing methods. The Corporation's influence on education depends upon the publishers to carry out the projects by the scholars that they finance. Another concern comes in Ogden's July letter where he says that the acknowledgment of the Corporation in West's pamphlet and its support for a conference "directly related" to its purpose in an attack on Basic implies grounds for a lawsuit. It is not clear what grounds he would have against Carnegie except to claim that it is violating its impartiality. Despite the drastic differences in politics, Ogden's case resembles the South African one. Where Hertzog complained about foreign interference in their schooling, Ogden's complaint has to do with American wealth interfering in the "free market" of ideas that traditionally resided within the protective fortress of Oxbridge. By tipping the scale toward one method rather than another—and in favor of one that comes from the peripheries—the Corporation is not just deciding against Ogden but changing the rules of the game on him.

The presumption that Ogden might have a legal case runs through all the rest of correspondence. Keppel sends Ogden a cautious response in August clarifying the charges made against him by the July 27 letter about Carnegie complicity in West's attacks. Keppel takes responsibility for organizing the conference, making West "merely" the covener by his request, and explains how "in our country" foundational support is understood as impartial. Ogden's initially accepted Keppel's explanation and its assurances of impartiality but claims that he could not attend the conference because it might prejudice a Foreign Office inquiry into "the proposed recognition of Basic English." While this appears to be a matter of polite face-saving, the excuse reinforces the nationalist stakes underlying this conflict. Ogden counterposes a private American foundation against the interests of an office of the British government. But this is a false balance. The fact is that neither anglophone power was capable of sponsoring a "World English" on its own, as West seems to have realized in setting up the conference to take place in New York and London. It is when this balance is tipped that Ogden takes the conflict to the next level.

When Ogden learns that Arthur Mayhew of the British Colonial Office plans to attend the conference in New York, he loses the legal politeness. In a long letter that he rushed to send to Keppel before the conference convenes in October, he excerpts directly from letters sent to him by friends in China, Egypt, Russia, and South America regarding West's pamphlet. Collectively, they can be summed up by the question one of his acolytes poses: "What have you done to put the Carnegie people against you?" Ogden uses these excerpts and a copy of a letter from Palmer to a Basic representative in Moscow as evidence that the conference is not impartial—as he has been assured by Keppel and Fife—but a consolidated attack on Basic. In losing his reserve, Ogden shows himself at his most pugnacious and litigious. In turn, Keppel had the Corporation lawyers review his own generally bland response, which was sent after the conference was completed, in which he emphasizes its "informal and tentative character."[48]

The excerpts included in Ogden's letter have no value other than mere gossip or as evidence of the significant impact of West's pamphlet globally in a short time. More importantly, these rants against West and Palmer reveal more directly than any of the other correspondence, the economic and political stakes involved in these competing claims for World English. In the letter from Egypt, Ogden's correspondent writes that

> the progress made by Basic in the last two years will be seriously retarded if you do not act promptly in dealing with the latest move of Longmans, whose textbooks are now being pushed here with the help of a preposterous attack on Basic by West and someone called Swenson, who seems to be his publicity manager in New York.[49]

The competition here is between West's New Method textbooks published by Longmans and Ogden's contracts with Routledge. The fact that the writer cannot seem to understand Swenson's role in the study, which is stated explicitly in the preface, suggests that it was not read carefully. And, as Thorndike predicted in August, the writer views the collaboration of Palmer and West as really a collaboration of publishers: "Palmer, I infer, is also in the game, and they hope to rope in Faucett (i.e. Oxford University Press)." The attribution of each linguist with a publisher and a sphere of influence (Egypt, Japan, India, etc.) complicates any move toward a World English. Obviously, the longstanding competition between Palmer and West was sufficiently well-known as to make their collaboration a sign of the seriousness with they view the threat of Basic: "Palmer and West are known to be as jealous as a couple of prima donnas, though the success of Basic may have brought them temporarily together; so the alliance may not last." It is true that Palmer and West were rivals who do not publish together after the conference; however, West was to reflect two years after that the most satisfying part of the Carnegie affair was the opportunity to work closely with Palmer and Faucett.

The writer suggests that Carnegie's role ("it has the imprimatur of the Carnegie, and has apparently been financed by them") is biased and warns that it "can have very serious consequences": "It is one thing to be up against another teaching method, but a rival simplified World English, backed from America, will play straight into the hands of nationalist opposition here which, as you are well aware, is largely under French influence." It is important to note that this was written two years before the Anglo-Egyptian Treaty normalized relations between the two countries. Despite Britain's presence in Egypt since 1882, French was still the lingua franca among the Egyptian elite who typically went to school in France and represented the "nationalist opposition" to the remaining British protectorate. As with South Africa, the Corporation is perceived as representing American influence within a British Dominion. In this case, it appears that "a rival simplified World English" would be interpreted as imperialist. While Basic English depends upon the connections and territories of the British Empire and draws much of its progressive rhetoric from pre-War new imperialism, it disavows these connections in order to present itself as transcending nationalist politics. Yet this delicate balance between rhetoric and reality would become more precarious if there was another claim to World English.

This concern about the reception of a "World English" by anti-colonial nationalists was also expressed by Mayhew. At first, as Ogden believed, he refused to attend the conference based on the August invitation from West. Mayhew, who was completing a year at Yale, wrote to Keppel about his conversation with West: "West agrees that the conference is supposed to be preliminary—clearing the air, demarcating fields of investigation, and framing, he hopes, an Agenda for *a more conclusive and authoritative conference* next year."[50] The latter conference would be held in London at the Colonial Office and be directed by Mayhew. It is here that the definition of the conference begins to assume the character of an "informal" gathering of experts. In letters of invitation, sent at the end of August—after his conversation with Mayhew—West was describing the conference as "wholly informal and tentative in character" with no plans for publication. Yet, notably, he still refers to it as "a Conference on English as a World Language."[51]

At the time, Mayhew was about to return to England and did not believe he would be allowed to return to New York. Under this belief, he notes that he was giving West a letter to be read at the conference that would clarify that the Colonial Office does not "view with any apprehension this movement towards coordination." According to Ogden, Mayhew reassured him that due to his objections "the original Agenda had been withdrawn; that World English was not to be discussed; that no Resolutions were to be formulated or published; and that the Conference would resolve itself into a preliminary discussion of whether a fully representative Conference should be called at a later date."[52] For Mayhew, British interests were being protected by casting the New York conference as "preliminary" and making the London conference with the Colonial Office and the Institute of Education as the "authoritative" meeting. Ogden, however, does not find this reassuring since the Institute director, Sir Percy Nunn, who had written favorably about Basic, was stepping down that year and was to be replaced by one of Keppel's "key men," Fred Clarke. For Ogden, the Carnegie takeover would be complete.

These letters from July to October 1934 reveal that the path toward the final description of the conference as an "informal" meeting whose "provisional" decisions will be only about teaching, not language, is more a reaction to Anglo criticism than a stated purpose. Ultimately, the controversies around the conference have more to do with a transatlantic struggle over possession of the English language than with word counts and ELT pedagogy. In organizing the conference, Keppel and Fife (if not West) are tactful in managing the anxious egos of their British associates, treating them deferentially while at the same time making their own plans to go ahead.

The Record

While Ogden was not physically in attendance at the conference when it convened on October 15 in the board room at the Carnegie Corporation, his litigious spirit hung over the meeting. The first couple of days of the conference revolved around the purpose of the meeting and the definition of their word list, while the last couple of days focused on how to implement it most effectively. For the former, they were concerned with avoiding the perception that they were meeting with the purpose of creating a World English, while for the latter, they were concerned with the best means of distributing a teaching list of English words around the world. That they did not recognize any conflict between these two activities speaks to the power of the consensus developed in the meeting. Rhetorically, they were capable of maintaining this distinction by repeatedly differentiating their project from that of Basic English. As long as they were not making an "abnormal" or "reformed" English, then they could safely invoke their project as purely pedagogical.

There were ten members in attendance on the first day, along with three observers. The absentees were the linguist Leonard Bloomfield, and Ogden and Richards. Attending were Keppel, West, Palmer, Faucett, Fife, Thorndike, Clarke, Loram, Mayhew, and Edward Sapir. Sapir and Bloomfield were invited mainly to lend legitimacy to the proceedings. Sapir had written about International Auxiliary Languages and even been involved with the New York chapter of the IALA, but had had not worked on questions about teaching language or World English. Other than a few comments on the first day, he is largely absent from the proceedings. Bloomfield also plays a legitimating role. After the conference, Palmer, Faucett, and West consult with Bloomfield in Chicago. The three observers were David Stevens from the Rockefeller Foundation, Walter A. Jessup from the Carnegie Corporation, and Janet Rankin Aiken. Despite Ogden's complaints about her attendance, Aiken was an active participant in the two days that she was present asking questions about word counts and making proposals for future research on grammar frequency. When it came to Basic English, she was silent, but then that could be said for almost the entire conference where Ogden and Basic were rarely mentioned by name yet references to "abnormal" or "reformed" English were rampant.

The controversy that preceded the conference was addressed at the beginning of the first meeting and then summarily dismissed. West began the conference with his account of the origins of the conference.

> Mr. West said that for some time past Mr. Palmer, Mr. Faucett and he had felt an increasing need of coordination in the work of English teaching; that this work of English teaching had appeared to them so important that it had got beyond the point at which individuals could make decisions regarding it and its future; that the whole matter should be reviewed by the best qualified persons available.

The root of the question, in his opinion, was whether a normal or abnormal form of the language was to be aimed at.[53]

West's summary glosses over the rivalry among the three experts and how it was resolved through the realization that they had a common enemy. Similarly, he only implies the conditions that lead to make "this work of English teaching" become "so important." One hint comes in the footnote in the *Bulletin* pamphlet cited in the last chapter where West refers to the "possible consequences" of declining English influence in Europe and Asia due to the decline of empire and the rise of militaristic nationalism. The other implication is that Basic English was imperiling their own projects making it necessary to remove it from any "individual." In this sense, inviting Ogden to the conference was also a way of asking him to relinquish control over his own, copyrighted language system. The final sentence on the "root of the question" overtly states that for West the conference was a referendum on Basic English. Recalling his essay on the problems of World English, the last sentence here remarks on the problem of creating a simplified English that does not sacrifice Englishness.

West's opening remarks are followed by remarks by Clarke, Sapir, Thorndike, and Mayhew that seek to distinguish their purpose from that of Ogden's. Clarke asked whether their purpose "was to settle a linguistic medium or a teaching medium." This raises a point of ambiguity in the calling of the conference—was it to discuss World English or teaching English? The distinction is an important one for the attendees, as Sapir says, "the two problems, the political and pedagogic must be clearly differentiated." It is in this context that Thorndike makes the comment quoted in chapter one: "the Conference should leave out the political aspect. Some universal form of English might ultimately result from its work, but that would be an accident." Their repeated disavowals of any political purpose are important for understanding World English as an apolitical "accident" of modern globalization.

Mayhew stands out at the conference as the member with the most expressed concern with this distinction between the political and the pedagogical. This begins with his response to West's opening remarks that "The Dependencies would welcome any process which would simplify the learning of standard English, but any abnormal or unstandard English would be resented" a thought that Clarke, with this experiences in South Africa and Canada, reinforced by saying that "the Dominions would strongly resent any abnormal form of limited vocabulary; they would consider that it implied limited intelligence." There is a repeated concern with "abnormal" and "simplified" as part of the presentation of this vocabulary. Faucett refers to "sufficient hostility" toward such limited vocabularies that it is quite clear how they stand on Basic English.

Any support for Basic English was mediated by concerns about the risk of any implied association. Loram spoke up most directly in support of Basic English a few times, once saying that he would like to hear the point of view from Basic. When Fife suggests that they adopt the first Agenda item: "Is it considered desirable that a limited English vocabulary be agreed upon as a common starting point of English study, in order to facilitate intelligibility among those who have learnt only a little English?" but eliminate the final clause, Loram expresses concern it "might embarrass exponents of Basic English." But even Loram considers it "inadvisable to let it be thought that we were determining a language." Sapir also expresses admiration for Basic before adding that he considers it "bogus."

Finally, Mayhew, Ogden's closest ally at the conference, concludes the discussion:

> Mr Ogden approached the problem as a philosopher. He originally began his system as a world language but is tending more and more to regard it as a first step. He is now enlisting more pedagogic help. If the conclusions of this Conference are agreeable, I hope that we may get Mr. Ogden's cooperation at a later date; but for the present we should leave Basic English out of account. We must avoid any conclusions as to the possibility of a World English.

He repeats many of the observations about Basic made by linguists and language teachers about Basic English as more of an experiment in utilitarianism than in language teaching. He also gets at the crux of Basic English's conflict with Palmer and West, which comes from the fact that it began as a world language before trying to compete as a means of teaching English which explains the shift in perception that Ogden frequently laments. But Mayhew's main point has to do with the dangers of the conference appearing as a collection of experts supporting a version of World English.

Yet for all of these qualifications there is a sense that they are only meeting because of Basic English and the possibility of a World English that it created. Most telling in this regard is the comment from the Carnegie representative, Walter Jessup, that the Conference "must try to capitalize what has been done by Basic English and make use of that which there is in common." It is ambiguous what Jessup thinks "has been done by Basic." It could refer to its value as an example of a subjective word list that is useful in the same way as Thorndike's objective word frequency lists are useful for adaptation. Or, it could allude to the value that West and Swenson acknowledge in their pamphlet about Ogden's arguments for the need for a World English.

All of this preliminary discussion about their definition and purpose in relation to Basic and World English leads to the conference's first resolution, proposed by Palmer, that they agree that "the learning of a limited vocabulary is to be regarded only as a step towards an unlimited vocabulary." The emphasis on a "stage" vocabulary clarifies their pedagogical purpose and distinguishes their word list from the political implications of a World English. This brings the purpose more in line with the traditional vocabulary lists from West and Palmer. However, the ambiguity between the pedagogical and the political is revealed in West's observation about the pedagogical value of standardized word lists:

> The further we are able to standardize the vocabulary the wider the range of communication we render possible. Thus, if we know that Mr. Palmer's pupils in Japan have learned a certain set of words and that same set is being taught in Africa, we can write a communication which will be understood by all who have learnt English in both countries.

Even when it is couched in the rhetoric of pedagogy, what does this describe except World English? It is through such rhetorical formulations that the conference "accidentally" creates a World English.

It is for this reason that Mayhew expresses his concerns about the conference, as he expresses in the Record and in letters, due to native perceptions of "World English" as inherently imperialist. Tracing his comments throughout the Record he appears to be policing the conference discussion and its resolutions for any references that might be interpreted as promoting World English. For instance, when Keppel suggests that it is necessary to "consider just how far it is important that the foreigner should speak exactly as does the Englishman," Mayhew is quick to jump in with "I thought that we ruled out abnormalities." When this leads to a linguistic discussion among Sapir, West, and Faucett on the definition of an abnormality, Mayhew repeats his point about abnormalities being ruled out, suggests that there are more important things to be discussed, and concludes with a proposal that the vocabulary "should deal essentially with the normal language." He repeats this role when the discussion turns to simplifying grammatical forms citing the agreement on the first day about ruling out abnormalities. When Aiken recommends a study on grammatical frequency his response appears incommensurate: "We must not give the ideas that we are trying to reform the English language." Mayhew's role is that of the British headmaster keeping the debate within its agreed upon rules of order. This impression of him as a British bull trying to protect Englishness from the "modernization" of irreverent Americans is reinforced when he speaks up against American forms of spelling and use of words (e.g., "sidewalk") being granted equivalence to British forms. In addition to the palpable Anglo-American tension, these exchanges reveal the divide between the modernists' preference for scientific and quantitative methods compared to the traditionalist's political concerns.

They also reveal that Mayhew's importance to the committee was not for his linguistic or pedagogical insights but rather for his position of power and access to global markets of teaching. This becomes more relevant in the last few days of the conference, which focus more on issues of publication, copyright, and distribution. While West had told Ogden that there would be no publication coming out of the conference, he meant that no publication of the October meeting; however, the product of the conference was to begin the process of creating a vocabulary list to be used by teachers of English to non-English speaking students and this list would have to be circulated somehow. The discussion over distribution was put on the agenda for the later London Conference and continues through correspondence for the following year until the Interim Report appears in 1936. Questions about distribution and publicity for their product are interesting for what the process reveals about the ambiguous position of this mixed, private-public, Anglo-American collaboration. As we have seen with Palmer, West, and Ogden, previously, if one developed a word list then the next step was to secure a publishing contract and then try to persuade educational departments and government ministries to adopt them. As we have seen with West, this can be complicated when the individual making the textbook is also part of the civil entity purchasing or recommending them. Yet the Corporation is not an individual like West, Palmer, or Faucett who can sell a product for profit, nor is it a governmental entity like the Colonial Office that has control over exams and syllabi. How can they protect it as intellectual property without it appearing to become private? The idea of putting a copyright on a language—even if it is not a "whole language"— evokes Ogden's restrictive use of copyright protection on Basic English. Not surprisingly, it is Aiken, a recipient of Ogden's litigiousness, who raises this problem of copyright preventing use of the list in English courses. They agree that it should be minimally priced with permission for use granted "to serious workers." Stevens, of the Rockefeller Foundation, with his experience of Chinese resistance to Basic English, raises the point that distributing it through governmental ministries "might arouse opposition and resentment." Mayhew, with his experience in India, also wants to avoid creating the impression that they are imposing the list.

Anglo-American cooperation comes through most clearly in the discussion over its distribution. The initial purpose is to send a draft of the list out to education departments and teachers for a survey of opinions on the usefulness of the list and to give them the opportunity to vote on certain questionable words. The principal concern is that it will be misunderstood. Loram points out that those in the field will need "some explanation of origins" and Fife believes "personal contact is necessary to explain the work." They decide to divide the world. Mayhew, who controls this part of the discussion, argues that the London Institute and the Advisory Committee "deal with materials for colonies, dominions, and India office" while China "might be approached through the US." They are sensitive to which side of the Anglo-American partnership each country is more receptive. The United States is responsible for domestic distribution, South America, and the Philippines and those part of Asia where the British are not welcome such as China, Japan, or Turkey. Even within their relative spheres they emphasize using "a personal touch" and "not organizations but people who will keep the pot boiling." As Clarke puts it, "We want two names for USA and let the two British and two Americans consult regarding the rest of the world." Even for those areas not mentioned they recommend that "West, Palmer, and Faucett suggest how to disperse to territories not already covered in resolutions." It is in this discussion that the power of the committee, which they have done so much to disavow, becomes apparent.

But from their perspective, judging from the discussions, it is the education departments, teachers, and ministries who hold all the power. In addition, they are concerned with resistance in England. One way they hope to make the list effective is by making it part of the examinations and syllabi. This makes bringing the list to Africa difficult because the exams for British African colonies were written in Cambridge. Mayhew points out that the "English examination bodies ... tend to regard English as a mother tongue" and therefore, "it is difficult for them simultaneously to treat English as a foreign language." This is an important quote for understanding the nature of what this conference is trying to do—produce a form of English that would represent the English language in the world but would not be "mother tongue" English (it is debatable if the Cambridge exam writers would consider Standard English to be the same thing).

What does one call such an English? Many of the concerns around definition come through in the discussion over the title. The Corporation, Keppel says, does not want its name on it (yet, despite his protests, "the Carnegie Report" became its de facto name). It is Keppel and West who help arrive at the final title. Keppel suggests saying to the teachers "whatever you do this nuclear list is necessary," to which West agrees "this is a nuclear list, a whatever-you-want-to-do-list." Keppel adds, to help the teachers feel like they can use local, specialized words, "You may consider special purposes beyond this list. Within the list the words are of general service." It is from this that Clarke suggests that this phrase "A General Service List" be used. The following day this is repeated when Palmer asks, "what is its name?" and Thorndike tells him it is the "Faucett-Palmer-West List or General Services List." (One can only imagine the furor that Ogden would have created if the former had been used.) As notable as the absence of one of the linguist's names is the absence of the word "English"—as in New Method English, Swensons's English, Little English, or Basic English. The word "general" anticipates any local objections regarding its application by distinguishing anything out of its purview as "specialized" words that would be included in a supplemental vocabulary. In this way, it builds on the Auxiliary/Native binary articulated by the Vocabulary Control movement.

As we have seen in previous chapters, the word list cannot be separated from the reader and textbook where its ideological potential is activated. The limited vocabulary functions as the supplement to the narrative form of the colonial reader, as that which is repressed in its creation and is supposed to be rendered invisible only to structure the narrative other according to its own ideological form. While the Carnegie Conference does not produce its own series of Readers to analyze in relation to its selected vocabulary, the members do discuss the role of literary fiction within a potential curriculum designed around its standardized word list. The discussion covers much of the material raised in Chapter 3 including West on canonical English literature, Palmer on parallel texts, and, speaking for Ogden, Keppel on the Basic translation of *Carl and Anna*. The topic of literature is raised when Mayhew asks about "stylistic values." This is in keeping with his concern to keep the list as conservative and traditional as possible. He suggests teaching "a little literary appreciation" at the end of secondary school, as has been typical of British education since Macaulay's time. West suggests using paraphrase with comparison between the substitution and the original. Palmer remarks that students tend to "prefer and misuse the stylistic phrases of the original" citing a phrase from Poe's "The Gold Bug" as an example. In a dig at Poe's difficult style, West remarks that this "tends to happen in the case of bad writers." Poe's stylistic value aside, Palmer's concern is that the presence of the original text will seduce readers into speaking a "stylistic" English that, as he notes in the Preface to "Gold Bug," comes out as a form of Babu English. This is both a similar and different problem to the one posed by Basic English. It is similar in that it presents an alternative, "unmanageable" pidgin form of English; it is different insofar as the literary original is Basic's opposite: where Basic presents a rational, logical, reduced form of English, literary English, especially Poe's, is baroque, emotional, figurative, idiomatic, and excessive. Mayhew recasts this debate as not between styles as between original and derivative work saying that he prefers abridgment over rewriting and would like to see "more original work in a limited vocabulary." Keppel suggests "collaboration between original writer and expert in limited vocabulary," such as H. G. Wells (who would do this for Basic English a few years later). There is also a concern with the content. Mayhew believes that the Advisory Committee will prefer "modern books from the past 30–40 years" because they believe "students need to study contemporary England." Faucett suggests that "the environment of the pupil" should be considered. The foreign student, he argues, might find more commonality with "the England of the past"; for example, "the Chinese can understand the pilgrimage in Chaucer better than they can factories." Faucett aptly reproduces the developmentalist perspective from the imperialist metropole in which the further one goes into the peripheries the further one goes back in time.[54] Fiction plays a double role in this process by acting as a historical translation that is also a mirror for the foreign student. Where criticism of colonial readers often remarks upon the disconnect between the reality represented in fiction exported to colonies in different cultures and climates, in this case, Faucett is arguing for colonial fiction as making a connection. West makes a different argument for using canonical literature: "The object is to give a picture of the real England including its present. Some older books are important for giving the real spirit." His emphasis on the "real" in fiction might be counterposed to the argument being made in the conference about language. They have gone through some difficulty to arrive at a proposal for a list of words that are simplified yet "real" English. The literary readers are also simplified yet "real." How does one create an auxiliary form without losing the "realness"—the spirit, the authenticity—of the original? Benjamin talks about the work's "aura" that is lost in mechanical reproduction. It is in the discussion of literature that we can see the subtext of the debate over the vocabulary list: how to create an auxiliary without losing its aura? The questions about the global commodity form arise in this debate. The local adaptation of a global form that is controlled and managed by the latter. It is also in this discussion that they are most open about the goals of teaching English—its purpose as a lingua franca, as West mentions with his example of the Japanese and African penpals, has an ambivalent relation to the traditional goal of dispersing a "picture of the real England." The fictional text acts as a site of anxiety for these colonial administrators: its language, setting, plot, character all present variations that have to be managed within this precarious dichotomy of auxiliary/native Englishes in such a way that the ideal pupil will learn the former and idealize the latter. This dichotomy suggests the divide that underlies their enterprise as it is also caught between the twin impulses of nationalism-imperialism and internationalism-globalism represented at the Conference by Mayhew and West, and, Ogden—the globalizing id that the empire's ego seeks to repress.

As well as the Conference accomplished its goals in coming to a series of agreements on the nature of the vocabulary to be circulated, it still needed to reinforce its boundaries. The spoken words at the Conference, recorded by stenographers in detailed Minutes, needed to be reviewed before being circulated. After reading West's compilation of the Minutes of the Conference, Keppel writes to West with a few suggestions—namely, to say that he did not make a comment that "all differences are necessarily abnormal," and to ask whether it is a good idea for Fife "to be on record doubting the practicability of Ogden's scheme."[55] Mayhew also wrote to West about the Minutes expressing his concern about any publicity before the word list has been finalized and is accompanied by Clarke's Preface otherwise it is "likely to result in serious misunderstandings of the aims and scope of the conference." Mayhew's own summary of the Conference for the Advisory Committee made it clear that it was only about teaching English in the "Near and Far East and Africa" and that "it did not concern itself with the position of English as a world language or as a medium of international communication and consequently it did not consider the desirability or practicability of any simplified or rationalised form of English."[56] Mayhew expresses the British interest in the Conference: to avoid offending Ogden or offending the bourgeois nationalists within the colonies. The risk for the latter would come in appearing to break from the principles of Indirect Rule. The risk for the former is create another controversy ahead of the conference in London.

Post-Conference: Ohio and London

The diverse, interdisciplinary group of linguists, educators, and administrators all went their separate ways after the Conference, which was widely viewed by those who attended as a success. The conference yielded several immediate outcomes—plans for further research by a sub-committee of experts composed of Palmer, Faucett, and West (with Thorndike in a key consultative role). This sub-committee would go to the University of Chicago to meet with Algernon Coleman, who had worked on teaching English in the Southwest to Native Americans, and then to Columbus to consult with the statisticians at the University of Ohio. The Conference had agreed upon a list of around 2,000 words, in normal English, with some American variants, that would come out of a synthesis of the various word lists produced over the past ten years. They also agreed that there should be a second Conference in either London or New York. There was a general consensus that there should be a second meeting to plan the next steps—reviewing the list, distributing it to teachers, and recording the responses—but where it would meet was not confirmed. While histories present these three meetings as a whole "Carnegie Conference," it is worth noting that they were more ad hoc than normally presented. This is due in part to how Keppel ran the Corporation in those days as a series of quick decisions made through personal contacts but it also reflects the tentative nature of the enterprise. As Mayhew's defensiveness suggests, there was always concern over the reception of the Conference's ideas in London. In November 1934, West wrote to Keppel about possible sites for the next meeting—basically choosing between New York and London—Keppel agreed on London after hearing from Mayhew at the end of November that the Advisory Committee had agreed to host the next conference at the University of London. The head of the committee at the time (until Clarke took over in 1935) was Sir Percy Nunn, an important professor of education who was an early proponent of Basic English. Evidently, Ogden had a strong influence on the committee. Many of its members were from Cambridge and were also indebted to Ogden's influential role as editor of several popular series at Routledge.

Ogden's last series of accusatory letters, including the one with accounts from around the world about the effect of the *Bulletin* pamphlet, had arrived just before the Conference. Keppel merely responded with a brief summary of the Conference, or, as he put it to Clarke, "told him what a jolly good time we had."[57] It is clear that they no longer considered it necessary to appease Ogden since they had made an effort at inviting him and the Conference had successfully defined its agenda in a way that does not threaten Basic (or at least does not bring cause for a lawsuit). They sent a summary of the Conference's agreements (not resolutions) to Ogden and Richards via Mayhew. Clarke wrote drafts of the

Preface with the intention of ameliorating Basic English. Keppel sees no point, as he writes, quite presciently: "I am not quite sure as to the wisdom ... of telling the world what Ogden has been trying to do. This may give him an opportunity, if he wishes, to start a row." Sure enough, within weeks of Keppel's letter, that's what he did.

Three events stoked controversy again: comments from Palmer, the article on Aiken's Little English, and a reference to Ogden in the Minutes. The first were some comments about the Conference from Palmer to the IRET in Japan. The correspondence only refers to Palmer's "incorrect and indiscreet statements" but never relates what he actually said that was so offensive to Ogden.[58] Palmer's comment was lamented by the Anglo-American contingent of Clarke, Keppel, and Fife to the extent that they did not want to support his travel from Japan to London as "nothing is to be gained by his participation" because of his "tendency to introduce non-pertinent matters into the discussion."[59] The second event was the Associated Press article about Aiken's Little English, which was discussed in Chapter 4. Ogden repeated his old accusation that her participation as an Observer tainted the entire Conference as anti-Basic. In response, Keppel noted that Corporation support for her work on grammar frequency came after she had compiled her word list. Nonetheless, it provided fuel for Ogden's claim that the Conference lacked any legitimacy, which was also the basis for his complaint about the fact that the conference Minutes listed him as an invitee but did not give his reasons for not participating. However, as Fife remarks, exasperated, this was impossible since Ogden previously requested that his reasons remain confidential.

The timing is the most important issue with these controversies as they all came about ahead of the London conference when Mayhew and Clarke were "conciliating opinion in England."[60] Notably, Ogden publishes his *Counter-Offensive* in May 1935, inspired, he claims, by West's further attacks on Basic in the most recent *Bulletin*, however, it also is perfectly timed ahead the London conference on June 11. In this way, despite all of their caution and prevention, the London Conference ended up having the same run-up of controversy as the first one in New York.

Originally, Fife and Keppel had not even considered it necessary to attend, saying that the "experts would do better by themselves."[61] But they changed their plans soon after these controversies were instigated. There were also extenuating circumstances with the experts beginning with Palmer's absence, and, significantly, Faucett had a nervous breakdown in March, the first in a series that persisted over the next few years.[62] West also seemed to be going through some personal problems at the time possibly due to the appearance of *Counter-Offensive*, which, as noted in the last chapter, was published as he was contemplating leaving Toronto for London. Keppel captured this state of affairs in his letter after the meeting: "West, who has had a good deal on his mind beside his hat, was in a very jumpy state, and Faucett was too ill to attend the meetings, but, thanks to Thorndike and Fife, the meetings were a real success." What had begun as a project marked by the collaboration of three experts on English language teaching had become most fully a Carnegie Corporation project headed by Keppel's key men. Maybe this should not come as a surprise as Keppel emphasizes the project's importance for the Corporation: "This is going to one of the most difficult jobs we ever tackled, but it may well prove to be the most useful."[63]

The London Conference had two main objectives—to finalize the list developed by West, Palmer, and Faucett in Ohio and to plan for the distribution of the list and the questionnaire after the report was completed. Fife was particularly concerned that this would not take as long as the ACE survey and he drew on that experience in framing the next steps. In addition to the four experts who would continue writing up the list, a "carry-on committee" consisting of Mayhew, Fife, and Clarke was designated with the remainder of the work to be done at the Institute. This transfer from a Corporation-initiated project to an educational institute that would operate (using Corporation funds) was typical for the time.

By July 1935, Faucett was well-enough to begin work on the vocabulary and Palmer also made it over to London so that the three experts could meet to finalize the report and, according to West, plan future projects such as a Thesaurus, a study of Stylistic values, a Study of Typical Errors, and "eventually perhaps an Oxford Dictionary of English for Foreigners." It would be left to Palmer's protégé, A. S. Hornsby, to complete these projects in the 1940s and 1950s. As with so much of this interwar history, its significance was more in their implications for future work than in what they produced at the time. After years of competing with one another and after all the controversy and personal difficulty of the past year, they found solace in collaboration. As West writes, they learned to value each other's strengths—"On word study Faucett is excellent; on grammar, idiom, collocations, and the detail within a word, both he and I need Palmer"—and to recognize the professional—and emotional—limits of working alone: "You will understand from this memorandum that there are here three men working in the same field, each possessing different and very complementary powers, who have got together and wish to stick together—, I personally believe that this is one of the most important outcomes of the Conference."[64] This is more poignant considering that Faucett would soon have another breakdown and that the War would interrupt any future projects including the planned revision of the Interim Report.

It was not until March 1936 that West could deliver the final product to Keppel. As a consequence of the Aiken affair the previous year, Keppel had emphasized that the Corporation should not be involved in the printing nor in copyright, preferring instead a noncommercial publisher. They found one in P. S. King & Co., which printed initially 2,000 copies with 700 to be delivered to the London Institute and 500 to Fife's "Committee on Modern Languages" with 800 for sale at 6 shillings a piece.[65]

Ogden made sure that it would not come out into the world easily. A newspaper article, "Basic English on the Offensive," lambasting the Carnegie Report and praising Basic English, appeared in April. Yet he no longer could provoke outrage, only a mixture of pity and respect. Fife noted that "the original author of this is undoubtedly Ogden" and "the article is so obviously biased and unfair that it will undoubtedly condemn itself." However, after two years of battling with him, Fife admits grudgingly that "Ogden is apparently as unforgiving as he is clever and resourceful."[66] The contrast with West's letter from the previous October could not be more striking. Where West had gone from being a combative outsider to a collaborator working with the primary educational institutions in New York and London, Ogden had lost the prestige that came with position at Cambridge as well as his influence with publishers. This state of affairs confirms I. A. Richards's lament about Ogden's battle with West that

> Admirable minds are seldom if ever at their best in controversy; enough examples, from Milton down, spring to mind to suggest that the impulse to reply destructively to attacks is indeed a temptation: something to be resisted, a movement to be refrained from whenever possible.[67]

At least in so far as it exposed the worst aspects of Ogden's eccentricities to the elite educational bodies in the United States and the UK, it appears that the battle with West and Carnegie had a more deleterious effect on Basic than the academic arguments in *Critical Examination*.

Ultimately, because of his objections to being listed in the Report as absent, Ogden does not even appear as a footnote in the final text circulated in the colonies and dependencies. However, as this archival history has shown, the role of Basic English was integral to its existence from the conception of a deterritorialized language to the impetus toward professionalization among English language teachers. While at times petty and personal, the controversy that ensued during the organization of the Conference shaped its negative definition and limited purpose—as "not World English" and as "provisional and experimental." Most importantly, Basic English established that there might be an Auxiliary English independent from English as a Mother Tongue. One of the unstated yet principal objectives of the *Interim Report* is to persuade educators and teachers that this was possible without falling into abnormalities. In these ways, Basic English appears as a subtext to the *Interim Report*, which, as we will see, is Janus-faced—with one face assuring its critics at home and the other persuading its critics abroad. Certainly, in most ELT histories, the Basic English controversy is merely a distraction of professional egos before the experts like Mayhew, Fife, and Clarke take over. In turning now to the Report itself, I am interested in how the controversy shaped the final product but not only negatively—in what it restrained it from saying— but also positively—in what the engagement with Basic made possible.

The Report

After the Conference there was a lot of attention from Keppel and Fife on Clarke's Introductory Statement. Since the rest of the Report would be written by West and Faucett, this was the one part that could be controlled by the Carnegie men. Also, since the Report would mainly consist of technical discussion of words and their definitions and uses, the Introduction would be the most accessible statement of purpose. It was also expected to be used as an explanatory document for agencies and representatives that would be distributing the report. For Fife and Keppel, Clarke's Introduction was important for avoiding misunderstanding, in particular, that teachers and educators might see it as an imposed word list, or authorizing a self-contained, abnormal form of English like Basic. Because of the controversy before the Conference, Clarke's first draft (shared with Mayhew, Fife, and Keppel in late December 1934) sought to establish a "distinction of our enterprise from that of Ogden, and make it easier for him to come in and to emphasize the provisional and tentative character of our effort."[68] Keppel suggested eliminating all reference to Ogden: "I'm not quite sure as to the wisdom … of telling the world what Ogden has been trying to do. This may give him an opportunity, if he wishes, to start a row." The Introduction can be read then as formalizing the Conference's disavowal of Basic English that is integral to the constitution of its version of English as a world language.

It does this primarily by emphasizing the Report as a teaching document interested in pedagogy and experimentation. Clarke's Introductory Statement describes it as "an examination of the part played by word lists in teaching" as if the existence and purpose of the lists themselves was under philosophic or linguistic scrutiny.[69] A peculiar description insofar as the report essentially consists of a lengthy word list. Hence, it appears as the list to end all lists, the list toward which all other lists go and then, as a result of its "investigation into the problems and principles involved in the framing of such word-lists," die. This ironic reading of Clarke's purpose comes with the perspective of hindsight. The Interim Report effectively ends the Vocabulary Control methodology. The later works that follow—Hornby's Oxford Dictionary and West's General Service List—are more aware of their specifically limited role that vocabulary plays in language teaching. Never again would the word list act as we have seen it behave in the 1920s as a central organizing principle for a method. For Clarke, writing this after the Conference in 1934, word lists and their problems are a way of naming their project in a way that distracts from the specter of World English and Ogden's litigiousness.

Not for long, though; Clarke devotes the following paragraph to distinguishing their purpose from that of Basic English. He quotes "Dr. Ballard's phrase" that the concern of the Conference is with "the simplification of teaching, not with the simplification of language," which reframes its purpose as pedagogical rather than linguistic. Admitting that "the report faces a practical issue of vast dimension and of great importance, political and cultural as well as educational," Clarke acknowledges the contested terrain it is entering without naming it directly.

Clarke then repeats the first sentence so as to eliminate any chance of misinterpretation: "It arises out of no desire to make English a *lingua franca* in the world *by reducing it* to a simplified or standardised form" (emphasis added). The dependent clause strategically modifies the statement so that there can be no doubt of their antagonism toward simplification yet leaves ambivalent their "desire" for English as a *lingua franca*. From the rest of the paragraph, it appears that the latter is assumed as a *fait accompli*. Instead, their purpose is to teach English to the "millions of children, youths, and adults throughout the world, who need English *in addition to their mother tongue* as a means of intercourse, or as an instrument of culture" (emphasis added). This sentence does two things— it reassures anyone concerned that they are promoting a World English to usurp native languages; and it redescribes English as an instrumentalized auxiliary language. This assumes that "mother tongues" cannot be a "means" or at all function as an auxiliary form. By reasserting the native/auxiliary dichotomy, the Interim Report replicates the anglophone ideology established in the word lists that constitute the General Service List.

The rest of the introduction explains the origins of the Conference, the preparation of the vocabulary, and the organization of the Interim Report. The fourth paragraph, where Keppel had suggested Clarke remove the reference to Ogden, describes the separate efforts in the 1920s by West, Palmer, Faucett, and Thorndike to establish "a scientific basis for English teaching."[70] The spirit of co-operation permeates Clarke's narrative with only gentle allusions to discord such as the "cross-purposes and confusion of methods and objectives" that "can work incalculable mischief." Of the problems that they sought to address, Clarke notes the problems of word lists that were encountered by Palmer and West such as the definition of a "word," word frequency, item counts, which we have discussed in previous chapters. Notably absent are the problems facing World English that were listed by Aiken and West and arose frequently at the Conference. Instead, what Clarke proposes is not a vocabulary as much as a program for co-operative experimentation. It is this sense that the Report seeks to initiate further study in English language teaching along scientific lines that it has been recognized by Howatt and Smith as helping to professionalize the field. But while its vocabulary control premises would pass out of fashion, the ideological assumption of English as an auxiliary language would persist.

The second part of the Report lists the subjects for future research that were raised at the Conference. This was important for establishing ELT as a science through consensus on areas of study and also to avoid duplication of research projects in diverse parts of the world. Not surprisingly, it depends upon quantitative measures to signal its scientific basis. There are frequency studies of grammar and speaking, and there are word counts for semantics and for words used in English language exams around the world. Some of these studies come from questions raised by Ogden such as word counts for idioms, synonyms, and words with wide semantic range. While Palmer and West addressed these by lending them word values, it was Basic English that created a system that took them fully into account by deploying the range of certain words' meanings as part of its reduction. In other words, they are having to study a number of these research items because of the provocation from Basic. This is more apparent when this list is compared to the original research items circulated by West ahead of the conference that asked for studies of learning with "abnormal" English. But in this final report Basic's presence has been elided in a number of ways. For instance, in the final item, an experiment with "Simplification by means of

Standardising and Regularising Enclitic Forms and Inflections" uses the word "regularising" to substitute for "abnormal forms." This item refers to the practice of using "un" as a universal negative prefix, as is suggested in Basic. Another item concerned with experimenting with a form like Basic is one that calls for a "study of style" from an experimental collaboration between a writer and a linguist using a simplified vocabulary. Ogden would probably say that such experiments have already been conducted with Lockhart's Basic Way Readers.

Traditional Vocabulary Control concerns with word lists and simplified readers appear in this list as well. Notably, number 8—"A study of the spoken language for frequency and range of word usage"—redresses the developmentalist ideology implicit in the first word lists that equate an English child to the adult English-language learner: "It has been suggested that records of the words used in speech by persons who have learned English as a second language may be even more valuable than records of children and others using English as vernacular."[71] This suggestion points to a few insights that undermine Vocabulary Control assumptions: the first and most obvious is that ESL learners might not be intellectual equivalent to children—though this suggestion reaffirms the fact that this had been implicit in the model of language learning used as a basis for the IRET and New Method word lists. But leaving aside the adult-child equivalency, there is significance in the distinction it makes between types of ESL "speech" and English "vernacular." What is ESL speech if it is not a form of English vernacular? It is an auxiliary language, not a version of mother tongue English. Yet what is its "value"? This would be for the purposes of making a word list for teaching English as an auxiliary language, but it already is an auxiliary language. The circularity of the auxiliary-native dichotomy is fully at work here: the ESL student produces auxiliary English "naturally" after learning English derived from the study of English children's vernacular; this "natural auxiliary" will be studied to produce materials for teaching English as an auxiliary language to the ESL student. Along with research items fourteen (frequency study of errors by ESL students), fifteen (study of difficulties in learning English in certain areas), and twenty (a study of the semantics of "Pidgin English"), there is an acknowledgment of the place of the student and a recognition that this word list is entering into relation with other Englishes. This makes apparent the primary concern of the *Interim Report* to "manage" the spread of Englishes in the world that runs throughout.

But where Part II, "Subjects of Research," points toward the future of World English, Part III, "Summary of the Proceedings," reviews its past in the discussion of purposes and criteria of vocabulary selection. They list nine purposes, offer their definition, and then explain how this list relates to that purpose. The purposes are: the "Island Vocabulary"; the "Foundation" Standpoint; the "Standardised Examination" Standpoint; Purification of Style; the Standpoint of the Practical Teacher; the Standpoint of the Educationist; the Standpoint of the Textbook Simplifier; the Standpoint of English as a Lingua Franca; the Tourist and Traveller Standpoint.[72] As a summary of the concerns expressed at the Conference, it does not represent the relative influence each possessed. For instance, the explanations for the Island Vocabulary—a euphemism for Basic English—and English as a *lingua franca* consist of a few sentences while the discussion of exams, style, and teachers is dense paragraphs.

However, the Island Vocabulary is given pride of place as the first purpose addressed. The definition they give comes almost directly from Ogden's advertisements for Basic:

> The exponents of this conception contemplate a small self-contained vocabulary, a complete language in itself, which will provide for all needs, in particular those of the adult, e.g. business-man, tourist, scientist, etc.

This purpose is dismissed briefly: "It was agreed that such a self-contained vocabulary was definitely ruled out of our terms of reference by the Conference." As we have seen from the Conference archive, while it was ruled out in the opening discussion it often threatened to return as part of the general discussion, often squashed by the hypersensitive Mayhew. I point this out to show how much the declarative sentence leaves out; this is not to say they did produce a self-contained vocabulary but to suggest the degree to which their purposes overlap and feed into one another so that it can never be simply "ruled out." This suggests a paradox when it is compared to the second purpose listed, the Foundation Standpoint. This is regarded favorably, as providing "a limited vocabulary" that can act "as a nucleus or starting-point" toward full English. However, this must be seen through the lens of West's theory of "surrender value," in which whatever is initially taught has to be valued by its utility if that is all that the student learns of the language. Doesn't this mean that any good teaching vocabulary acts as a self-contained vocabulary insofar as its strives toward maximum value? Of course, the key word for this part of the report is "*purposes* in vocabulary selection" and it is true that making a self-contained vocabulary was never the stated purpose yet that does not mean it was so easily "ruled out." Yet there is a further irony in the title itself as the depiction of Basic as an "island vocabulary" deflects from the fact that Standard English, too, is the vocabulary of an island.

Just as they are concerned with distancing themselves from modernist abnormal Englishes, they also have a cautionary attitude toward those defending "traditional" English. The audience here are the "English examination bodies" that Mayhew mentions at the Conference who "tend to regard English as a mother tongue."[73] As a consequence, they write exams focusing on the "rare and tricky" parts of speech rather than "plain English."[74] Because they need to persuade this group to adopt their list, their criticism is couched in ameliorative language such as "We believe that the prescription of any supplementary word-list in this field would be undesirable."[75] However cautious their criticism may be, the distinction they draw here significant. By taking on the English that appears in exams, they are effectively taking on official standardization, splitting the standard of "foreign English" from that of the Standard English "at home." This has been the fine distinction that they have been trying to make since initiating the Conference: avoiding the Scylla of Standard English and the Charybdis of Abnormal Englishes. Instead, they embrace an International Standard English, also referred to by the generic epithet, "Plain English."

While they criticize prescriptivism on the part of the examiners, they embrace it in the purpose titled "Purification of Style." Here they lament the degradation of language due to the usual suspects of "cheap journalism" and "the cinema" though they add "the foreigner's preference for slang and rare variants."[76] The last part recalls Palmer's argument that Babu English arises from the misuse of literary styles. In this case, they see a selected vocabulary like the General Service List as "an opportunity of purging the language" of material that can be misused. Instead, they admit words for clarity and "on the literary side we must similarly provide for adequate expression of elementary feeling and emotional states."[77] This "purpose" recalls the use of simplified language in West's New Method Readers—it seeks the appropriate fit between emotion and word, avoids psychology, and emphasizes action. It is questionable if there is a difference between the "simple" in the "simple, straightforward style" they advocate and the "simple" in their literary simplifications. I believe that they see these as the same. That is why they do not consider the Simplifications a "dumbing down" but rather as an improvement on the original.

This is not the only direct statement that they make about the vocabulary as having a purpose other than just teaching. For purpose 8, "the standpoint of English as a lingua franca," they do not negate this approach as they do with "Island Vocabulary." They recognize that English has already taken on this role in "certain countries where there is multiplicity of languages." While it was not their purpose to create a lingua franca vocabulary, they admit that "our work will be found useful ... for such a lingua franca."[78] Its usefulness will come in providing a coherent structure for an otherwise unruly version of English. They are careful here to avoid any sense that they are imposing a prescriptivist vocabulary, simply stating that it could be useful "if it be practicable and desirable." Instead, they adopt the tone expressed by Thorndike at the conference regarding the "accident" of English as a world language. The goal here has never been with how to spread English but how to manage it, or as it is put here, "provide a structural basis."

For all of the awareness of the foreign language learner noted in the research agenda, the final "purpose" listed is remarkably limited in how it imagines this subject. Titled as "the Tourist and Traveller Standpoint," and described as word lists that "emphasize the prospective travel-needs of certain classes of people." This standpoint is dismissed since they "are unable to predict that all our pupils will have such needs." This is the closest that they come to signaling the perceived class position of their students. Unlike the Filtration Theory that was aimed at the native elite mostly serving in government or education, this vocabulary seeks, as its title suggests, a "general" audience, at least those who are able to afford schooling. It also indicates that the auxiliary form of English they are creating here does not necessarily have "England" as its referent. Their cautious support for English as a lingua franca suggests as much; they see English as having more of a role in multilingual contexts, as an intermediary among natives, than in engaging with the English or England. But when seen in terms of the invention of the native that has occurred in the making of word lists, then this appears to deny the native any attempt at becoming other than a native. In this sense, it recalls Jamaica Kincaid's insight that "every native of every place is a potential tourist" yet "some natives ... cannot go anywhere."[79]

This uneven distribution of globality is cultivated in the criteria for vocabulary selection. In establishing word value they derive seven criteria. The first one, "word-frequency," is familiar from Objective, statistical lists such as Thorndike's and the second, "structural value," derives from the insights of West's lists. And criteria D, E, and F all reflect the principle of "coverage" that West, Palmer, and Ogden all used in their subjective lists. However, coverage means something different now for West and Palmer, whose lists were directed toward regional Englishes, not World English as Ogden intended. In this case, then, there is a new principle, criteria C, used: "universality in respect to geographic area."

For "Universality," they take into account "the geographical distribution of the need of the word" along with six factors: "Ascendant words, American variants, Squeamishness, Religious Objections, Moral Concepts, and Names of Peoples." By "ascendant words" they refer to words that are not widely present but where its spread seems inevitable. This category accounts for the problems West notes in Swenson's simplified list on the dubious usefulness of the word "automobile" in Egypt. The examples they give here are "*Telephone, Belt, Scout, Park,* also words connected with games and sports."[80] While this category might seem most obviously suited toward technology, only the first example has to do with a technology (and since the first transcontinental cable was laid in 1915, it appears a strange choice for "ascendant"). The other terms are all cultural factors: "Belt" refers to form of dress suited for a Westernized office, "scout" to the spread of Baden Powell's nationalistic Boy Scout program, and "Park" (assuming we are not referring to an "automobile") refers to a Westernized model of urban space. All three refer to ways in which culture and nature are reconfigured in modern terms.[81]

It is in the paragraph on "American Variants" that the institutional pressures of adoption come into play. This section recalls West's observation about the problems of having an American-English-based version of World English adopted by British-trained teachers. This is an instance where the changing face of empire becomes plain: while the United States, in the form of the Carnegie Corporation and the data collection by Thorndike and others controls the product, the British world system, despite the frailty of its second empire, control distribution. The result is the compromised form of a deracinated English that makes up the global word. The primacy of British sensibilities comes through in the decision to only use American words that "have already some sanction in England." The report describes this issue as "very delicate ground" and as a result they have "been extremely cautious" and only allowed "a very small number of words." Basically, in the tradition of committees everywhere that have been faced with a controversial issue they punted on it, calling for some future "competent committee" to "make further investigation of this subject." Underlying this deferral is an awareness that the future English that this committee will have to investigate is destined to be quite different in its balance of power.

For the consideration of "squeamishness" they obscurely refer to "variations which exist in regard to standards of politeness and decency in the very wide area which we have to consider in this work." Since other forms of offensive words are addressed in the following considerations, it appears that the word "squeamish," with its association with nausea, suggests a physical level of discomfort with words regarding the body, sex or sexuality, or bodily functions. This recalls West's rationale, included in *The Critical Examination*, for omitting "breast" in his word list "owing to the special conditions of Girls' Schools in the Near Eastern countries," where, he writes, "the English teachers in many such schools are men, and the girls tend to be rather sex-conscious."[82] West also suggests omitting "kiss" because it might be objected to in "Turkey, Palestine, Egypt, Sudan, Tropical Africa, India, Burma, Ceylon, Siam, Malaya, and China."[83] West's awareness comes from his experience in Bengal where British textbooks were scrutinized for examples of Christianity or other forms of cultural imperialism.[84]

Similarly, for "religious considerations" they confront the fact that "English is essentially a Christian language and deeply infused with Christian symbolism and figurative uses." Their concern here is both ideological and pragmatic: they want to avoid giving offense to non-Christians, but they do not want to have a list that is too long because of a need to give equal representation to diverse religious terms. As a result, they exclude Christian words such as "Chapel, Mission, Angel" but parenthetically argue that "Devil" is not objectionable when it is used as a "human personification of spiritual beings." It is not clear why "Devil" is acceptable and "Angel" is not considering that both are Angels. Their religious consideration also excludes words that might give offense such as "Ham" and "Beef," which "are excluded in deference to hierarchical Moslem and Hindu feelings."

A similar liberal attitude is expressed in the fourth consideration, "Moral Concepts," where they refer to the diverse "moral code[s] of different peoples" and therefore only select words that are "universally approved (or disapproved)" such as "Responsibility, Punctuality, Discipline, Vice."[85] Each of these terms implies a secular Western bias with assumptions about individualism (responsibility), temporality (punctuality), hierarchical order (discipline), and, as alluded to in the section on "squeamishness," immorality (vice). It is clear that the committee perceives each of these presumably universal terms as expressive of a nonideological order that is neither the Christian bias of the Missionaries nor the Anglicist bias of British nineteenth-century education. While that may be the case, these specific words also aptly describe the qualities of an ideal laborer who avoids vice, takes responsibility for his own work, follows commands, and is on time.

All of these considerations reflect the paradoxes inherent in having a criterion of universality that respects a cultural relativist worldview as part of a limited vocabulary that is also for general use. As with "Religious Objections," their criteria for "Names of Peoples," face the problem of either expanding the word list immoderately or only to include the most important and relevant. The first would defeat the purpose of the list and the second would open it up to criticism. As they do with religion, they resolve by elimination: they exclude all names of nationalities from the General Service List, leaving it up to the textbook writers for specific localities to include relevant names in the supplemental lists. Even "the word *English* is included as the name of the language" only, and it not intended as a reference to a nationality. Their negative definition of universality assumes that it is in not stating something that the list becomes unobjectionably neutral. Of course, this is to mistake doing nothing for saying something since obviously the negation is coming from somewhere. The privileged perspective here is granted to the makers of the list in the metropole to identify the presumed offence of words like "kiss," "ham," or the universal value of "punctuality." In many ways, this is an exemplary document of Indirect Rule in that their solution to nationalist criticism is not to deny them but to consign them to the status of supplements just as self-rule was always deferred within the need to maintain late imperialism.

The dependence on supplemental lists to resolve their contradictions of a General Word List for local uses comes through in the criteria "subject range." The nine examples for use in more specialized lessons include "classroom words," "business words," "application for employment," "letter-writing," "military terms," "agricultural terms," "mechanics," "professional words," and "customs of the Far East and Tropical Countries."[86] In keeping with the purpose of a neutral universality they use business words, for example, that refer to the "general purchasing public" rather than the vocabulary of specific tradespeople. But this section reveals the reasons that the committee imagines lay behind the worldwide adoption of English. This is evident in the title of the section "application for employment" as they write: "a very large number of those who learn English do so in the hope of ultimate official or commercial employment."[87] This refers to the tradition of educating an elite class in English for employment in the Civil Service or as middle management for global trade yet now its possibility is expanded beyond this narrow class. Significantly, the words they include in this sub-topic, "Appoint, Dismiss, Resign," have to do with the exercise of power around matters of inclusion and exclusion, which ideologically reinforces the power associated in this regard with English itself.

In this way, their subject categories not only suggest the privileging of a managerial class, but it also contributes to its reproduction as well. For instance, in part six, "words connected with Agriculture," they anticipate a redistribution of a global population undergoing the pressures of modernity:

> While we recognise that perhaps the majority of our pupils live in an agricultural environment, we have to remember that English is in the main used for intercommunication between the country and the town, and that a large proportion of our pupils live in towns. We have, therefore, tried to make our list

neutral, excluding urban phenomena which do not affect the rural child, and rural words which would be useless to the urban learner.

Despite repeating their principle of universality through exclusion, it is made clear that English has a role as an intermediary between rural and urban populations with the privilege tilted toward the latter. It is here that the globalist rather than the imperialist ideology of English is made more apparent. English increasingly becomes marked as the language of modernity, if not with empire or Britishness specifically. The traditional and the modern are connected to the rural and urban with the role of English clearly associated with the urban. English does not just exist in the urban space but functions as a mode of translating between the past and the present. As they write in the following section on "Words connected with Mechanics": "One of the important reasons for learning English is the need to discuss or acquire knowledge of mechanical matters" because "That part of the world which is our special concern is rapidly becoming more mechanised." In keeping with the Orientalist assumptions about English based in Macaulay's Minute of 1815, they note: "The mother-tongue of our pupils is often deficient in informative reading on these subjects and in many cases it lacks the necessary terminology."[88]

Because of the significance of this subject for the teaching of English as a foreign language they have intervened more fully in this aspect of the word list. Referring to Thorndike's and Horn's lists, the existing "objective" word lists are based in literature and periodicals from the nineteenth and early twentieth centuries so that they are lacking specifically in modern technological terms and reflect "an unmechanical world." Their observation suggests a closer cultural tie than otherwise noted; that is, if English was "unmechanical" only one generation previous then why would it not be possible for these other mother tongues to adapt to modernity at the same pace as English? This is also evident in the final category discussed in "subject range," "Customs of the Far East and Tropical Countries." For instance, "the four-wheeled *Wagon* is excluded because of the bad country roads in these areas, *Cart* being preferred."[89] The list positions the foreign language as premodern and unable to adapt to modernity. Though at the same time, as in this example of the Wagon/Cart, blind to the fact that colonialism left its effect on these areas through its roads, building and maintaining only those that were necessary for bringing natural resources to the ports. Instead, their landscapes are imagined, as if it were static. In some cases, such as technology, modern words are to be included, while in some cases, such as customs, they are fixed in a premodern environment. Also, if English was able to adapt to include new words for modernity why are other languages not able to expand in the same way? In this sense, the debate over language is not so different from that of the Anglicists and Orientalists a hundred years previously where English appears as an adaptable and diverse form in contrast to the static, and soon to be extinct, species of foreign languages.

The main body of the *Interim Report* consists of word lists organized in the form of the questionnaire used by the consultants at the conference. The words are divided into various lists of nouns, verbs, adverbs with designated semantic categories. For example, section four, list twenty, contains nouns for "transportation, travel, etc." Within the list the words are divided into categories of "inclusion, suspense, doubtful, and excluded" so that the teacher can see all the options within a managed selection. Initially, the committee sought an "included" list of approximately 2,000 words. Each word is accompanied by a number indicating word-frequency, which is arrived at by Faucett-Maki's list (a synthesis of the Thorndike and Horn lists). In this way, the committee allows for frequency to be part of the consideration by teachers, though in keeping with Palmer's and West's skepticism of objective word counts it is recommended to the teachers that the numbers "not be allowed to influence your independent judgment unduly."[90] The purpose here is to use the statistical words derived from the center as the basis for a selective list based in the teacher's opinion of their regional necessity.

The limitations of this selection are evident by the organizational categories that the teachers are given. The nouns are organized according to purpose and functionality beginning with "Time," "Nature," and "Mainly Human," and concluding with words used for "the Furnished Home," "Business, Industry, Commerce," and "Government, Peace, War."[91] As discussed in Chapter 2, statistical word lists like Thorndike's function ideologically as a mode of social reproduction while a subjective word list like Basic's imagines its language system as part of a new social order. In this regard, the Carnegie Report's General Service Word List signals its agnosticism about the two methods by using word frequency as the basis of the list and then allowing the teachers to rate and offer suggestions. This suggests it ambivalence about the degree to which it wants to be prescribing anything resembling a "view." This entire history of the conference and the making of the word lists are an exercise in disavowal and deferral—whether it is in the caution over offending Ogden, or of openly supporting a view toward World English, or in claiming responsibility for the document as a product of US corporatism or British Imperialism. The ambivalence in the word list between subjective and objective methods is another

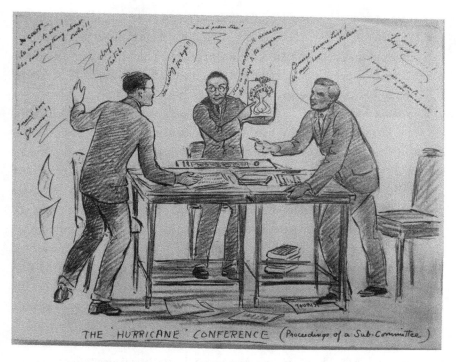

Figure 10 "The 'Hurricane' Conference." Cartoon. From left to right: Michael West, Harold Palmer, and Lawrence Faucett. Warwick ELT Archive.

disavowal of intentionality. But in another sense, even as they seek to remove any association of Britishness from "English" or offend any world cultures, the vocabulary unambiguously refers to a world in which Western norms of space, time, technology, and consumption appear as inextricable from the language. It amounts to what Bourdieu calls "doxa—an agreed account of how the world works. The more this account is unspoken and taken for granted, the more secure that regime of power."[92]

A cartoon sketch of West, Palmer, and Faucett making the word list as the Carnegie Conference sub-committee humanizes this banal process of "word-counting." Titled "The 'Hurricane' Conference," (see Figure 10) it depicts West, Palmer, and Faucett around a conference table arguing for certain words to be included: West declares "I must have glimmer," Palmer, "I need 'palm-tree,'" and Faucett, "We must have 'nevertheless.'" The title refers to debates over inclusion of "hurricane." Other floating voice balloons have other phrases that parody their respective styles, thus Palmer, who was the most pedantic of the group is speaking jargon, "that is an unopposite accretion, let us refer to the diagram," and pointing to a mock diagram of "Construction Patterns." West parodies the objective word list methodology by complaining that "the rating is too high!!" and Faucett shows the associative logic inherent to the subjective method: "I want 'mosquito' if we have 'malaria.'" As quoted earlier, West wrote to Keppel that the best part of the sub-committee was working together and collaborating after all of these years working as rivals or in relative isolation and that sense of humor comes through in this self-parody. In fact, the cartoon gestures at the innate absurdity of the entire enterprise of word lists and vocabulary control itself as Faucett's "If ... then" logic implies a list that extends all the way to full English.

Nevertheless (if I may use that word), the examples here, "palm tree," "mosquito/malaria," the word under Faucett's foot, "tourist," and even the title, "hurricane," all point to the global south as the subject under construction through this list. The ambivalence of the General Service List toward any social change is captured in its name, mocked here by Faucett whose "General Service List!" indicates its emptiness as a slogan. Ultimately, this emptiness is, like so much else about the conference, a form of disavowal as misdirection that becomes implicit in a particular type of ideological view of Global English as an accident.

Conclusion

After the *Interim Report* was delivered to the Carnegie Corporation in 1936, it was circulated around the world accompanied by a survey. In the following years, 1937–8, the main task was organizing the correspondence and responses from teachers and education ministers. On the US side, the Carnegie records show the distribution to areas that were deemed the responsibility of Fife including 341 copies sent to the Philippines, Puerto Rico, Hawaii, Latin America, and China. On the British side, Mayhew stated in 1938 that the list was "being widely used in the colonies." However, the Advisory Committee still insisted on distributing the Basic English list as well in order to avoid the appearance of making any preferential decision.[93] The ambivalence suggests the indecision over their purpose—are they maintaining an old colonial order or passing into a new phase of internationalism?—and the transatlantic power relations at the heart of the conference. To Mayhew, for all of its troubling internationalism, Basic English is one of "our"—that is British—lists and the Carnegie Report is too American even though it does the most toward reinforcing an imperial identity.

Judging from the reviews of the *Interim Report*, its readers were able to distinguish between Carnegie and Basic, which is what the Conference members had desired. Positive reviews in the journals *American Speech* and *English Studies in Japan*, and an English-language newspaper in Egypt, the *Egyptian Gazette*, appreciate it as a teaching document similar to Thorndike's elementary teaching vocabularies.[94] They all recognize its necessity whether for US immigrants or for use as a "starter vocabulary" in Egyptian or Japanese schools. The review in the *Egyptian Gazette* criticizes its grammatical examples before humorously quoting the Report's criticism of traditional Examiners who are interested in the "tricky and rare" parts of language. But in all the reviews there was recognition of the significant role of the Carnegie Corporation, the names of the experts, and the metropolitan locations for the two conferences as establishing the legitimacy of the list.

The provisional nature of the *Interim Report* contained in the title, and that was often stated in the Conference, meant that there was an expectation for a definitive version. This task was originally intended to be done by Faucett who was to incorporate the suggestions from the survey and revise into a final word list. However, his illness, first seen in 1935, returned in 1936 and forced him to retire while his daughter took over the job of collecting and organizing the correspondence. At the same time, Clarke had succeeded Nunn as the head of the London Institute of Education and, like Mayhew, sought to regain British control over English language teaching by demanding that the editor be someone "on our side" of the Atlantic.[95] After consulting with Keppel and Fife, they finally came back to the man who originated the entire project, Michael West, who had left the University of Toronto in 1935 and was in London, now with Palmer as well, publishing and writing textbooks. West agreed that the revision would be done "under the supervision of the Institute of Education" thus completing the project's transatlantic exchange of authority from the Carnegie Corporation.[96]

Before undertaking the revision, West submitted to the Corporation a formal memorandum on the history of the Conference and the *Interim Report*. Listing his reasons for organizing the conference, West first cites the "Linguistic war in Balkans and Near East. French and German being subsidised in Sofia and Istanbul" and the risks of English's "waning prestige" amid the rise of anti-colonial nationalism."[97] Ogden, too, is revised in this account. West lists him as one of the innovators in the field of limited vocabularies—along with Palmer, West, Thorndike, Aiken, and Swenson—and reduces the controversy over his non-attendance to a simple statement: "Ogden was not there. If he had been there I doubt if he would have been persuadable because he is an enthusiast." But

West recognizes the persistence of Basic English, especially within the British Foreign Office, in summing up the "present position": "Basic has achieved some success but is too small; most schools want something 'bigger than Basic, smaller than Carnegie.'" He even suggests co-ordinating with Basic as part of further experimentation before recalling that Ogden "is probably rather a difficult man, and even under the best of circumstances it would not have been easy to make him co-operative." Fittingly, West concludes with a parenthetical note about Ogden, writing that he is "now on reasonably friendly terms with him."

West's letter was written in June 1939, months before the World War that would impede him from completing the revision for another fourteen years. Five years after promoting the conference as about "World English," he writes humbly that "The ideal of English as a World Language is a very fascinating one, but a little heady." The Internationalist spirit of the interwar period expressed in *Bilingualism,* symbolized by Keppel's leadership at Carnegie, and captured in Ogden and Richards's aspirations for Basic English, appears distant and naïve from the perspective of 1939.[98]

However, in a few short years, due to the war effort, the language learning practices developed during this period would be infused with unprecedented resources and expertise in order to train soldiers and intelligence agents in European languages.[99] The British Council, semi-officially formed in 1935, at the same time as the Carnegie Conference, would gain permanent status in 1941 and begin developing teaching materials based in the simplified English schemes from Carnegie. The Cambridge Lower Exam, introduced in 1940, created a standard for English proficiency that was based on a simplified English, including the use of Basic English texts. Among figures in the ELT profession, the Carnegie Report was later criticized for technical issues over its use of objective or subjective modes of word rating.[100] Palmer's former assistant at IRET, and one of the compilers of the Carnegie list, A.S. Hornby, published the *Advanced Learners Dictionary of Current English* in 1948. He began it while at IRET and acknowledges the Carnegie list as its predecessor. Hornby's dictionary has remained in print in one form or another ever since, as Howatt remarks, "for a long time it held the field alone, and won a definitive status informally bestowed by the profession. One might say that, just as Johnson 'fixed' the English of the eighteenth century, Hornby 'fixed' English as a foreign language."[101] West's *General Service List* would also remain in print and be adapted as language teaching methods developed over the later twentieth century.

Carnegie's significance does not reside in its influence, direct or indirect, onto specific artifacts of ELT or Global English. Even if West had never completed revising it, the Conference was important because of how it professionalized the field of ELT, synthesized methods, and expanded the scope of English teaching beyond regionalized, "foreign" language teaching. All of this was not possible without the impetus of Basic English. But one cannot get this from reading the *Interim Report* alone. Reading it through the Conference record shows experts dealing with English in relation to its colonial past (as represented through Mayhew), its global future (in Basic), and its nationalist and anti-colonial present (West). They are able to negotiate through these multiple and contradictory contexts by way of their conception of an auxiliary language, "Plain English." The Conference record allows us to see an early and rare expression of the Anglophone ideology that would coincide with versions of late twentieth-century globalization. By itself, the Report appears as a teaching document, but when read along with the correspondence and the Minutes, it might be seen as expressing a desire for World English in tension with an anxiety over its success. At the time, the battle with Ogden was more tactical than philosophical: the question had more to do with how to achieve it most effectively: through Ogden's manifestoes and populist appeals or the Corporation's institutional social engineering. Their Plain English defeated Basic English by strategically using education and a tone of experimentation and provisionality to make the achievement of World English a mere accident of their Conference. Yet viewed through the perspective of Global English nearly a hundred years later, the battle defined the rhetorical conditions that would come to define debates over linguistic imperialism, English as a lingua franca, and World English.

Notes

1. Memo, Oct. 18, 1934, Box 140, Folder 7, CCNY. "In reply to an inquiry by FPK, West said that the suggestion of a conference was made by Sandiford while FPK was in Toronto."
2. "Record of an Informal Conference on the Teaching of English to Non-English-Knowing Pupils," Box 140, Folder 6, CCNY. Hereafter "Record."
3. *Carnegie Corporation of New York: Charter, Constitution and Bylaws* (Carnegie Corporation of New York, 1911). Accessed at https://library.columbia.edu/libraries/rbml/units/carnegie/ccny/history.html.
4. *Carnegie Corporation of New York: Historical Note*, https://library.columbia.edu/libraries/rbml/units/carnegie/ccny/history.html. Accessed August 10, 2021.

5 See Richard Glotzer, "Influence of Carnegie"; "Frederick P. Keppel and Carnegie Corporation's Interwar Area Experts: An Overview," *American Educational History Journal* 33, no. 1 (2006): 47–56. "A Long Shadow: Frederick P. Keppel, the Carnegie Corporation and the Dominions and Colonies Fund Area Experts 1923–1943," *History of Education* 38, no. 5 (2009): 621–48.
6 Glotzer, "Influence of Carnegie," 93–4.
7 See H. J. Carman, "Dean of Columbia College," in Charles Dollard, *Appreciations of Frederick Paul Keppel* (New York: Columbia University Press, 1951).
8 Glotzer, "Influence of Carnegie," 49.
9 Quoted by Glotzer, "Influence of Carnegie," 49.
10 Ibid., 627.
11 Glotzer, "Frederick P. Keppel" 2006, 49.
12 Glotzer, "Long Shadow," 630.
13 Quoted by Edward Berman, "American Influence on African Education: The Role of the Phelps-Stokes Fund's Education Commissions," *Comparative Education Review* 15, no. 2 (1971): 132.
14 Glotzer, "Influence of Carnegie," 52. "Between August, 1920, and March, 1921, the African Education Commission Visited Sierre Leone, Liberia, the Gold Coast, Nigeria, Cameroons, the Belgian Congo, Angola, and South Africa" (Berman, "American Influence," 135).
15 Quoted in Glotzer, "Influence of Carnegie," 5.
16 Glotzer, "Influence," 98.
17 Glotzer, "Long Shadow," 639.
18 Ibid.
19 CCNY book 2008, p. 4.
20 The only female exceptions to this rule were Mabel Carbey and Margaret Mead. See Glotzer, "Long Shadow," 621–2.
21 Ibid.
22 Glotzer "Long Shadow," 631. See Lagemann, *The Politics of Knowledge*, 100–3.
23 Peter Axelrod, *Making a Middle Class: Student Life in English Canada during the Thirties* (Montreal: McGill-Queen's University Press, 1990), 57.
24 Glotzer, "Long Shadow," 624.
25 Angus McLaren, "Stemming the Flood of Defective Aliens," in *The History of Immigration and Racism in Canada: Essential Readings,* ed. Barrington Walker (Toronto: Canadian Scholars Press, 2008), 191.
26 Quoted in McLaren, 197, 189–204.
27 Ibid.
28 Ibid. McLaren points out that Sandiford could only make this claim after dismissing as anomalous those tests that showed Chinese and Japanese students doing better than whites.

29 Correspondence from Keppel to Ogden, Aug. 15, 1934, Box 280, CCNY. Sandiford suggested putting part of the grant toward a "fundamental language study." In Corporation files, conference material is listed as "English Language Study."
30 Robert Herndon Fife, "Trends in Modern Language Teaching," *The French Review* 1, no. 2 (1928): 5–17.
31 Robert Herndon Fife, "Summary of Reports on the Modern Languages," *Modern Language Journal* 15, no. 5 (1931): 374.
32 Glotzer, "Influence," 104. Clarke also started *The British Journal of Education Studies*.
33 As a reviewer recollects nearly twenty years after his death: "[Clarke] was extremely influential in bringing to the fore both comparative studies in education and educational sociology: for him the work of Mead and Benedict, Fromm, Kardiner and Malinowski were adjuncts to his experience, whilst his own publications contain some of the most comprehensive statements of the culture pattern hypothesis" J. W. Tibble, Review of "Sir Fred Clarke: Master Teacher, 1880–1952 by F. W. Mitchell," *British Journal of Educational Studies* 15, no. 3 (1967): 336.
34 For instance, Tibble criticizes Clarke's cultural relativism as akin to "Rousseau's social authoritarian position" and, Judges, in an otherwise positive memorial upon Clarke's death, writes that "He could not be indifferent or entirely objective; so he was something less and yet more than a scholar." For both Judges and Tibble the fact that Clarke had "a political message" and was a "reformer through and through" are seen as critical faults. See Tibble, "Review," 336; A. V. Judges, "The Late Sir Fred Clarke," *British Journal of Educational Studies* 1, no. 1 (1952): 7.
35 Correspondence from Fife to West, July 2, 1934, Box 140, Folder 7, CCNY.
36 Correspondence from West to Keppel, July 5, 1934, Box 140, Folder 7, CCNY.
37 Correspondence from Keppel to West, July 10, 1934, Box 140, Folder 7, CCNY.
38 The first woman hired as an assistant professor was in 1929 and the first to be tenured was Ruth Benedict in 1937. Another, unstated, rationale might have to do with cost: by restricting membership to men, they could affordably hold the conference receptions and dinners at Keppel's restricted Century Club. Keppel also belonged to the inclusive Town Hall which he suggests as a possibility if it will be a mixed party, or as he put it "a 'cock and hen' party." See Correspondence from Keppel to West, July 25, 1934, Box 140, Folder 7, CCNY.
39 Correspondence from Keppel to West, June 1934, Box 140, Folder 7, CCNY. As if to drive home the point, the file heading for Carnegie would refer to him as "Professor Richardson." See copy of correspondence from IAR to West, 4 Aug. 34, Box 140, Folder 7, CCNY.
40 In his one positive observation about Basic, Fife is quite prophetic: he notes that a useful by-product of Basic will be for use in the radio, which in fact, becomes the case as it influences the vocabulary of the Voice of America broadcasts after the war. Correspondence from Fife to Keppel, Nov. 30, 1932, Box 280, CCNY.

41 L. H. Robbins, "850 English Words: A World Tongue," *The New York Times*, Nov. 20, 1932, 149.
42 Correspondence from May to Keppel, Nov. 25, 1932. Box 280, CCNY.
43 Correspondence from May to Keppel, Jan. 16, 1933, Box 280, CCNY. For more on May and IHR, see Dennis Bryson, "Mark A. May: Scientific Administrator, Human Engineer," *History of the Human Sciences* 28, no. 3 (2015): 80–114.
44 Correspondence from Richards to West, 4 Aug. 34, Box 140, Folder 7, CCNY. Underlining in original.
45 Correspondence from West to Ogden, Aug. 7, 34, Box 280, CCNY.
46 Memo, Aug. 13, 1934, Box 280, CCNY.
47 Memo, Aug. 18, 1934, Box 280, CCNY.
48 Correspondence from Root Clark, Buckner, and Ballantine to Keppel, Oct. 22, 1934, Box 280, CCNY.
49 Correspondence from Ogden to Keppel, Oct. 5, 1934, Box 280, CCNY.
50 Correspondence from Mayhew to Keppel, 20 Aug. 34, Folder 7, Box 140, CCNY. Emphasis added.
51 Correspondence from West to invitees, Aug. 24, 1934, Box 140, Folder 7, CCNY.
52 Correspondence from Ogden to Keppel, Sept. 28, 1934, Box 280, CCNY.
53 Record of an Informal Conference on the Teaching of English to Non-English-Knowing Pupils, Box 140, Folder 6, CCNY. Because these quotations are from the official Record of the meeting all speaking quotations are in the third person. To avoid too many notes, let it be understood that all subsequent references to the events from the conference in this chapter are from this record.
54 This is a common trope in colonial discourse; see Anne McClintock, *Imperial Leather* (New York: Routledge, 1995), 10.
55 Correspondence from Keppel to West, Nov. 13, 1934, Box 140, Folder 7, CCNY.
56 Arthur Mayhew, "A Note on the Conference on the Teaching of English" for the Advisory Committee on Education in the Colonies, Nov. 9, 1934, Box 140, Folder 7, CCNY.
57 Correspondence from Keppel to Clarke, Oct. 22, 1934, Box 140, Folder 7, CCNY.
58 Correspondence from Fife to Keppel, May 23, 1935, Box 140, Folder 6, CCNY.
59 Correspondence from Fife to West, March 15, 1935, Box 140, Folder 6, CCNY. Despite this, Palmer did attend the London Conference.
60 Correspondence from Fife to Keppel, May 23, 1935, Box 140, Folder 7, CCNY.
61 Memo Fife to Russell, May 10, 1935. Keppel was on a tour of Australia and the Middle East and was supposed to attend an event elsewhere in England on the date of the London Conference.
62 See Smith, *Pioneers of ELT*, vol. IV, xxi. Among the three experts, Keppel had identified Faucett as the one who might be a "key man" in the future and he supported the family long after the Interim Report was completed. See Box 142, CCNY.
63 Correspondence from Keppel to Russell, June 20, 1934, Box 140, Folder 7, CCNY.

64 Correspondence from West to Keppel, Oct. 3, 1935, Box 140, Folder 8, CCNY.
65 Budget Interim Report on Vocabulary Selection Box 140, Folder 6, CCNY.
66 Correspondence from Fife to Keppel, April 22, 1936, Box 140, Folder 8, CCNY.
67 Richards, "Commentary," 226.
68 Correspondence from Clarke to Keppel, Dec. 26, 1934, Box 140, Folder 7, CCNY.
69 Lawrence Faucett, Harold Palmer, Edward Thorndike, and Michael West, *Interim Report on Vocabulary Selection for the Teaching of English as a Foreign Language*, in *Teaching English as a Foreign Language, 1912-1936*, in Smith, *Pioneers of ELT*, vol. v, 389. Hereafter referred to as the *Interim Report*.
70 Faucett et al., *Interim Report*, 390.
71 Ibid., 394.
72 Ibid., 397-9.
73 *Record of an Informal Conference*, Box 140, Folder 6, CCNY.
74 Faucett et al., *Interim Report*, 397.
75 Ibid., 398.
76 Ibid.
77 Ibid.
78 Ibid., 399.
79 Jamaica Kincaid, *A Small Place* (New York: Farrar, Straus, Giroux, 1988), 18.
80 Faucett et al., *Interim Report*, 402.
81 Faucett et al., *Interim Report*, 402-3. All quotations in this paragraph refer to these pages.
82 West and Swenson, *Critical Examination*, 39 n.27.
83 Ibid., 30.
84 On the use of English as a means of reproducing a colonial-national mode of gender and sexuality for women see Chandra, *Sexual Life of English*.
85 Ibid., 403.
86 Ibid., 403-5.
87 Ibid., 404.
88 Ibid.
89 Ibid., 405.
90 Ibid., 418.
91 Ibid., 419.
92 Pierre Bourdieu, *Outline of a Theory of Practice* (Cambridge: Cambridge University Press, 1977), 167.
93 Notes on Past Interest of Corporation in Simplifying English Teaching, 1945, Box 55, CCNY.
94 Katherine M. Cook, "Review of Interim Report on Vocabulary Selection," *American Speech* 11, no. 3 (1936): 258-9. T. Sawamura, "Review of Interim Report on Vocabulary Selection," *Studies in English Literature* 17, no.4 (1937): 635-6 Reprint

from *English Society of Japan*, n.d.; "Plain English First," *Egyptian Gazette*, n.d., Box 140, Folder 8, CCNY.
95   Correspondence from Clarke to Keppel, Feb. 25, 1937, Box 140, Folder 8, CCNY.
96   Correspondence from Fife to Clarke, April 5, 1939, Box 140, Folder 8, CCNY.
97   West, "A Memorandum," June 1939, Box 140, Folder 8, CCNY.
98   Maybe it should not be so surprising given that on the same October day that the conference was first held in New York City, there was a congressional hearing downtown on the "un-American activities" of the Friends of New Germany. According to the *Chicago Tribune*, "300 members of the organization interrupted the proceedings several times with jeers and shouts of 'Heil Hitler'. A fistfight almost broke out between Jews and Nazi sympathizers when the hearing let out into the hall." *Chicago Tribune*, October 18, 1934, 20.
99   Howatt, *History of ELT* (2004), 303.
100 Ibid., 290.
101 Ibid., 296.

6

After Carnegie: Masking English

"It [Basic English] was made the official medium of communication throughout the world by the Air and Sea Control, and by 2020 there was hardly anyone in the world who could not talk and understand it."
— H. G. Wells, *The Shape of Things to Come* (1933)

"If World English is to be valued because of its soul, the artificial language should set out to make itself soulless: it should be soul-neutral."
— Michael West, "English as a World Language" (1934)

Ogden's Mask

In 1943, in an effort to shore up the allied effort during the Second World War, Winston Churchill was awarded an honorary degree from Harvard University where he gave a speech designed to act as "a public declaration to the world of Anglo-American unity and amity." Churchill famously evoked the English language as that shared commonality that could be used to dominate the post-war world: "I do not see why we should not try to spread our common language even more widely throughout the globe and, without seeking selfish advantage over any, possess ourselves of this invaluable amenity and birthright." A long admirer of Basic English, Churchill evokes Richards and Ogden as "gentlemen" at the "head-stream" of the future:

> Gentlemen, I make you my compliments. I do not wish to exaggerate, but you are the head-stream of what might well be a mighty fertilising and health-giving river. It would certainly be a grand convenience for us all to be able to move freely about the world—as we shall be able to do more freely than ever before as the science of the world develops—be able to move freely about the world, and be able to find everywhere a medium, albeit primitive, of intercourse and

understanding. Might it not also be an advantage to many races, and an aid to the building-up of our new structure for preserving peace?

The power of the common language will be a necessity since, as he says, in one of his most-often quoted phrases: "The empires of the future are the empires of the mind."[1] Later in the twentieth century, Churchill's speech would often be cited as an originary moment for Global English that anticipates the persistence of British imperial power into a postmodern, American-dominated world of information and knowledge. His speech made headlines and led to the formation of an interdepartmental cabinet committee that met several times until Churchill's defeat in the 1945 elections led to Basic English's official demise. Indicative of Basic's political association with Churchill is the relief expressed by the BBC controller for overseas services who wrote that "It seems to us likely that the recent change of Government here may result in the whole question [of Basic English] being put on a high shelf in a dark corner."[2]

It could be said that this was the fate for Basic English everywhere, not just at the BBC. As Richards later remarked, "The real headache of the future will be what can be said about Basic and *why* with Churchill's Harvard speech, that ALL went down the drain."[3] In 1943, Basic English was relatively dormant in comparison to the burst of production from the 1930s. The war had put on hold the 1939 plans by the Foreign Office for implementation of Basic (and the Carnegie List). Richards had relocated to Harvard before the war. For Ogden in particular, the "Empire of Minds" speech proved ruinous. As a result of Churchill's statement of support, the American enthusiasts of Basic English withdrew their financial support once they perceived that Basic English would have the full backing of the British Government. Also, having worked as a one-man operation for so long, Ogden bristled at government bureaucracy, while the government subcommittee was shocked by his budget requests. (Maybe not surprisingly, Ogden had an "immediate and intense dislike"[4] of the committee's chairman, Professor B. Ifor Evans.) It certainly did not help his cause that following Churchill's speech, Ogden greeted reporters at his apartment wearing a Greek mask. Refusing to answer their questions, he simply appeared in doorways wearing the different Greek masks that he collected. His eccentric performance was recorded in the popular news magazine, the *Picture Post* (see Figure 11). As his friend P. Sargant Florence regretfully recalled, "This may have seemed to Cabinet Ministers an odd way of greeting new responsibilities."[5]

Ogden's friends were familiar with his propensity toward wearing his Greek masks in conversations. As Mary Adams recalled, "he would wear a mask while

Figure 11 Ogden receiving reporters in his Greek mask. *Picture Post*, 23 October 1943.[6]

he talked to you—and often put a mask on you" because, Ogden would say, "this enables me to talk in terms of ideas and not in terms of personalities. I blot you out. I only listen to what you have to say and the ideas that you have."[7] As a prosthesis that separates words from the context of the speaker the mask represented an ideal scene of communication. The mask motif was part of the modernist aesthetic that defined Ogden and Richards's intellectual milieu. For example, the poet Ezra Pound (who wrote a celebrated review of Ogden's *Debabelization*) had described the act of translation as a "complete mask of the self," which also suggests the purpose of Ogden's own use of his Greek mask.[8] On that fateful day in 1943, it must have seemed to Ogden that the newspapers that sought to interview him represented the exact opposite of the ideal communicative situation that he hoped to create with the mask and, it should be added, with Basic English. To Ogden, mass journalism used language to confuse, persuade, excite, but not to communicate. In fact, one of Ogden's Basic English assignments directed students to translate newspaper articles into his more rational vocabulary; not only would this assignment teach the student the Basic English vocabulary, but it would reveal the fallacy of "word magic" in journalism. Ogden's mask represents the ideal condition in which Basic English would operate as a language: as a device that filters out individual personalities or cultural, national, and linguistic histories—all those concerns about the local context that Aiken, West, and Swenson raised about the suitability of Basic as a World Language.

For this reason, it makes sense that for all of its failures in being implemented as a language system, Basic English's immediate impact after the war was felt in its influence on radio and the nascent field of machine translation. Yunte Huang has written about the legacy of Basic English on the 1,500-word vocabulary used by the Voice of America radio program "Special English" that he grew up listening to in China.[9] In a related sense, at Harvard, Richards and Christine Gibson developed the *Language through Pictures* series that was to become the longest surviving Basic English textbook. Of course, Ogden broke with Richards over his adaptation of Basic even though Richards's experiments in film and sound proved that he was correct in foreseeing the applicability of Basic English to new educational technologies.[10]

As I discuss in Chapter 3, Rita Raley has argued for the "homology between the rationale of Global English and machine translation" while Lydia Liu has traced the impact of Basic English throughout the development of mid-century Information Theory. The most well-known instance comes in an exchange of letters from Warren Weaver and the founder of cybernetics, Norbert Wiener. For Wiener, the connotations of individual languages would be impossible for a machine to translate. He notes that Basic has suggested possibilities in the "mechanization of speech" but that "you must remember that in certain respects Basic English is the reverse of mechanical and throws upon such words as *get* a burden which is much greater than most words carry in conventional English." Weaver responds that Basic English was based on the combination of words to make up for its lack of verbs such as "*get up, get over, get back*" which, Weaver theorizes, could be taken as "single words" for a vocabulary of 4 million, which is "not so formidable a number to a modern computer."[11] Liu observes that Weaver views Basic as a statistical system and Wiener's argument "suggests a largely semantic understanding of Basic."[12]

The distinction that Liu makes resembles the vocabulary control debates over word list construction discussed in Chapters 2 and 4. Wiener's criticism of Basic's adequacy suggests West and Swenson's argument that Basic English produces more learning items than its 850-word list promises because of the extra burden put upon individual words. The idea that idioms such as Weaver's two word combinations should be counted as individual items was anticipated by Ogden who made this argument in the Preface to the Basic version of Poe's "Gold Bug." The difference is that West and Swenson were arguing that this burden was too much for a human learner whereas Weaver's point is that this is not such a great burden for a computer. Liu's insight about the difference between Wiener and Weaver's uses of Basic English can be taken as a paradox of Basic that was also played out in the distinction between the views of Basic English as a tool for teaching (by Richards but also by Lockhart, West, Swenson, Aiken) and Ogden's view of Basic as a universal language that can be used as a corrective for Word Magic in all of its forms.[13]

Ultimately, Basic English's legacy has been as an innovator and a disruptor. It was an innovator in the use of media like radio, the phonograph and film for language pedagogy and in its description of a language of the future; and it was a disruptor of the field of English Language Teaching. As Liu and others have noted, Basic English anticipated post-war media studies' recognition of the ways that language adapts to new forms of technology and media. It is in these many ways, through its failure, that Basic English was an experiment in reimagining our relation to language in an age of technology. This is quite different from how its success had been imagined in the middle of the century. For instance, in 1933 H. G. Wells cast it in *The Shape of Things to Come* as the utopian language of 2020, while in 1944, a year after Churchill's speech, George Orwell evoked Basic English as the totalitarian language used by the dystopian state in *1984*. Weaver's interpretation of Basic as a rational model of translation-as-decoding draws from Well's idealized version of Basic while Huang's evocation of his childhood experience of Basic English through the VOA suggests Basic English more along the lines of Orwellian Newspeak. Despite their differences, they each draw on the idea of Basic English as a kind of mask that hides the "complete self" in a form of translation.

However, it is important to recognize that the most lasting impact of Basic English and West and Palmer's Simplified Englishes on contemporary Global English was through a figure less well known than Churchill or even Ogden. The assistant secretary at the University of Cambridge Local Examinations Syndicate (UCLES) from 1925 to 1945 was Jack Roach, who had joined UCLES after a long career in the Indian Army. As I noted in Chapter 1, there was little centralized government investment in promoting English until the mid-1930s, but until then, it was Roach who strategized how to use the CLE "for the reaffirmation and spread' of British influence" and to "realise his 'modest ambition of making English the world language.'"[14] As ELT historians Weir, Vidakovic and Galaczi have argued, the Simplification and Vocabulary Control movements influenced his decision to introduce a Lower Certificate in English (LCE) in 1939. This test would not include as much reading and writing as the CLE and would make it possible to expand the number of candidates worldwide who could take the exam. The LCE brought UCLES and the British Council together in this endeavor in 1941 including using Basic English books as preparation for the LCE exam. This had the effect of re-starting the dormant controversy. At the inaugural meeting of the British Council, Professor Daniel Jones, the famous phoneticist who had brought Palmer to the University of London during the First World War, argued that the British Council could not associate itself with an exam "in something which might not be English."[15] They resolved to use the phrase "Simple English" instead and agreed to only use those Basic texts that read "naturally." By offering the lower exam, UCLES and the British Council made possible the expansion of English to Kachru's "outer circles" that would take full effect in the 1960s. Although it removed all signs of Basic English (or basic-sounding English) from its exams, it was not as easy to remove Ogden's ideological view of English as a neutral, instrumental auxiliary language that would shape its promotion for the rest of the century.[16]

This history of the making of World English during the interwar period demonstrates the ways in which this conception of English as a language synonymous with neoliberalism that is part of the contemporary "entrenched ideological constructions of English ... as entity, as commodity, as capital with global convertibility"[17] was made possible as a response to the conditions of late imperialism. Reading the present through the past, it is possible to understand why defenses of Global English—as "accidental," as "neutral," as necessary for "modernity"—stay so persistently the same over the past century. The conditions of late imperialism, a nascent international economy, and vocabulary control methods produced arguments for English as an international auxiliary language that appeared rational and scientific. When it is viewed in the tradition of colonial linguistics and IALs like Esperanto rather than as part of a specifically English-language history, Global English appears as a structure designed for efficiency and flexibility. As the examples of West, Palmer, and Ogden illustrate, they created such language systems that promoted scientific efficiency over nationality, and they used modern methods of marketing and international foundations as external support to legitimatize English as a necessary language to participate in modernity.

This might be best illustrated by conceiving of the post-world war history of Global English into three overlapping phases that derived their framework from the rhetoric of this period.[18] The first phase witnessed the

Cold War implementation of English through the British Council and US-sponsored agencies aligning English with freedom, individualism, and capitalist democracy. It is also a period where English was adopted by many postcolonial governments as an official or diplomatic language. The language teaching materials produced during the 1930s and the vocabulary control method provided the groundwork for post-war ESL. The second phase, in the late twentieth-century, when English becomes associated more with economic opportunity rather than political or national identity, is anticipated by West's arguments in *Bilingualism* that English become available to a wider population that needs English to participate economically in the international "Great Society" of the future. The third phase, our contemporary moment, views language politics through the lens of technology, the role of social media, and machine translation. While some have interpreted the present as not only "post-human" and "post-global" but also "post-English," to some critical observers of language politics in Artificial Intelligence and machine translation technologies, it also signals a new phase of English hegemony. A sign of the persistence of these interwar concerns can be seen in the contrast between the two dominant methods of machine translation: Google's statistical, quantitative methods, versus a rule-based SYSTRAN method, as used by Babel Fish, which replicate the debate over Thorndike's objective, statistical methods and Ogden's subjective, rule-based Basic English word list. As Raley has argued, Google Translate still depends upon English as a common language for interlingual translations granting Global English a form of "network power."[19] This power is not so different from that attributed to English as a language of wider communication that pertains to Lemaire's *Vocabulaire Practique* or the simplified word lists discussed in Chapter 2. Whenever we engage in debates over the role of Global English, whether it is a form of linguistic imperialism, or an integral element of a technological, global economy, the terms remain shaped by the interwar definition of auxiliary English.

As a consequence, the controversies and debates of the 1930s also put into place the framework for criticizing this ideological form of global English. The range of Anglophone ideologies—from the imperial, monolingualist models of Global English to the pluralist multilingualism of World Englishes—are all at play during this early conception of English as a world language. The interwar formulation of an instrumental form of English also relates to the pluralist views of English that develop in the late twentieth century. West's economic arguments for the highest "surrender value" in English language education argued for competency at all levels of education, not just standard proficiency at the highest. The emphasis on reading rather than speaking counters privileging standard English pronunciation that resulted from the Direct Method. The following statement by Ruanni Tupas about pluralist multilingualism could also apply to West's *Bilingualism*: "it has demolished the idea of the supremacy of a monolith English language ... on the other hand, it has divested the language of its colonial moorings, thus subtly affirming and perpetuating the hegemonic power of English today."[20] This paradox comes out of a concern with correcting imperial prejudices and countering local, nationalist anxieties of that imperialism. Where West was responding to the imperatives of the Dual Mandate and anti-colonial sentiments in Bengal, contemporary pluralist arguments for equality of languages seek to correct for monolingual biases and balance the needs of individual agents operating as economic actors within neoliberal globalization. The fact is that even if we concede English as a plurality, those differences in varieties coincide with existing global inequalities.[21] Understanding World English as an intentional object should help us to make this distinction between "English *per se* and linguistic hegemony" as part of our ongoing discussions over the status and meaning of English as a world language.[22]

West's Mask

In the wake of Churchill's speech, questions about supporting Basic English were revived at the Carnegie Corporation. At this point, most of the men and women of 1934 were no longer around. West was still productively working in London (and would do so into the 1960s); Palmer left the IRET in Japan and returned to England where he lectured occasionally and wrote materials for Longman before dying in 1949;[23] Faucett returned to the United States and turned his attention to moral philosophy and comparative philology.[24] Among the New York contingent, Aiken, Keppel, and Thorndike had all passed away and Fife had retired from Columbia. As a result, there was scarcely anyone left at Carnegie when David Stevens, a former supporter of Basic English with the Rockefeller Foundation, and now with the General Education Board, approached Robert Lester, the Secretary of Carnegie, with a plan to revive Basic English after Churchill's speech. Lester was dismissive, summarizing the pre-war controversy as belonging to the "department of utter confusion."

> Some think Basic English should be developed simply as a means of giving instruction to non-English speaking persons; others believe it should be promoted as an international diplomatic language. There has been great variety of opinion as to selection of words ... As a matter of fact, the whole business seems to belong to the department of utter confusion.[25]

On the other side of a world war, these pre-war controversies over word lists appeared trivial and naive, as did the faith, so closely identified with Keppel's time at the Corporation, that a single foundation, acting in the image of a leading figure and his cohort, could effect global social change through education alone.[26]

However, the work that Keppel had described ten years previously as one of the Corporation's "most difficult" and "most important" jobs had not entirely disappeared. After the war, West picked up the revision of the *Interim Report* that he had barely started in 1939. The final product, published by Longman, *The General Service List of English Words* appeared in 1953 and it would become an influential part of early ESL course design.[27] In his introduction to *The General Service List*, West returns to the principles of auxiliary English first laid out in *Bilingualism* almost thirty years before. He explains that one of the factors he considered in vocabulary selection is that of "Intensive and Emotional words," since, he writes, "the foreigner is learning English *to express ideas rather than emotion; for his emotional expression he has the mother-tongue.*" West repeats the dichotomies of emotion and intelligence, mother tongue and auxiliary, technology and literature that were embodied in the vocabulary control debates. The inner space of the non-English speaker remains an independent spiritual space while the external space of "ideas" was the domain of English. This time, however, West even goes so far as to state as a matter of fact that "English is a rather unemotional language."[28] This sentiment is not meant as an accurate description of the English language itself as much as it reflects West's understanding that any World English needs to distinguish itself from normative, standard English. As he wrote about international languages in 1934:

> We need a language which is so simple that everyone can learn it, and yet it must be capable (unlike World English) of ranging over the whole field of ideas. Essentially it must be a language of practical and formal discussion, of commerce and diplomacy. *It need have not emotional values and nuances*; on the contrary it should avoid them. It should be a language in which it is impossible to lose one's temper (as impossible as in algebra), and impossible to mean less or more or other than one says. If World English is to be valued because of its soul, the artificial language should set out to make itself soulless: it should be soul-neutral.

The Carnegie Conference represented an attempt at creating a "soul-neutral" World English. By casting "unemotional" English as an auxiliary supplement to the unreasoned mother tongue identity of the speaker, West defines its role as an auxiliary language in the post-war world.

In this way, West's claims for an "unemotional English" are not so different from Ogden's claims for Basic English as a language system divorced from the worlds of dialect and vernacular. These masks of English persist nearly a hundred years later. They were invented through these interwar debates over word lists and methods of ELT, over the fitness of English as a regional, foreign language or a universal, second language. By seeing the masks as constructed through the discursive frame of institutions, disciplines, markets, and even individual personalities, this history and analysis offer a means of understanding these modern and postmodern masks of English as prostheses of power. The counterpart to this "soul-neutral" English has been a valorization of vernaculars and particular uses of English. But this response has already been anticipated by West in *Bilingualism* where he valorizes national vernaculars as part of an argument for the role of an auxiliary language. This was also implicit in the examination of word lists and mother tongues in Chapter 2; the interwar discourse of auxiliary languages also had as its object the production of its Other—primitive languages for Palmer and Ogden, "national" languages for West.[29] The auxiliary needs these "mother tongues" in order to fashion itself as a contingent language and as part of an ideological disavowal of its structuring dominance.

Nearly a hundred years after the Carnegie Conference, English has passed through several phases as an international language from its role as the ideological counterpart to the cold war and economic neoliberalism to its current iteration as a *lingua franca* in a post-human and post-global world order. Arguments for an instrumental form of English can be traced to the requirement of English for the Indian Civil Service that informed the 1854 reforms. As West observes in *Bilingualism*, the lingering presence of the Anglicist argument for English— and English literature—as a means of moral uplift impeded these reforms from taking place in the British Indian curriculum. The *Interim Report* and *General Service List* sought to resolve this problem by standardizing a normative model of English that can also act as a technical language for the world.

When West submitted the *Interim Report* to Keppel in 1936, he also made him a gift of his own 1913 prose translation of troubadour poetry, *Claire de Lune and Other Troubadour Romances*. Notably, Pound's comment about translation as a "mask for the self" was referring to his youthful translations of troubadour poetry. West does not cast his translation in such Poundian terms; instead, he describes it humorously as "an antidote to the report": "You will notice the vocabulary is not limited, and the opinions expressed therein are not liable to give rise to any controversy!"[30] Indeed, while it is possible that Pound or other translators might object to his traditional, Victorian interpretation, such complaints would lack the stakes involved in creating a universal language as part of a worldwide colonial system.

As a gift, West's translation acts as the exact opposite to the *Interim Report*. It is a "full English" not a simplified English; if the *Interim Report* seeks to remove the "intensive, emotional words" from English, then West's translation seeks to infuse such words *into* English. Rather than seeking to distinguish and separate English from other languages, the translation seeks to merge English with its Provençal "other." There is a further irony in the fact that the troubadours represented the first vernacular literature to appear in print while the *Interim Report* represents the other end of this historical language continuum: the resolution of these vernaculars into a "new Latin." As an originary text, the Troubadours share status with vernaculars and mother tongues, a kind of excessive speech that supplements the limited vocabulary of the auxiliary language represented by the *Interim Report*. Where the Troubadours represent English's multilingual origins, the Carnegie Conference marks its monolingual present. Instead of addition through translation, auxiliary English depends upon the opposite process of simplification through the process of removing those emotional, intensive words associated with literature and the mother tongue. The Troubadours and the Carnegie Report represent the paradox that the vocabulary control movement inherited from colonial linguistics, namely, the ambivalent relationship between the mother tongue and an imperialist language of wider communication. Over time it becomes difficult to disentangle them from one another or even identify which came first. Contemporary concepts like English as a Lingua Franca, World Englishes, Global English, Netlish, World Literature in English, and even Standard English depend upon a shared term "English" that has become increasingly hard to define.

West's translation mimics Ogden's Greek mask as another "mask of the self." Over forty years ago, Gauri Viswanathan memorably described the colonial discipline of English as a "mask of conquest." She was using the metaphor to evoke the irony of humanist education being deployed for colonial dominance. It may be that Ogden's performance in his Greek mask was a reminder that while the conditions have changed, the "English mask" remains. The English of the future would "blot out" individual cultures, histories and strive for its "soul-neutral" ideal. At the same time, the mask suggests performance, speaking one's own language through its structures. Understanding the Anglophone as such a mask might help to understand its place in the world, as a means of maintaining hierarchies of status, repressing language rights, and managing other forms of inequality. The mask metaphor also serves as a reminder of the contingency of language and to signal the importance of the performance that ultimately determines whether it is a mask that obscures or reveals.

Notes

1. Winston Churchill, "The Gift of a Common Tongue." International Churchill Society. *WinstonChurchill.org*. https://winstonchurchill.org/resources/speeches/1941-1945-war-leader/the-price-of-greatness-is-responsibility/.
2. K. E. Garay, ""Empires of the Mind"? C. K. Ogden, Winston Churchill, and Basic English," *Communications Historiques* 23, no. 1 (1988): 289.
3. Russo, *I. A. Richards*, p. 776, n. 33.
4. Quoted in Garay, "Empires of the Mind?," 289.
5. P. Sargant Florence, "Cambridge 1909–1919 and Its Aftermath," in *Collective Memoir*, 44, note.
6. C. K. Ogden, "Can Basic English Be a World Language?" *Picture Post* 21, no. 2, Oct. 23, 1943, 23+. Picture Post Historical Archive, 1938-1957, link.gale.com/apps/doc/EL1800013364/PIPO?u=wash43584&sid=PIPO&xid=e515b960. Accessed Feb. 3, 2021.
7. Quoted in Florence, *Collective Memoir*, 44.
8. Quoted in Stuart Y. McDougal, *Ezra Pound and the Troubadour Tradition* (Princeton: Princeton University Press, 1972) 6. The quote is from Pound, *Gaudier-Brzesca* (New York: New Directions Press, 1974), 85.
9. Yunte Huang, "Basic English, Chinglish, and Translocal Dialect," 76. Created in 1959, "Special English" still exists as "Learning English," a controlled vocabulary of English.
10. See Liu, *Freudian Robot*, 88.
11. For more on Basic English and the Weaver-Wiener letters, see Liu, *Freudian Robot*, 85–6; Raley, "Machine Translation and Global English," 291.
12. Liu, *Freudian Robot*, 86.
13. On the Cambridge obsession with accuracy also associated with Russell and Wittgenstein, see Quigley, *Modernist Fiction and Vagueness*; McElvenny, *Language and Meaning*, 18–24.
14. Cyril J. Weir and Barry O'Sullivan, *Assessing English*, 13. This includes direct quotations from Roach's writing in 1929 and 1956.

15 Ibid., 24.
16 Weir and O'Sullivan write about the expansion in the 1960s: "the eventual decision for CPE to offer a more language focused route from 1966 onwards was groundbreaking, and reflected a developing interest in the *use of English* among the language teaching profession and applied linguistics. It again signified the increased importance accorded to English as a global means of communication rather an object of study for accessing British culture." See Weir and O'Sullivan, *Assessing English*, 32.
17 Quoted in Thomas Ricento, "The Promise of Global English," in Peter A. Kraus and François Grin, *The Politics of Multilingualism: Europeanisation, Globalisation, and Linguistic Governance* (Amsterdam-Philadelphia: John Benjamins Publishing Company, 2018), 202.
18 I am basing this sketch on Phillipson's from "English, the *Lingua Nullius* of Global Hegemony," in Kraus and Grin, *The Politics of Multilingualism*, 282–3.
19 Raley, Rita, "Another Kind of Global English," *Minnesota Review*, no. 78 (2012): 108.
20 Ruanni Tupas and Rani Rubdy, "Introduction: From World Englishes to Unequal Englishes," in *Unequal Englishes*, 2.
21 Ricento, "The Promise of Global English," 211.
22 Grin, "Fashionable Terms," 274.
23 Smith, *Pioneers of ELT*, vol. II, xvi.
24 Ibid., vol. IV, xxii.
25 Memo of phone conversation between David Stevens and Robert M. Lester (RML), Dec. 7, 1945, Box 55, CCNY.
26 On the changes at Carnegie after the war, Lagemann, *The Politics of Knowledge*, 147–53.
27 On the legacy of West's *General Service List* including its contributors and the response, see Howatt 289–90, 297. Howatt makes clear that the "spadework" (297) from the 1930s provided the basis for the first ELT books in the 1950s.
28 Michael P. West, ed., *A General Service List of English Words* (London: Longmans, 1953), x. Emphasis added.
29 See Kubota, "Inequalities of Englishes," 23–6. Mufti, *Forget English!*, 173.
30 Correspondence from West to Keppel, March 25, 1936, Box 140, Folder 8, CCNY.

Bibliography

Archives

[CCNY] Carnegie Corporation of New York Records. Columbia University Rare Book and Manuscript Library, New York, NY.
[Warwick] History of ELT Archive, Warwick Centre for Applied Linguistics, University of Warwick, UK.

References

Aiken, Janet Rankin. "'Basic' and World English." *American Speech* 8, no. 4 (December 1933): 17–21.
Aiken, Janet Rankin. *Commonsense Grammar*. New York: Thomas Y. Crowell Co., 1936.
Aiken, Janet Rankin. "English as the International Language." *American Speech* 9, no. 2 (April 1934): 98–110.
Aiken, Janet Rankin and Margaret Bryant. *The Psychology of English*. New York: Columbia University Press, 1940.
Aiken, Janet Rankin. *Surely Goodness: Sixty-six Little Sketches of Nineteen Ways to Become Good at Living*. Ridgefield, CT: Quarry Books, 1942.
Aiken, Jean Sherwood. *Everyday English: Book II*. Boston: Educational Publishing Company, 1906.
Allender, Tim. *Ruling through Education: Schooling in Colonial Punjab*. Sydney: New Dawn Press, 2006.
Anderson, Benedict. *Imagined Communities: Reflections on the Origin and Spread of Nationalism*. London: Verso, 1983.
Anderson, Dorothée. "A Biographical Essay." In *This Language-Learning Business*. Edited by Roland Mackin and Peter Strevens. London: Oxford University Press, 1969. 133–61.
Annamalai, E. "Nation-building in a Globalised World: Language Choice and Education in India." In *Decolonisation, Globalistion: Language-in-Education Policy and Practice*. Edited by Angel M. Y. Lin and Peter Martin. Clevedon, UK: Multilingual Matters, 2005. 20–37.
Appuhn, Karl. "Microhistory." In Methods & Theory/Periods/Regions, Nations, Peoples/ Europe & the World. Edited by Peter N. Stearns, 105–12. Vol. 1 of *Encyclopedia of*

European Social History. Detroit, MI: Charles Scribner's Sons, 2001. *Gale eBooks* (accessed February 12, 2021). https://link.gale.com/apps/doc/CX3460500023/GVRL?u=viva_gmu&sid=GVRL&xid=1518d00d.

Arrighi, Giovanni. *The Long Twentieth Century: Money, Power, and the Origins of Our Times*. New York: Verso, 2010.

Ashcroft, Bill. *Caliban's Voice: The Transformation of English in Post-Colonial Literatures*. New York: Routledge, 2009.

Auerbach, Erich. *Literary Language and Its Public in Late Latin Antiquity and in the Middle Ages*. Translated by Ralph Manheim. Princeton: Princeton University Press, 1993.

Axelrod, Peter. *Making a Middle Class: Student Life in English Canada during the Thirties*. Montreal: McGill-Queen's University Press, 1990.

Baer, Ben Conisbee. *Indigenous Vanguards: Education, National Liberation, and the Limits of Modernism*. New York: Columbia University Press, 2019.

Baldwin, Melinda. "Scientific Autonomy, Public Accountability, and the Rise of 'Peer Review' in the Cold War United States." *Isis* 109, no. 3 (2018): 538–58.

Ballantyne, Tony. "Empire, Knowledge and Culture: From Proto-Globalization to Modern Globalization." In *Globalization in World History*. Edited by A. G. Hopkins. London: Pimlico, 2002.

Baloji, Sammy and Maarten Couttenier. "The Charles Lemaire Expedition Revisited: Sammy Baloji as a Portraitist of Present Humans in Congo Far West." *African Arts* 47, no. 1 (Spring 2014): 66–81.

Baudelaire, Charles. *Edgar Allan Poe: sa vie et ses ouvrages*. Edited by W. T. Bandy. Toronto: University of Toronto Press, 2016.

Bellenoit, Hayden J. A. *Missionary Education in Late Colonial India, 1860–1920*. Empires in Perspective Series. Vol.3. London: Pickering and Chatto, 2007.

Belmihoub, Kamal. "English in a Multilingual Algeria." *World Englishes* 37, no. 2 (2018): 207–27.

Benrabah, Mohamed. *Language Conflict in Algeria: From Colonialism to Post-Independence*. Bristol: Multilingual Matters, 2013.

Berns, Margie, ed. *Concise Encyclopedia of Applied Linguistics*. 1st Edition. London: Elsevier, 2009.

Blommaert, Jan. *The Sociolinguistics of Globalization*. Cambridge: Cambridge University Press, 2010.

Boldrini, Lucia. "Translating the Middle Ages: Modernism and the Ideal of a Common Language." *Translation and Literature* 12, no. 1 (Spring 2003): 41–68.

Bonfiglio, Thomas Paul. *Mother Tongues and Nations: The Invention of the Native Speaker*. Boston: De Gruyter, 2010. Accessed November 21, 2019. ProQuest Ebook Central.

Bongers, Herman. *The History and Principles of Vocabulary Control: As It Affects the Teaching of Foreign Languages in General and of English in Particular*. Woerden, HL: Wocopi, 1947.

Bourdieu, Pierre. *Outline of a Theory of Practice*. Cambridge: Cambridge University Press, 1977.

Bourdieu, Pierre. *The Rules of Art: Genesis and Structure of the Literary Field*. Translated by Susan Emanuel. Stanford: Stanford University Press, 1996.

Bradshaw, David. *A Concise Companion to Modernism*. Malden, MA: Blackwell Publishing, 2003.

Bradshaw, David, and Kevin J. H. Dettmar. *A Companion to Modernist Literature and Culture*. Malden, MA: Blackwell Publishing, 2006.

Brutt-Griffler, Janina. *World English: A Study of Its Development*. Clevedon, UK: Multilingual Matters, 2002.

Bryson, Dennis. "Mark A. May: Scientific Administrator, Human Engineer." *History of the Human Sciences* 28, no. 3 (2015): 80–114.

Burton, Antoinette and Hofmyer, Isabel, eds. *Ten Books That Shaped the British Empire: Creating an Imperial Commons*. Durham, NC: Duke University Press, 2014.

Campbell, Carl. "Education and Black Consciousness: The Amazing Captain J. O. Cutteridge in Trinidad and Tabago, 1921–42." *The Journal of Caribbean History* 18, no.1 (May 1983).

Canagarajah, Suresh. *Translingual Practice: Global Englishes and Cosmopolitan Relations*. London: Routledge, 2013.

Carter, Robert and Michael McCarthy, *Vocabulary and Language Teaching*. London: Longman, 1988.

Casanova, Pascale. *The World Republic of Letters*. Trans. M. B. DeBevoise. Cambridge: Harvard University Press, 2004.

Chakrabarty, Dipesh. *Provincializing Europe: Postcolonial Thought and Historical Difference*. Princeton: Princeton University Press, 2008.

Chandra, Shefali. *The Sexual Life of English: Languages of Caste and Desire in India*. Durham: Duke University Press, 2012.

Chatterjee, Partha. "The Curious Career of Liberalism in India." *Modern Intellectual History* 8, no.3 (2011): 687–96.

Chatterjee, Partha. *The Nation and Its Fragments*. Princeton, NJ: Princeton University Press, 1993.

Chatterjee, Partha, ed. *Texts of Power: Emerging Disciplines in Colonial Bengal*. Minneapolis: University of Minnesota Press, 1995.

Chatterjee, Rimi. *Empires of the Mind: A History of Oxford University Press in India under the Raj*. New Delhi: Oxford University Press, 2006.

Chaudhary, Latika. "Caste, Colonialism, and Schooling." In *A New Economic History of Colonial India*. Edited by Latika Chaudhary, Bishnupriya Gupta, Tirthankar Roy, Anand Swamy. London: Routledge, 2016. 161-78.

Chaudhary, Shreesh. "First Textbooks in English in India." In *Language Policy and Education in India: Documents, Contexts and Debates*. Edited by M. Sridhar and Sunita Mishra. London: Routledge, 2017. 147–65.

Cheah, Pheng. *What Is a World?: On Postcolonial Literature as World Literature*. Durham: Duke University Press, 2016.

Churchill, Winston. "The Gift of a Common Tongue." International Churchill Society. *WinstonChurchill.org*. https://winstonchurchill.org/resources/speeches/1941-1945-war-leader/the-price-of-greatness-is-responsibility/.

Clifford, Geraldine Jonçich. *The Sane Positivist; a Biography of Edward L. Thorndike*. Middletown, Connecticut: Wesleyan University Press, 1968.

Cochran, Robert. *Louise Pound: Scholar, Athlete, Feminist Pioneer*. Lincoln: University of Nebraska Press, 2009.

Cohn, Bernard S. *Colonialism and Its Forms of Knowledge: The British in India*. Princeton, NJ: Princeton University Press, 1996.

Cooper, James Fenimore, and Michael Philip WEST. *The Deerslayer ... Brought within the Vocabulary of New Method Reader 4 by Michael West, Etc. (Second Edition, Reset and Re-Illustrated.)*. [New Method Supplementary Reader.]. London: Longmans, 1959.

Crehan, Kate. "Gramsci's Concept of Common Sense: A Useful Concept for Anthropologists?" *Journal of Italian Studies* 16, no. 2 (2011): 273–87.

Crooke, Nigel, ed. *Transmission of Knowledge in South Asia: Essays on Education, Religion, History, and Politics*. Delhi: Oxford University Press, 1996.

Crystal, David. *The Stories of English*. New York: Overlook Press, 2004.

Crystal, David. *English as a Global Language*. Cambridge: Cambridge University Press, 2003.

Damrosch, David. *What Is World Literature?* Princeton: Princeton University Press, 2003.

Darnell, Regna. *Edward Sapir: Linguist, Anthropologist, Humanist*. Berkeley: University of California Press, 1990.

Davies, Alan. *The Native Speaker: Myth and Reality*. Clevedon, UK: Multilingual Matters, Ltd., 2003.

DeRocher, James, Murray S. Miron, Sam M. Patton, and Charles C. Pratt. *The Counting of Words: A Review of the Techniques and Theory of Word Counts*. Prepared for the Defense Language Institute. Syracuse, NY: Syracuse University Research Corporation, 1973.

Dollard, Charles. *Appreciations of Frederick Paul Keppel*. New York: Columbia University Press, 1951.

Doloughan, Fiona. *English as a Literature in Translation*. London: Bloomsbury, 2016.

Ellen, Roy, Ernest Gellner, Grazyna Kubica, and Janusz Mucha, eds. *Malinowski between Two Worlds: The Polish Roots of an Anthropological Tradition*. Cambridge: Cambridge University Press, 1988.

Errington, Joseph. *Linguistics in a Colonial Context: A Story of Language, Meaning, and Power*. London: Blackwell, 2008.

Esplin, Emron. "Cosmopolitan Poe: An Introduction." *The Comparatist*, no.35 (2011): 98–210.

Esplin, Emron, and Margarida Vale De Gato. "Introduction: Poe in/and Translation." In *Translated Poe*. Edited by Emron Esplin and Margarida Vale De Gato. Bethlehem, PA: Lehigh University Press, 2014. xi–xxi.

Esty, Jed. *Unseasonable Youth: Modernism, Colonialism, and the Fiction of Development*. Oxford: Oxford University Press, 2012.

Evans, Stephen. "Macaulay's Minute Revisited: Colonial Language Policy in Nineteenth-century India." *Journal of Multilingual and Multicultural Development* 23, no. 4 (2002): 260–81.

Fabian, Johannes. *Language and Colonial Power*. Cambridge: Cambridge University Press, 1986.

Falk, Julia S. *Women, Language and Linguistics: Three American Stories from the First Half of the Twentieth Century*. London: Routledge, 1999.

Falk, Julia S. "Words without Grammar: Linguists and the International Auxiliary Language Movement in the United States." *Language and Communication* 15, no. 3 (1995): 241–59.

Faucett, Lawrence, Harold Palmer, Edward Thorndike, and Michael West. *Interim Report on Vocabulary Selection for the Teaching of English as a Foreign Language*. London: P. S. King, 1936. Reprinted in *Teaching English as a Foreign Language, 1912–1936: Pioneers of ELT*, vol. V, edited by Richard C. Smith. London: Routledge, 2003. 383–503.

Fife, Robert Herndon (R. H.). "Summary of Reports on the Modern Languages." *Modern Language Journal* 15, no. 5 (1931): 372–5.

Fife, Robert Herndon. *A Summary of Reports on the Modern Foreign Languages*. Publications of the American and Canadian Committees on Modern Languages/Modern Foreign Language Study, 18. New York: Macmillan, 1931.

Fife, Robert Herndon (R. H.). "Trends in Modern Language Teaching." *The French Review* 1, no. 2 (1928): 5–17.

Fischer-Tiné, Harald, and Michael Mann. *Colonialism as Civilizing Mission: Cultural Ideology in British India*. Anthem South Asian Studies. London: Wimbledon Publishers, 2004.

Florence, P. Sargant, and J. R. L. Andeson, eds. *C. K. Ogden: A Collective Memoir*. London: Pemberton Publishing Co. Ltd., 1977.

Frank, Leonhard. *Carl and Anna*. Translated into Basic English by L. W. Lockhart. Second Edition. London: Kegan Paul, Trench, Trubner and Co., Ltd., 1933.

Frank, Leonhard. *Carl and Anna*. Translated by Cyrus Brooks. London: G. P. Putnam's sons, 1929.

Fraser, Robert. *Book History through Postcolonial Eyes: Rewriting the Script*. London: Routledge, 2008.

Fraser, Robert. "School Readers in the Empire and the Creation of Postcolonial Taste." In *Books without Borders, Volume 1: The Cross-National Dimension in Print Culture*. Edited by Robert Fraser and Mary Hammond, Palgrave Macmillan, 2008. 89–106.

Friedman, Thomas. *The World Is Flat: A Brief History of the Twenty-First Century*. New York: Farrar, Straus, Giroux, 2005.

Galef, Bennet G. "Edward Thorndike: Revolutionary Psychologist, Ambiguous Biologist." *American Psychologist* 53, no. 10 (1998).

Garay, K. E. "'Empires of the Mind'? C. K. Ogden, Winston Churchill and Basic English." *Historical Papers/Communications historiques* 23, no. 1 (1988): 280–91.

Garvía, Roberto. *Esperanto and Its Rivals: The Struggle for an International Language.* Philadelphia: University of Pennsylvania Press, 2015.

Ghosh, Durba. *Gentlemanly Terrorists: Political Violence and the Colonial State in India, 1919-1947.* Cambridge: Cambridge University Press, 2017.

Gikandi, Simon. "Provincializing English." *PMLA* 129, no. 1 (2014): 7–17.

Gikandi, Simon. *Writing in Limbo: Modernism and Caribbean Literature.* Ithaca, N. Y: Cornell University Press, 1992.

Glotzer, Richard. "The Influence of Carnegie Corporation and Teachers College, Columbia, in the Interwar Dominions: The Case for Decentralized Education." *Historical Studies in Education/Revue d'histoire de l'education* 1, nos. 1/2 (2000): 93–111.

Glotzer, Richard. "Frederick P. Keppel and Carnegie Corporation's Interwar Area Experts: An Overview." *American Educational History Journal* 33, no. 1 (2006): 47–56.

Glotzer, Richard. "A Long Shadow: Frederick P. Keppel, the Carnegie Corporation and the Dominions and Colonies Fund Area Experts 1923-1943." *History of Education* 38, no. 5 (2009): 621–48.

Gogaku Kyōiku Kenkyūjo (Japan). *Interim Report on Vocabulary Selection: Submitted to the Seventh Annual Conference of English Teachers.* Tokyo: The Institute, 1930.

Gordin, Michael D. *Scientific Babel: How Science Was Done before and after Global English.* Chicago: University of Chicago Press, 2015.

Gordon, W. Terrence. *C. K. Ogden and Linguistics.* 5 Volumes. London: Routledge/Thoemmes Press, 1994.

Gordon, W. Terrence. "Linguistics and Semiotics I: The Impact of Ogden & Richards' *The Meaning of Meaning*" In *History of the Language Sciences: An International Handbook on the Evolution of the Study of Language from the Beginnings to the Present.* Edited by Sylvain Auroux, E.F.K. Koerner, Hans- Josef Niederehe and Kees Versteegh. New York: De Gruyter Mouton, 2008. 2579–88. https://doi.org/10.1515/9783110167368.3.39.2579.

Goswami, Manu. *Producing India: From Colonial Economy to National Space.* Chicago: University of Chicago, 2004.

Graddol, David. *English Next.* London: British Council, 2006.

Greenfeld, Liah. *The Spirit of Capitalism: Nationalism and Economic Growth.* Cambridge: Harvard University Press, 2001.

Grin, François. "On Some Fashionable Terms in Multilingualism Research: Critical Assessment and Implications for Language Policy." In *The Politics of Multilingualism: Europeanisation, Globalisation, and Linguistic Governance.* Edited by Peter A. Kraus, and François Grin. Amsterdam-Philadelphia: John Benjamins Publishing Company, 2018. 247–74.

Halliday, M. A. K. "Written Language, Standard Language, Global Language." In *The Handbook of World Englishes.* Edited by Braj B. Kachru, Yamuna Kachru, and Cecil L. Nelson. London: Blackwell, 2006. 349–65.

Hochschild, Adam. *King Leopold's Ghost: A Story of Greed, Terror, and Heroism in Colonial Africa*. New York: Mariner Books, 1998.

Holborow, Marnie. *The Politics of English*. London: Sage, 1999.

Holborow, Marnie. "Language, Ideology, and Neoliberalism." *Journal of Language and Politics* 6, no. 1 (2007): 51–73.

Howatt, Anthony P. R. *A History of English Language Teaching*. New York: Oxford University Press, 1984.

Howatt, Anthony P. R. with H. G. Widdowson. *A History of English Language Teaching*. Second Edition. Oxford Applied Linguistics. Oxford: Oxford University Press, 2004.

Huang, Yunte. "Basic English, Chinglish, and Translocal Dialect." In *English and Ethnicity*. Edited by Janina Brutt-Griffler and Catherine Evans Davies. New York: Palgrave Macmillan, 2006. 75–103.

Huang, Yunte. *Transpacific Displacement: Ethnography, Translation, and Intertextual Travel in Twentieth-century American Literature*. Berkeley: University of California Press, 2002.

Huddart, David. *Involuntary Associations: Postcolonial Studies and World Englishes*. Liverpool: Liverpool University Press, 2014.

Hutchins, W. John, ed. *Early Years in Machine Translation*. Philadelphia: John Benjamins Publishing Co., 2000.

Ichikawa, Sanki. *Collected Writings of Sanki Ichikawa*. The Institute for Research in Language Teaching. Tokyo: Kaitakusha, 1966.

James, Allan. "Theorising English and Globalisation: Semiodiversity and Linguistic Structure in Global English, World Englishes and Lingua Franca English." *Apples: Journal of Applied Linguistics* 3, no. 1 (2009): 79–92.

Jespersen, Otto. *Language: Its Nature, Development, and Origin*. New York: Norton, 1964.

Jespersen, Otto. *How to Teach a Foreign Language*. Translated by Sophia Yhlen-Olsen Bertelsen. London: George Allen and Unwin, Ltd., 1904:1967.

Jespersen, Otto. *An International Language*. New York: Norton, 1929.

Joseph, John E., and Talbot J. Taylor, eds. *Ideologies of Language*. London: Routledge, 1990.

Joshi, Priya. *In Another Country: Colonialism, Culture, and the English Novel in India*. New York: Columbia University Press, 2002.

Joshi, Svati. *Rethinking English: Essays in Literature, Language, History*. Delhi: Oxford University Press, 1995.

Kennedy, J. Gerald. *Strange Nation: Literary Nationalism and Cultural Conflict in the Age of Poe*. Oxford: Oxford University Press, 2016.

Kennedy, J. Gerald, and Liliane Weissberg, eds. *Romancing the Shadow: Poe and Race*. Oxford: Oxford University Press, 2001.

Keppel, Frederick Paul. *Philanthropy and Learning*. New York: Columbia University Press, 1936.

Kincaid, Jamaica. *A Small Place*. New York: Farrar, Straus, Giroux, 1988.

Kiselman, Christer. "Esperanto: Its Origins and Early History." In *Prace Komisji Spraw Europejskich PAU*. Edited by Andrzej Pelczar. Krakow: Polska Akademia Umiejeno, 2008.

Koeneke, Rodney. *Empires of the Mind: I. A. Richards and Basic English in China, 1929-1979*. Stanford: Stanford University Press, 2004.

Kraus, Peter A., and François Grin. *The Politics of Multilingualism: Europeanisation, Globalisation, and Linguistic Governance*. Amsterdam-Philadelphia: John Benjamins Publishing Company, 2018.

Krishnaswamy, N. and Archana S. Burde. *The Politics of Indians' English: Linguistic Colonialism and the Expanding English Empire*. Delhi: Oxford University Press, 1998.

Kroskrity, Paul, ed. *Regimes of Language: Ideologies, Polities and Identities*. Santa Fe, NM: School of American Research Press, 2000.

Kumar, Krishna. "Origins of India's 'Textbook Culture.'" *Comparative Education Review* 32, no. 4 (1988): 452-64. https://doi.org/10.1086/446796.

Kumar, Krishna. *The Political Agenda of Education: A Study of Colonialist and Nationalist Ideas*. New Delhi: Sage Publications, 2005.

LaDousa, Chaise. *Hindi Is Our Ground, English Is Our Sky: Education, Language, and Social Class in Contemporary India*. New York: Berghahn Books, 2014.

Lagemann, Ellen Condliffe. *The Politics of Knowledge: The Carnegie Corporation, Philanthropy, and Public Policy*. Wesleyan, CT: Wesleyan University Press, 1989.

Landau, Paul. "Language." In *Missions and Empire*. Edited by Norman Etherington. Oxford: Oxford University Press, 2005. 194-215.

Langendoen, D. Terence. *The London School of Linguistics: A Study of the Linguistic Theories of B. Malinowski and J.R. Firth*. Boston: M.I.T Press, 1968.

Léger, Benoit. "*Traduction négative et traduction littérale: les traducteurs de Poe en 1857.*" *Études françaises*, no. 432 (2007): 85-98.

Lemaire, Charles. *The Geographic Journal* vol 29 (1907) *Tra Mez-Afriko. (A travers l'Afrique centrale) Par le Commdt*. Lemaire, Charles. *Vocabulaire Pratique: Francais, Anglais, Zanzibarite (Swahili), Fiote, Kibangi-Irébou, Mongo, Bangala*. Second Edition. Brussels: CH. Bulens, 1897.

Liu, Lydia H., ed. *Tokens of Exchange: The Problem of Translation in Global Circulations*. Durham: Duke University Press, 1999.

Liu, Lydia H. *The Freudian Robot: Digital Media and the Future of the Unconscious*. Chicago: University of Chicago Press.

Lockhart, L. W. *The Basic Way Reading Books*, Book One. London: Evans Bros. Ltd., 1939.

Macaulay, Thomas. "Document Fourteen: Minute Recorded in the General Department by Thomas Babington Macaulay, Law Member of the Governor-General's Council, dated 2 February 1835." In *The Great Indian Education Debate: Documents Relating to the Orientalist-Anglicist Controversy, 1781-1843*. Edited by Lynn Zastoupil and Martin Moir. Richmond, UK: Curzon, 1999. 161-74.

Mair, Christian. *Twentieth-Century English: History, Variation, and Standardization.* Cambridge, UK: Cambridge University Press, 2006.

Mair, Christian, ed. *The Politics of English as a World Language: New Horizons in Postcolonial Cultural Studies.* Cross/cultures 65. Amsterdam; New York, NY: Rodopi, 2003.

Mangan, J. A. *The Imperial Curriculum: Racial Images and Education in the British Colonial Experience.* London: Routledge, 1993.

May, Stephen, ed. *Language Rights.* The International Library of Essays on Rights. New York: Routledge, 2017.

McClintock, Anne. *Imperial Leather: Race, Gender, and Sexuality in the Colonial Contest.* New York: Routledge, 1995.

McCrea, Barry. *Languages of the Night: Minor Languages and the Literary Imagination in Twentieth-Century Ireland and Europe.* New Haven: Yale University Press, 2015.

McCrum, Robert. *Globish: How English Became the World's Language.* New York: Norton, 2010.

McDonald, Peter D. *Artefacts of Writing: Ideas of the State and Communities of Letters from Matthew Arnold to Xu Bing.* First edition. Oxford: Oxford University Press, 2017.

McDougal, Stuart Y. *Ezra Pound and the Troubadour Tradition.* Princeton: Princeton University Press, 1972.

McElvenny, James. *Language and Meaning in the Age of Modernism: C.K. Ogden and His Contemporaries.* Edinburgh: Edinburgh University Press, 2018.

McKee, Clayton Tyler. "Translation and Audience: Edgar Allen Poe's 'The Gold Bug.'" *International Journal of Comparative Literature and Translation Studies* 5, no. 4 (2017): 1–10.

McLaren, Angus. "Stemming the Flood of Defective Aliens." In *The History of Immigration and Racism in Canada: Essential Readings.* Edited by Barrington Walker. Toronto: Canadian Scholars Press, 2008. 189–204.

Mignolo, Walter. "Nebrija in the New World. The Question of the Letter, the Colonization of American Languages, and the Discontinuity of the Classical Tradition." *L'Homme* 32, no. 122 (1992): 185–207.

Miller, Joshua. *Accented America: The Cultural Politics of Multilingual Modernism.* New York: Oxford University Press, 2011.

Mills, John A. *Control: A History of Behavioral Psychology.* New York: New York University Press, 1998.

Misak, Cheryl. *Frank Ramsey: A Sheer Excess of Powers.* Oxford: Oxford University Press, 2020.

Mitchell, Linda C. "Grammar Wars: Seventeenth- and Eighteenth-Century England." In *The Handbook of World Englishes.* Edited by Braj Kachru, Yamuna Kachru, and Cecil L. Nelson. London: Routledge, 2006. 475–95.

Moretti, Franco. *Distant Reading.* London: Verso, 2013.

Morrison, Toni. *Playing in the Dark: Whiteness and the Literary Imagination.* Cambridge, MA: Harvard University Press, 1992.

Mufti, Amir. *Forget English! Orientalisms and World Literature.* Cambridge: Harvard University Press, 2016.

Mukherjee, Alok. "Early English Textbooks and Language Policies in India." In *Language Policy and Education in India: Documents, Contexts and Debates.* Edited by M. Sridhar and Sunita Mishra. London: Routledge, 2017. 9–25.

Mulhern, Francis. *The Moment of "Scrutiny."* London: Verso, 1981.

Murata, Kumiko and Jenkins, Jennifer, eds. *Global Englishes in Asian Contexts: Current and Future Debates.* New York: Palgrave MacMillan, 2009.

Murdoch, Brian. "War, Identity, Truth and Love: Leonhard Frank's *Karl Und Anna.*" *Forum for Modern Language Studies* 37, no. 1 (2002): 49–62.

Nadeau, Jean-Benoît and Julie Barlow. *The Story of French.* New York: St. Martin's Press, 2006.

Nero, Shondel J., and Dohra Ahmad. *Vernaculars in the Classroom: Paradoxes, Pedagogy, Possibilities* New York, NY: Routledge, 2014.

North, Michael. *The Dialect of Modernism: Race, Language and Twentieth Century Literature.* New York: Oxford University Press, 1994.

Northrup, David. *How English Became the Global Language.* New York: Palgrave, 2013.

Ogden, C. K. *Debabelization.* Psyche Miniatures. General Series, no. 36. London: Kegan Paul, Trench, Trubner & Co., 1931.

Ogden, C. K. *The System of Basic English.* London: Orthological Institute, 1934.

Ogden, C. K. "Can Basic English Be a World Language?" *Picture Post* 21, no. 2, 23 Oct. 1943, 23+. Picture Post Historical Archive, 1938-1957, link.gale.com/apps/doc/EL1800013364/PIPO?u=wash43584&sid=PIPO&xid=e515b960. Accessed 3 Feb. 2021.

Ogden, C. K. (Charles Kay). *Basic English: An International Second Language*, edited by E. C. Graham (New York: Harcourt, Brace and World, 1968).

Ogden, C. K. *C. K. Ogden and Linguistics.* 5 vols. Edited by W. Terrence Gordon. London: Routledge/Thoemmes Press, 1994.

Ogden, C. K. and I. A. Richards. *The Meaning of Meaning: A Study of the Influence of Language Upon Thought and the Science of Symbolism.* New York: HBJ, 1989.

Ogden, C. K, Paul Desdemaines Hugon, and L. W Lockhart. *Basic English versus the Artificial Languages.* Psyche Miniatures. General Series, No. 78. London: K. Paul, Trench, Trubner and Co, 1935.

Orde, Anne. *The Eclipse of Great Britain: The United States and British Imperial Decline, 1895–1956.* New York: St. Martin's Press, 1996.

Palmer, Harold. *Principles of Language Study.* London: George Harrap & Co., 1921. Reprinted in Richard C. Smith, *Teaching English as a Foreign Language, 1912–1936.* Pioneers of ELT. Vol. II. London: Routledge, 2003. 1–186.

Palmer, Harold. *The Gold Beetle, This Being the Simplified Version by Harold Palmer of the Gold Bug by Edgar Allan Poe*, vol. 1. Tokyo: Institute for Research in English Teaching, 1932.

Palmer, Harold. *The Gold Beetle, This Being the Simplified Version by Harold E. Palmer of The Gold Bug by Edgar Allan Poe*. Tokyo: Institute for Research in English Teaching, 1932.

Palmer, Harold. *The Grading and Simplifying of Literary Material: A Memorandum*. Tokyo, Institute for Research in English Teaching, 1934. Reprinted in Richard C. Smith, *Teaching English as a Foreign Language, 1912–1936. Pioneers of ELT*. Vol. V. London: Routledge, 2003. 257–368.

Palmer, Harold. "History and Present State of the Movement towards Vocabulary Control." *The Bulletin of the Institute for Research in English Teaching*, no. 120, pp. 14–17, no. 121, Tokyo, 1936, 19–23. Reprinted in Richard C. Smith, *Teaching English as a Foreign Language, 1912–1936. Pioneers of ELT*. Vol. V. London: Routledge, 2003. 369–80.

Palmer, Harold. *The Principles of Language Study*. London, Harrap, 1921. Reprinted in Richard C. Smith, *Teaching English as a Foreign Language, 1912–1936. Pioneers of ELT*. Vol. II. London: Routledge, 2003. 1–186.

Palmer, Harold and H. Vere Redman. *This Language-Learning Business*. Oxford: Oxford University Press, 1969.

Parsons, Timothy. *The Second British Empire: In the Crucible of the Twentieth Century* Lanham, Maryland: Rowman & Littlefield, 2014.

Pennycook, Alastair. *The Cultural Politics of English as an International Language*. London: Longman, 1994.

Pennycook, Alastair. *English and the Discourses of Colonialism*. London: Routledge, 1998.

Pennycook, Alastair. "Beyond Homogeny and Heterogeny." In *The Politics of English as a World Language: New Horizons in Postcolonial Cultural Studies*. Edited by Christian Mair, 3–17. Cross/cultures 65. Amsterdam: Rodopi, 2003.

Pennycook, Alastair. "English as a Language Always in Translation." *European Journal of Language Studies* 12, no. 1 (2008): 33–47.

Phillipson, Robert. *Linguistic Imperialism*. Oxford Applied Linguistics. New York: Oxford University Press, 1992.

Phillipson, Robert. *Linguistic Imperialism Continued*. London: Routledge, 2009.

Phillipson, Robert. "English: From British Empire to Corporate Empire." *Sociolinguistic Studies* 5, no.3 (2013): 456. 441–64. doi: 10.1558/sols.v5i3.441.

Phillipson, Robert. English, the *Lingua Nullius* of Global Hegemony. In Peter A. Kraus, and François Grin, *The Politics of Multilingualism: Europeanisation, Globalisation, and Linguistic Governance*. Amsterdam-Philadelphia: John Benjamins Publishing Company, 2018. 275–304.

Poe, Edgar Allan. "The Gold-Bug." In *Collected Works of Edgar Allan Poe, Tales and Sketches, 1843–1849*. Edited by Thomas Ollive Mabbott. Cambridge: Belknap Press of Harvard University Press, 1978. 799–847.

Poncelet, Marc. "Colonial Ideology, Colonial Sciences, and Colonial Sociology in Belgium." *The American Sociologist* 51, no. 148 (2020): 148–71.

Pugach, Sara. *Africa in Translation: A History of Colonial Linguistics in Germany and Beyond,1814–1945*. Ann Arbor: University of Michigan Press, 2012.

Quigley, Megan. *Modernist Fiction and Vagueness: Philosophy, Form, and Language*. Cambridge: Cambridge, University Press, 2015.

Rafael, Vicente L. *Motherless Tongues: The Insurgency of Language and Wars of Translation*. Durham: Duke University Press, 2016.

Raley, Rita. "Machine Translation and Global English." *The Yale Journal of Criticism* 16, no. 2 (2003): 291–313.

Raley, Rita. "Another Kind of Global English." *Minnesota Review*, no. 78 (2012): 105–12.

Rapatahana, Vaughan, and Pauline Bunce. *English Language as Hydra Its Impacts on Non-English Language Cultures*. Bristol: Multilingual Matters, 2012.

Ricento, Thomas. "The Promise of Global English." In Peter A. Kraus and François Grin, *The Politics of Multilingualism: Europeanisation, Globalisation, and Linguistic Governance*. Amsterdam-Philadelphia: John Benjamins Publishing Company, 2018. 201–22.

Richards, I. A. *Practical Criticism: A Study of Literary Judgment*. New York: Harcourt, 1929.

Richards, I. A. *Basic Rules of Reason*. London: Kegan, Paul, 1933.

Richards, I. A. *Basic in Teaching: East and West*. London: Kegan, Paul, 1935.

Richards, I. A. *Basic English and Its Uses*. New York: Norton, 1943.

Richards, I. A. *Mencius on the Mind: Experiments in Multiple Definition*. London: Kegan, Paul, 1932; Richmond, UK: Curzon, 1997.

Richards, Jack C. and Theodore Rogers. *Approaches and Methods in Language Teaching*. 2nd Edition. Cambridge: Cambridge University Press, 2001.

Rolls, Alistair and Clara Sitbon. "'Traduit de l'américain' from Poe to the *Série Noire*: Baudelaire's Greatest Hoax?" *Modern and Contemporary France* 21, no. 1 (2013): 37–53.

Rosenheim, Shawn James. *The Cryptographic Imagination: Secret Writing from Edgar Poe to the Internet*. Baltimore: Johns Hopkins University Press, 1997.

Rossiter, A. P. *The Gold Insect. Being the "Gold Bug" Put into Basic English*. London: Kegan Paul, 1932.

Russo, John Paul. *I. A. Richards: His Life and Work*. New York: Routledge, 1989.

Samarin, William. "Language in the Colonization of Central Africa, 1880–1900." *Canadian Journal of African Studies/Revue Canadienne des Études Africaines* 23, no. 2 (1989): 232–49.

Saraceni, Mario. *World Englishes: A Critical Analysis*. London: Bloomsbury, 2015.

Sartori, Andrew. *Bengal in Concept History*. Chicago: University of Chicago, 2008.

Schmitt, Norbert. *Vocabulary in Language Teaching*. New York: Cambridge University Press, 2000.

Scott, Walter. *Ivanhoe*. New York: Barnes and Noble, 2005.

Scott, Walter and Michael West. *Ivanhoe*. New Method Readers. Supplementary Reader: Grade Six. London: Longman and Greens, 1945.

Sen, Satadru. *Colonial Childhoods: The Juvenile Periphery of India, 1850–1945*. Chicago: Anthem Press, 2005.

Sen, Satadru. "A Juvenile Periphery: The Geographies of Literary Childhood in Colonial Bengal." *Journal of Colonialism and Colonial History* 5, no. 1 (2004). n.p.

Sengupta, Indra and Daud Ali, eds. *Knowledge Production, Pedagogy, and Institutions in Colonial India*. London: Palgrave Macmillan, 2011.

Sengupta, Parna. "An Object Lesson in Colonial Pedagogy." *Comparative Studies in Society and History* 45, no. 1 (2003): 96–121.

Seth, Sanjay. *Subject Lessons: The Western Education of Colonial India*. Durham: Duke University Press, 2007.

Shen, Shuang. *Cosmopolitan Publics: Anglophone Print Culture in Semi-colonial Shanghai*. New Brunswick, NJ: Rutgers University Press, 2009.

Shiach, Morag. "'To Purify the Dialect of the Tribe': Modernism and Language Reform." *Modernism/Modernity* 14, no. 1 (2007): 21–34.

Shih, Shu-mei. *The Lure of the Modern: Writing Modernism in Semicolonial China, 1917–1937*. Berkeley: University of California Press, 2001.

Slaughter, Joseph. *Human Rights, Incorporated: The World Novel, Narrative Form, and International Law*. New York: Fordham, 2007.

Smith, Richard C. *Teaching English as a Foreign Language, 1912–1936: Pioneers of ELT*. 5 Volumes. Logos Studies in Language and Linguistics. London: Routledge, 2003.

Sollors, Werner. *Multilingual America: Transnationalism, Ethnicity, and the Languages of American Literature*. New York: New York University Press, 1998.

Sommers, Doris. *Bilingual Games: Some Literary Investigations*. New York: Palgrave, 2003.

Spivak, Gayatri. *An Aesthetic Education in the Era of Globalization*. Cambridge: Harvard University Press, 2012.

Sridhar, M., and Sunita Mishra. *Language Policy and Education in India: Documents, Contexts and Debates*. London, England: Routledge, 2017.

Stolzenberg, Nomi M. "Bentham's Theory of Fictions: A 'Curious Double Language.'" *Cardozo Studies in Law and Literature* 11, no. 2 (1999): 223–61.

Szymura, Jerzy. "Bronislaw Malinowski's 'Ethnographic Theory of Language.'" In *Linguistic Thought in England, 1914–1945*. Edited by Roy Harris. London: Duckworth, 1988. 106–31.

Talib, Ismail S. *The Language of Postcolonial Literatures: An Introduction*. London: Routledge, 2002.

Tignor, Robert L. "In the Grip of Politics: The Ford Motor Company of Egypt, 1945–1960." *Middle East Journal* 44, no. 3 (1990): 383–98. Accessed July 3, 2021. http://www.jstor.org/stable/4328139.

Toner, Jennifer Dilalla. "The 'Remarkable Effect' of 'Silly Words': Dialect and Signature in 'The Gold-Bug.'" *Arizona Quarterly* 49, no. 1 (1993): 1–20.

Tong, Q. S. "The Bathos of Universalism: I. A. Richards and His Basic English." In *Tokens of Exchange: The Problem of Translation in Global Circulations*. Edited by Lydia H. Liu. Durham: Duke University Press, 1999. 331–54.

Tsu, Jing. *Sound and Script in Chinese Diaspora*. Cambridge: Harvard University Press, 2010.

Tupas, Ruanni, ed. *Unequal Englishes: The Politics of Englishes Today*. London: Palgrave Macmillan, 2015.

Vadde, Aarthi. "Language's Hopes: Global Modernism and the Science of Debabelization." *The New Modernist Studies*. Edited by Douglas Mao. Cambridge: Cambridge University Press, 2021. 200–24.

Varughese, E. Dawson. *Beyond the Postcolonial: World Englishes Literature*. New York: Palgrave, 2012.

Viaene, Vincent. "King Leopold's Imperialism and the Origins of the Belgian Colonial Party, 1860–1905." *The Journal of Modern History* 80, no. 4 (December 2008): 741–90.

Vines, Lois Davis. "Poe Translations in France." In *Translated Poe*. Edited by Emron Esplin and Margarida Vale De Gato. Lanham, MD: Rowan and Littlefield, 2014. 47–55.

Vines, Lois Davis, ed. *Poe Abroad: Influence, Reputation, Affinities*. Iowa City: University of Iowa Press, 1999.

Viswanathan, Gauri. *Masks of Conquest: Literary Study and British Rule in India*. New York: Columbia University Press, 1989.

Walkowitz, Rebecca. *Born Translated: The Contemporary Novel in an Age of World Literature*. New York: Columbia University Press, 2015.

Walkowitz, Rebecca. "Response." *Interventions* 20, no. 3 (2018): 361–5.

Wallaert, Ineke. "The Translation of Sociolects: A Paradigm of Ideological Issues in Translation?" *Language across Boundaries*. Edited by Janet Cotterill and Anne Ife, Continuum, 2001. 171–84.

Wallas, Graham. *The Great Society: A Psychological Analysis*. London: MacMillan, 1914.

Wee, Lionel. *Language without Rights*. New York: Oxford University Press, 2011.

Weir, Cyril J., and Barry O'Sullivan. *Assessing English on the Global Stage: The British Council and English Language Testing, 1941–2016*. Sheffield, UK: Equinox Publishing, 2017.

Weissberg, Liliane. "Black, White, Gold." In *Romancing the Shadow: Poe and Race*. Edited by Gerald J. Kennedy and Liliane Weissberg. Oxford: Oxford University Press, 2001. 127–56.

West, Michael. *Education and Psychology*. London: Longmans, 1914.

West, Michael. *Indian School Management and Inspection: A Practical Handbook*. Bombay: K & J Cooper, 1920.

West, Michael. "English as a World Language." *American Speech* 9, no. 3 (Oct. 1934): 163–74.

West, Michael. *A General Service List of English Words with Semantic Frequencies and a Supplementary Word-List for the Writing of Popular Science and Technology*. London: Longman, 1953.

West, Michael. *The Teaching of English: A Guide to the New Method Series*. London: Longmans 1953.

West, Michael. *Learning to Read a Foreign Language and Other Essays on Language-Teaching*. London: Longmans, 1955.

West, Michael. "The Gold Bug." In *Tales of Mystery and Imagination: Edgar Allan Poe*, simplified by Roland John and Michael West. Longman Classics Stage 4. London: Longman, 1988, 15–27.

West, Michael. *Bilingualism (with Special Reference to Bengal)*, Bureau of Education, India, Occasional Reports, no. 13, Calcutta: Government of India Central Publication Branch. Reprinted in Richard C. Smith, *Teaching English as a Foreign Language, 1912–1936. Pioneers of ELT*. Vol. III. London: Routledge, 2003. 1–392.

West, Michael. *New Method Reader VI: For Teaching English Reading to Foreign Children* London: Longman, n.d.

West, Michael, Elaine Swenson, et al. *A Critical Examination of Basic English*. Bulletin no. 2. The Department of Educational Research, Ontario College of Education, University of Toronto, 1934.

Whalen, Terence. "Average Racism: Poe, Slavery, and the Wages of Literary Nationalism." In *Romancing the Shadow: Poe and Race*. Edited by Gerald J. Kennedy and Liliane Weissberg. Oxford: Oxford University Press, 2001, pp. 3–40.

Whitehead, Clive. *Colonial Educators: The British Indian and Colonial Education Service 1858–1983*. London, GBR: I.B. Tauris, 2003. ProQuest ebrary. Web. 6 February 2015. Princeton University Press, 2006.

Willinsky, John. *Empire of Words: The Reign of the OED*. Princeton, NJ: Princeton University Press, 1994.

Whalen, Terence. "Average Racism: Poe, Slavery, and the Wages of Literary Nationalism." In *Romancing the Shadow: Poe and Race*. Edited by Gerald J. Kennedy and Liliane Weissberg. Oxford: Oxford University Press, 2001. 3–40.

Williams, Michael. "'The Language of the Cipher': Interpretation in 'The Gold Bug.'" *American Literature* 53, no. 4 (1982): 646–60.

Woods, Carly S. *Debating Women: Gender, Education, and Spaces for Argument, 1835–1945*. East Lansing: Michigan State Press, 2018.

Xie, Ming. "Trying to Be on Both Sides of the Mirror at Once: I. A. Richards, Multiple Definition, and Comparative Method." *Comparative Literature Studies* 44, no. 3 (2007): 279–97.

Yadav, Alok. *Before the Empire of English: Literature, Provinciality, and Nationalism in Eighteenth-Century Britain*. New York: Palgrave, 2004.

Yildiz, Yasemin. *Beyond the Mother Tongue the Postmonolingual Condition*. New York: Fordham University Press, 2012.

Zastoupil, Lynn and Martin Moir. *The Great Indian Education Debate: Documents Relating to the Orientalist-Anglicist Controversy, 1781–1843*. Richmond, UK: Curzon Press, 1999.

Index

abnormal/reformed English 176, 195, 198, 208, 210, 213. *See also* normal English
abstraction 120, 128, 131, 156
Adams, Mary 232
Africa 42, 46, 93, 115, 200
    Africans 7, 33, 37, 41, 60, 203
    British African colonies 200
    education in 5, 7–8
    ELT in 15
    (tribal) languages 36, 76 n.10
    Native Africans 181
    Oxford (publisher) in 15, 17, 95
    postcolonial 27 n.52
    South Africa (*see* South Africa)
    Tropical Africa 216
African-American 127–8, 136
Aiken, Janet Rankin xv–xvi, 146–8, 150–6, 158–60, 166, 169–70, 173 n.38, 177, 188–9, 195, 198, 207, 210, 234–5, 238
    "Basic English and World English" 150, 152, 154
    Commonsense English 151
    Commonsense Grammar 156
    "English as an International Language" 152–3
    English Present and Past 151
    "Little English" 147, 154–5, 170, 201, 205
    A New Plan of English Grammar 151
    and Ogden 152–3, 169
    The Psychology of English 151, 156
    Surely Goodness: Sixty-six Little Sketches of Nineteen Ways to Become Good at Living 172 n.23
    "Swenson's English" 147, 153–4, 159, 170, 201
    Why English Sounds Change 151
American Indian languages 4, 62
Anderson, Benedict 33
Anderson, J. L. R. 147

Anglicists 13, 49, 216, 219, 240. *See also* Orientalists
Anglo-American 187, 199–200, 205, 231
Anglophone xvi, 8, 66, 87, 91, 163, 177, 192, 210, 224, 237, 242
Anglophone Caribbean 92
Anglophone empire 6–8
Anglo-Saxon values 7, 177, 180
Annamalai, E. 47–8
anthropology 31, 60, 62–3, 65
anti-colonial nationalist movements 7, 46, 51, 75, 177–8, 193, 222
anti-realist literature 89
applied linguistics xvii, 12, 19, 109, 171 n.2, 243 n.16
Appuhn, Karl xviii n.5
Arabic language 52, 99
Arrighi, Giovanni 8
    The Long Twentieth Century: Money, Power, and the Origins of Our Times 25 n.22
Artificial Intelligence 237
artificial languages 5, 17–20, 34–5, 42, 98, 155, 157, 160, 168, 170
Ashcroft, Bill xiii
Asia 8, 11, 104, 173 n.42, 196, 200. *See also* specific countries
assimilation 52, 55–6, 178, 180
Associated Press, on Aiken's "Little English" 154–5, 205
associationism 44
Australia 113
auxiliary English xiv, xvii, 4, 87, 93, 103, 123, 190, 203, 208, 237, 239, 241
auxiliary language 4, 19–20, 23, 31, 34–5, 45, 57, 60, 66, 74–5, 87, 95–7, 100–1, 104, 108, 111, 117–18, 127, 132–4, 148, 157, 161, 165, 171, 178, 209–11, 236, 240–1. *See also* non-auxiliary languages
    Sapir on 35

Babu English 122, 160, 202, 213
Balfour, Lord Alfred 151
Banerjea, Surendra Nath 52
Bangala language 38, 41
barbarian languages 32, 43
Basic Dictionary 106, 163
Basic English 60, 74, 98, 106–8, 110,
    112–13, 115, 117, 122, 124, 131, 145,
    148, 150, 153–4, 157–9, 162, 165,
    175, 190, 193, 195–8, 202, 204–5,
    208, 221, 223–4, 233–4, 236
  Basic English Applied: Science 109
  Basic English Readers 106, 108
  "The Basic Error of Basic English" 165
  in China 11, 20, 160, 188, 200
  criticism of 148, 153–5, 160, 164–8, 189
  decline of 146, 232
  direction-words from 70–1
  in Japan 74
  legacy of 234–5
  and Malinowski 63–5
  and modernity 117
  operation-words from 69–70
  textbooks 84, 109, 111, 168, 234
  word lists 68–9 (*see also* word lists)
Basic Science word lists 107
Baudelaire, Charles, translations of 125, 129–30
behaviorism 24, 32, 44
  behaviorist psychology 31, 66, 184
Belgian Colonialism xv, 37, 40
  colonial policies 40–1
Belgian Congo 36–7, 136
Bell, Andrew 26 n.43
Bellenoit, J. A. Hayden 79 n.63
Bell-Lancaster system 26 n.43. *See also* filtration method/Filtration Theory
Benedict, Ruth 226 n.38
Bengali language 52
Benjamin, Walter 203
Bentham, Jeremy 21, 69
Bentinck, William 14
Berlitz method 10, 73
Bhattacharya, Sabyasachi 52
bilingualism 49, 52, 100. *See also* monolingual/monolingualism; multilingual/multilingualism
Bloomfield, Laurence xvii, 171 n.2, 195

An Introduction to the Study of Language 44
Boas, Franz, "Americanization Study" 178
Bonfiglio, Thomas Paul, *Mother Tongues and Nations: The Invention of the Native Speaker* xix n.8
Bongers, Herman 106
  History and Principles of Vocabulary Control 107
Bourdieu, Pierre 170, 220
Britain/UK
  Advisory Committee on Education 3–4, 200, 202–4, 221
  after Great War 7
  British Colonialism (in India) xv, 6–7, 17, 33, 50
  British Committee for Relations with Other Countries 8
  British Council xvii, xviii n.3, 236–7
    Tilley Report (blue-print for) 8
  British Dominions 177, 179, 183, 193, 196
  British Empire 8, 27 n.46, 46, 75, 93, 178, 193
  British English 4
  and bureaucracy 179, 232
  imperialism 51, 54, 219
  interwar period xiv, xvi–xvii, 3, 6–8, 31, 35, 178, 236
  Kegan Paul publisher 23, 84, 89, 166
  literary education 91
  Macmillan publisher 89, 95
  readers/reading habits 88–9
  Routledge publisher 21, 23, 192, 204
Brutt-Griffler, Janina 5, 7
  World English 24 n.5
Bryant, Margaret 156
Bulletin, IRET 12, 65, 86, 150, 158, 168, 196, 204–5
Burke, Edmund, *Reflections on the French Revolution* 15, 89
Burma 164, 216
Burton, Antoinette 27 n.46, 92
business, language and 11, 19–20, 50, 113, 217
Butler, Nicholas Murray 180

Campbell, George 138 n.34
  Philosophy of Rhetoric 47
Canada 92–3, 113–14, 161, 183–4, 186, 196

Index

canonical literature/works 15, 84, 87, 95–6, 108, 155, 202
capitalism 33, 51, 116, 184
Carbey, Mabel 182, 225 n.20
Carnegie, Andrew 178, 181
Carnegie, Arthur 5
Carnegie Conference xvi–xvii, 3–5, 8, 17, 28 n.63, 35, 67, 112, 145–7, 154–6, 161, 170–1, 178, 183, 240
    Anglo-American cooperation 187, 199–200, 205
    British cooperation 187
    Carnegie Report/Interim Report xiv, 8, 161, 176–8, 185–6, 189, 199, 201, 207–22, 224, 239–41
    "General Service List" 156, 176, 201, 209–10, 213, 216, 219, 221, 223, 239–40, 243 n.27
    Phillipson on 8
    post-conference in Ohio and London 203–8
    records 194–208, 221, 224
    resolution by Palmer 198
    and West 175–7
Carnegie Corporation (archives) xiv, xvi, 5, 8, 17, 24 n.2, 67, 146, 148, 155, 158, 176–86, 189, 193–4, 215, 221–2, 238–9
    and international education 5–6
    Keppel's vision on 6 (*see also* Keppel, Frederick Paul)
    promoting education 178–82
    Report of the Carnegie Commission on the Poor White Problem 182
    and South Africa 181–3, 186–7
Carnegie Corporation of New York (CCNY) 177
Castilian grammar 32
Cattier, Félicien 41
Certificate of Proficiency in English (CPE) 172 n.8
Ceylon 164, 216
Chandra, Shefali, *The Sexual Life of English: Languages of Caste and Desire in India*. 228 n.84
Chatterjee, Partha 51, 54
Chaudhary, Latika 14, 47, 79 n.63
childhood, image of (in Bengali magazines) 95–6
China 18, 113, 136, 200, 216, 221

Basic English in 11, 20, 160, 188, 200
    Richards' engagement with 28 n.63, 35, 65, 112, 158
    Rockefeller foundation's interests in 25 n.23
Christian/Christianity 91, 172 n.23, 216
    Christian words 216
    civilization 33, 62
Churchill, Winston 146, 231–2
    Harvard speech 232, 235, 238
civilization 113, 115
    Christian 62
    modern 23
    Western 62–3
Clarke, Frederick 8, 177, 182–3, 185–6, 194–6, 200–1, 203–6, 210, 222
    death of 226 nn.33–4
    Introductory Statement 208–9
classical language teaching method 9–10, 47
Cohn, Bernard 58
Colonialism and Its Forms of Knowledge: The British in India 77 n.31
Coleman, Algernon 204
collaborations 8, 147, 159, 169, 193, 199, 202, 206, 211
colonial education 8, 17, 25 n.23, 56, 93, 105, 149
    in Africa 7
    Belgian policies 38
    Bellenoit on 79 n.63
    British 47, 93, 95, 179, 182
    in India 50, 84, 92
    pay for results system 93
colonialism xiv, xvi, 33, 36, 95
    British (*see* Britain/UK, British Colonialism (in India))
    colonial knowledge 36, 58, 92
    colonial policy 40–1, 88
    German linguistic 76 n.10
    Liberal 7, 55, 57
colonial linguistics xv, 31–6, 42, 74, 87, 236, 241
colonial readers 103, 126, 201–2
commercialism 51, 166
commodity 133, 136, 164, 202, 236
    commodity narratives 106–18
common language 19, 103, 231–2, 237
common-sense simple English 167–8

comparative philology 34, 238
constructed languages 18
Cooper, James Fenimore
  The Deerslayer 15, 96
  The Prairie 90
Crawford, F. Marion 89–90
Crookshank, F. G. 63
cryptography/English as code 118, 126, 133–6
Crystal, David 6
cultural identity 97, 132
cultural imperialism/imperialist 6, 28 n.63, 35, 46, 216
cultural language 53, 57
cultural nationalism 32, 51, 55, 97
cultural relativism 62, 226 n.34
curriculum 3, 10, 12, 23, 46, 48, 55–6, 90, 94, 102, 157, 201
  British Indian 240
  oral-based 10
Cutteridge, James Oliver 93–6, 138 n.34
  language teaching by 93–4
  Nelson's Geography of the West Indies and Adjacent Lands 92
  Nelson's West Indian Maths 92
  Nelson's West Indian Readers 1–6, 92–5

Darwin, Charles 19
  Origins of the Species 34
Das, C. R. 52
Defoe, Daniel, *Robinson Crusoe* 15, 84–5, 88, 96
developmentalist model 34–5, 87, 105, 113, 202, 211
Dewey, John 86, 93
dialects 33, 98, 122–3, 127–30, 152, 240
dichotomy 17, 31, 49, 52, 60, 99, 109, 118, 203, 210–11, 239
Dickens, Charles 88, 90, 119
  David Copperfield 15, 96–8, 101
dictionaries 4, 19, 32, 34, 61, 74, 83, 102, 106, 146, 163, 206, 209, 223
didactic works 88–9, 108
diplomatic language 6, 237, 239
direct language teaching method 9–10, 12, 14, 49, 55, 84, 93–4, 238
dominant languages 33, 38, 136. *See also* nondominant languages
Dual Mandate education policy 6–7, 95, 238

Dutch 33
Dutrieux, *Vocabulaire francais-kisouahili* 38
Dyche, Thomas, *Guide to the English Tongue* 88

Eastern languages 111
École Coloniale Supérieure. *See* Université Coloniale de Beglique
economy/economics xiv, xviii n.8, 11, 17, 24, 31, 50, 115. *See also* commodity
  and English in Japan 11
  ethical political economy 51–2
  Fordist 179–80
  global 7, 237
  power of US 6, 8
  of UK 8, 25 n.22
education (English) 55
  colonial (*see* colonial education)
  Dual Mandate policy 6–7, 95, 238
  educational psychology 24, 44–5, 49, 55–6 (*see also* psychology)
  Imperialist 48
  Indian 13–14, 46–52, 79 n.64, 84, 88, 92
  Japanese 11–12, 74
  liberal models of 24
  oral-based curriculum 10
  primary/secondary 13–14, 46–8
  progressive 3, 93–4, 182, 185
  promotion of 8, 178–82 (*see also* South Africa)
  vocational 94
Egypt 7–8, 156–7, 173 n.30, 192–3, 215–16
Egyptian Gazette newspaper 222
Eldridge, R. C. 73
elites 5, 7, 11, 13, 32, 48, 50–1, 56, 79 n.64, 107, 127, 149, 158, 180–1, 193, 207, 214, 217
employment 159, 217
England 8–9, 13, 26 n.43, 88–9, 93–4, 96, 102–3, 186–7, 194, 200, 202, 214–15, 238
English as a Lingua Franca (ELF) xvii, 7, 209, 212–14, 224, 241
English as an International Language xvii, 31, 146, 152–3, 161
English Language Teaching (ELT) xv–xvii,

3–4, 8, 15, 17, 20–1, 23, 31, 35, 47, 56, 84, 106, 112, 145, 149–50, 185, 191, 194, 206, 210, 223–5, 240. *See also* language teaching
  in Africa 15
  in India 13–17
  in Japan 11–12, 24, 74
English-only ideology 7, 49
Errington, Joseph 32–3
  Linguistics in a Colonial World 31, 76 n.11
  on philological theories 34
  reducing speech to writing 33, 35, 65, 74
ESL teaching method 32, 93, 101, 211, 237, 239
Esperanto language 9–10, 17–19, 34, 41–2, 45, 134, 145, 148, 150, 170, 189, 236
ethnographic/ethnography 43–4, 57, 62–4, 114, 140 n.85
eugenics movement/eugenicists 56, 184
Europe/European 40, 42, 48, 53–4, 113, 115, 157, 161–2, 164, 196
  European languages 18, 32–4, 38, 67, 111
  lingua franca 38
  linguistic diversity in 54
Evans, B. Ifor 232
Evans Brothers publisher 112
existing languages 4, 41, 48

Fabian, Johannes 37–8, 40–1, 53
Falk, Julia 150, 173 n.38
Faraday, Michael, *The Chemical History of a Candle* 107
Faucett, Lawrence xv, 15, 74, 147, 149–50, 162, 177, 188, 191, 193, 195, 197, 200, 202, 204–7, 210, 221–2, 227 n.62, 238
  The 'Hurricane' Conference 220–1
  Oxford English Course 4, 15, 27 n.52, 74, 84
Fawkes, K. M. 159
Fetishism 63
fiction, genre 69–70, 88–9, 95–6, 101, 104, 121, 126, 201–3
Fife, Robert Herndon 3, 24 n.3, 155, 170, 177, 185, 187–9, 190, 192, 194–5, 197, 200, 205–8, 221–2, 226 n.40, 238

ACE survey 185–6, 206
"Committee on Modern Languages" 207
"Trends in Modern Language Teaching" 185
figurative language 128, 151, 190
filtration method/Filtration Theory 14, 26 n.43, 48–52, 105, 182, 214
Fiote language 38
First World War 3–6, 9, 19, 21, 48, 93, 110, 179, 185, 236. *See also* Second World War
Firth, J. R. 21
Florence, P. Sargant 232
folk material 92–5
foreign language 122, 185–6, 214, 219, 224
  English as xv, 7, 75, 101, 200, 213, 218, 223
  French as 36
  translation of 112
France
  English for 4
  French Algeria 76 n.9
  French English 122, 127
  French language 6, 9, 33, 36–8, 41, 76 n.9, 129, 133, 141 n.122, 193
Frank, Leonhard, *Carl and Anna* (*Karl und Anna*) 84, 108–12, 201
Fraser, Robert 88, 93, 138 n.34
Freud, Sigmund 53, 63
full English 12, 20, 65, 149, 157, 160, 169, 212

Galef, Bennet 44
  on Thorndike 44–5
gender xiv, 57, 79 n.61, 114, 117, 228 n.84
genres 88–9, 95
  adventure stories 95, 127
  Bildungsroman 95, 97–8
  exploration 95–6
  melodramatic works 88–9, 97, 110
  romance/romantic 84, 88–9, 97, 103
Germany/Germans 33, 110, 151, 173 n.42, 175, 184, 222
  Germanic languages 54, 163, 185
  linguistic colonialism 76 n.10
  romantic novel 84, 110
Ghosh, Durba, *Gentlemanly Terrorists: Political Violence and the Colonial State in India, 1919–1947* 80 n.84

Gibson, Christine 20, 149
Gikandi, Simon xiii
global economy 7, 237. *See also* economy/economics
Global English xvii n.2, xix n.9, 4, 53, 84–5, 96, 142 n.138, 146–7, 190, 221, 223, 232, 234–7, 241
  as anglophone empire 6–8
  Crystal on 6
globalization 36, 54, 196, 224, 238
Glotzer, Richard 179–83
Google Translate 237
Gordin, Michael 18–19
Gordon, W. Terrence 21, 60, 147
Graddol, David, *English Next* xviii n.3
grammars 22, 34–5, 64, 74, 83, 90, 93–4, 151, 154, 163, 195
  Aiken's *Commonsense Grammar* 156
  Castilian 32
  grammar frequency 154–5, 195, 205, 210
  grammar-translation language teaching method 9, 32
  grammatical method of language teaching 84, 93, 169
  Latin 32–3
  native 33
Gramsci 67, 73
Greek language 9, 21, 62, 124, 232–3, 241
Greenfeld, Liah 11
  on *bushido* ethic 11
Greet, William 191
Grin, François xiii, 238
guides, language 36–41, 74

Haggard, Rider 127
  King Solomon's Mines 89, 96
Haldane, J. B. S., *Science and Well-Being* 107
Halliday, M. A. K. 124
Hatfield, H. S., *Electricity and Magnetism* 107
hegemony, English xvi, 67, 73, 92, 237–8
Herder, Johann Gottfried 34
hierarchies, linguistic xiv, 33, 35, 57, 131–2
Hindi language 74, 160
Hindu 95, 216
Hochschild, Adam, *King Leopold's Ghost: A Story of Greed, Terror, and Heroism in Colonial Africa* 77 n.42
Hofmyer, Isabel 27 n.46, 92
Holborow, Marnie xiii, 73
Horn, Ernest 74, 86, 149, 168, 218
  Basic Writing word list 66
Hornby, A. S. 12, 206, 223
  Oxford Dictionary 209
Howatt, A. P. R. xvi, 11, 24, 26 n.29, 146–7, 171 n.1, 210, 223
  behaviorist 78 n.53
  History of English Language Teaching xx n.19, 24 n.4
  view on *New Method Readers* 101
Huang, Yunte 234–5
Huq, A. K. Fazlul 52
The 'Hurricane' Conference 220–1
Hyde, Douglas 53

Ichikawa, Sanki, *Kenkuysha's English Classics* 83
ideology, language and 7, 45–6, 72–3, 84–5, 108–9, 132, 134, 136, 177–9, 210, 218, 221, 224, 236–7
Ido 19, 34, 148, 170
imperialism 6, 34, 74, 193, 217, 238
  British 51, 54, 219
  colonial 17
  cultural 6, 28 n.63, 35, 46, 216
  imperial language 32, 58
  late 6, 54, 75, 236
  linguistic 224, 237
  New Imperialism 7, 9, 24, 193
India 4, 7, 54, 102–3, 113, 115, 193, 216. *See also* Britain/UK, British Colonialism (in India)
  Basic English in 160
  Bell-Lancaster system 26 n.43
  Bengal/Bengali 13–15, 17, 23, 45–6, 48, 51–2, 56, 58, 60, 91, 95, 102, 136, 145, 216
  books in 88
  Calcutta 13, 17, 48, 50, 103
  Calcutta University Commission 90
  Calcutta University Report (1919) 46
  dyarchy 52, 57
  education system in 13–14, 46–52, 79 n.64, 84, 88, 92
  ELT in 13–17
  English Education Act (1835) 26 n.43

English for Indian Civil Service 14, 88,
   92, 94, 137 n.24
epistemological space 58
Government of India Act (1919) 52,
   54–5, 57
Hindustani 33
Hunter Commission Report (1882) 46
Indian Education Service (IES) 12–13,
   17, 48–9
language policy in 46
language teaching by West in 13–17,
   45, 48–51, 102
Longmans publisher in 15, 17, 27 n.51,
   84, 89, 95, 137 n.14, 149, 192, 238–9
Montague Reforms (1919) 46
Oxford University Press 89, 95
Provincial Education Service (PES) 48
Raleigh Commission (1904) 46
readers/reading habits 88–91
Rowlatt Acts in 7, 52
Swadeshi movement 51
Wood's Despatch (1854) 46–7, 49, 90
indigenous languages 32–3
Indirect Rule 7, 45–58, 94, 203, 217
individualism 96–8, 103–6, 216, 237
industrialization 50, 53, 96
Informal Conference on the Teaching of
   English to Non-English-Knowing
   Pupils, record of 227 n.53
Information Theory 234
Institute for Research in English Teaching
   (IRET), Tokyo 4, 12, 20, 65–6, 74,
   86, 119, 129, 205, 211
   Simplified Series 122
   1,000 word "Plain English" 147
instrumental language 69, 126, 135
inter-cultural lingua franca 37
intermediary language 32–3, 132, 218
International Auxiliary Languages (IALs)
   xiv, 31, 34, 96, 106, 112–13, 145,
   148, 150, 160, 170, 195, 236
international English xv, xvii, 5–6, 9, 11,
   19, 35, 46, 53–4, 150, 152, 156,
   160–1, 164, 171, 176
internationalism 6, 9, 11, 19, 35, 53–4,
   113, 158, 178, 181, 203, 221
international language 18, 20, 23, 31, 41,
   108, 110, 124, 145–6, 153, 161, 163,
   165, 239–40
International Phonetic Alphabet 120

international words 116–17, 162–3, 165
invented language 24, 134, 147, 153
Ireland 7, 33
Irish language 53

Jamaica 54
James, William, *Principles of Psychology*
   44
Japan 193, 200, 205
   ELT (by Palmer) in 11–12, 24, 35, 45,
      65, 74, 148
   English Studies in Japan journal 222
   Japanese English 122
Jespersen, Otto xv, 10, 19, 34–5, 43, 45
Jessup, Walter A. 177, 195, 197
Johnson, Burgess 191
Johnson, Samuel 223
   Dictionary 32
Jones, Daniel 9–10, 236
Jones, William 33–4
Joshi, Priya 88–9, 95
Joyce, James 20
   Finnegans Wake 23, 146

Kachru, Braj xiii, 236
Kalidasa, *Sakuntala* 103
Kansas test 57
Kelly, F. J. 57
Keppel, Frederick Paul 5–6, 24 n.6, 154–5,
   170, 173 n.38, 175, 177–9, 188–90,
   193–5, 198, 201–2, 204–8, 210,
   221–3, 226 n.38, 227 n.61, 238–40
   education and positions 180–1
   "key men" of 177, 183–6, 227 n.62
   and Ogden 189, 191–2, 226 n.29
   and Thorndike 183–4, 191
   and West 187–8, 201, 224 n.1, 226 n.39
Kibanga language 38
Kincaid, Jamaica 214
Krapp, George Philip
   The English Language in America 151
   Modern English 151
Kumar, Krishna 102

Lamb, Charles 119
   Essays 15, 89
Langendoen, D. Terence 65
language acquisition 12, 36, 43, 65, 171 n.2
language education 5, 7–8, 55, 149, 182,
   237. *See also* education (English)

for immigrants 173 n.39
  on postcolonial studies of xix n.9
language learning 9, 32, 44–5, 86, 150, 158, 168, 190, 211
  Lemaire's interest in 36, 42
  natural learning 42
Language of Wider Communication (LWC) 32–3, 38, 41–2, 65, 76 n.9, 237, 241
language policy 33
  Belgian 37–8, 42
  in India 46, 79 n.61
  US–Philippines 7
language system 18, 84, 108, 159, 170, 240
  copyrighted 196
  international 145
  organized 31
  standardized 152
  transformative 20
language teaching xv, xvii, 3–6, 9, 23, 34–5, 45, 67, 74, 88, 101, 145, 185, 189, 195, 197, 209. *See also* English Language Teaching (ELT)
  classical/grammar-translation method 9–10, 32, 47
  direct method 9–10, 12, 14, 49, 55, 84, 93–4, 238
  grammatical method 84, 169
  in India by West 13–17, 23, 45, 48–50, 102, 148, 160, 175
  in Japan by Palmer 11–12, 24, 35, 45, 65, 74, 148
  materials 24, 112, 156, 237
Latin language 9, 32, 52, 54, 99, 124
  grammars 32–3
Lauwerys, J. A. 109
Lawrence, John 83
Léger, Benoit 129, 141 n.126
Lemaire, Charles (French Esperanto) 19, 36, 41, 45, 57, 77 n.42, 78 n.46, 136
  Belga Sonorilo magazine 41
  in Belgian Army 37
  colonial career 40
  in Congo (Congo Free State) 37–8, 40–1
  early life 37
  and Esperanto 41–2
  imperial *tiers-parti* 37, 41
  language guide 38–41
  and Palmer Method 42–5
  Vocabulaire Pratique 36–42, 67, 237
Lester, Robert M. 238
Liberal colonialism 7, 55, 57
limited English 149, 197
limited vocabulary 31, 75 n.3, 86, 124, 126, 196, 198, 201–2, 212, 216, 241
Lingala language 37
lingua franca 7, 37, 41, 203, 209, 213. *See also* English as a Lingua Franca (ELF)
  European 38
  French 193
  inter-cultural 37
  international 54
  universal 45
linguistics xiv, 3, 86, 196
  applied xvii, 12, 109, 171 n.2, 243 n.16
  British 20, 64
  colonial xv, 31–6, 236, 241
  distribution 130–1
  diversity 35, 54
  female linguists 148, 173 n.38, 187
  imperialism 224, 237
  linguistic hierarchies xiv, 33, 35, 57, 131–2
  revolutions 146
  Saussurean 24
  sociolinguistics xviii n.8, 132
  symbols 86, 119–22
  women in 148
link language 32
literary criticism 122, 129
literary material 86, 91, 108, 118, 120–1
literature 10, 47, 105, 201–2, 218, 239
  anti-realist 89
  Bengali children's 95–6
  canonical 15, 84, 87, 95–6, 108, 155, 202
  English 47, 91, 201, 240
  Indian 92
  simplified literature 175
  vernacular 91, 241
  world xix n.9, 84, 110
Liu, Lydia 234–5
Li, Victor 62
Lockhart, Leonora Wilhelmina 109–10, 139 n.66, 147–8, 173 n.38, 235
  Basic Way Readers 211

The Basic Way Reading Books 108,
  112–18
 early life 109
 translation of *Karl und Anna* 110
 Woods on 109
 *Word Economy: A Study in Applied
  Linguistics* 109
London, Carnegie Conference in 203–8
Loram, Charles T. 177, 182–3, 195, 197,
  200
Lower Certificate in English (LCE) 236
Lowth, Robert *Introduction to English
  Grammar* 32
Lugard, Lord, *Dual Mandate* 7

Macaulay, Thomas 13, 53, 55, 60, 158, 218
 Filtration Theory 14, 49–52, 105
 Minutes of the Conference 49, 175,
  203, 218
machine translation 134, 234, 237
Macmillan, *Golden Treasury* 89, 95
Maki, Itsu 74, 147
Makin, Ronald 36
Malaya 164, 216
 Malay language 33, 74
Malherbe, Ernest Gideon, Poor White
  Commission Report 182
Malinowski, Bronislaw 20–1, 60
 and Basic English 63–5
 context of situation 64–5
 Coral Gardens 64
 and primitive languages 63–4
 structural functionalism 63
 "The Problem of Meaning in Primitive
  Languages" 63–4
 Word Magic 64
Marx, Karl 63
Matsukata Kojirohe 11, 26 n.29
Mayhew, Arthur 177, 187–8, 192–200,
  202, 204–5, 208, 212, 221, 224
 Education in the Colonial Empire 4
 The Education of India 4
 English examination bodies 200, 213
 and West 194, 203
May, Mark 189–90
McClaren, Angus 184, 225 n.28
McElvenny, James 20
McKee, Clayton 129–30
Mead, Margaret 225 n.20

Mencken, H. L. 152
Meyer v Nebraska 186
The Middle East 46
Mignolo, Walter, on Nebrija 32
Miller, Joshua 7
Milton, John 102
 "Samson" poem 103–5
minimal language 18, 67
Minimum Adequate Vocabulary (M.A.V)
  156
modernism/modernity xiv, xix n.9, xviii
  n.6, 7, 23–4, 31, 51–4, 57, 65, 75,
  96, 99, 101–3, 105–6, 115, 117, 158,
  165, 167, 217–18, 236
 Asian 96
 globalization 196
 modernist aesthetic 233
 modernization 179, 199
 West's view on 53–4
Mongo language 38
monolingual/monolingualism 10, 23,
  52, 237–8. *See also* bilingualism;
  multilingual/multilingualism
Montrose Colony eugenics movement 56
Moore, Adelyn. *See* Ogden, C. K.
Morrison, Toni 127–8
Moslem 216
mother tongue xix n.8, xv, 31–2, 35, 45–6,
  57, 60, 65–6, 87, 97, 104, 109, 118,
  127–8, 133, 157, 160, 166, 200,
  208–9, 211, 213, 218, 240–1
Mouchak magazine 95
Mufti, Aamir xii
Mukherjee, Alok 46
Mulhern, Frances 166
multilingual/multilingualism 23, 38, 40,
  42, 52, 54–5, 57, 96–7, 99, 101,
  103, 133, 214, 237–8, 241. *See
  also* bilingualism; monolingual/
  monolingualism
Murdoch, Brian 110, 112
Murray, Lindsley, *English Grammar* 47

Nahuatl 32–3
nationalism 19, 54, 161, 173 n.42, 175
 Bengali anti-colonial 46, 51, 60, 94
 cultural 32, 51, 97
 European 33–4
 Indian 51

Irish xiv
Japanese 11–12
militaristic 196
national languages 11, 32, 42, 54, 57, 65, 87, 123, 127, 158, 240
national/nationalist identity 34, 52, 54, 74, 111, 182, 190, 237
native English 122, 203
native languages 13, 33, 37–8, 99, 118, 157, 160, 209
native-primitive-national languages 63
native-speakers 10, 122
Nebraska 151, 185–6
Nebrija, Anton de 32
neoliberalism 236, 238, 240
new education psychology 56
New Imperialism 7, 9, 24, 193
non-auxiliary languages 32, 127, 129. *See also* auxiliary language
nondominant languages 33. *See also* dominant languages
non-linguistic contexts 64, 146
non-native languages 32, 67
non-native speakers/speaking instructors 4, 14, 49, 73, 122
normal English 106, 169, 198, 204. *See also* abnormal/reformed English
Norman 99, 124
nouns 18, 69, 123, 219
Novial language 19, 34, 145, 148
Nunn, Percy 3, 194, 204, 222

Ogden, C. K. xiv, 4–5, 9, 35, 46, 66, 74, 107, 110, 112, 119, 125–7, 130, 133, 135, 139 n.65, 145–6, 149–50, 152, 155–6, 158–9, 162–5, 171, 175, 177, 190, 193–8, 201, 203–5, 208, 211, 214, 219, 222–4
and Aiken 152–3, 169
artificial languages 5, 18–20
Basic English xiv–xvi, 4–5, 11, 17–23, 72, 111, 113, 119, 146–7, 159, 186–7, 190, 212, 233–4
in China 11, 20
copyrighted system 20, 199
fictional/non-fictional texts 108
word lists 66, 68, 84, 106–7
Basic English: An International Second Language 27 n.56, 69, 108
direction-words from 70–1

operation-words from 69–70
"Basic English on the Offensive" 207
Bentham's Theory of Fictions 21
Cambridge Heretic Society group 21
controversy 147, 150, 154–5, 159, 171, 188
Counter-Offensive: An Exposure of Certain Misrepresentations of Basic English xvi, 146–8, 154, 159, 166–70, 189, 205–6
counter to *Critical Examination* 169
criticism of West 146
Debabelization 233
"The Gold Insect" 86, 163
Greek mask 231–8, 241
heretic 20–3
Heretics club 109, 167
interests of 22
and Keppel 189, 191–2, 226 n.29
Meaning of Meaning xv, 18, 22, 31, 58–65, 125, 167
Orthological Institutes 23, 108, 148, 155, 159, 169
Psyche series 21, 23, 65, 84, 167
subjective method of word selection 67–73, 119–21, 168, 197, 221, 223, 237
and West 189, 191–2, 199
Word Magic 58, 61, 63–4, 69, 72, 100–1, 234–5
Orde, Anne 6
Orientalists 13, 49, 123, 218–19. *See also* Anglicists
Orwell, George 235
Ostwald, Wilhelm 19
O'Sullivan, Barry, *Assessing English on the Global Stage: The British Council and the English Language Testing, 1941–2016* 243 n.16

Palestine 164, 216
Pali language 47
Palmer, Harold xiv, xvii, 4–5, 8, 15, 21, 23–4, 35, 45, 57, 60, 65–6, 83, 108, 112, 145, 147–8, 159, 162, 169, 177, 185–6, 188, 192, 195, 197, 199–201, 204–6, 210, 213–14, 219, 222–3, 236, 238
alogs 119–20
Basic English 84

deletion and replacement 121
early life and education 9
escape from Belgium 42
and French 129
"The Gold Beetle" 86
The Grading and Simplifying of Literary Material: A Memorandum xv, 86–7, 118–23, 128–9
"habit" 44
The 'Hurricane' Conference 220–1
Interim Report on Vocabulary Selection 74
IRET 4, 12, 20, 153
language teaching xv, 9–10
in Japan 5, 11–12, 45, 65
On Learning to Read Foreign Languages 149
on material (narrative) 120–1
miologs 73–4, 119–20
monologs 73–4, 119
Palmer Method 5, 9–12, 17, 36, 83, 119, 123, 150
and Lemaire 42–5
"Plain English" 166
Poe Test (translation) 118–36
polylogs 73–4, 119
The Principles of Language Study xv, 9, 31, 35–6, 42–5, 86
"savage" 43–4
The Scientific Study and Teaching of Languages 9–10, 42, 86, 119
simplification-clarification-translation 121–3, 129
Simplified Readers (*see* Simplified Readers)
simplified texts 121–3, 127, 130
spontaneous capacity 43
and West 192–3
word lists 73–4
Parsons, Timothy 7
Second British Empire 25 n.16, 54
pedagogy/pedagogical 10, 12, 44, 93, 119, 177, 185, 194–6, 198–9, 209
conventional language 148
peer review 147, 171 n.6
Peirce, Charles Sanders 22
tripartite theory 60–1
Pennycook, Alastair xviii n.8, 56, 84–5, 158
on Palmer's achievement 9

Phelps-Stokes Fund organization 179, 181
Phelp-Stokes, Anselm 181–2
Philippines 33, 200, 221
American language policy in 7
Survey of Education in the Philippines 7
Phillipson, Robert xviii n.8, 8, 56, 84–5
philology 33–5, 83, 88, 151–2
comparative 34, 238
philosophical language 162
philosophy of language 31, 60, 65
phonetics 10, 24, 42, 83, 93–4, 103, 129
photographs 113–15
Pidgin English 19, 122, 211
Plain English xvii, 122, 131, 147, 166, 213, 224
Poe, Edgar Allan, "The Gold-Bug"/"The Gold Beetle" xv, 86–7, 107, 118, 201, 235
cryptography/English as code 118, 126, 133–6
translation of 123–36
Jupiter (fictional character) 127–33
politics, language 33, 118, 131, 141 n.114, 160, 237
positivist view of language 31, 34–5, 45, 66
Pound, Ezra 233, 240–1
Cantos 23, 146
Pound, Louise 148, 151–2
American Speech journal 150–2, 154, 156, 222
Powell, Baden 215
prescriptivism 151, 213–14
primitivism/primitive languages 32, 45, 58–65
Malinowski's interest in 63–4
progressive education 3, 93–4, 182, 185
progressivism 53
pronunciation 14, 18, 55, 83, 92, 94, 103–4, 238
Protestant 38, 180
P. S. King & Co. 207
psychology xiv, 13, 21, 23–4, 55, 65, 93, 189, 213. *See also* education, educational psychology
animal 44
behaviorist 31, 66, 184
comparative 44
educational 24, 44–5, 49, 55–6
social 53, 64
Pugach, Sara 76 n.11

Africa in Translation: A History of Colonial Linguistics in Germany and Beyond, 1814–1945 76 n.10

race/racism/racist 33–4, 62, 76 n.11, 87, 93–4, 115, 128, 136, 178, 184–5. See also "other"
Raley, Rita 134, 234, 237
Rangmashal magazine 95
Rankin, Jean Sherwood 148, 151–2
 Everyday English 151
readers/reading habits 88–91, 95, 101–2, 106
reading material 91, 94–5
realism/reality effect 87, 103, 155
Reform Movement, principles of 10
regionalism 95, 149
reification 33, 45, 61
religion 22, 41, 55, 57, 62, 91. See also specific religions
 religious considerations 216
 Religious Objections 214, 216
Reynold, G. M. W. 88
Richards, I. A. 4, 20–1, 23, 28 n.63, 46, 69, 74, 110, 112, 145, 147, 156, 158, 162, 169–70, 188, 190, 195, 204, 207, 231–5
 Basic in Teaching: East and West 27 n.62, 109
 Basic Rules of Reason 72, 109
 engagement with China 28 n.63, 35, 65, 112, 158
 The Interim Report on Vocabulary Selection 167
 Language through Pictures series 148–9, 234
 Meaning of Meaning xv, 31, 58–65, 125, 167
 minimal language 18
 Word Magic 58, 61, 63–4, 72, 101
Roach, Jack 235
Rockefeller Foundation 8, 25 n.23, 108, 179, 181, 188, 195, 200, 238
Rossiter, Arthur Percival 86, 109, 124–5, 130, 132
rote memorization 10
Roy, Rammohan 49, 51
Russell, Bertrand 20, 109
Russell, Dora 139 n.65
Russell, F. L. 159
Russell, James E. 182

Samarin, William 37
Sandesh magazine 95
Sandiford, Peter 175, 183–5, 224 n.1, 225 n.28
 Educational Psychology 183
 fundamental language study 226 n.29
Sanskrit language 47, 52
Sapir, Edward 4, 35, 190, 195–8
Saraceni, Mario, *World Englishes: A Critical Analysis* xviii n.8
Saussure, Ferdinand de 24, 61–2, 64
Saxon 99–100, 124
Schleicher, August 34
Schleyer, Johan Martin 18
Schmitt, Norbert 10
 Vocabulary in Language Teaching 75 n.3
scientific language 19, 107, 124–7, 154
Scott, Emmett 181
Scott, Walter, *Ivanhoe* 89, 96, 98–101
second language 43, 57, 85, 157, 160, 211, 240. See also third language
Second World War 146, 171 n.2, 173 n.42, 231. See also First World War
self-contained vocabulary 212
self-expression 53, 97
self-rule 7, 217
semantics 22, 124
 Lady Welby's view on 23
semiotics 18, 21, 23, 27 n.62, 61
Sen, Satadru 95–6
Seth, Sanjay 79 n.63, 92
Shakespeare, William 83–4, 109, 125
shared language 6, 72
Shaw, George Bernard 22, 151
Siam 164, 216
simple English xvii, 167–8, 236
simplicity of words 35
simplification, language 3, 23, 35, 121–3, 127, 129–30, 135, 158, 189, 209, 213, 235
simplified English 9, 36, 56, 121, 128, 147, 152–5, 157, 163, 196, 223, 235
simplified German 19
simplified languages 19, 36, 152, 213
simplified literature 175

Simplified Readers xiv–xv, 5, 15, 24, 83–7, 90, 98, 119, 123, 145, 211
skepticism 69, 74, 131–2, 168, 219
Slavonic English 122
Smith, Richard C. 13–14, 24 n.5, 48, 149, 210
  Teaching English as a Foreign Language, 1912–1936: Pioneers of ELT xviii n.4, 26 n.34, 27 n.51, 27 n.54, 227 n.62
  on West 48–50
social psychology 53, 64
sociolinguistics xviii n.8, 132
sociology 62
  educational 226 n.33
"soul-neutral" English 240–2
source language 120, 134
South Africa 177, 196
  and Carnegie Corporation 181–3, 186–7
  South African Institute of Race Relations (SAIRR) 182
South America 148, 192, 200
Spanish 32–3, 133, 185
  Spanish-Mexican 33
Sparrow, Mighty, "Dan Is the Man (in the Van)" song 92–4
specialized language 52–3
specialized vocabularies 32, 107
speech, language as 64, 127, 131–2, 157
  ESL 211
Spencer, Herbert 62
Srinivasachari, C. S. 94
Standard English 106–7, 111–12, 117, 122, 129–30, 134, 153, 157, 161, 196, 200, 212–13, 238–9, 241
standardization, language xiv–xv, xix n.9, 9, 32–4, 130, 134, 213
Standard Pronunciation 55, 92
Stanley, Henry Morton 37
Stevens, David 188, 195, 200, 238
Stolzenberg, Nomi 21
structuralism 152
Study of Typical Errors project 206
stylistics/stylistic value 121–3, 201–2
  study of 206
Sudan 164, 216
Swahili language 33, 38, 41–2, 74
Swenson, Elaine xv–xvi, 146–8, 150, 152, 154, 156, 166, 169–70, 173 n.38, 177, 188–9, 193, 198, 215, 234–5
  A Critical Examination of Basic English xv, 146, 148, 150, 158–66, 189, 207, 215
  "Learning Items" 163–4, 168
  West on 173 n.38
  900-word "Swenson English" 153
syntax 32, 35

Tagore, Rabindranath 102–5
  Fruit Gathering 104
  Gitanjali 104
target languages 10, 120, 134
Teacher's College at Columbia 13, 50, 67, 179, 181, 186
technical language 65, 240
technology 19, 106, 114, 165, 215, 218, 220, 234–5, 237
territorial identity 33–4, 67
textbooks xv, 3, 10, 14–15, 17, 20, 46, 67, 73, 84–5, 87–90, 92, 94–6, 102, 109, 111, 149, 151, 158, 160, 222. *See also specific publishers*
  Basic English 84, 109, 111, 168, 234
  British 88, 92
  commercial 149
  educational 112
  paper empire 92
  textbook culture 102
theories of language 5, 22, 31–2, 60, 65, 85
  evolutionary 34, 54
Thesaurus project 206
third language 55, 160. *See also* second language
Thomas Nelson and Sons, Canada 92
Thorndike, Edward 50, 55–7, 66, 72–4, 91, 125–6, 147, 149, 162, 177, 183, 188, 193, 195–7, 201, 204, 206, 210, 214, 218, 222, 238
  animal psychology (puzzle-box experiments) 44
  Galef on 44–5
  and Keppel 183–4, 191
  Montrose Colony eugenics movement 56, 184
  objective word lists 66–7, 86, 119–21, 155, 168, 197, 214, 218–19, 223, 237
  Teacher's Word Book 3, 66, 90–1
  textbooks 67

thoughts, language and 21–3, 60, 190
Tibble, J.W. 226 nn.33–4
totalitarian language 235
trade 6, 11, 13, 47, 64, 101, 114–15, 147, 166, 217
transactional language 45
transatlantic methods xvi, 3, 5–6, 8, 15, 17, 194
translations xv, 10, 21, 95, 99, 104, 106–8, 110–12, 120–2, 218, 240
  Basic translation 124–6
  of Baudelaire 125, 129–30
  French 129, 141 n.122
  Google Translate 237
  interlingual 237
  for *Le Magasin de demoiselles* 129
  machine translation 134, 234, 237
  non-expert 139 n.62
  of Rossiter 124–5, 130
  translation-as-decoding 235
  translators 20, 37, 51, 77 n.31, 98, 124, 129, 241
  of troubadour poetry 240–1
tribal languages 36, 53, 63
Trouillot, Michel Rolph, "North Atlantic Universals" xvi
Tupas, Ruanni xiii, 238
Turkey 149, 164, 200, 216

The United States xvi, 6–7, 17, 50, 89, 93, 154, 177, 179, 185, 200, 207, 238
  Bilingualism in 15
  "English-Only" states 185
  female linguists in 148
  immigrants and 178
  international/world power 6–8
  language policy in Philippines 7
  post-Carnegie Conference in Ohio 203–8
  South Carolina 136
universalism 51–2, 149
universal language 18, 111, 126, 235, 241
Université Coloniale de Beglique 78 n.58
University of Cambridge Local Examinations Syndicate (UCLES) 172 n.8, 235–6
Urdu language 160
utilitarian/utilitarianism 10, 21, 35, 47, 52, 66, 70, 120, 161, 197

vernacular language xix n.9, 10, 13–14, 32–4, 46–9, 51, 54, 57, 87–8, 91, 122–3, 127, 129–33, 136, 158, 161, 182, 211, 241
Viaene, Vincent 37, 41, 77 n.42
Victoria, Lady Welby 22–3
Viswanathan, Gauri, *Masks of Conquest: Literary Study and British Rule in India* xii, 47, 91, 241
Vocabulary Control xv, xvii, 4–5, 31–6, 63, 65–6, 73, 83–7, 91, 106, 110, 112, 118–19, 121, 123–4, 134, 136, 165, 201, 209–11, 221, 234–6
vocabulary lists 32, 198–9, 202
vocabulary selection, purposes/criteria of 211–12
  Foundation Standpoint 212
  "Intensive and Emotional words" 239
  Island Vocabulary 212–13
  Purification of Style 212–13
  self-contained vocabulary 212
  Standpoint of English as a Lingua Franca 212–13
  Tourist and Traveller Standpoint 212, 214
vocational education 94
Volapük language 17–19, 170
von Humboldt, Alexander 34

Walkowitz, Rebecca xiii
Wallaert, Ineke 129–30, 141 n.122
Wallas, Graham, *The Great Society* 53
Washington, Booker T. 181
Watson, J. B., "Psychology as the Behaviorist Views It" 44
Weaver, Warren 134, 234–5
Weir, Cyril J., *Assessing English on the Global Stage: The British Council and English Language Testing, 1941–2016* 243 n.16
Weissberg, Liliane 127–8, 135
Wells, H. G. 102, 202
  The Shape of Things to Come 235
  "The Country of the Blind" 103
Weltdeutsch language 19
West, Michael Philip xiv, xvi–xvii, 3, 5, 8, 15, 21, 23, 35, 66, 86, 108, 112, 133, 135, 145–9, 152, 157, 167, 169–70, 185–6, 188–91, 195–8, 203–4, 206–7, 210, 214, 219, 222–4, 234–6
  adaptations of (novels/poems) 15,

84–6, 89, 97–101, 103–4, 129 (see also specific novels)
awareness/omission of words 216
Basic English 86
on Bengalis 51
Bilingualism (with Special Reference to Bengal) xv, 14–15, 31, 45–58, 65, 78 n.59, 89, 94, 96–7, 99, 101, 103, 126, 157–8, 160, 168–9, 223, 237–40
experiments with Bengali students 57–8
individual reading profile 59
"Bilingualism and National Culture" 54
and Carnegie Conference 175–7
A Critical Examination of Basic English xv, 146, 148, 150, 158–66, 189, 207, 215
criticism by Ogden 146
Definition Dictionary 147
early life and education 12
Educational Psychology 49–50
"English as a World Language" xvii, 148, 150, 156–8
fallacy of renationalization 55–6, 58
filtration method/Filtration Theory 14, 26 n.43, 48–52, 105
"General Service List" 156, 176, 201, 209–10, 213, 216, 219, 221, 223, 239–40, 243 n.27
"The Gold Bug" 86, 101
The 'Hurricane' Conference 220–1
and Keppel 187–8, 201, 224 n.1, 226 n.39
language teaching
in Dacca 46, 48
in India 13–17, 23, 45, 48–51, 148, 175
Learning to Read a Foreign Language 15, 50, 149
On Learning to Speak a Foreign Language 150
and Mayhew 194, 203
on multilingualism 54–5
New Method 3, 5, 14, 52, 54–6, 66, 86–7, 92–3, 126, 149–50, 160, 166, 168, 179, 192, 201, 211
New Method Conversations 150
New Method Dictionary 146
New Method Readers xv, 15–17, 27 n.52, 46, 84–5, 88–106, 110, 113, 119, 122, 132, 158, 213
and Ogden 189, 191–2, 199
Oxford dissertation 14, 46, 50
and Palmer 192–3
"reading-first" concept 12, 14, 45, 84
reading method 55–7
Robinson Crusoe 15, 84–5, 88, 96
and Smith 48–50
"surrender value" 50–1, 56, 212, 237
on Swenson 173 n.38
translation acts 240–1
view on modernity 53–4
Word Magic 58, 61, 101
Wiener, Norbert 234–5
Wilf, Jose de Magellanes 159
Williams, Eric 92
Williams, Michael 128, 131
Wittgenstein, Ludwig 20–1
Wood, Charles 14
Wood, Gillen D'Arcy 99
Woods, Carly S. 109
Debating Women: Gender, Education, and Spaces for Argument, 1835–1945 139 n.66
word count/word counting 66, 107, 121, 149, 152, 159, 162, 164–5, 167–8, 171, 188–9, 194–5, 210, 219
word definition xvi, 12, 73–4, 120, 125, 162
word lists xiv–xv, 5, 15, 20, 23–4, 31, 36–8, 45, 65–74, 82 n.128, 85, 87, 165, 195, 209–11, 219, 240
Basic English 68–9
Basic Science 107
Basic Words 165
of Faucett-Maki 74, 147, 219
frequency-based 66–8, 73–4, 91, 121, 123, 135, 197, 210–11, 214, 219
General Word List, criteria 217
geographical distribution of words 214–16
International 162
objective list (Thorndike) 66–7, 86, 119–21, 155, 168, 197, 214, 218–19, 223, 237
Palmer's criticism of 73–4
pedagogical 75, 84, 148
religious consideration 216
standardized 198, 201

statistical 125, 167, 219, 237
subjective list (Ogden) 67–73, 119–21, 168, 197, 221, 223, 237
supplementary 87, 213
universality 158, 161, 214, 216–18
Wordsworth, William 102, 105
"Upon Westminster Bridge" poem 103–4
world literature xix n.9, 84, 110
World Literature in English (WLE) xii, 241
Wren, Percival Christopher 10, 15
Wyatt, Horace, advice to teachers 10

Yutang, Lin 139 n.62, 160

Zamenhof, Ludwik Lejzer (Doktoro Esperanto) 18–19